Designing Rubrics for
K-6 Classroom Assessment

Designing Rubrics for K-6 Classroom Assessment

Debbie Rickards
Alief Independent School District
Houston, Texas

and

Earl Cheek, Jr.
Louisiana State University and
A&M College

Christopher-Gordon Publishers, Inc.
Norwood, Massachusetts

The Bill Harp Professional Teacher's Library
An Imprint of
Christopher-Gordon Publishers, Inc.
1502 Providence Highway, Suite #12
Norwood, MA 02062
(800) 934-8322

Printed in the United States of America

10 9 8 7 6 5 4 3 2 1   04 03 02 01 00 99

Library of Congress Catalog Card Number: 98-073519
ISBN: 0-926842-86-2

Acknowledgments

We want to thank those people at Christopher-Gordon Publishers who assisted us throughout this project. We are particularly grateful to Sue Canavan, who believed in the viability of this text, and to Jacob Schulz for his valuable contributions during the latter stages of this project. Also, we thank Kristen Tatum for her excellent assistance in reviewing the final manuscript for this text.

This text would not have been possible without the work of an exceptional group of educators. We thank Dr. Kerry Laster, Martha Maple and the excellent faculty at Shreve Island Elementary School in Shreveport, Louisiana. Appreciation is also due to those educators who contributed rubrics for inclusion in this text: Carol Hankins, Kerry Laster, and Georgia Nemeth.

Dedication

To Dan Rickards and Pam Hautot,
for all your support along the way

—D. R.

To the students at Louisiana State University
and A&M College in Reading Education

—E. C.

Contents

PREFACE

Teachers must always be cognizant of each student's progress at all stages of the instructional process. There are many avenues open to the classroom teacher that will facilitate the acquisition of this knowledge. For example, teachers may use formal assessment procedures such as achievement tests, or informal assessment procedures such as observational checklists can be used. Perhaps the most effective way to properly utilize assessment information is through both formal and informal means. One component of an effective classroom assessment program is the use of rubrics. Rubrics can be distinguished from other assessment procedures by their carefully written criteria that delineate various levels of proficiency that may be found among students on a common skill or task.

The primary purpose of this text is to explicate the development and use of rubrics for classroom assessment. Additionally, we explain the use of rubrics and how they fit into an effective assessment program. We follow the journey of one elementary school as its teachers strived to provide appropriate and authentic learning activities for all students. As more is revealed about the school, you will understand more clearly how the faculty integrated authentic assessment as an integral part of their instructional process and how the use of rubrics played a crucial role in this process.

The nine chapters that comprise this text begin with an introduction to the use of rubrics at Red River Elementary School and end with a discussion of the principal's role in providing the leadership essential to the creation of a creative and innovative school environment.

Chapters 1, 2, and 3 introduce the concept of rubrics, provide the reader with a rationale for using rubrics, describe how to develop rubrics, and suggest ways to involve students in the use of rubrics. Components of Chapter 1 include an introduction to rubrics and the participation of Red River Elementary School, a brief discussion of traditional and authentic assessment, and an in-depth discussion of the use of rubrics. How to develop and use rubrics is discussed in Chapter 2, with particular emphasis on developing rubrics within a planned unit of study, describing scoring criteria, selecting assessment anchors, using rubrics effectively in the classroom, grading, and using rubrics to guide instruction. Chapter 3 discusses the introduction of rubrics to students, the use of anchor papers, and designing rubrics with students.

In Chapters 4, 5, and 6, we discuss the use of rubrics in reading, writing, and the three content areas of math, social studies, and science. Sample rubrics are provided as models for rubric development. In Chapter 4, rubrics for use in reading are presented, with particular emphasis on oral reading, comprehension, and student engagement in reading tasks. The use of rubrics in writing is discussed in Chapter 5, with emphasis on written content and written mechanics. Chapter 6 focuses on the use of rubrics for math, social studies, and science.

Chapters 7, 8, and 9 demonstrate the effective use of rubrics with special needs students, explain how to use rubrics to facilitate communication with parents, and describe the administrator's role in the implementation of an effective schoolwide assessment program. Accommodating students with special needs is the theme of Chapter 7, with special attention devoted to at-risk readers and students with exceptionalities. An integral part of this chapter is the use of rubrics to assess each student's instructional needs. In Chapter 8, the focus is on effective communication with parents. We discuss topics such as parents and evaluation, the impact of parental involvement on schools, and the development of a parental involvement plan. The purpose of Chapter 9 is to discuss the role of the administrator in setting the tone for an effective assessment program, with emphasis on the principal as an agent of change. A major portion of this chapter is devoted to an interview with the principal and a classroom teacher from one of this country's most highly decorated elementary schools, which has implemented many of the ideas that we discuss in this text.

Each chapter of this text opens with an overview, thoroughly discusses each point presented in the table of contents, and closes with a summary. *Designing Rubrics for K-6 Classroom Assessment* is part of the Christopher-Gordon series entitled **The Bill Harp Professional Teacher's Library.**

CHAPTER 1

Introduction to Rubrics

Introduction

It is crucial that classroom teachers be aware of their students' abilities at all stages of the instructional process. There are various ways of obtaining this information through the use of formal assessment procedures such as achievement tests, and/or in conjunction with informal assessment procedures such as observation checklists. Thus, rubrics are just one component of an effective classroom assessment program. They are distinguished from other assessment tools by their carefully written criteria that delineate various levels of proficiency that may be found among students on a common skill or task. In addition, rubrics demonstrate to the students and their parents various levels of proficiency ranging from unsatisfactory to exemplary.

The primary purpose of this text is to elaborate on the development and use of rubrics for classroom assessment. An explanation of the use of rubrics and how they fit into a total authentic assessment program will be explored by examining the journey of one elementary school and the process its faculty moved through to provide appropriate and authentic learning activities for all students. As we learn more about the school, we will see how the school faculty members integrated authentic assessment as an integral part of their instructional framework and how rubrics became an essential component of daily instructional planning and assessment.

Red River Elementary School

Red River Elementary School is a suburban elementary school in the southeastern United States. While it is unique in several respects, it is representative of many schools across the country. The school has approximately 600 students from prekindergarten through fifth grade. These students come from diverse racial, ethnic, and socioeconomic backgrounds. They span the spectrum of ability levels, though many students attend Red River Elementary School because of their significant learning problems. The school faculty makes adaptations and modifications for children with learning difficulties and promotes full inclusion for its special education population. In addition, a number of gifted and talented students attend the school. Its staff is highly skilled and dedicated to meeting the needs of all learners. In short, Red River Elementary School differs little from other schools throughout the nation in its need to address the academic growth of a very diverse student population in all areas of the curriculum.

Red River Elementary's Journey to Authenticity

In the mid-1980s, Red River Elementary School was known for its mastery learning language arts program. Teachers used a highly structured instructional format, with scripted lessons in reading, writing, and spelling. Students mastered skills well, but there was little excitement or motivation for learning among the students and teachers. With the arrival of a new school principal and a desire to investigate more current research on teaching and learning, the school staff began to work together to explore the most effective instructional practices.

Faculty study groups were formed to study the professional literature on the writing process, integrated instruction, and authentic learning tasks. Teachers attended workshops and conferences to learn more about innovative topics and teaching strategies. In addition, a series of graduate courses emphasizing more current instructional practices became available on campus to help teachers gain additional knowledge about new theories and trends. Slowly, the staff began to adopt new assumptions about teaching and learning. The faculty at Red River Elementary soon believed that learning activities should be (a) child-centered, soliciting the students' own interests; (b) experiential, with students learning by doing whenever possible; (c) reflective, with opportunities for students to look back and reflect; (d) holistic, with instruction proceeding from the whole to its parts; (e) social and collaborative; (f) democratic; (g) cognitive, with activities designed to develop true understanding of concepts and higher-order thinking; (h) psycholinguistic, with language being the primary tool for learning; (i) rigorous and challenging, with students making choices and accepting responsibility for their own learning; (j) developmental; (k) constructive, whereby students gradually construct their own understandings in a productive learning environment; and (l) authentic, with real ideas in purposeful contexts (Zemelman, Daniels, & Hyde, 1993).

Authenticity is ubiquitous at Red River School. Teachers strive to ensure that learning activities in all curricular areas are meaningful and have application to real-life situations. In reading, authenticity means that children read unabridged books with natural language, not simplified and contrived texts. In writing, students write for authentic purposes—stories, letters, messages, informational pieces—to communicate to real audiences. In math, children investigate fractions by dividing a pizza, for example, rather than completing fractions problems in a workbook. Students may study a unit on the rain forest as a way to integrate a topic of current interest into the areas of science, social studies, reading, and writing. In other words, authentic activities are centered around topics that students care about, so that learning is meaningful and motivating.

Traditional versus Authentic Assessment

What are the purposes of assessment? Two answers are immediately apparent. First, we assess student learning in order to provide information on each student's progress to his or her parents, the school administration, and the public. Second, and perhaps most important, we assess student progress to guide our instruction. While the public seemed quite satisfied with the traditional grading system and many school boards mandate it, many teachers at Red River Elementary were displeased because their innovative teaching strategies were not always congruent with the objective tests they administered, such as achievement tests or state-mandated criterion-referenced instruments. They found that authentic learning activities require authentic assessment practices.

With authentic assessment, teachers avoid what has traditionally been done to evaluate student progress—administer a test and assign grades on report cards. While grading may be required (grading issues will be addressed in the next chapter), traditional objective tests by themselves are inadequate for measuring the complex and higher-order activities seen in classrooms where teachers stress authenticity. Many objective tests encourage memorization of isolated facts. A grade of 82 on an objective test, for example, provides little information concerning a student's strengths and learning needs. In addition, traditional assessment typically does not encourage student self-reflection. Figure 1.1 contrasts traditional assessment with more authentic assessment practices.

TRADITIONAL ASSESSMENT . . .	AUTHENTIC ASSESSMENT . . .
• is usually in the form of tests.	• entails many methods and forms.
• occurs as the teacher assesses students (teacher to students).	• occurs as the teacher assesses with students.
• is typically done at the end of an instructional unit.	• is a continuous process throughout a unit of study.
• assigns number grades to student work often based upon test scores.	• is multi-dimensional.
• is objective.	• is flexible.
• often focuses on isolated skills or facts.	• taps higher-order thinking skills and integration of knowledge.
• assesses knowledge.	• integrates knowledge and processes.
• has one answer or solution.	• encourages multiple solutions.
• is usually administered to a group of students.	• is often individualized to meet specific learner needs.
• does not encourage student reflection on work.	• encourages student self-reflection.

Figure 1.1   Traditional versus Authentic Assessment

As teachers at Red River Elementary School adopted more authentic instructional activities for their students, they worked to provide more authentic means of assessing student progress. The teachers knew that, with both traditional and authentic assessment, it was essential to identify goals and objectives for units of study and then formulate opportunities to determine whether students had reached those goals and objectives. Because they were dissatisfied with the reliance on traditional means of assessment, Red River faculty members began to experiment with various forms of authentic assessment and collect student work in portfolios.

Portfolios

Portfolios are purposeful collections of student work. They are designed to exhibit each student's efforts, achievements, and development in one or more curricular areas. The portfolio includes an ongoing, representative assortment of work samples and generally includes contributions from both the student and teacher. For example, one student's reading portfolio might include a list of the books that he or she has read during the school year, written responses to books read, teacher notes about reading conferences with the student, a reading interest survey, story retellings, and audiotapes of oral reading. Portfolios provide a thorough and complex picture of a student's performance over time.

Forms of Authentic Assessment

Authentic assessment takes many forms. Teachers select the assessment format that correlates best with a particular learning task. Among the forms of authentic assessment are running records, anecdotal notes, writing samples, retellings, learning logs, checklists, and rubrics. We will explain each assessment form briefly.

Running Records A running record is a procedure for coding and scoring a student's oral reading, and it serves as a tool for analyzing a child's reading behaviors. Running records are an authentic assessment tool because they assess how a student reads a genuine, not contrived, text. They are called running records because the teacher records a student's reading "on the run," with no advance preparation necessary. When taking a running record, the student and teacher read the same text, though the teacher doesn't need a separate copy. As the student reads, the teacher watches while recording the reading behaviors on a blank sheet of paper. All accurate reading is recorded with a check; other codes signify a miscue. A segment of a running record is seen below.

> Text: Little pig, little pig, let me come in.
>
> Child: Little little pig, little pig, let us come.
>
> Code: ✓R ✓ ✓ ✓ ✓ $\frac{us}{me}$ ✓ $\frac{—}{in}$

In this sample, the child repeated, substituted, and omitted words. As teachers take a running record of longer texts, they can (a) compute a percentage of accurate oral reading, and (b) analyze the miscues to find problem areas or evidence of effective strategy usage. (For more information on running records, see Clay, 1993.)

Anecdotal Notes   Anecdotal notes are dated written observations concerning a particular student's attitudes, needs, strengths, progress, and strategies that the teacher believes are important for a better understanding of that child. Anecdotal notes record brief statements that, when accumulated over time, provide a more complete picture of a student's learning than can be achieved through numerical grades in a grade book. They can be taken for any subject matter or skill area. An anecdotal note taken after a writing conference might look like the one shown in Figure 1.2.

> Robert 11/14
>
> Wrote about his new puppy. Easy to understand and shows humor. Good use of capitalization and use of conventional spelling. Needs review on punctuation at end of sentences.

Figure 1.2   Anecdotal Note

Writing Samples   Writing samples collected over the school year provide an authentic means of assessing a student's growth in writing. When studying and comparing writing samples over the course of the school year, the teacher can observe each child's progress (or continuing problem areas) in written content and writing mechanics.

Figures 1.3 and 1.4 illustrate a first grader's writing progress over the course of several months. Figure 1.3 reads, "We are in October, Halloween." At the time that this sample was obtained, the teacher noted that the writer appeared reluctant to take risks with writing. In this sample, the student simply copied print from around his classroom. However, he did put a capital letter at the beginning

Figure 1.3   October

Figure 1.4   December

of his sentence. Two months later (see Figure 1.4), this child wrote, "I like my ornament. It is good. It is good to me." At this time, he was writing more text and using sound/symbol relationships for phonetic spelling. Although he did not use punctuation at the end of his sentences, he drew boxes to indicate the sentence units.

These two writing activities help to demonstrate the advantages of obtaining samples of student writing. Each sample alone provides evidence of this child's skills and abilities at a particular time in his first grade year. A comparison of the two samples shows his progress as he moved to more detailed content and more accurate spelling and punctuation.

Story Retellings   An effective strategy for assessing comprehension of a reading selection is to ask students to retell a selection in their own words. Either oral or written, retellings help teachers determine each student's understanding of the material read. Teachers can prompt with questions such as, "What happened next?" or "What else do you remember?" to ensure that students respond with specific information. This process enables teachers to assess students' understanding of a story's characters, setting, problem, sequence of events, and the ending. In addition, teachers can evaluate a student's comprehension of the main ideas and important details given in an informational text.

Learning Logs   In the areas of math, social studies, and science, learning logs can be used. Learning logs are journals in which students communicate their knowledge of the content in a particular unit of study. As students write daily about what they have learned, they demonstrate understandings and misunderstandings of the content presented. Teachers then assess each student's comprehension of the subject area and determine points that need clarification. The example in Figure 1.5 illustrates a typical learning log entry in response to a science unit on animals.

Checklists   Checklists, as the name implies, are lists of skills or strategies appropriate for a unit of study. They are used by the teacher to determine which skills or strategy students are using appropriately. Either the student uses the skill or doesn't. To develop a checklist, the teacher must first determine the essential

> Vertebrates are animals with backbones. Backbones are spines. There are 5 kinds of vertebrates — fish, birds, mammals, anfibians, and reptiles. Humans are mammals. We have backbones so were vertebrates to.

Figure 1.5   Learning Log Entry

elements in a student product or a unit of study, and then list these elements in a column. For assessment, the teacher observes a student's behavior or product and checks off the elements that are observed. An example of a checklist for an intermediate grade writing sample is seen in Figure 1.6. A checklist such as this is valuable because the teacher is specific about his or her expectations, and students can refer to the checklist to analyze their own writing.

Name _____

Date _____

Title of Piece _____

This writing has . . .

_____ a title

_____ indentation

_____ topic sentence

_____ subject/verb agreement

_____ correct spelling

_____ capitalization

_____ punctuation

_____ a conclusion

_____ neat handwriting

Figure 1.6   Writing Checklist

Rubrics

Rubrics are another form of authentic assessment that help improve instruction and learning. They can be used with the other forms of assessment described above to give a thorough and complex picture of an individual's work.

What is a Rubric?

Rubrics are scoring guides that use specific written criteria to distinguish among levels of student proficiency on a common task. Like checklists, they specify the essential elements of a process or product. Unlike checklists, they allow for the assessment of the depth of knowledge or degree of proficiency for a particular student on a specific skill or task. In other words, the distinguishing characteristic of rubrics, and their major advantage, consists of the descriptions of the levels of proficiency for each objective.

How Does a Rubric Differ from a Checklist?

Consider the writing checklist in Figure 1.6. It is quite easy for the teacher to determine whether a student's written piece has a title. Either it does or it doesn't. But for the other objectives enumerated in the checklist, a "yes, it is evident" or "no, it isn't evident" seems insufficient. For example, suppose a student indents some paragraphs but not others. Should the teacher check off that objective? What if the child uses capital letters at the beginning of sentences but not for proper names? How does the teacher address that distinction using the checklist? In other words, the disadvantage of a checklist is that it doesn't allow for different levels of achievement for any given objective.

Levels of Proficiency

Let us examine one objective in the writing checklist above—capitalization. Some students will use capital letters appropriately all of the time, and others will use capital letters inappropriately or not at all. A rubric for the objective of capitalization would distinguish the different levels of proficiency that a teacher might find in students' written work and provide students with information about exemplary work. A rubric divided into four levels of proficiency is shown in Figure 1.7. The numbers aren't necessary but are provided to help you more easily distinguish the different levels. As you read the criteria for each level, you can readily observe how this rubric would facilitate assessment and would guide instruc-

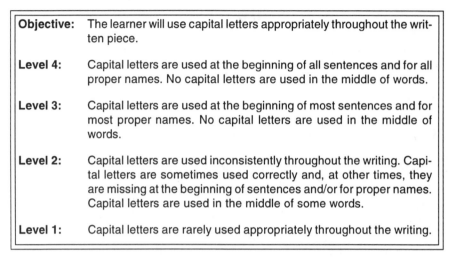

Objective:	The learner will use capital letters appropriately throughout the written piece.
Level 4:	Capital letters are used at the beginning of all sentences and for all proper names. No capital letters are used in the middle of words.
Level 3:	Capital letters are used at the beginning of most sentences and for most proper names. No capital letters are used in the middle of words.
Level 2:	Capital letters are used inconsistently throughout the writing. Capital letters are sometimes used correctly and, at other times, they are missing at the beginning of sentences and/or for proper names. Capital letters are used in the middle of some words.
Level 1:	Capital letters are rarely used appropriately throughout the writing.

Figure 1.7   Capitalization Rubric

tional planning because it distinguishes among a task's different levels of proficiency.

Advantages of Rubrics

Rubrics have several advantages that make them excellent tools for classroom assessment. First, the development of a rubric requires the careful reflection of the teacher. The teacher must plan goals, objectives, and assessment criteria before the unit is taught. This is advantageous because the teacher then knows (a) what needs to be taught, (b) what students must learn, and (c) what separates excellent and average student work from work that requires additional teacher attention.

A second advantage occurs when the teacher introduces the rubric to students (and parents) at the beginning of a unit of study. Students benefit from being aware of the criteria for assessment, parents understand the teacher's expectations, and everyone can work toward achieving the highest level of achievement. As the unit progresses, the teacher can monitor student progress to assist students who may be having difficulties.

Student self-evaluation is a natural extension of a rubric. Rubrics easily translate into a tool that allows students to become more responsible for reaching higher levels of achievement. This advantage will be discussed fully in Chapter 3.

Rubrics foster collaboration. Teachers can work together to develop rubrics, and rubrics can also be designed by students collaboratively with their teacher. Parents become partners in the learning process because they are made aware of the unit objectives, tasks, and the criteria for exemplary work prior to the unit of study. In this way, parents are better able to support their child and the teacher.

With the explicit criteria provided in a rubric, subjectivity is reduced and assessment is made more objective. This is particularly crucial for assessing those skills and tasks that aren't easily quantifiable.

Finally, rubrics can include both process and product evaluation. In traditional assessment, teachers usually measure only each student's product—the end result of the learning. With rubrics, however, behaviors that relate to the learning process—participation, on-task behavior, and appropriate use of materials, for example—can be more easily assessed.

One Example from Red River Elementary

Ms. Richards is a second grade teacher at Red River Elementary. One of her favorite language arts units features Readers Theater. Readers Theater is similar to an old-time radio show because the actors read their parts using only their voices to "act." It is a preferred language arts activity for Ms. Richards because it is easy, motivational, requires no costumes or stage sets, and provides an audience for student readers. Readers Theater is designed to develop word recognition, fluency, phrasing, and expression as students read their assigned parts. In preparation for a performance, students spend several days in rehearsal by reading and rereading their parts so that they can read with fluency and expression. During a Readers Theater performance, a group of students stands in front of the audience and each student reads with expression from a script.

Before introducing the unit to her students, Ms. Richards selected appropriate Readers Theater scripts, decided upon the length of the unit, and planned daily lessons. Most important, she determined the objectives that would be addressed throughout the unit. She selected three objectives dealing with the Readers Theater final performance: (a) reading with fluency and expression, (b) using a speaking voice that was easily heard, and (c) using the standing position appropriate for a performance. In addition, one of the unit objectives dealt with on-task behavior during rehearsals.

For each of the objectives, Ms. Richards described four levels of proficiency (see Figure 1.8). By familiarizing her students with the unit objectives and levels of proficiency, the second graders were able to strive for the best level of performance and evaluate their own learning behavior and Readers Theater performance by reflecting on the objectives.

	Objective: The learner will read with fluency and expression.	Objective: The learner will speak in a voice that is easy to hear.	Objective: The learner will use Readers Theater posture.	Objective: The learner will stay on task during rehearsals.
4	Student read with fluency and expression through all of the performance.	Student's voice was easy to hear through all of the performance.	Student used Readers Theater posture through all of the performance.	Student stayed on task during all of the rehearsals.
3	Student read with fluency and expression through most of the performance, though the reading lacked expression for one or two lines.	Student's voice was easy to hear through most of the performance. At several points, the audience could not hear the performance.	Student used Readers Theater posture through most of the performance, but moved into another posture once or twice.	Student stayed on task during most of the rehearsals.
2	Student read with fluency and expression through approximately half of his/her lines.	Student's voice was easy to hear through approximately half or less of the performance.	Student used Readers Theater posture occasionally, but typically stood in a different posture.	Student stayed on task during some of the rehearsals, but needed reminders to attend to the task.
1	Student read word-by-word with no fluency and/or expression.	Student's voice could not be heard through the performance.	Student did not use Readers Theater posture through the performance.	Student rarely stayed on task during the rehearsals and needed regular teacher direction to return to work.

Figure 1.8   Readers Theater Rubric

A Word of Caution

Throughout this text, we present various rubrics that address many instructional areas and span many grade levels. As you begin to use rubrics in your own classrooms, remember that the rubrics within this book are models only. Because the rubrics illustrated here may not address the objectives that you find important, or may not meet the needs of your particular students, we urge you to continually adapt and refine any rubric so that it aligns better with your instructional program.

Chapter 2

Developing and Using Rubrics

Mr. Martin is a fifth grade teacher at Red River Elementary School. Every year since he began teaching fifth grade, he has taught a science unit on mammals. He wanted to develop unit plans that differed from his traditional approach of lecturing, reading the textbook, and giving an objective test at the end of the unit of study. In this chapter, we will examine how Mr. Martin prepared his unit so that learner objectives and activities were more integrated and authentic. In addition, we will observe how he planned rubrics for this unit of study, organized his classroom to encourage a collaborative and challenging learning atmosphere, and converted his rubric assessment scores to the traditional numerical grades required by his school district. Finally, Mr. Martin's use of the rubric to meet individual student's needs will be examined.

Developing a Rubric

Step 1: Plan a Unit of Study

Mr. Martin taught this unit on mammals as part of his school district's recommended topics for fifth grade science. Besides the specific information about mammals that he wanted his students to learn, he also wanted to integrate reading, writing, and math into the unit. Mr. Martin's first steps in planning were to decide upon the important goals and objectives for this unit of study and then determine what student activities would be most appropriate for each goal and objective. He began by asking himself, "What are the goals and objectives I want my students to reach by completing this unit?" Next, he made a map of his unit plan (see Figure 2.1).

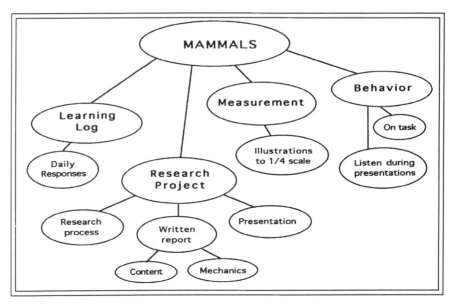

Figure 2.1   Unit Map

This map helped Mr. Martin organize his ideas for the unit into four major goals. First, he knew that it would be necessary to teach some specific information about mammals—for example, characteristics of mammals, similarities and differences between mammals and other animals, and varieties of mammals. Instead of assessing this knowledge with a test as he had done in the past, Mr. Martin decided to have the students record what they learned daily in their learning logs. In addition, Mr. Martin wanted to introduce the procedures for a research report and have students research a mammal of their choice. During the research, Mr. Martin wanted students to find accurate and adequate information about their mammal and to use multiple sources. The end result of the research would be a written report and a presentation. He expected the written report to be thorough, well-written, and contain accurate written mechanics. To integrate math into this science unit, Mr. Martin decided that students would make illustrations of their chosen mammals drawn to 1/4 scale. Finally, he wanted to assess student behavior as they attended to instruction, completed their research, and listened to presentations.

Mr. Martin estimated that the unit would take approximately four weeks to complete. He decided that the first five days would be spent on understanding important scientific information about mammals. He would use the science text and informational trade books to teach this information. At the end of each day during the first week, students would complete their learning logs to explain what they had understood. Mr. Martin also decided that the best way to explain the research project was for him to complete a research project along with his students. He decided that for approximately the next 7 to 8 days, he would do a short lesson at the beginning of each science class in which he modeled the research process for the class. Mr. Martin wanted all reports to have specific information on each mammal's appearance, reproduction/offspring, size, habitat, diet, and unique characteristics. He would model locating reference materials, organizing and taking notes, and using the notes for the final written product. After each day's mini-lesson, the students would locate reference materials, take notes, and work on their final written report. As the reports were nearing completion, Mr. Martin planned a mini-lesson on drawing to a 1/4 scale. He expected that students would need 1 or 2 days to complete their illustrations. Because he did not want the students simply to read their written reports for their presentations, he also prepared a mini-lesson so that they would understand how to use notes on index cards to guide them through their oral reports. During the final week of the unit, five students would give an oral presentation each day and answer questions about their mammal.

Now Mr. Martin knew his role, expectations, and the activities that the students would attempt during this science unit. Consider his goals and objectives, which are shown in Figure 2.2.

Step 2: Choosing the Number of Levels of Proficiency

Once his learning objectives were established, Mr. Martin created a set of criteria—a rubric—for assessing students' processes, products, and behavior. He knew that since a rubric is distinguished by varying levels of proficiency for each learning objective, he first had to decide how many levels of proficiency he wanted for each objective. In other words, how many scoring points were appropriate for assessing student performance on each objective?

Before beginning our discussion, we want to reiterate that it is not necessary to assign numbers to each level of proficiency. Well-written descriptions are the critical component of rubrics; numbers are provided in this discussion to make it easier for you to understand the range of proficiency levels. When numbers are used in the rubrics provided in this book, the higher the number, the more exemplary is the performance or task.

Goals	Objectives
To record information in a learning log	1. The learner will record accurate and complete information in a learning log.
To complete a research project	1. The learner will use multiple resources. 2. The learner will take adequate notes. 3. The learner's written report will be well-organized and contain sufficient information. 4. The written report will have correct capitalization, usage, punctuation, and spelling. 5. The presentation will give sufficient and pertinent information to the audience. 6. The presentation will be easy to hear.
To make an illustration to 1/4 scale	1. The learner will draw a picture of his or her chosen mammal accurately to 1/4 scale.
To exhibit proper behavior throughout the unit	1. The learner will listen attentively during instruction. 2. The learner will remain on task throughout the research project. 3. The learner will listen attentively during presentations.

Figure 2.2   Goals and Objectives

The appropriate number of levels of proficiency is determined by the teacher's preference and how broad the levels of performance might be among students. A three-point scale is often the easiest to use, but Mr. Martin believed that a three-point scale would not distinguish sufficiently between his expected levels of performance. In addition, Mr. Martin thought that it would be too easy to assign a score of 2 to much of his students' work—work that was neither exemplary nor unsatisfactory. Because he preferred more discriminating rubrics, he chose 4 levels of proficiency to describe student work, and to use a score of 0 for work that was not attempted. In this way, Mr. Martin could distinguish among excellent work, good work, acceptable work, inadequate work, and no work.

Step 3: Describing Scoring Criteria for Each Level of Proficiency

For each objective, Mr. Martin's next task was to describe the scoring criteria for each level of proficiency. This step is the nexus of developing rubrics. For each objective, Mr. Martin described the 4 levels of proficiency that he anticipated finding among his students' work. The first rubric that he developed concerned the students' entries in their daily learning logs. Mr. Martin began this rubric by rewriting the goal and objective. His initial decision was to determine whether he would assess the learning logs daily or at the end of the five-day recording period. After he decided that he would use the rubric for all five learning log entries, he then described the criteria for each level of proficiency to be used for student evaluation. As he wrote the descriptions, he kept in mind that he wanted a score of 4 to describe excellent work; 3 to describe good work; 2 to describe acceptable work; and 1 to describe inadequate work. Observe how Mr. Martin distinguished among levels of proficiency for learning log entries in his rubric, which is shown in Figure 2.3.

Goal: To record information in learning log	
Objective: The learner will record accurate and complete information in a learning log.	
4	Information on all five learning log entries was thorough and accurate. No misunderstanding of the content was evident.
3	Information on four learning log entries was thorough and accurate. No significant misunderstanding of the content was evident.
2	Information on three learning log entries was thorough and accurate OR information on entries showed understanding of the main points but lacked details.
1	Information was scant and/or showed significant misunderstanding of the content.
0	No information was recorded in the learning log.

Figure 2.3 Rubric for Learning Log Entries

Mr. Martin continued this procedure for the remaining goals and objectives. As he wrote and rewrote the rubric descriptions, he was able to reflect on his intentions and better clarify his objectives for the students. For example, he did not want to assess the illustrations of mammals by how well each child drew; instead, he wanted to evaluate each student's ability to compute the size of an animal to a 1/4 scale. Therefore, the criteria he developed dealt only with the mathematical issue, not the quality of the artwork. Mr. Martin's rubric for the mammal illustrations is shown in Figure 2.4.

Goal: To make illustrations to 1/4 scale	
Objective: The learner will draw a picture of his or her chosen mammal accurately to 1/4 scale.	
4	The drawing was accurately reduced to 1/4 scale. The student used math to compute the reduction.
3	The drawing was reduced near 1/4 scale. The student used math accurately to compute the reduction.
2	The drawing was reduced but was not near 1/4 scale. The student used math accurately to compute the reduction.
1	The student made an illustration but used math inaccurately OR did not attempt to use math to compute the reduction.

Figure 2.4   Rubric for Mammal Illustration

Mr. Martin's rubric for student behavior is shown in Figure 2.5. Because this goal had three objectives, Mr. Martin arranged this rubric in a grid format using his computer's word processing program, with the objectives across the top of the grid and the scoring points on the left side. As he prepared this behavior rubric, he realized that a score of 1 was sufficient for the lowest scoring point on this rubric. Read Figure 2.5 to see how Mr. Martin distinguished among levels of proficiency for student behavior.

Mr. Martin used the same grid format for assessing student performance on the various aspects of the research process. Again, to distinguish among levels of proficiency for each learner objective, he considered his criteria for excellent, good, acceptable, and inadequate work. Mr. Martin's rubric for the research project is shown in Figure 2.6. The unit objectives are shown across the top of the rubric.

While Mr. Martin was developing this rubric, he was able to clarify several concerns that he had not previously considered. For example, he had not thought about the number of sources that he wanted the students to use as they researched their mammals. As

Goal: To exhibit proper behavior through the science unit on mammals	The learner will listen attentively during instruction.	The learner will remain on task throughout the research project.	The learner will listen attentively during presentations.
Score Point 4	The student was attentive throughout all of the instruction.	The student stayed on task throughout all of the research project.	The student was attentive throughout all of the presentations.
Score Point 3	The student was attentive, but was distracted several times throughout the instruction. The student returned to the instruction without teacher intervention.	The student stayed on task throughout most of the research project but was distracted from the work several times. The student returned to work without teacher intervention.	The student was attentive, but was distracted several times throughout the presentations. The student returned to the presentations without teacher intervention.
Score Point 2	The student was usually attentive, but needed occasional reminders to attend to the instruction.	The student stayed on task throughout some of the research project, but needed occasional reminders to attend to work.	The student was usually attentive, but needed occasional reminders to attend to the presentations.
Score Point 1	The student was inattentive and needed regular teacher direction to attend to the instruction.	The student had difficulty staying on task and needed regular teacher direction to return to work.	The student was inattentive and needed regular teacher direction to attend to the presentations.

Figure 2.5   Behavior Rubric

he developed the rubric, he was able to determine that four sources would be representative of excellent achievement, three for good achievement, and so on. In addition, his first draft of the rubric did not make it clear that he wanted the students to work from notes for their presentation instead of reading their written reports. Mr. Martin found that the process of rubric-writing was helpful not only for considering assessment criteria, but for considering lesson specifics as well.

	The learner will use multiple sources.	The learner will take adequate notes.	The written report will be well-organized and contain sufficient information.	The written report will have correct capitalization, usage, punctuation, and spelling.	The presentation will give sufficient and pertinent information to the audience.	The presentation will be easy to hear.
4	Information came from 4 or more sources.	Many details were apparent in notes in all categories (appearance, reproduction/offspring, habitat, diet, and unique characteristics).	The report was well-organized and contained thorough and accurate information.	Accurate capitalization, punctuation, usage, and spelling were used throughout the written report.	The presentation was well-organized and contained thorough and accurate information. The student did not read his/her report.	All of the presentation was easy to hear from the back of the classroom.
3	Information came from 3 sources.	Many details were evident in most, but not all, of the categories.	The report was well-organized. Many details were evident but some important information was missing in 1 or 2 categories.	Several errors were evident, but the errors did not interfere with a reader's comprehension.	The presentation was well-organized, but some important information was missing. The student did not read his/her report.	Most of the presentation was easy to hear from the back of the classroom.
2	Information came from 2 sources.	Notes were evident in all categories, but details were lacking.	The report was sometimes difficult to understand. Important information was missing in 3 or more categories.	Errors were evident, and several of the errors made it difficult for a reader to understand parts of the report.	The presentation was easy to understand, but details were missing OR the student read his/her report.	Some of the presentation was easy to hear from the back of the room.
1	Information came from 1 source.	Few notes were taken.	The report was difficult to understand. Important information was missing in all categories.	Many errors were evident throughout the written report that made it difficult for a reader to understand.	The presentation was difficult to understand and incomplete. Important information was missing.	Little of the presentation was easy to hear from the back of the room.
0	No sources were used.	No notes were taken.	No written report was done.	No written report was done.	No presentation was given.	No presentation was given.

Figure 2.6   Rubric for Research Project

Step 4: Selecting Assessment Anchors

Assessment anchors provide models of expected student work and/ or performance for each scoring point on a rubric. This step is optional and will be discussed thoroughly in the next chapter.

Step 5: Revising the Rubric

Mr. Martin was excited about his new approach to this science unit. The activities and assessment practices were more authentic, and he anticipated that the students would be more motivated about the topic. Despite his enthusiasm, Mr. Martin knew that the rubrics he designed would require continuous revisions in the years to come to meet the needs of the students he would have in the future. In other words, once a rubric is created, it will need to continuously undergo thorough adaptations and modifications to better align with the diverse needs of future students and/or different goals and objectives.

Summary

To develop rubrics for his science unit on mammals, Mr. Martin first thoroughly planned this unit of study. He had to reflect on goals, objectives, unit design, available resources, timelines, as well as teacher and student activities. He then decided upon the number of levels of proficiency (i.e., the number of scoring points) per objective. Next, and most important, he described the scoring criteria for each level for every objective. Finally, he selected assessment anchors. Mr. Martin realized that revisions to his rubrics may be necessary in the future.

Various Formats for Rubrics

The rubrics we've shown for Mr. Martin's science unit illustrate several different formats for rubric development. Depending on the goal, Mr. Martin either had scoring points between 0 and 4 or between 1 and 4. In addition, he used different forms, based upon the number of objectives for a particular goal. He found that if he had only one objective per goal, he simply described the scoring criteria in a list under the objective (as seen in Figures 2.3 and 2.4). Mr. Martin found that if a goal had more than one objective, his scoring criteria were clearer if he used a grid to list the objectives and scoring criteria on one sheet of paper (as seen in Figures 2.5 and 2.6).

Mr. Martin's behavior rubric contained similar descriptions on all four levels of proficiency throughout all three objectives. In other words, for each objective, the description was similar at each scoring point. When this occurs, a rubric could be simplified to appear as in Figure 2.7.

Goal: To exhibit proper behavior through the science unit

Objectives   **Score**

   1. Listen attentively during instruction   _____

   2. Remain on task throughout research project   _____

   3. Listen attentively during presentations   _____

Scoring Key

4 = Always

3 = Usually, but was distracted several times. No teacher intervention was
     necessary.

2 = Sometimes, but needed occasional reminders to attend.

1 = Rarely, and needed regular teacher direction to attend.

Figure 2.7   Alternate Rubric Format

As you develop rubrics, you will decide the number of levels of proficiency appropriate for a particular objective. You will also choose the format for describing your scoring criteria for each level of proficiency. Various formats are included throughout the book.

A Classroom Using Rubrics

In years past, Mr. Martin presented this science unit with a traditional approach to instruction and assessment. Each day, he lectured to impart information to his fifth graders about mammals. Mr. Martin led class discussions and controlled the direction and amount of student talk. Students were required to read the science textbook and turn in written answers to questions in the textbook. The questions generally focused on factual recall, and student responses were short and simple. Mr. Martin valued silence during seatwork time, and collaboration among the students was discouraged. Grades from written assignments were recorded in Mr.

Martin's grade book, but students' final grades were derived in large part from their ability to answer multiple choice and short answer questions on an objective test administered to all students at the end of the unit. Once the test was complete, Mr. Martin and the students moved on to another unit of study.

By contrast, Mr. Martin's new plans for this science unit were very different from his traditional approach. On the first day of the unit, Mr. Martin introduced his goals, objectives, timeline, and assessment rubrics to the class. In this way, the students knew his expectations at the beginning of instruction. Mr. Martin still had some specific information about mammals to teach to the class, but instead of a lecture and textbook approach, he primarily used trade books and cooperative learning. In place of the short answers to textbook questions, students now wrote detailed information in their learning logs.

The assessment rubrics were posted in the classroom throughout the unit to aid in teacher and student reflection. At the end of the first week, Mr. Martin asked his students to assess themselves on the rubric related to learning logs, then, to encourage excellent work, they were allowed to revise their logs if they were dissatisfied with their entries. Mr. Martin also encouraged students to assess their listening skills during instruction on the behavior rubric. After student self-assessment, Mr. Martin scored his students' progress on the appropriate elements of the rubrics.

When the research project began on the second week of the four-week unit, Mr. Martin modeled the research process by demonstrating, rather than telling, his students what to do. Students were able to assume control of the learning process by choosing a mammal to research and proceeding at their own pace as they conducted their research. Mr. Martin had obtained many resources for student research—for example, trade books, encyclopedias, nature magazines—and students were allowed to select their own resources, collaborate, and help one another. Mr. Martin served as a facilitator during this time by assisting, encouraging, and redirecting his students as needed. He took anecdotal notes concerning students' research processes, writing skills, and behavior. Because he so clearly understood his expectations, Mr. Martin was able to evaluate student progress daily and give immediate assistance to those in need. Furthermore, because the students clearly understood the expectations, they were able to continually reflect on their own progress.

As written reports were nearing completion, Mr. Martin encouraged students to help each other revise and edit their reports for content and mechanics. A writing checklist posted in the classroom helped students check for grammar, punctuation, and capitalization errors. Dictionaries were available for spelling, and students also referred to the class Word Wall and to a chart with words related to mammals to confirm or correct their spellings.

Students were allowed to choose the materials for their illustrations. Some used watercolors, others used markers, colored pencils, or crayons. Rulers and measuring tapes were available for measurement. Students were spread out across the classroom as they worked on their illustrations, some at their desks and others on the floor. Again, collaboration and conversation were encouraged. When the illustrations were complete, students evaluated themselves on the illustration rubric, and then Mr. Martin assessed each student. The illustrations were displayed in the hall near the classroom with a sign that explained the math objective to interested observers.

Students sat on the carpeted section of the floor to listen to presentations. Mr. Martin and his students were encouraging and gave positive feedback to each speaker. In this way, students learned about other mammals in addition to the one that each had researched. As before, students first self-assessed before Mr. Martin scored the rubric related to the research project.

Though he had worked very hard to prepare this unit, Mr. Martin knew that his work was worth the effort. With the multidimensional and interdisciplinary approach to the study of mammals, the learning was more meaningful to his students and was more authentic. His assessment was on-going, flexible, and individualized. Mr. Martin was sure that the students produced better work because of their increased motivation and collaboration, their thorough understanding of his expectations and the components of exemplary work, their continuous reflection on their own work, and his immediate response to students with problems. Because of the success of this unit, Mr. Martin intended to make more use of integrated, authentic learning activities and assessment rubrics in other units of study. He also shared his new approach with other fifth grade teachers at Red River Elementary to encourage collaboration among the school staff as they planned future units.

Grading Issues

With reluctance, we address the issue of grading. When authentic assessment practices are implemented, numerical grading becomes unnecessary. Rubrics and other authentic assessment tools replace traditional grades. As we've stated before, authentic assessment provides a more accurate and meaningful picture of each student's growth over time. In fact, translating a rubric scoring point to a numerical grade is contrary to the purpose and philosophy of authentic assessment.

We are realists, however, and realize that no matter what a particular teacher's philosophy toward authentic assessment is, numerical grading is typically mandated by school districts. We may not like it, but most classroom teachers must assign numerical grades to assignments and letter grades on report cards. We will see how Mr. Martin used his rubric rating scale scores and converted them to numerical grades because his school district required traditional grading. In this way, though not ideal, rubrics complemented more traditional grading practices.

Mr. Martin's Grading System Using Rubrics

Before Mr. Martin introduced the science unit to his students, he considered the issue of grading. With each objective, he first determined how his grades would be categorized into subjects. He decided that learning log information would be one science grade; the illustration would be a math grade; the three behavior objectives would convert to three conduct grades; objectives related to the written report would be used for science and language grades; and the presentation scores would be used for another language grade.

Mr. Martin chose a rubric rating scale of 4 points on each objective not only to distinguish between different levels of proficiency, but also to easily convert to numerical grades. He decided that each scoring point readily corresponded to his district's range of scores for a grade of A, B, C, and D. Mr. Martin's district considered an A to be earned with a numerical grade from 93 to 100; B from 85 to 92; C from 78 to 84; and D from 70 to 78. Mr. Martin's initial point assignment is shown in Figure 2.8. If a student obtained a score point of 3 on the rubric related to the mammal illustration, for example, he or she would earn a math numerical grade of 90 (which corresponded to a letter grade of B in Mr. Martin's district).

Rubric Scoring Point	Numerical Grade	Letter Grade
4	100	A
3	90	B
2	80	C
1	70	D

Figure 2.8   Grade Conversion Chart

Let's look at several of Mr. Martin's rubrics related to this science unit to further explore his grading decisions. The rubrics related to learning log entries (see Figure 2.3) and mammal illustrations (see Figure 2.4) are easy to use in determining numerical grades because there is only one objective per rubric. The scoring points readily convert to the numerical grades shown in Figure 2.7. That is, a score point of 4 equals a numerical grade of 100; a score point of 3 equals a numerical grade of 90; and so on.

The rubric related to behavior (see Figure 2.5) could be graded in one of two ways. Mr. Martin chose to take three conduct grades from this rubric using his numerical grading scale, but he easily could have elected to take one overall behavior grade. To take one grade, he first would assign a rubric score to each of the three objectives. Then he would convert the three scoring points to numerical grades using his grade conversion chart. Last, he would average the three numerical scores. For example, suppose a student received a scoring point of 3 on the first behavior objective; 2 on the second objective; and 4 on the last objective. Mr. Martin first would assign a numerical grade to each scoring point (90, 80, and 100) and then average the three numbers for a final behavior grade of 90. Mr. Martin used this averaging procedure for assigning numerical grades for each student's written report and presentation.

Mr. Martin could have elected to weigh one objective more heavily than the other objectives related to the same goal. Referring again to the behavior rubric (see Figure 2.5), suppose Mr. Martin wanted the objective related to on-task behavior to count twice as much as the other two objectives. In this case, he first would obtain numerical grade conversions for the three scoring points, double the grade for the second objective, and divide the sum by 4. In the example described in the preceding paragraph, the numerical grades for one student were 90, 80, and 100 on the behavior rubric. Mr. Martin doubled the second score (to 160), added the 3 numbers (90 + 160 + 100 = 350), and divided the total by 4. In this case, the student's final behavior grade was 87.

Three Cautions

The example of Mr. Martin's grading system is an illustration only. If your school or district does not require traditional numerical grades, we urge you to eliminate their use from your practice. If you are required to use numerical and/or letter grades, you may wish to assign points differently than Mr. Martin did. Use your professional judgment to align your rubric scoring points with your school district's grading scale.

If you do use rubrics for grading purposes, you won't want to assign numerical grades for every rubric you use. You will use some rubrics only for the purpose of monitoring student performance or for helping you to determine teaching points to address in future instruction. Again, your professional judgment is necessary for determining the rubrics appropriate for use as grading tools.

One last word about numerical grades—don't use percentages to determine grades from rubrics. If you assign a student a score of 2, for example, on a four-point rubric, you cannot then say he or she received 2 out of 4 points for a grade of 50%. On a four-point rubric, a score of 2 means acceptable work, and in no way corresponds to a numerical grade of 50.

Using Rubrics to Guide Instruction

Now that the procedures for designing rubrics have been fully discussed, one major advantage of rubrics becomes apparent. Mr. Martin used the process of rubric development to thoroughly plan his unit—goals, objectives, activities, resources, and assessment. In other words, the process guided his instruction because he had to consider the content to teach, the important goals and objectives, and what separated excellent and average work from work that required additional teacher attention.

In addition, rubrics were advantageous for Mr. Martin's students because they allowed him to better meet individual learner's needs. As he monitored the students as they completed their research projects, Mr. Martin could provide additional help to students who encountered problems and give guidance as students had questions. That is, Mr. Martin's thorough understanding of his expectations allowed him to adapt his instruction to help all learners achieve high levels of achievement.

Collaboration with Other Faculty

In a school setting where the use of rubrics for assessing students' work is being considered, it is critical that this be seen as a collaborative process. The school districts that have used rubrics successfully have relied heavily upon collaboration among teachers. Although we are using an example of one teacher, Mr. Martin, and his fifth grade science class, we are assuming that he is not alone in his efforts to use rubrics and other authentic assessment measures to evaluate student performance. In fact, we strongly suggest that teachers work collaboratively in their school to design rubrics appropriate for authentic units of study.

CHAPTER 3

Introducing Rubrics to Students

One advantage of using rubrics is that students know the teacher's expectations and the criteria for grading prior to the beginning of the unit of study. Mr. Martin, as discussed in Chapter 2, found that his students not only learned more because of their immersion in authentic activities, but they produced better work because they were clear about his goals, objectives, timeline, and assessment procedures. As this chapter proceeds, we will begin by following Mr. Martin and his class as they continue working on the science unit related to mammals.

Sharing Rubrics with Students

As explained in Chapter 2, Mr. Martin planned his unit by selecting goals and objectives, choosing student activities, estimating timelines for completion, and designing assessment rubrics. Mr. Martin presented the unit plans to his students on the first day of the unit of study. He began by explaining procedures, learning objectives, his expectations, his role, and the students' roles and responsibilities. To introduce the four rubrics to be used with this unit, Mr. Martin reproduced them on chart paper and displayed them throughout the classroom. When he presented each rubric to the class using the charts, he read each objective, interpreted the criteria at each scoring point, and explained his grading system. He then answered students' questions concerning any aspect of this science unit before he proceeded to his first lesson on the characteristics of mammals. In addition, Mr. Martin sent a note to parents explaining his purposes and objectives for the unit, and he included copies of the four rubrics so that parents would also understand his expectations and assessment criteria.

Mr. Martin knew that students would need repeated exposure to the rubrics so that they could internalize the information and use it effectively. Therefore, he began each lesson with a review of the objectives and rubric(s) pertinent to that day's study. For example, during the first week the class completed information in their learning logs. So every day of this week, Mr. Martin began by reviewing the rubric related to learning log entries and the section of the behavior rubric related to attentive listening during instruction. As he reviewed the assessment criteria for each objective with his students, Mr. Martin encouraged them to reflect on their own achievement and consider ways to continue excellent work and improve any other work that was less than excellent.

Anchor Papers

Definition and Uses

Not only are the scoring criteria provided in a rubric useful to guide teachers in assessing student work by comparing each individual's work to the criteria, they also help students gain a more thorough understanding of the teacher's expectations. However, an additional step to ensure more consistent teacher assessment and better student understanding is for the teacher to provide models that help to clarify the criteria for each scoring point. This can be accomplished through the use of anchor papers.

Anchor papers are actual samples of student work that correspond to the various levels of proficiency represented on a rubric. Referring again to Mr. Martin's mammal unit, he expected students to have three products at the end of the unit: learning log entries, a written research report, and an illustration. To utilize anchor papers during this science unit, Mr. Martin provided four learning log samples, four written reports, and four illustrations, with each sample corresponding to one scoring point on a rubric. In other words, one sample for each learning objective would meet the criteria for a score of 4, another for a score of 3, and so on. These anchor papers were introduced with the rubric and referred to routinely as the unit progressed. (Obviously, these anchor papers would not be available during the first year Mr. Martin implemented this unit but would be selected from student work to be used in subsequent years.)

Anchor papers provide models of student products, but they cannot be used for those objectives in which no product is produced. For example, Mr. Martin's students had no written product related to his objectives for student behavior and the research presentation. For objectives such as these in which a performance, not a product, is assessed, we suggest the use of what we have termed performance anchors. With performance anchors, as with anchor papers, teachers provide a model for each scoring point per learning objective. The difference is that the teacher must provide a visual model of each scoring point. The teacher could produce an audio or video tape with performances that represent each scoring point on a particular rubric. For example, Mr. Martin could videotape four research presentations that corresponded to four rubric scoring points. (As stated previously, these performance anchor videos would not be available during the first year of implementing a new unit of study.)

Collaboration with Faculty in Selection of Anchors

Just as we encourage the collaboration among staff members in the development of rubrics, collaboration is also important in the selection of anchor papers and performance anchors. Before beginning the long journey to authenticity, the teachers at Red River Elementary School decided to work as a team to develop the best assessment program possible for their school. A critical part of this process was the use of anchor papers and performance anchors.

Teachers collected the work of their students and spent many hours determining which of their students' work best represented the criteria established in their rubrics. Thus, rubrics often were developed by the teachers collaboratively first, and then anchor papers and performance anchors were carefully selected from the students' work to represent a framework within which each teacher could evaluate their student's efforts. As a result, consistency of evaluation can be maintained within grade levels and across grade levels within a school setting.

Collaboration with Students in Selection of Anchors

It can be beneficial for students in the intermediate grades (or above), who have a thorough understanding of a rubric's scoring criteria, to collaborate with the teacher in the selection of anchor papers or performance anchors. Students then develop a better understanding of the critical elements necessary for proficiency.

We will again use Mr. Martin's science unit to illustrate our point. Suppose that Mr. Martin wanted his students to select anchor papers for his objective concerning written mechanics—capitalization, usage, punctuation, and spelling. He would first collect writings from research reports done by students in previous years and delete the students' names so that the samples were anonymous. Small groups of students would then study several of the writing samples and assess the samples according to the rubric's scoring criteria for written mechanics. In essence, the students would be scoring the samples according to the rubric criteria. Each group would seek to select a representative sample for each scoring point (an anchor paper) and justify their choice to the rest of the class. After the small groups scored their writing samples, Mr. Martin would reconvene his class, and students in each group would share the representative anchor papers they had chosen. Mr. Martin would help his students reach a consensus so that one anchor paper was selected for each scoring point. These anchor papers would then be posted and used for reference as the rubric was discussed.

Students can also help the teacher select performance anchors. Instead of choosing a representative paper for each scoring point, groups of students could role-play the expected performance for each level of proficiency on a rubric. A simple illustration of this process can be shown with Mr. Martin's objective concerning how well the audience could hear student presentations of their research reports. Each small group would discuss and then act out the expected behavior for each scoring point. The class would then agree on a representative performance that was easy to hear throughout all of the presentation (score point 4); one that was easy to hear throughout most of the presentation (score point 3); and so on. In this way, students would demonstrate their understanding of the scoring criteria by selecting performance anchors.

The process of student selection of anchor papers and performance anchors is time-consuming, and teachers probably would not want to have students go through this process for each objective on every rubric. However, because the process is so beneficial for helping students become discriminating thinkers about quality work, we recommend that teachers provide regular opportunities for students to select anchors for teacher-designed rubrics.

Designing Rubrics with Students

In the previous discussions, we've described how teachers select scoring criteria as they design rubrics. Another possibility with older students is to have the students write the scoring criteria themselves.. As with student selection of anchors discussed above, students gain a more critical understanding of the elements that distinguish between different levels of proficiency as they write a rubric's scoring criteria.

To accomplish this, the teacher would begin by introducing the goals and objectives for a unit of study. A rubric form would be given to small groups of students with only the scoring points and unit objectives included. Just as the groups worked to select anchors as we've explained above, the students in each group would work together to write scoring criteria for each scoring point. Then the class would meet to reach consensus on the descriptions for the rubric.

Rubric-writing is often difficult, and the task of writing scoring criteria may be very challenging for students initially. A great deal of teacher guidance and input will be required. As students become more proficient and develop a deeper understanding of the functions of rubrics, the teacher's task will be easier and the quality of the student-written rubrics will increase.

Student Self-Assessment

An additional advantage of using rubrics is that they facilitate student self-assessment. Self-monitoring allows students to analyze their own attitudes, efforts, and learning processes so that they can use that knowledge to further their own learning. They reflect on their own work to determine what they have done well and what they could do better. Through discussion with others and guidance from the teacher, students who have contemplated the quality of their work are more likely to understand what they can do so that their work is improved.

In addition, student self-assessment provides information to teachers so that they can gain additional insights into individual students. Teachers learn how students view themselves as learners, and this knowledge can help teachers better address the needs of each student. Careful analysis of student self-assessment information assists teachers in learning as much as possible about individual student's learning strategies, motivation, self-concept, and other learning-related information (Cheek, Flippo, & Lindsey, 1997).

Rubrics easily facilitate the use of student self-monitoring. There is very little preparation required for the teacher to create a form for self-assessment. All that is needed is to record the unit objectives and the scoring points on one sheet of paper. Remember Ms. Richards' unit on Readers Theater described in Chapter 1? We will use that rubric (see Figure 1.8) to illustrate the format for converting a rubric into a self-assessment tool.

Ms. Richards had four objectives for her Readers Theater unit: (a) The learner will read with fluency and expression, (b) the learner will speak in a voice that is easy to hear, (c) the learner will use Readers Theater posture, and (d) the learner will stay on task during rehearsals. If this rubric were used with intermediate grade students, a self-assessment form might be similar to the one seen in Figure 3.1. With this form, students would simply circle the num-

Figure 3.1 Sample Self-Assessment Form for Use with Intermediate Grade Students

ber that corresponded with their perception of their performance on each unit objective. The original rubric should be thoroughly familiar to the students and available to them as they assess their own learning.

Younger children, or those with special learning needs, may need a visual aid to help them with self-assessment. If you feel that your students may be confused by using numbers to assess their achievement, then illustrations can be used to correspond with your scoring points. An example is shown in Figure 3.2 that uses pictures for student self-assessment. This sample again is related to Ms. Richards' Readers Theater unit.

Another element to include in a self-assessment form is a comment section. If you include a space on your self-assessment form

I read with fluency and expression.

I spoke in a voice that was easy to hear.

I used Readers Theater posture.

I stayed on task during rehearsals.

Figure 3.2 Sample Self-Assessment Form for Use with Younger Students

so that students can write comments about their performance, students must reflect more deeply about the quality of their work. In addition, you may gain a better insight into students' perceptions of their achievement and motivation.

CHAPTER 4

Using Rubrics in Reading

As the teachers at Red River Elementary School moved away from the traditional forms of assessment, they realized that their use of workbook pages and the end-of-unit tests was inadequate for giving them a rich picture of each student's reading strategies, strengths, and areas of need. Through their faculty study groups, the staff identified various areas in which authentic reading assessment could be utilized. Teachers kept reading portfolios on each student, utilized running records to analyze reading strategies, wrote anecdotal notes of their observations, and assessed comprehension through story retellings. Throughout all of their new assessment practices, the use of rubrics played a major role in standardizing grading issues and making explicit their assessment criteria.

In this chapter, we will look at a sampling of the rubrics that were used at Red River Elementary School to assess student competencies and needs in reading. As we've cautioned before, the rubrics presented here are illustrations only. They may not address all areas that you find important, or they may need revision to meet the needs of your particular students. In addition, you must teach your students the rubric's criteria before you use it for assessment purposes.

Oral Reading Rubrics

Red River teachers created several rubrics to help them assess a student's oral reading. Not only were they focusing on oral reading fluency, they were also concerned with each student's effective use of strategies to identify unknown words and to correct miscues. One example of a rubric for scoring the oral reading behaviors of primary-aged students is shown in Figure 4.1.

To score a 4, the student should:

— Use taught strategies effectively (reading; using first sound; looking at picture; think what makes sense, sounds right, and looks right).

— Locate and read known words.

— Locate unknown words.

— Read fairly fluently and be able to discuss what was read in some detail.

To score a 3, the student should:

— Attempt taught strategies, usually successfully.

— Locate and read known words.

— Locate some unknown words.

— Read somewhat less fluently and discuss what was read, perhaps in less detail.

To score a 2, the student should:

— Attempt strategies if prompted, perhaps not successfully.

— Locate fewer known words.

— Attempt to locate unknown words, but may not be sure what to look for.

— Read haltingly, word by word, with less discussion of what was read.

To score a 1, the student should:

— Not attempt taught strategies.

— Locate few or no unknown words.

— Read very laboriously, knowing few sight words.

— Have little or no discussion of what was read.

Figure 4.1   Oral Reading Rubric
(Developed by Georgia Nemeth, Alief ISD, Houston, Texas)

Another rubric for the assessment of oral reading miscues is shown in Figure 4.2. This rubric helps a teacher consider the significance of an oral reading error as a student attempts to construct meaning.

The rubric in Figure 4.3 grew out of a second grade teacher's concern about grading issues. In Ms. Smith's classroom, and in many

Objective: When miscues occur, the student will employ strategies so that errors do not disrupt comprehension.

Score Point 4:

The student consistently recognizes miscues that disrupt meaning, and consistently self-corrects those miscues or makes logical substitutions to maintain meaning.

Score Point 3:

The student usually recognizes miscues that disrupt meaning and usually self-corrects those miscues or makes logical substitutions to maintain meaning.

Score Point 2:

The student recognizes miscues that disrupt meaning but has no consistent strategy to self-correct errors.

Score Point 1:

The student does not recognize errors that disrupt meaning and usually substitutes words that don't make sense and/or makes omissions that disrupt meaning.

Figure 4.2   Rubric for Meaning Construction During Oral Reading

other classrooms at Red River Elementary, small groups of students worked with their teacher on texts at each group's instructional level. Ms. Smith knew that students need to be grouped heterogeneously throughout most of the school day, but she believed that flexible, homogeneous grouping was necessary for short periods of instruction so she could guide the learners through the skills and strategies each group needed to become better readers. She organized this daily period of guided reading after a model proposed by Fountas and Pinnell (1996). Ms. Smith took running records daily to analyze the reading strategies each student applied and to consider teaching points for instructional purposes. Though she felt that her instructional practices in reading and reading assessment were authentic, her district required that student progress be reported by numerical grades. (See Chapter 2 for a further discussion of grading issues.) Ms. Smith's grading dilemma was this: If students were working with texts at their instructional level, how should she assign grades to students who were working on a text that was below grade level expectations? In other words, students working on texts at their instructional level should be making good grades on activities correlating with the text. But how should the grades that are reported to parents and administrators reflect that a student is functioning below grade level? To solve this dilemma, Ms. Smith created the oral reading rubric shown in Figure 4.3 to differentiate the grading for students working on texts below grade level. Her grade conversion chart is shown in Figure 4.4.

If reading a text appropriate for current grade level . . .	If reading a text approximately a half year below current grade level . . .	If reading a text approximately a year below current grade level . . .	**Objective:** When reading a passage at an instructional level, the reader will have automatic recognition of the words.	**Objective:** When miscues occur, the reader will employ strategies so that miscues do not interfere with comprehension.
4	3	2	The reader primarily reads fluently and recognizes the words within the passage.	The reader consistently recognizes miscues that interfere with meaning, and self-corrects those miscues or makes logical substitutions to maintain meaning.
3	2	1	The reader reads fluently throughout most of the passage and has automatic recognition of most of the words.	The reader usually recognizes miscues that interfere with comprehension and usually self-corrects those miscues or makes logical substitutions to maintain meaning.
2	1		The reader reads slowly in an attempt to determine the words within the passage and/or has difficulty with word recognition.	The reader recognizes miscues that disrupt meaning but has no consistent strategy to self-correct errors.
1			The reader has difficulty with many of the words in the passage (indicating that the text was too difficult).	The reader does not recognize errors that disrupt meaning and usually substitutes words that do not make sense and/or makes omissions that interfere with comprehension.

Figure 4.3   Differentiated Oral Reading Rubric

Rubric Score	Grade
4	95
3	85
2	75
1	65

Figure 4.4   Grade Conversions for Differentiated Oral Reading Rubric

Comprehension Rubrics

Traditional comprehension assessment typically has been conducted by having the students respond to oral or written questions. The questions are generally at a factual level, and student responses often show little evidence of higher-level thinking. The three examples shown next will illustrate how teachers at Red River Elementary School used rubrics to make the assessment of comprehension more authentic and meaningful.

The fourth grade teachers wanted a simple rubric to help them teach and assess higher-level comprehension skills. Figure 4.5 shows the rubric they created. This rubric would be appropriate for any group of readers in grade 1 and above. To ensure that this rubric was utilized in an objective manner, teachers supported their rubric assessments with anecdotal notes of their observations of each student's comprehension skills and strategies.

The reader will employ higher-level comprehension when reading by . . .

                                           Score

(a) making connections to self and other texts;   _____

(b) supporting statements and conclusions
with information from the text;   _____

(c) identifying points of view; and   _____

(d) predicting and confirming ideas.   _____

Scoring Criteria:

4 = consistently and effectively

3 = often, usually effectively

2 = sometimes; not always effectively

1 = rarely, or when attempted, is ineffective

Figure 4.5   Higher-Level Comprehension Rubric

Story grammar, also known as story elements, refers to the components of a fictional story. Stories contain characters, a setting, a sequence of events, a problem or goal, and a resolution. Red River teachers taught story grammar to help students better comprehend the important elements in stories they heard and read, and teachers assessed each student's understanding through retellings. As discussed in Chapter 1, story retellings are an effective means of assessing comprehension, and the retellings can be either oral or written. Two rubrics shown in Figures 4.6 and 4.7 are appropriate for the assessment of comprehension through story retelling.

Score Point 4

Without prompting, the student correctly tells the characters and setting, and fully describes the story's problem and solution. Events are described thoroughly and sequenced accurately.

Score Point 3

With a minimum of prompting, the student correctly identifies the characters and setting. He/she explains the story's problem and solution. Events are described and sequenced accurately.

Score Point 2

With prompting, the student identifies the characters, setting, problem, solution, and events, though the information is minimal and may contain slight inaccuracies.

Score Point 1

Even with prompting, the student does not identify the necessary story elements, and/or information contains significant inaccuracies.

Figure 4.6   Rubric for Oral Story Retelling

Retellings are also a useful device for assessing a student's comprehension of nonfiction material. In this instance, the teacher evaluates each child's retelling of the main points and supporting details given in the informational text. Figure 4.8 shows a rubric for the assessment of retelling of a nonfiction text.

Rubrics for Assessing Student Engagement in Reading Activities

The staff of Red River Elementary understood that engagement in reading is important for the development of lifelong readers. There-

Score Point 4

The student correctly writes the characters and setting, and fully describes the story's problem and solution. Events are described thoroughly and sequenced accurately.

Score Point 3

The student correctly identifies the characters and setting. He/she explains the story's problem and solution. Events are described and sequenced accurately.

Score Point 2

The student identifies the characters, setting, problem, solution, and events, though the information is minimal and may contain slight inaccuracies.

Score Point 1

The student does not identify the necessary story elements, and/or the information contains significant inaccuracies.

Figure 4.7   Rubric for Written Story Retellings

Score Point 4

The reader fully explains the piece's main points and supporting details.

Score Point 3

The reader adequately explains the piece's main points and supporting details.

Score Point 2

The reader explains most of the main points but is unclear about the supporting details. The retelling contains slight inaccuracies and/or minimal information.

Score Point 1

The reader does not correctly identify the main points or supporting details. Information is minimal and inaccurate.

Figure 4.8   Rubric for Retelling of a Nonfiction Piece

fore, a major goal of teachers at Red River was the thorough immersion of students in reading for enjoyment and discussions about reading.

The principal scheduled a time daily for the schoolwide participation in sustained silent reading, an activity commonly called DEAR (Drop Everything and Read). Figure 4.9 illustrates a rubric for the assessment of student engagement during DEAR.

Objective: During sustained silent reading, the reader will engage fully with a variety of texts.	
4	The reader stays consistently on task and engages fully with the text. The student reads a variety of genres and attempts books at various difficulty levels.
3	The reader stays consistently on task and engages fully with the text. The student usually reads books among a limited variety of genres and difficulty levels.
2	The reader is often, but not always, on task while reading and/or the choice of books is consistently limited in variety of genres and difficulty levels.
1	The reader has difficulty staying on task while reading.

Figure 4.9 Rubric for Sustained Silent Reading

In addition, teachers at Red River assessed students' engagement in reading through their participation in literature study groups and their written responses in literature journals. Rubrics for both areas are shown in Figures 4.10 and 4.11.

4	The learner participates frequently in literature discussion groups. Responses are pertinent and reflect careful attention to the text.
3	The learner participates occasionally in literature discussion groups. Responses are usually pertinent and reflect attention to the text.
2	The learner participates infrequently in literature discussion groups, and/or responses are often off-topic or irrelevant to the discussion.
1	The learner rarely participates in class discussions, and/or responses are usually off-topic or irrelevant.

Figure 4.10 Rubric for Participation in Literature Discussion Groups
(Adapted from a rubric by Kerry Laster, Ph.D., Caddo Parish Schools, Shreveport, LA)

4	The written response is clearly organized and focused. The ideas flow logically and main points are well-elaborated. The responses show a clear understanding of the content of the text. Responses reflect the student's opinions with well-supported arguments.
3	The responses are organized but may be occasionally unfocused. Main points are somewhat elaborated. The responses show an understanding of the content of the text. Responses reflect the student's opinions, but opinions may have insufficient support.
2	The responses present a minimal amount of information and lack organization. Responses show a limited understanding of the content of the text. The student's opinions are absent or unsupported.
1	Responses reflect no pertinent information, or they only briefly mention the topic or some key words. Responses reflect serious misunderstanding of the content of the text. The student's opinions are absent.

Figure 4.11   Rubric for Written Responses to Texts
(Adapted from a rubric by Kerry Laster, Ph.D., Caddo Parish Schools, Shreveport, LA)

Summary

As you can see, rubrics can play an important role in the assessment of authentic reading activities. This chapter has illustrated rubrics for oral reading fluency, effective use of reading strategies, comprehension, and engagement in reading. Rubrics are by no means limited to these areas of reading, though we hope that you can utilize the samples given here to design reading-related rubrics for your classroom.

CHAPTER 5

Using Rubrics in Writing

When evaluating student writing, teachers at Red River Elementary were troubled about the subjective nature of writing assessment. They felt that they too often made judgments about the quality of writing based upon an indeterminate "feel" for how well the piece was written. They also were concerned that a student's problems with written mechanics (capitalization, punctuation, handwriting) sometimes detracted from the teacher's assessment of the written content. In addition, students were generally poorly informed about how their writing would be evaluated, and thus had insufficient information about how to improve a particular piece of writing. Red River staff again turned to rubrics to solve these dilemmas concerning the assessment of student writing.

In this chapter, we will look at several rubrics written for the assessment of student writing. Evaluation of content will be considered first, and evaluation of mechanics will follow. Finally, rubrics for the assessment of the writing of first graders will be given separately because of the emerging and rapidly-changing nature of first grade writing. As with all the rubrics in this book, you must judge the appropriateness of a particular rubric in terms of your teaching objectives and the needs of your students.

Rubrics for Written Content

The content of a student's writing is the major focus of writing instruction at Red River Elementary School. Typically, students select topics of their own choice, complete a rough draft, revise and edit, confer with other students and the teacher, and then write a final copy. Instruction focuses primarily on helping students to write original pieces, stay on topic, use a variety of interesting words, and organize their writing into a coherent whole.

The four rubrics that follow relate to the content of a student's written piece. The first deals specifically with the development of ideas within the written piece (see Figure 5.1). The second rubric helps with assessment of the organization of the piece (see Figure 5.2). Word choice can be assessed with the rubric shown in Figure 5.3, and a rubric for language use is seen in Figure 5.4.

4	The writer's ideas are original and suit the purpose of the writing. Ideas are focused on one topic and are clearly developed. Specific details support the topic and add to the reader's understanding.
3	Most of the writer's ideas are original and suit the purpose for writing. Most ideas are focused on one topic, though the piece may include some irrelevant information. There are some details that support the topic and add to the reader's understanding.
2	Few of the writer's ideas are original and the purpose for writing is unclear. The ideas focus on multiple topics, and many details are nonspecific or irrelevant. The reader understands some of the writer's ideas but is confused.
1	Ideas are unoriginal. The writer has no focus for the writing and the purpose is unclear. Ideas are unrelated and/or undeveloped. The reader is confused.
0	The student makes no attempt to write.

Figure 5.1   Rubric for Written Content

4	The writer uses a strong lead. Ideas are presented in a logical order with a strong beginning, middle, and end. The writer effectively uses transition words to connect ideas.
3	The writer uses an adequate lead. Ideas are presented in a logical order with a beginning, middle, and end. The writer uses some transition words to connect ideas.
2	The writer uses a poor or no lead. The piece lacks a clear idea of a logical order, and/or it lacks a beginning, middle, or end. Few transition words are used to connect ideas.
1	The writer has no main idea, no logical order, and no transition words. There may be insufficient information to evaluate the writer's organization.
0	The student makes no attempt to write.

Figure 5.2   Rubric for the Organization of Written Piece

4	The writer uses effective description and figurative language. Word choice is creative and varied. The words strengthen the writer's ideas.
3	The writer's use of description and figurative language is generally effective. The word choice is somewhat varied and helps make the writer's meaning clear.
2	The writer uses some description and figurative language, but the use is generally ineffective to strengthen the piece of writing. Word choice may be overused and/or redundant. There is little variety of word choice.
1	The piece lacks any clear description and figurative language. The writer's choice of words confuses the meaning and/or detracts from the message. There is no variety of word choice.
0	The student makes no attempt to write.

Figure 5.3   Rubric for Vocabulary Usage

4	The writer uses complete sentences throughout all of the writing. Sentence length is varied and adds interest to the piece. Subject/verb agreement is correct.
3	The writer uses complete sentences throughout most of the writing. Sentence length is somewhat varied. Subject/verb agreement is correct.
2	The writing contains some run-on sentences and/or sentence fragments. There is little variety in sentence length. There are errors in subject/verb agreement.
1	There are many incomplete and/or run-on sentences. There is no variety in sentence length. Frequent errors in subject/verb agreement occur throughout the piece.
0	The student makes no attempt to write.

Figure 5.4   Rubric for Language Use

Rubrics for Written Mechanics

The mechanics of writing are the conventions of a written piece—punctuation, spelling, capitalization, and handwriting. During instruction and assessment, the content of the writing is paramount. Without a writer's attention to conventions, however, the reader may misinterpret or be unable to understand the writer's message. The rubrics shown in this section deal with various aspects of written mechanics. A capitalization rubric has been shown previously in Chapter 1 (see Figure 1.7).

Two rubrics for punctuation are seen in Figures 5.5 and 5.6. You can modify the rubric easily to meet the writing development of your students by listing the punctuation that you expect your students to use. For example, a second grade teacher may list the appropriate use of periods, question marks, and exclamation marks as objectives, whereas a third grade teacher may add commas and quotation marks to the list of expected usage. Figure 5.5 presents a general rubric for the assessment of punctuation usage; Figure 5.6 assesses punctuation usage more specifically.

Objective: The writer will use punctuation appropriately throughout the written piece.	
4	Punctuation is used correctly throughout all of the written piece.
3	Punctuation is used correctly throughout most of the written piece, and the errors do not interfere with the reader's understanding of the text.
2	Correct punctuation is used inconsistently throughout the written piece, but the errors do not significantly interfere with the reader's understanding.
1	Correct punctuation is rarely used throughout the written piece, and/or errors significantly interfere with the reader's understanding.

Figure 5.5   Punctuation Rubric

The writer correctly uses . . .

	Score
Ending punctuation	_____
Commas	_____
Quotation marks	_____

Scoring Criteria:

4 = all of the time

3 = most of the time; errors do not interfere with a reader's understanding

2 = some of the time; errors do not significantly interfere with a reader's understanding

1 = rarely; errors interfere with a reader's understanding of the text

0 = never

Figure 5.6   Punctuation Rubric

Figures 5.7 and 5.8 are examples of rubrics for scoring a student's spelling in a written piece. The first spelling rubric (see Figure 5.7) is useful for evaluating a student's spelling on a rough draft. At this point in the writing process, the teacher is judging a student's spelling by (a) how well the student correctly spells high frequency and grade appropriate words, and (b) how well he or she uses effective strategies to spell unfamiliar words. The second rubric (see Figure 5.8) is appropriate to use for assessing spelling in a final draft of a piece, where spelling errors in the rough draft have been corrected.

	High Frequency Words/Grade Appropriate Spelling	Strategy Usage for Spelling Unfamiliar Words
4	The writer correctly spells high frequency and grade appropriate words throughout all of the written piece.	The writer's effective use of strategies to spell unfamiliar words is evident throughout all of the written piece.
3	The writer correctly spells high frequency and grade appropriate words throughout most of the written piece. Errors do not interfere with the reader's ability to understand the text.	The writer's effective use of strategies to spell unfamiliar words is evident throughout most of the written piece. Errors do not interfere with the reader's ability to understand the text.
2	The writer correctly spells high frequency and grade appropriate words throughout some of the written piece. Errors do not significantly interfere with the reader's ability to understand the text.	The writer's effective use of strategies to spell unfamiliar words is evident throughout some of the written piece. Errors do not significantly interfere with the reader's ability to understand the text.
1	The writer rarely spells high frequency and grade appropriate words correctly. Understanding of the text is difficult due to spelling errors.	The writer's use of strategies to spell unfamiliar words is ineffective throughout most of the written piece. Understanding of the text is difficult due to spelling errors.

Figure 5.7   Spelling Rubric for Rough Draft

	The writer uses . . .
Score Point 4	Correct spelling throughout all of the final copy.
Score Point 3	Correct spelling throughout most of the final copy. Spelling errors do not interfere with the reader's understanding.
Score Point 2	Correct spelling throughout some of the final copy. Spelling errors do not significantly interfere with the reader's understanding.
Score Point 1	Correct spelling rarely throughout the final copy, and/or spelling errors significantly interfere with the reader's understanding.

Figure 5.8   Spelling Rubric for Final Copy

Handwriting is another convention of writing that can be assessed through the use of a rubric. Figure 5.9 shows a rubric that can be used to judge a student's placement of letters on the line, spacing between letters and words, and formation and size of letters.

	Letters are placed on the lines correctly throughout . . .	Spacing between letters and words is used correctly throughout . . .	Letters are formed correctly throughout . . .	Letters are the correct size throughout . . .
4	All of the writing.	All of the writing.	All of the writing.	All of the writing.
3	Most of the writing.	Most of the writing.	Most of the writing.	Most of the writing.
2	Some of the writing.	Some of the writing.	Some of the writing.	Some of the writing.
1	Little or none of the writing.	Little or none of the writing.	Little or none of the writing.	Little or none of the writing.

Figure 5.9   Handwriting Rubric

Rubrics for First Grade Writing

The first grade teachers at Red River Elementary utilized some of the rubrics delineated in the examples above, but they found that a static writing rubric was inadequate for assessing the rapidly changing writing of their emergent writers. The three rubrics shown in Figures 5.10 to 5.12 demonstrate how the first grade teachers collaborated to develop rubrics that changed as their students became more knowledgeable and proficient with writing.

	The writer will . . .
Score Point 3	—Use spaces between words. —Form letters correctly. —Use phonetic beginning and ending sounds in words. —Write a complete thought or a series of thoughts.
Score Point 2	—Use phonetic beginning sounds. —Have a coherent message (including labeled drawings). —Form most letters correctly, with few reversals.
Score Point 1	—Draw but not write. —Use random letters for spelling. —Have no complete thought or message.
Score Point 0	—Give no response.

Figure 5.10   Rubric for First Grade Writing, Fall
(Developed by Georgia Nemeth, Alief ISD, Houston, Texas)

	The writer will . . .
Score Point 3	—Write multiple sentences on one topic. —Use capital letters and periods appropriately most of the time. —Use appropriate beginning, medial, and ending sounds. —Use spacing between words.
Score Point 2	—Write one or two complete sentences on one topic. —Use capital letters and periods inconsistently. —Use beginning and ending sounds appropriately. —Use spacing between words.
Score Point 1	—Write sentence fragments or unconnected words. —Use capital letters and periods incorrectly or rarely. —Have little or no graphophonic match. —Use spacing incorrectly.
Score Point 0	—Give no response.

Figure 5.11   Rubric for First Grade Writing, Winter
(Developed by Georgia Nemeth, Alief ISD, Houston, Texas)

	The writer will . . .
Score Point 3	—Use appropriate capital letters and periods most of the time. —Write multiple sentences using details and/or description. —Spell known words correctly and use transitional invented spelling.
Score Point 2	—Use capital letters and periods most of the time. —Write multiple sentences on one topic. —Use phonetic spelling with correct beginning, medial, and ending sounds.
Score Point 1	—Use capital letters and periods inconsistently. —Write one or two complete sentences or no complete sentences. —Use only beginning and ending sounds or no graphophonic match.
Score Point 0	—Give no response.

Figure 5.12 Rubric for First Grade Writing, Spring
(Developed by Georgia Nemeth, Alief ISD, Houston, Texas)

Summary

This chapter has contained examples of rubrics for the assessment of writing. Rubrics for various aspects of written content and mechanics have been included. First grade writing rubrics for fall, winter, and spring were designed to help the teacher assess the changing writing of emergent writers.

Typically, we've included a single rubric for each aspect of writing. To facilitate their use, though, you may wish to combine the rubrics into a different format. The rubric in Figure 5.13 illustrates a way to consolidate four aspects of written mechanics into one form. As always, the rubrics you develop will be based upon the needs of your students.

	Punctuation	Capitalization	Spelling	Handwriting
4	Punctuation is used appropriately throughout all of the writing.	Capital letters are used appropriately throughout all of the writing.	Words are spelled correctly throughout all of the writing.	Letters are well-formed and easy to read throughout all of the writing.
3	Punctuation is used appropriately throughout most of the writing. Errors do not interfere with a reader's understanding of the text.	Capital letters are used appropriately throughout most of the writing. Errors do not interfere with a reader's understanding of the text.	Words are spelled correctly throughout most of the writing. Errors do not interfere with a reader's understanding of the text.	Letters are well-formed and easy to read throughout most of the writing. Errors do not interfere with a reader's understanding of the text.
2	Punctuation is used appropriately throughout some of the writing. Errors do not significantly interfere with a reader's understanding of the text.	Capital letters are used appropriately throughout some of the writing. Errors do not significantly interfere with a reader's understanding of the text.	Words are spelled correctly throughout some of the writing. Errors do not significantly interfere with a reader's understanding of the text.	Letters are well-formed and easy to read throughout some of the writing. Errors do not significantly interfere with a reader's understanding of the text.
1	Punctuation rarely is used appropriately throughout the writing. It is difficult for a reader to understand the text due to the errors.	Capital letters rarely are used appropriately throughout the writing. It is difficult for a reader to understand the text due to the errors.	Words rarely are spelled correctly throughout the writing. It is difficult for a reader to understand the text due to the errors.	Letters rarely are well-formed and easy to read throughout the writing. It is difficult for a reader to understand the text due to the errors.

Figure 5.13   Rubric for Written Mechanics

CHAPTER 6

Using Rubrics in the Content Areas

Teachers at Red River Elementary School integrated language arts into the content areas of math, social studies, and science whenever possible. Besides using computation and problem-solving skills in math, for example, students were asked to write about their strategic mathematical thinking. In science, teachers required that students record hypotheses, observations, and conclusions. Children read, researched, and wrote about topics examined in social studies. In all content areas, learning logs were used routinely for students to record information that they understood. Mr. Martin's science unit on mammals, described in Chapter 2, is a detailed example of how rubrics can be developed and used in the content areas.

In this chapter, we will discuss the use of rubrics with thematic units that integrate the language arts with social studies, science, and/or math. Two sample rubrics will demonstrate how they can be used to assess student progress in each content area. Because these content areas cover a wide range of objectives and learning processes, you will need to develop rubrics for your classroom that assess the particular content that your students study.

Rubrics for Math

Quantitative assessment in math equates to assigning numerical scores to an assigned task. This is simple to determine for those activities that can be assessed quantitatively. In other words, it is easy to determine a percentage of correct answers on a math facts worksheet. Either the student is right or wrong. Teachers of math often must look beyond a numerical score, however, to assess a student's thinking, to look for areas of confusion, and to determine further teaching points. For example, the assessment of problem-solving is more difficult because the students have more than a right or wrong answer; their logic must also be assessed. Two examples described below will illustrate the use of rubrics for problem-solving in math.

Ms. Short, a third grade teacher at Red River, designed a simple rubric to evaluate her student's problem-solving skills. After students recorded their problem-solving attempts in their learning logs, Ms. Short used the rubric seen in Figure 6.1 for assessment.

Objective: The student will apply logic to accurately solve a given mathematical problem.	
3	The student solved the problem accurately and logically.
2	The student solved the problem logically, but not accurately.
1	The student solved the problem neither accurately nor logically.

Figure 6.1   Simple Problem-Solving Rubric

An example will help illustrate how Ms. Short used this rubric. Ms. Short asked her students to solve the problem seen in Figure 6.2 and record their work and solution. Some students described how they would divide four children into twelve cupcakes for a total of three cupcakes per child. These students received a score point of 3 on Ms. Short's rubric. Other students understood that division was the correct mathematical operation, but they computed the solution incorrectly, receiving a score point of 2. Students

> Matthew invited three friends to help him celebrate his birthday by spending the night at his house. His father had baked a dozen cupcakes for Matthew and his guests. How many cupcakes could each boy have if they each had an equal amount?

Figure 6.2   Ms. Short's Math Example

received a score point of 1 if they could neither logically nor accurately solve the problem.

A more complex rubric is shown in Figure 6.3. This rubric gives more detailed information for the assessment of problem-solving.

1	2	3	4
The student . . . –writes something on the paper. –shows a minimal attempt to solve the problem. –clearly does not understand the problem.	The student . . . –starts using a strategy but is unsuccessful in following through. –describes steps which are not logical and cannot be easily followed. –shows some signs of having a process. –shows some computation. –has no solution or an incorrect solution.	The student . . . –uses a strategy. –shows logical steps. –has a stated process. –arrives at a solution but has some gaps in the process. –has a solution, but it may not be correct.	The student . . . –uses a strategy. –shows logical steps. –has a clearly stated process. –explains completely, with few, if any, gaps. –identifies the correct solution.

Figure 6.3   Complex Problem-Solving Rubric
(Developed by Carol Hankins, Alief ISD, Houston, Texas)

Rubrics for Social Studies

As mentioned previously, all students in first through fifth grade at Red River Elementary routinely completed learning log entries in social studies and science. Learning logs give students an opportunity to review and synthesize the information they've learned during a particular lesson, and the entries help the teacher assess the extent of student learning and the need for further instruction or clarification. A rubric for learning logs is repeated in Figure 6.4. (This rubric was previously described as part of Mr. Martin's science unit in Chapter 2.)

Many teachers at Red River Elementary used the rubric shown in Figure 6.5 to assess student learning during social studies research projects. We will again use a classroom illustration to help clarify the use of this rubric. The rubric, however, is appropriate for use in contexts other than the social studies project described next.

Score	Objective: The learner will record accurate and complete information in a learning log.
4	Information was thorough and accurate. No misunderstanding of the content was evident.
3	Information was thorough and accurate. No significant misunderstanding of the content was evident.
2	Information was accurate and showed understanding of the main points, but the information lacked details.
1	Information was scant and/or showed significant misunderstanding of the content.
0	No information was recorded in the learning log.

Figure 6.4   Learning Log Rubric

The fourth grade students at Red River participated in a social studies research project that their teachers labeled "Design a Stamp." This project integrated the language arts and social studies by requiring students to read biographies of significant Americans from the past and present, select one noted individual, design a stamp, and write a letter to the Postmaster General proposing the stamp for distribution and justifying their choice. The letters would show evidence that each student used accurate and relevant information, communicated ideas clearly, formulated generalizations, and drew reasonable conclusions. The Design a Stamp project occurred over approximately a two- to three-week period, with the teachers presenting lessons throughout the unit to help the students be successful. Mini-lessons focused on topics such as biographies, encyclopedia usage, technology, design of stamps, business letter format, and presentations. Teachers introduced the scoring rubric (see Figure 6.5) at the beginning of the unit, and students and teachers assessed performance at the end of the project.

Rubrics for Science

As we've stated previously, the elementary content areas cover many topics, processes, and objectives, and the science curriculum is no exception. We will use a first grade unit on organisms to demonstrate how rubrics can be used to assess student work in science, but obviously you must adapt these rubrics to suit the science units that you teach.

	Objective: The learner uses accurate and relevant information gained during research.	Objective: The learner communicates ideas clearly.	Objective: The learner understands and completes the assignment.	Objective: The learner formulates generalizations and draws conclusions.
4	There is consistent use of relevant and accurate information.	There is a clear and complete presentation of ideas in a manner appropriate to the task.	The work exceeds requirements for completion.	Generalizations and conclusions are valid and supported by enough evidence to make them plausible.
3	There is generally relevant and accurate information; minor errors do not reflect conceptual misunderstanding.	There is generally a clear presentation in a manner appropriate to the task.	The work meets requirements for completion.	Generalizations and conclusions are, for the most part, valid and supported by enough evidence to make them plausible.
2	There is use of some relevant and accurate information; errors cause confusion.	There is generally a clear presentation of ideas, although the presentation may not be supported by the evidence.	The work meets some but not all of the requirements for completion.	Generalizations and conclusions are occasionally valid and supported by evidence.
1	There is use of little relevant and accurate information.	There is generally an unclear presentation of ideas.	The work does not meet minimum requirements.	Few or no generalizations are valid and supported by evidence.

Figure 6.5   Social Studies Research Rubric

The first graders at Red River Elementary participated in a science unit on organisms. They studied both plants and animals, conducted many hands-on experiments and activities, and recorded their learning in various ways. The rubric shown in Figure 6.6 shows a rubric for scoring each student's science products after the class completed several lessons on seeds and plants. For this rubric, the teachers first wanted the students to write about the discoveries they made about seeds, such as how the students helped seeds to grow, how the seeds first changed when they were planted, ways they continued to change, what the students did to take care of the plants, similarities among the plants, differences among the plants, the plants' needs, and so on. Next, the students were required to illustrate and label their observations. Teachers gave students specific criteria to include in their illustrations.

	Discoveries	Drawings/ Changes	Drawings/ Characteristics	Descriptions
4	Includes 5 or more discoveries from planting seeds.	Drawings illustrate the changes in the seed and plant, and they are in the correct sequence.	Drawings illustrate more than one characteristic of the seed and plant.	Many words are included, and they describe and support the drawings.
3	Includes 4 discoveries from planting seeds.	Drawings illustrate more than 3 changes, and the majority are sequenced correctly.		Some words describe and support the drawings.
2	Includes 3 discoveries from planting seeds.	Drawings illustrate 2–3 changes but are not sequenced correctly.	Drawings illustrate one characteristic of the seed and plant.	Only a few words are included, but they do describe and support the drawings.
1	Includes only 1 discovery from planting seeds.	Drawings illustrate only 1 change in the seeds.		Words are included, but they do not support the drawings.
0	Makes no attempt to complete the activity.	Makes no attempt to complete the activity.	Drawings do not illustrate any characteristic of the seed and plant.	No words are included in the drawings.

Figure 6.6   Science Rubric for Plant Task
(Adapted from a rubric by Carol Hankins, Alief ISD, Houston, Texas)

As this science unit progressed, the first graders learned more about plants, studied various animals, and compared and contrasted

0	1	2	3	4
Makes no attempt to complete the activity.	Makes no comparisons.	Makes some comparisons, but they are not based on the experiences in the unit, and the items being compared are not related.	Draws on experiences to make some comparisons. The items being compared are related.	Draws on experiences to make many comparisons.
	Does not show characteristics about the different organisms.	Shows 1–2 characteristics about one of the organisms.	Shows 1–2 characteristics about more than one organism.	Shows more than two characteristics about the different organisms.
	Does not identify any similarities between plants and animals.	Identifies 1–2 similarities between plants and animals.	Identifies 3–4 similarities between plants and animals.	Identifies more than 4 similarities between plants and animals.
	Does not identify any differences between plants and animals.	Identifies 1–2 differences between plants and animals.	Identifies 3–4 differences between plants and animals.	Identifies more than 4 differences between plants and animals.
		Does not list any basic needs that are common to plants and animals.	Lists 1–2 basic needs that are common to plants and animals.	Lists more than 2 basic needs that are common to plants and animals.
	Does not use the Venn diagram correctly.	Draws the Venn diagram, but similarities and differences are not located in the right places.	Demonstrates near proficiency in using a Venn diagram to compare and contrast.	Demonstrates proficiency in using a Venn diagram to compare and contrast.

Figure 6.7   Rubric for Organism Comparison
(Developed by Carol Hankins, Alief ISD, Houston, Texas)

plants and animals. The next rubric (see Figure 6.7) was developed to assess each student's understanding of the similarities and differences between plants and animals. Students were asked to write comparative descriptions and use a Venn diagram. You will notice that this rubric uses a slightly different format than the preceding rubrics, in which the descriptors have been written horizontally across the page. The descriptors for each level of proficiency in Figure 6.7 are read in a vertical fashion.

Summary

The six rubrics included in this chapter were designed to be used in the content areas of math, social studies, and science. Reading and writing skills were integrated into the content of the lessons and into the assessment rubrics whenever possible. We hope that the illustrations provided here will be helpful as you develop content area rubrics for other topics, goals, and objectives in math, social studies, and science.

CHAPTER 7

Accommodating Students with Special Needs

In this chapter, we are concerned with the needs of students who, for various reasons, may require certain modifications and accommodations in their instructional programs. For our purposes, the phrase "students with special needs" is used in its broadest sense to include a wide variety of special circumstances of which teachers should be aware. For example, many students in regular education may have special needs, such as at-risk readers, as well as those children who have been identified with exceptionalities under P.L. 101-476 (The Individuals with Disabilities Act), or those students whose needs must be addressed under Section 504 of The Rehabilitation Act of 1973. In any case, we believe that assessment becomes particularly crucial in planning appropriate instruction for these students.

As already stated earlier in this text, assessment is the key to providing effective instruction to students. It is particularly critical when planning appropriate instruction for students with special needs. We believe that the use of rubrics provides a framework for assessment that is especially useful in assessing the performance of those students with special needs. The information obtained from rubrics allows teachers to provide more appropriate instruction by modifying the student's instructional program in an effort to better accommodate each student's special needs.

In this chapter, we will take a broad approach to our discussion. Many teachers struggle as they attempt to provide appropriate instruction to special needs students. Because of this difficulty, coupled with the many legal and instructional issues related to students with special needs, we will not only describe rubrics, but broader instructional and assessment issues as well.

Historical Factors Affecting Special Needs Students

Since the needs of students have intensified in recent years and your responsibilities to your students have increased, we believe that it is important to examine some of these factors and their impact on classroom instruction and how that instruction is assessed.

Prior to the passage of P.L. 94-142 in 1975, students typically received the same instruction and were all assessed by the same instrument (usually a standardized test). Those students who were identified as "special," in other words placed in special education, were taught primarily in special settings away from the regular classroom. As a result, the regular classroom teacher was not responsible for providing appropriate instruction to those students. After the passage of P.L. 94-142, this changed dramatically because those students who had been placed in special/self-contained classrooms began to be integrated into the regular classroom. As this process intensified, teachers recognized the need for modifying instruction for those students and/or for applying alternative assessment procedures. It was during this period that a subtle shift away from formal assessment techniques such as standardized tests to more informal assessment techniques began to occur. Not only were those students who were identified with exceptionalities affected, but so were other regular education students with special needs. As a result of all this activity, teachers focused more on the needs of every student in the classroom, resulting in modifications of instructional plans and the use of informal assessment tools that examined growth over time.

During the 1970s and the 1980s, there was an intense effort to meet the growing needs of an increasingly diverse population in our schools. The role of the classroom teacher has become more of a facilitator of instruction rather than delivering instruction to groups of students viewed as empty vessels. As a result, the need for more appropriate and diverse assessment procedures has also increased.

In 1990, P.L. 94-142 was reauthorized by Congress as P.L 101-476, The Individuals with Disabilities Act (IDEA). At about this same time, the Office of Civil Rights began to more vigorously enforce Section 504 of The Rehabilitation Act of 1973, which was designed to prevent discrimination against individuals with handicaps of any type that affected their ability to perform adequately at school or in the workplace. The impact on schools receiving federal funds was immediate and wide-ranging. In order to comply with Section 504, schools and teachers were required to provide appropriate modifications in the instructional program of some students in order to accommodate their needs. Although Section 504 does not provide for the allocation of funds for its implementation, it greatly increases the number of students who are eligible for special modifications of their instructional plans and appropriate accommodations when required.

Models of Instruction for Special Needs Students

As a result of the passage of P.L. 94-142 and its reauthorization as P.L. 101-476, students with exceptionalities have been provided appropriate instruction primarily through the implementation of two somewhat different models. These models are the Mainstreaming Model and the Full Inclusion Model.

The Mainstreaming Model is the older of the two models and is more widely used at this time. Its purpose is to place students in their least restrictive environment, typically the regular classroom setting, for part or all of the day. Students in this model receive services from both a teacher trained to work with exceptional children and the classroom teacher. This model represents an effort to allow exceptional children to learn and socialize with regular education children in a normal classroom setting. One of the primary principles of the Mainstreaming Model is the emphasis on collaboration between the special education teacher and the regular classroom teacher.

In recent years, another model has emerged that has a radically different perspective on providing equal access to students with exceptionalities. The primary purpose of the Full Inclusion Model is to eliminate the separateness endemic in schools caused by the use of resources and self-contained special education programs for those students identified with exceptionalities. It is a model that supports inclusion rather than exclusion. In this model, students are not removed from the classroom for special instruction, and they remain in the regular classroom throughout the day. The regular education teacher assumes the primary responsibility for instruction and provides appropriate modifications to accommodate the needs of each student.

In the following sections of this chapter, four categories of students with special needs that comprise the largest segments of our diverse population, including both regular education students and those with exceptionalities, will be identified. A brief discussion of the characteristics of students in each category, with information on modifying instruction to accommodate student needs, and the role of rubrics in assessing their strengths and weaknesses is presented. Although there are a number of categories of students who have special needs, these four categories were selected because of their prevalence in the regular classroom.

At-Risk Readers

As a classroom teacher, you frequently may have noticed that some of your students have great difficulties with the traditional literacy activities that are the central focus of the reading/language arts program in place in the classroom. These students are able to function in the classroom and complete activities; however, through close observation and ongoing discussions with these students, it is more and more apparent that some students are unable to make a connection with the literacy activities. These same students are quite capable in many areas and are able to participate in discussions and activities that require speaking, listening, interaction, and reasoning, but seem unable to make these connections during formal literacy instruction. These students are exhibiting the behavioral characteristics of at-risk readers.

Who are at-risk readers? At-risk readers can be from any type of home environment. Typically, when we discuss at-risk readers, we are also thinking of at-risk students, but that is not always accurate. Although the vast majority of at-risk readers are also at-risk students, some are not. At-risk readers are students who are unable to bridge the gap between oral language and print in effective and productive ways. This may be due to such factors as cultural differences, language deficits or differences, socioeconomic conditions, and child abuse typically characteristic of at-risk students. In the instance of at-risk readers from more print rich environments with adequate resources, factors such as lack of motivation, interest, and a lack of self-confidence in their abilities to successfully engage in meaningful literacy activities may exist. Typically, at-risk readers focus so intensely on decoding and attempting to read the words in the text that comprehension becomes secondary and frequently results in their failure to gain adequate meaning from the text.

Modifying Instruction for At-Risk Readers

Since many school districts do not utilize special programs in modifying instruction for at-risk readers, the responsibility falls on the regular education teacher. You must first consider the type of literacy programs that will be used for your primary literacy activities, then evaluate the program in reference to the at-risk readers in your classroom. You will then have to make adjustments in your program in order to achieve the greatest success for all students. Three components of an effective literacy program for at-risk readers are (a) student motivation, (b) integrating various instructional techniques into the literacy program, and (c) flexible grouping.

Finding ways to motivate students can often be the most difficult task that a teacher will ever have to face. Students' attitudes toward literacy and school tend to be formed at an early age, so you may have to use a variety of techniques before achieving any degree of success.

One technique that would greatly increase intrinsic motivation would be to provide reading opportunities that allow students to undertake literacy activities without formal evaluation. Students would be allowed to read high-interest materials, then complete activities such as drawing pictures about the story, making puppets, taping themselves while reading orally, and participating in writing activities. Such informal assessment procedures as keeping records of students' interests, activities, work habits, interaction with text, and behavior during literacy activities could greatly assist you in making informed decisions in adjusting literacy lessons when appropriate.

Another technique that would serve to motivate students would be to allow them to work with peers as their partners. In this process, the students are working together toward the achievement of a common goal. Many students are more highly motivated when working with others because of the dynamics of group interaction. Another valuable aspect of peer interaction is the development of self-responsibility for their own literacy learning.

An alternative to utilizing one primary literacy program in a classroom is eclecticism. Since a teacher cannot predict which literacy technique will more adequately meet the needs of each student, utilizing a variety of techniques would seem to be in the best interest of students. Some of the strategies that can be integrated into daily classroom literacy instruction are (a) reading orally to students, (b) choral reading, (c) reading environmental print, (d) assisted reading, (e) individualized reading programs, (f) cloze tasks, (g) phonics, (h) skills instruction, (i) vocabulary building activities, and (j) journal writing.

In order to successfully implement an eclectic literacy program, time, space, and classroom resources must be efficiently managed. This can be best accomplished by thorough planning and preparation, assessing specific student needs and weaknesses, and being more knowledgeable about a variety of instructional methods and strategies.

Flexible grouping of students allows you to implement an eclectic literacy program in your classrooms, as well as to support the motivational process. Three major grouping techniques that should be a part of every successful literacy program are (a) whole class activities, (b) peer cooperative groups, and (c) intense instruction groups.

Whole class instruction can be effectively used in certain closely monitored situations. Modeling comprehension and vocabulary building exercises for students can be appropriate for whole group instruction. Whole class group instruction is useful for more in-depth lessons, individual instruction can be provided to students as part of the whole group activity, and at-risk readers do not lose self-respect by being identified as less able readers.

Peer cooperative grouping provides an immediate support system for students, especially at-risk readers. Frequently, students require assistance, but teachers are engaged and unable to stop immediately to assist them, thus the use of small collaborative groups would serve to provide a continuous instructional flow. Additionally, a variety of literacy activities could be used because the collaboration among better readers and at-risk readers would create a type of support system similar to scaffolding.

Intense instruction groups would be formed when students exhibit persistent problems in a specific area of literacy development. These groups would focus on specific skills or areas of concern that continue to be a problem for particular students. The primary purpose of this grouping format would be to assist in the development of strategies that can be used to enhance literacy learning. Any student experiencing a problem in a certain area would be invited to participate, thus avoiding isolating individual students into what would effectively be an ability group.

Using Rubrics to Assess At-Risk Readers

The primary purpose of assessment in teaching at-risk readers is to determine the student's current location in the literacy learning process, specifically in relationship to grade level performance, knowledge of grade appropriate vocabulary, and ability to apply skills and strategies as needed in interacting with text material.

Since there are more at-risk readers than any other category of students with special needs in our schools, it is crucial that teachers are aware of their at-risk readers' progress at any given point in the school year. Teacher awareness of progress is the key to providing effective instruction for at-risk readers. Rubrics, in conjunction with other assessment tools, can provide some of the information that teachers must have to modify instruction to accommodate the needs of their students. By using rubrics, teachers can assess the progress that students have made over specific periods of time. Since many at-risk readers typically have greater difficulty with comprehension, we have identified three rubrics that relate directly to their specific needs. These can be used with various types of reading materials to assess progress in comprehension. (See Figures 7.1 to 7.3.)

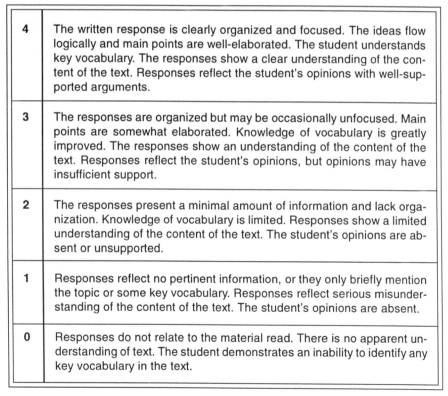

4	The written response is clearly organized and focused. The ideas flow logically and main points are well-elaborated. The student understands key vocabulary. The responses show a clear understanding of the content of the text. Responses reflect the student's opinions with well-supported arguments.
3	The responses are organized but may be occasionally unfocused. Main points are somewhat elaborated. Knowledge of vocabulary is greatly improved. The responses show an understanding of the content of the text. Responses reflect the student's opinions, but opinions may have insufficient support.
2	The responses present a minimal amount of information and lack organization. Knowledge of vocabulary is limited. Responses show a limited understanding of the content of the text. The student's opinions are absent or unsupported.
1	Responses reflect no pertinent information, or they only briefly mention the topic or some key vocabulary. Responses reflect serious misunderstanding of the content of the text. The student's opinions are absent.
0	Responses do not relate to the material read. There is no apparent understanding of text. The student demonstrates an inability to identify any key vocabulary in the text.

Figure 7.1   Rubric for At-Risk Reader's Written Responses to Text
(Adapted from a rubric by Kerry Laster, Ph.D., Caddo Parish Schools, Shreveport, LA)

4	The student correctly writes the primary details and the main idea, describes the characters and setting, and fully describes the story's problem and solution. Events are described thoroughly and sequenced accurately.
3	The student correctly identifies many details and the main idea. He/she explains the story's problem and solution. Events are described and sequenced accurately.
2	The student identifies some details, but not the main idea. The information is minimal and contains inaccuracies.
1	The student does not identify details and the main idea, and/or the information contains significant inaccuracies.
0	Responses do not relate to the story. The student demonstrates no apparent understanding of the text.

Figure 7.2   Rubric for At-Risk Reader's Written Story Retelling

4	Without prompting, the student correctly describes the characters, setting, details, and main idea, and fully relates the story's problem and solution. Events are described thoroughly and sequenced accurately. The student knows key vocabulary thoroughly.
3	With a minimum of prompting, the student correctly identifies the characters, setting, details, and main idea. He/she explains the story's problem and solution. Events are described and sequenced accurately. The student understands most of the vocabulary.
2	With prompting, the student identifies the characters, setting, problem, solution, events, details, and main idea, although the information is minimal and may contain slight inaccuracies. Knowledge of vocabulary is improved.
1	Even with prompting, the student does not identify the necessary story elements, and/or information contains significant inaccuracies. Knowledge of vocabulary is weak.
0	Responses do not relate to the story. No apparent understanding of the text or vocabulary is evident.

Figure 7.3   Rubric for At-Risk Reader's Oral Story Retelling

Students with Exceptionalities

In this section, we have selected three categories of students who have been identified with exceptionalities as defined within the parameters of P.L. 94-142 and its reauthorization as P.L. 101-476, and who are entitled to special services as specified by these guidelines. These three categories constitute the largest concentration of students within the exceptional children area. They consist of children who are learning disabled, have mild disabilities, and have emotional and behavioral disorders. These students who have been identified with exceptionalities have individualized instructional plans known as IEPs (Individualized Education Program) that specifically address each individual's educational goals and objectives.

Learning Disabled

According to the U.S. Office of Education (1977), the term "specific learning disability" means a disorder in one or more of the basic psychological processes involved in using spoken or written language that may result in the inability to perform certain activities such as reading, writing, thinking, and spelling at even a minimally effective level. Included under this definition are such conditions as perceptual handicaps, brain injury, minimal brain disfunction, dyslexia, and developmental aphasia; excluded conditions are visual, hearing, or motor handicaps; mental retardation; and environmental, cultural, or economic disadvantage.

Some of the characteristics exhibited by students with a learning disability include such areas as poor reading and writing skills, reversals of letters and words, a tendency toward poor coordination, repetitions of errors, difficulty in following directions, and inconsistent performances in affected areas.

Mild Disabilities

Students with mild disabilities tend to perform at significantly lower levels in academic areas such as reading and writing than other students of the same age. According to Grossman, writing for the American Association on Mental Deficiency (1983), mental retardation is directly related to below-average intellectual capabilities resulting in deficits in adaptive behavior, and is manifested in the child's developmental period.

Characteristics exhibited by students with mild disabilities include significant difficulty in reading, writing, and spelling; much slower development in processes related to language, creativity, and conceptual abilities; and considerably slower progress in school as compared to other children.

Emotional and Behavioral Disorders

Students with emotional and behavioral disorders often exhibit appropriate behavior for long periods of time, and then, for little or no apparent reason, erupt into erratic or disruptive behavior that can significantly affect learning in the classroom. Bower (1960) defines emotional and behavioral disorders as a condition in which one or more of the following characteristics over a period of time and to a significant degree adversely affects educational performance. These characteristics include an inability to learn that is inexplicable by intellectual, sensory, and health factors; an inability to develop a satisfactory rapport with other students and teachers; inappropriate behavior in normal situations; a general mood of unhappiness or depression; and a tendency to develop physical symptoms or fears related to personal or school problems.

Modifying Instruction for Children with Exceptionalities

In the inclusive classroom setting, teachers must assume the responsibility for modifying literacy instruction to accommodate the needs of children with exceptionalities. Ebeling, Deschenes, and Sprague (1994) recommend the following elements in an inclusive activity-based curriculum to accommodate the needs of children with exceptionalities.

Membership in a regular education classroom will be the least restrictive environment for most students with exceptionalities. Membership means that students are included within a classroom of students of approximately the same chronological age. That is, students with disabilities who are age 8 attend a third grade regular education class. Within an inclusive program, students are removed from class only when absolutely necessary. Teachers should provide instruction within a co-teaching model, and should work together collaboratively in a variety of situations.

Authentic assessment is conducted within natural school, community, and home settings to determine specific skills a student needs to learn. Portfolios can be kept of observational records, permanent products, and adaptations or modifications used to determine the student's growth over time.

Students should be grouped differently for different activities. One-on-one instruction is appropriate for teaching some activities to some students. Cooperative learning groups are increasingly being implemented in inclusive classrooms and encourage students to work together to achieve common goals.

Thematic approaches concentrate on teaching a variety of skills within a particular theme, and involve projects that students address over several days or weeks. Individuals, small groups, or entire classes can collaborate on projects within a thematic instructional format.

In the regular education classroom, modifications should be designed and implemented. When planning the student's schedule, teachers should consult the IEP (Individualized Education Program) to target daily or weekly opportunities to teach, support, or adapt activities for each exceptional student.

Using Rubrics to Assess Children with Exceptionalities

Assessment is especially crucial when teaching students with exceptionalities because of the many modifications in instructional planning essential to accommodating the needs of your students. One of the key components of the instructional process is the Individualized Education Program (IEP). These are instructional plans that are required for each exceptional student in your classroom. These IEPs identify your student's primary exceptionality and, in some situations, a secondary exceptionality. Within the context of the IEP, suggestions for modifications to accommodate the special instructional needs of each student are explicated. In order to determine the progress of your exceptional students, assessment is critical. Rubrics, in conjunction with other assessment tools, provide a valuable source of assessment information regarding the students' growth over time.

Included for your perusal are three partial sets of IEPs that relate to children who are learning disabled, have mild disabilities, and have emotional and behavioral disorders. The IEPs show traditional special education techniques combined with more authentic assessment practices. Corresponding rubrics are appropriate to each exceptionality based on specific objectives on each student's IEP. You will note that the rubrics are similar to ones used elsewhere in this book, but they have been adapted to meet the requirements of each student with special educational needs.

IEP for Sarah, a Student with a Learning Disability

GENERAL STUDENT INFORMATION   (Include needed curriculum adaptations/modifications, instructional methods, specialized equipment, media/materials, health needs, and social/emotional needs of the student.)

Sarah is a 9 year old second grader participating in the full inclusion program at Red River Elementary. Sarah's primary exceptionality is learning disabled with a secondary exceptionality of speech impairments: articulation. Sarah has made progress in the second grade in both reading and math. She must be given preferential seating, individual/small group testing, and repeated directions. In math, story problems should be read aloud. For required standardized testing, the following modifications should be given for Sarah to do her best: repeated directions, extended time, tests read aloud except for reading comprehension, and individual/small group setting. Reading remains a weakness. She has good listening comprehension skills and oral expression skills. Her reading is labored and her decoding skills are poor. She has good use of context clues. Sarah's written language skills are improving. It has been beneficial for her to have a quick list of words as references. She is usually able to read her writings and self-correct her mistakes. Sarah's handwriting is excellent. She is very meticulous in her work and is a perfectionist. Sarah gets along well with her peers and adults; however, at times she becomes angry when the work given is difficult for her. She often wants to give up, but encouragement usually helps in getting her to finish her work. Sarah has been receiving speech therapy to remediate a mild articulation disorder since September 1996. Language, voice, and fluency skills are adequate for chronological age level expectations.

Figure 7.4   General Student Information on Sarah's IEP

Annual Goal:	Sarah will increase basic reading skills to a 3.5 level.	
Short-Term Objectives	**Proficiency**	**Evaluation Criteria**
1. Sarah will recognize and read a list of words presented weekly	With 80% accuracy on 4 of 5 trials.	Teacher/therapist observations
2. Given ability-level reading selections, Sarah will answer basic comprehension questions (main idea, details, sequence, characters, etc.)	With a score of 3 or above on 4 of 5 trials using a rubric related to comprehension of text material.	Teacher/therapist observations, rubric
3. When given a common word list, Sarah will decode common word families	With 80% accuracy on 4 of 5 trials.	Teacher/therapist observations
4. When presented with words in random order, Sarah will be able to read basic sight words	On 3 of 6 trials of four 9-week periods.	Teacher checklists

Figure 7.5   Reading Goals and Objectives on Sarah's IEP

Annual Goal:	Sarah will increase basic written language skills to the 3.0 level.	
Short-Term Objectives	**Proficiency**	**Evaluation Criteria**
1. On teacher command, Sarah will write four basic types of sentences (statements, commands, questions, and exclamations)	With 80% accuracy on 4 of 5 trials.	Completed work samples
2. Sarah will write creative stories using given ideas or story starters on 8 of 10 trials on teacher command	With a score of 3 or above on a rubric for assessing written language usage.	Completed work samples; rubric
3. Sarah will use words from her reading program in complete sentences and spell the words	With 80% accuracy on 4 of 5 trials.	Teacher/therapist observation

Figure 7.6   Written Language Goals and Objectives on Sarah's IEP

4	The reader understands effective descriptive and figurative language. Word choice is creative and varied.
3	The reader's grasp of descriptive and figurative language is generally effective. Word choice is somewhat varied and helps make the reader's meaning clear.
2	The reader uses some description and figurative language, but the use is generally ineffective to indicate understanding of the text. Word choice may be overused and/or redundant. There is little variety of word choice.
1	The reader's choice of words confuses the meaning and/or detracts from the message. There is no variety of word choice.
0	The student makes no attempt to pronounce vocabulary in story.

Figure 7.7   Rubric for Assessing Sarah's Comprehension of Text Material as Related to Her IEP Objectives

4	The student correctly writes the main idea, details, and characters, and fully describes the story's problem and solution. Events are described thoroughly and sequenced accurately.
3	The student correctly identifies the main idea, details, and characters. He/she explains the story's problem and solution. Events are described and sequenced accurately.
2	The student identifies main idea, details, sequence, and characters, though the information is minimal and may contain slight inaccuracies.
1	The student does not identify the main idea, details, sequence, or characters and/or the information contains significant inaccuracies.

Figure 7.8   Rubric for Assessing Sarah's Written Story Retellings as Related to Her IEP Objectives

4	The writer uses complete sentences throughout all of the writing. Sentence length is varied and adds interest to the piece. Subject/verb agreement is correct. Conventions are accurately included.
3	The writer uses complete sentences throughout most of the writing. Sentence length is somewhat varied. Subject/verb agreement is correct, and conventions are included.
2	The writing contains some run-on sentences and/or sentence fragments. There is little variety in sentence length. There are errors in subject/verb agreement. Some conventions are included.
1	There are many incomplete and /or run-on sentences. There is no variety in sentence length. Frequent errors in subject/verb agreement occur throughout the piece. Conventions are ignored.
0	The student makes no attempt to write.

Figure 7.9   Rubric for Assessing Sarah's Written Language Use as Related to Her IEP Objectives

IEP for Jane, a Student with Mild Disabilities

GENERAL STUDENT INFORMATION (Include needed curriculum adaptations/modifications, instructional methods, specialized equipment, media/materials, health needs, and social/emotional needs of the student.)

Jane is an 8 year old first grade student at Red River Elementary School. She goes to a first grade class for social studies, science, enrichments, and field trips. She receives APE twice a week. Jane is on Ritalin for attending skills. Weaknesses noted include moderately impaired intellectual functioning, moderate academic deficits, mildly delayed adaptive behavior, and severe gross motor deficits.

Jane is in good health, has good school attendance, and has a supportive family. She has made some academic progress this year. She gives initial sounds using a wall chart but is inconsistent; matches pictures to initial letters and sounds; reads some basic preprimer sight words; does not pay close attention to stories; and is not able to give good details. Jane does a good job on answering 'wh' questions when focused. She writes her name in a hurry without correct form, size, or position. She can also print letters, numbers to 10 without a model, and numbers to 35 with a model. She adds sums to 6 using touch math. She isn't consistent in identifying coins. Jane knows 21 of 26 capital letters and 14 of 26 small letters.

Jane responds very well to treats and special privileges. Her ability to comply with teacher directives and requests is closely related to the treats, privileges, and tokens. Jane's social skills are improving. She speaks to students when sitting by them. She continues to ask questions she knows the answers to.

Jane's activities need to be modeled, and materials need to be simple and uncluttered. Manipulatives for math and touch math are recommended. She should be given clear, concise directions, having her repeat the process step-by-step for understanding and reinforcement. Use of a computer, language master, and tape recorder are beneficial to success.

Figure 7.10   General Student Information on Jane's IEP

Annual Goal: Jane will increase her reading skill in the area of word recognition.		
Short-Term Objectives	**Proficiency**	**Evaluation Criteria**
1. Jane will give sounds to letters that are presented individually on flash cards	2 out of 3 trials with 75% accuracy.	Teacher checklists
2. When given appropriate stimulus pictures, Jane will group pictures according to a common initial sound	On 4 of 5 trials with 80% accuracy.	Teacher checklists
3. When presented with preprimer words in random order, Jane will be able to read basic sight words	With a score of 3 or above on a rubric related to sight word acquisition in 4 of 5 trials.	Teacher checklists; rubric
4. Jane will identify significant details in a story read orally retelling on 3 of 4 trials	By obtaining a score of 3 or above on a rubric that assesses oral story.	Rubric
5. When asked by the teacher, Jane will orally tell a story depicted by a set of pictures	With 85% accuracy on 2 of 3 trials.	Teacher checklists
6. When given a common word list, Jane will decode common word families	With 80% accuracy on 2 of 3 trials.	Teacher checklists

Figure 7.11 Reading Goals and Objectives on Jane's IEP

4	The student's recognition of sight words is effective and enhances meaning.
3	The student's use of sight words is generally effective.
2	Some sight words are pronounced correctly, but the student's use of sight words is generally ineffective to enhance meaning.
1	The student's pronunciation of words confuses the meaning of sight words.
0	The student makes no attempt to pronounce sight words.

Figure 7.12   Rubric for Assessing Jane's Acquisition of Sight Words as Related to Her IEP Objectives

4	Without prompting, the student correctly identifies the details and main idea. The use of basic vocabulary is accurate.
3	With a minimum of prompting, the student correctly identifies details and the main idea. Use of basic vocabulary is significantly improved with infrequent errors.
2	With prompting, the student identifies the details and main idea, though the information is minimal and may contain slight inaccuracies. Use of basic vocabulary is improved, but frequently inaccurate.
1	Even with prompting, the student does not identify the necessary story elements, such as detail and main idea, and/or information contains significant inaccuracies. Use of basic vocabulary is inaccurate.

Figure 7.13   Rubric for Assessing Jane's Oral Story Retelling as Related to Her IEP Objectives

IEP for Bill, a Student with Emotional Behavior Disorders

GENERAL STUDENT INFORMATION   (Include needed curriculum adaptations/modifications, instructional methods, specialized equipment, media/materials, health needs, and social/emotional needs of the student.)

Bill is a 10 year old student participating in the full inclusion program at Red River Elementary School. Bill has a primary exceptionality of Emotional Behavior Disorders. He does not have a secondary exceptionality. Bill loves to read and work on the computer. On October 1, 1998, a conference was held with Bill to discuss behavioral concerns. At that time, a new behavior modification plan was written. The plan includes rules that Bill will follow. Failure to follow these rules will result in his being removed from the classroom immediately. Rewards include praise, stickers, notes home, extra reading and computer time, and typing work on Fridays. Bill responds well to verbal praise and notes. Over the past few weeks, Bill's classroom behavior has improved. He will place himself in time out when he becomes upset. Bill is easily distracted and requires redirecting. However, this has improved over the past weeks. He enjoys math and science and excels in every area, when attempting his work. When Bill is corrected, he becomes verbally aggressive at times. It is important not to respond to this behavior. Bill is given a checklist format of required morning activities. This organizer is given to him daily. Bill needs verbal cues for appropriate size, spacing, and formation of letters and numbers. In addition, he has begun to use a pencil grip.

Figure 7.14   General Student Information on Bill's IEP

Annual Goal: Bill will increase his writing skills.		
Short-Term Objectives	**Proficiency**	**Evaluation Criteria**
1. On teacher command, Bill will write his complete name and address	With a score of 3 or above on a rubric related to written language in 2 of 3 trials.	Completed work samples, rubric
2. When asked by the teacher, Bill will write the date in proper form	With a score of 3 or above on a rubric related to written language in 2 of 3 trials.	Completed work samples, rubric
3. Bill will print upper- and lower-case letters within the lines from teacher dictation	With a score of 3 or above on a rubric related to handwriting in 4 of 5 trials of 3 nine-week periods.	Completed work samples, rubric
4. Bill will copy from the board in left-right progression on teacher command	With a score of 3 or above on a rubric related to handwriting in 4 of 5 trials of 3 nine-week periods.	Completed work samples, rubric

Figure 7.15 Written Language Goals and Objectives on Bill's IEP

Annual Goal: Bill will write assigned task using correct form, spacing, and alignment.		
Short-Term Objectives	**Proficiency**	**Evaluation Criteria**
1. Given classroom assignments requiring short answers, Bill will complete assignments with legible handwriting	With a score of 3 or above on a rubric related to handwriting in 4 of 5 trials of 4 nine-week periods.	Completed work samples, rubric

Figure 7.16 Fine Motor Goals and Objectives on Bill's IEP

4	The student writes his/her name and address correctly with no errors. The date is copied from the board correctly.
3	The student writes his/her name and address with one or two errors in upper- and lower-case letters. The date is copied with only one or two errors.
2	The student writes his/her name and address, but confuses some upper- and lower-case letters. The date is copied but in incorrect order.
1	The student attempts to write his/her name and address but is unable to distinguish upper- and lower-case letters. The student does not copy the date correctly.
0	The student makes no attempt to write his/her name and address or copy the date from the board.

Figure 7.17   Rubric for Assessing Bill's Written Language Usage as Related to His IEP Objectives

4	The student writes legibly from the teacher's dictation. He/she uses appropriate left-to-right progression and stays within the lines on the paper.
3	The student's ability to write from teacher's dictation using appropriate left-to-right progression is generally legible. The student stays within lines on the paper with limited errors.
2	The student writes from teacher's dictation, but experiences periodic regression in left-to-right progression. The writing is sometimes illegible and is frequently outside the lines.
1	The student attempts to write from teacher's dictation, but is unable to distinguish the left side of the paper from the right. The writing is generally illegible and is outside the lines on the paper.
0	The student makes no attempt to write.

Figure 7.18   Rubric for Assessing Bill's Handwriting as Related to His IEP Objectives

Summary

As we've shown, rubrics can be an integral part of the instructional and assessment program for students with special educational needs. For students placed in special education programs, many goals and objectives delineated in each IEP can be assessed through the use of rubrics, in contrast with the traditional quantitative measures typically used in IEP evaluation criteria.

In this way, assessment is made more authentic, growth over time is more easily documented, and instruction can be modified to better meet the needs of each learner.

CHAPTER 8

Communicating
with Parents

Successful communication with the parents of your students sets the tone for each child's success in school. As the teacher, you have the responsibility for establishing positive communication with parents and involving them in the instructional and assessment process. This chapter includes extensive information dealing with the parent/teacher communication process. We begin with the impact of parental involvement on schools, recommend ways to communicate with parents, and provide suggestions for parent conferences. We end with recommendations from the National PTA (1997) for developing a parental involvement plan for your school. While this chapter deals with general issues related to parent involvement, the necessity of involving parents in an assessment program that includes rubrics should be evident.

Background Information

Although the teacher is ultimately responsible for providing an atmosphere that is conducive to learning, another crucial component in the instructional process is establishing effective communication with parents. In a great many situations, the support or lack of support of parents is the key to the child's success in school. Parents instill in their children the desire to learn by showing an interest in learning themselves. This, in turn, is transmitted to their children. When parents are indifferent toward school and learning, their children see no value in attending school. Such an attitude increases the difficulty of providing appropriate instruction for students, and also increases the likelihood of their failure.

Parents need to spend time with their children, providing them with both vicarious and actual experiences. Most important is the obligation of parents to provide a role model that reflects a positive approach to learning and life in general.

Encouraging reading at home is especially important to the development of a successful learner. Responsible parents should provide good reading materials. It is especially crucial that children from at-risk situations have the opportunity to be exposed to books and other materials that will enhance their opportunities to become effective readers.

Also important is the responsibility of parents to become involved in school activities—to show their children that they are concerned about learning. Teachers need this parent support. Most of the really effective instructional programs exist in communities where there is good rapport between parents and teachers. In these instances, parents are visible, as well as positive, because they provide ideas and experiences and occasionally help out in the classroom. Parents and teachers may not always agree, but it is important for both to work together to promote good instructional programs.

The establishment of effective communication with parents becomes even more critical when new or different instructional approaches, materials, and particularly assessment techniques are implemented either schoolwide or in just one teacher's classroom. No matter what else is going on in the classroom, parents ultimately want to know how their child will be evaluated on the work they complete in the classroom. This is true of all parents regardless of any distinguishing characteristics that may set them apart.

The vast majority of parents are accustomed to a relatively stable and standard evaluation system that has been used in schools for many years. Therefore, it is absolutely essential for teachers who contemplate using rubrics in their classrooms, whether partially or totally, to communicate to the parents how they will be used to evaluate their children.

If you are planning to use rubrics as part of a less traditional evaluation system, such as portfolios, you must be prepared to explicate your system to the parents of your students. It is difficult enough to effectively communicate a child's progress to parents without the added burden of a complicated evaluation system. Remember that parents typically relate their own school experiences to those of their children. As we have already discussed earlier in this text, the use of rubrics is one way of assessing a student's progress over time. We believe that it holds great promise in assessing a student's growth in many areas.

Parents and Evaluation

Involving your parents in the evaluation process will lessen the likelihood that misunderstandings will occur. As teachers, we are concerned with growth and students' progress over time, such as during a grading period, semester, or year; however, parents are typically more interested in the product than the process. These different perspectives can result in a situation in which faulty communication may lead to misinterpretations of your evaluation system, causing tensions that need not have occurred had there been adequate communication. How then can miscommunication between you and your parents be avoided?

Fredericks and Rasinski (1990) suggest that parents be invited to become active participants in the evaluation process. They believe that the involvement of parents in the evaluation process should be an integral part of any such program. Parents should be involved as a natural extension of the reading and language arts program and not considered to be just an "add-on" to the ongoing process. Another point to consider is conducting comprehensive parent assessment procedures. This involves taking all assessment measures from all aspects of the curriculum. By addressing assessment and evaluation on a regular basis, rather than once or twice a year, parents will more readily understand that appropriate evaluation does result in sound curricular decisions. In the final analysis, parents' participation in the evaluation process should be approached systematically. In other words, get parents involved; but you must realize that parents cannot participate fully as an active partner in the evaluation process without sufficient time or training. Your primary goal is to get parents involved and keep them involved.

Fredericks and Rasinski (1990) suggest six ways to encourage parent participation in the evaluation process. First of all, at the beginning of the school year, invite parents to indicate to you their expectations for their child. Ascertain the kind of progress that each parent expects, then record the parents' responses and refer to them regularly. Next, ask parents to participate in designing an evaluation instrument that rates home assignments. Develop a brief questionnaire that can be attached to homework assignments and that allows parents to address such factors as difficulty level, the students' comprehension of the assignment and procedures to be followed, appropriateness, and any recommendations for future procedural changes in assignments. A third suggestion is to provide parents with frequent summary sheets that can be used weekly or biweekly to allow parents to record their observations regarding their child's progress. This information is particularly useful when conducting phone or in-person conferences. Another suggestion is for teachers to develop a series of sheets with questions that parents can complete periodically. Each sheet would enable parents to ask questions regarding their child's progress and would have additional spaces for your responses. In addition, you may want to ask parents to periodically generate a list of things that their children have learned. It would also be helpful to ask parents to provide information about lessons that their children had difficulty understanding. These could be submitted at various times during the year, and then discussed with the parents. A final suggestion is to invite parents to visit your classroom and observe the instruction taking place. Parents should be encouraged to discuss their perceptions of their child's strengths and weaknesses during the class. These perceptions could be recorded and discussed later in the year.

In the preceding section of this chapter, we have discussed the vital issue of parental involvement in the evaluation aspects of your curriculum. We believe that it is essential to communicate effectively with your parents in order to provide the most supportive environment possible for your students. As already discussed in the beginning chapters of this text, the use of rubrics in evaluating students' progress is somewhat controversial and even different from the more traditional grading system that has typically been used in our schools. Interestingly enough, rubrics can be used as part of a more innovative approach to evaluation, as an integral part of a portfolio assessment system encouraging the notion of authenticity and growth over time, or rubrics can be used separately as part of a more traditional approach to evaluation encompassing the notion of a product-driven curriculum with grades. Realistically, however, rubrics are often used in a combination of ways encompassing both portfolios and product-driven systems in an effort to provide comprehensible and relevant evaluation information to many segments of our communities, especially parents.

Since we agree that effective communication between the schoolwide community and parents is essential to the success of any innovative program, we will examine next the impact of parental involvement on schools and their programs.

Impact of Parental Involvement on Schools

What is the impact of parental involvement on schools? We have already discussed its impact on evaluation issues, but now we must explore the broader issue of the schoolwide community. In order to implement innovative programs in an effort to provide more opportunities for student success, such as the use of rubrics in evaluating progress over time within the framework of an authentic system, it is important to examine this issue from the perspective of what research suggests.

In a comprehensive review of the research related to the impact of parental involvement on student success, Henderson and Berla (1995) found that the research supported a number of important conclusions. One significant finding was that students do better in school when their parents are involved regardless of educational level, socioeconomic status, ethnicity, or race. Moreover, the performance of students increases in increments equivalent to the participation of their parents. Thus, the more extensive the parents' participation, the more successful the student's performance. Not only do students have better grades when there is a high level of parental participation, they have better attendance and are more apt to complete their homework assignments. A direct result of parental involvement is more appropriate behavior and a more positive attitude toward school, resulting in higher graduation rates and increased enrollments in post-secondary education. An important aspect of parental involvement is that it should be well-planned, inclusive, and comprehensive. When parents are active in the school community, teachers have higher opinions of those parents and higher expectations of children whose parents collaborate with them. Schoolwide programs that strongly encourage and actively seek parental involvement typically result in higher achievement for at-risk children that can equal those levels attained by children from higher socioeconomic backgrounds. Additionally, those children who are the most seriously behind often make the most significant gains. In these situations where cultural diversity is an issue, these children have a tendency to achieve at higher levels when there is close collaboration between teachers and parents. This has the effect of bridging the gap somewhat between school and home. As parental involvement increases, the use of alcohol and antisocial behavior decreases. An absence of or a low level of parental involvement typically results in lower achievement for many students. The benefits of parental involvement are not confined to just the early grades, but are also essential for all ages and grade levels. In fact, with parental support, middle school and high school students make more successful transitions, maintain the quality of their work, and are more realistic in planning their future, while those students whose parents are not involved face a greater risk of not completing school. In conclusion, the most important predictor of success in school is not socioeconomic status, but is the extent to which the parents are involved in creating a home environment conducive to learning, have reasonable expectations for achievement in school, and are involved in schoolwide activities and the community.

As an integral part of their survey of the research on parental involvement, Henderson and Berla (1995) also investigated the relationship between parental involvement and school quality. For example, schools that not only encourage, but also seek parental involvement tended to have teachers whose morale was improved and who were more highly regarded by parents. In addition, schools with greater parental support received more support from their parents and the community. Schools with extensive parental support outperformed equivalent schools that had little or no parental involvement. When parental support is an integral part of a school, even those schools with a history of poor performance will see dramatic improvements in their students' performances. Inner-city schools that promote parental support and involvement are more of a determining factor in gaining this support than other factors such as parent education programs, family size, marital status, and student grade level.

Henderson and Berla (1995) also examined the impact of parental involvement on a school's program design. As the relationship between parents and schools intensifies and becomes a comprehensive, well-planned partnership, student achievement increases. Schools with high at-risk populations that feature home visits are typically more successful in generating parental involvement than those schools that require parents to visit them. However, parental involvement at school does result in significantly better achievement for their children. When schools communicate frequently and effectively with their parents, the result is greater involvement, greater respect for the teachers' instructional programs, and a more positive attitude toward the school. Schools that encourage and assist parents in helping their children with schoolwork usually receive greater parental support and involvement than those that do not. The effectiveness of a school's program is dependent upon successful collaboration between the principal, teachers, and parents. When schools treat parents as partners, parents are more likely to become involved and become more effective contributors to the school. Many schools are unable to implement a viable parental involvement program because the principals and teachers have received little or no training prior to joining the schoolwide community. Parental involvement is an essential component of any school's program design, but it is just one facet of an effective school program that encompasses successful instruction and comprehensive planning.

Communication Between Home and School

A primary principle in the communication process between home and school should emphasize that this is a collaborative effort emphasizing the two-way sharing of information about students. As teachers and administrators, we must remember that effective communication enhances the learning environment through the development of relationships between parents and the school. As these relationships develop, many problems are not only solved, but may even be prevented. As these relationships become more meaningful and stronger, students benefit because a collaborative effort is underway to enhance the learning environment.

The National PTA (1997) has identified several indicators of successful communication between home and school. For example, successful programs use many types of communication tools regularly in an effort to facilitate two-way interaction between home and school. These successful programs provide many opportunities for parents and teachers to collaborate and to discuss students' strengths and weaknesses. They also provide useful information about school activities, specific programs for students, and information outlining school and teacher expectations. Other characteristics of successful programs include mailing progress reports and report cards to parents; providing appropriate support services and follow-up conferences; disseminating information on school reforms, policies, discipline procedures, assessment tools, school goals and objectives; and including parents in the decision-making process. In a successful program, conferences are conducted at least twice a year. These conferences should be convenient for parents, accommodate parents whose primary language is not English, and consider child care needs. When problems with students develop, parents and teachers should communicate immediately. Students' work should be distributed for parental comment at regular intervals, and it is important to communicate with parents regarding positive student behavior and progress, not just misbehavior and failure. Successful programs provide parents with opportunities to interact with the principal and any other administrators at school, and informal activities involving parents, teachers, staff, and community members should be encouraged. Another characteristic of a successful program is a staff development program that teaches the importance of regular two-way communication between the home and school.

An important element in keeping communication open between home and school is the desire by parents to assist in the learning process. Frequently, parents feel frustrated because they want to help their children learn, but are not sure how to accomplish it. We are responsible for initiating and fostering this desire by parents to actively participate in the learning process. Again, communication is the key. Invite parents into the process by enlisting their help, especially with assigned schoolwork. Parents want to help, so create a collaborative team to help students learn.

Some indicators of successful programs that result in greater student learning are identified by the National PTA (1997). These include seeking and encouraging parents to participate in decision-making that affects students. Parents should always be informed of the expectations for students in their school work, and should be provided with information that will assist them to support learning at home, provide assistance as needed, monitor homework, and give feedback to teachers. Teachers should regularly assign interactive homework that will require students to discuss with their parents what they are learning in school. Successful schools involve parents in setting goals each year, and encourage the development of an individualized education plan for each student with parents as full partners.

Conferencing with Parents

Conferencing with parents is one of the most vital components in an effective school setting. Schools that work, or are effective, have successful parental involvement, and a primary cornerstone of that involvement is the teacher-parent conference. This is your opportunity to begin developing a concrete and stable relationship with your parents. Remember that a teacher-parent conference is an occasion to develop trust between parents and yourself. It is not only the teacher's opportunity to learn more about their students' background and home environment, but is also a chance for the parents to learn more about the school, the other children in your class, and you. This is the time to lay down the foundation of a collaborative relationship that will enhance learning in your classroom. Remember that a trusting and collaborative relationship between you and your parents is vital to the learning process.

Preparation is a primary ingredient in a successful teacher-parent conference. Before the conference begins, you should be prepared to discuss your instructional plans for the entire class and individual students. It is especially essential that you outline your expectations for the class and individual students. Of course, expectations may vary based on special circumstances. For example, you may have students who are affected by federal regulations pertaining to exceptionalities or disabilities. Be familiar with each student's past academic performance, favorite topics, special interests, and any special social or behavioral circumstances that are relevant to the school setting. Conferences held at the beginning of the year will typically take the form of establishing a collaborative relationship and developing rapport. Future conferences will become more focused and centered on the student, but should continue to emphasize collaboration and trust. In preparing for conferences, it is important to inform the students that you will be meeting with their parents. You may want to have a mini-conference with individual students before meeting with their parents to ask them for their suggestions regarding the teacher-parent conferences. They may have some specific topics that they would like to have included in the conference. It is also essential that students develop a sense of trust with you, and asking for their input into teacher-parent conferences will enhance that trust.

During the conference, you should make every effort to start your conference on time. Many parents make a concerted effort to attend conferences despite many distractions and schedule conflicts. You should be as considerate of their time constraints as they are of yours. Always start the conference in a positive way. Perhaps you could relate a situation in which the parents' child was particularly successful, or performed at a higher level than usual. You may want to conduct the conference by using a prepared list or outline of topics that you would like to discuss with the parents. This will save time and keep the conference focused on the student. This should be conducted as a collaborative conference with input from parents in addition to your list of items to discuss. As the facilitator in the conference, part of your responsibility is to listen carefully to the parents for their perspectives about their child's progress.

After the conference, it is important to reflect on the interaction that occurred. Was it mostly positive and balanced, or was it mostly negative, with you and the parents talking at each other rather than interacting in a collaborative manner? If the latter occurred, be better prepared next time and be a more effective facilitator. Additionally, it is a good idea to discuss relevant aspects of the teacher-parent conference with the student. When teachers and parents collaborate, students develop a greater sense of worth and trust and become more successful (North Carolina Department of Public Instruction, 1997).

Losen and Diament (1978) have identified a number of pitfalls that teachers should avoid when conducting a teacher-parent conference. For example, teachers exhibit a tendency to view themselves as the sole authority regarding appropriate instruction and other related topics in their classroom, and therefore parents should unquestionably accept their suggestions. As you can imagine, this authoritarian stance does not readily lead to a development of trust and collaboration. Teachers should be willing to acknowledge the limits of their knowledge in many instances. Another unique characteristic of teachers is our overuse of jargon. We have a tendency to use terminology that may not facilitate communication with our parents. Rather than fostering collaboration, it frequently has the opposite effect of causing parents to feel that the problem is too great for them to comprehend, and should be left to the experts, us. This has a negative effect on collaborative efforts between teachers and parents, and creates unnecessary tensions.

Another type of defense mechanism, or pitfall, that teachers frequently fall prey to in conferences is excessive interpretation. Some teachers have a tendency to attempt to provide answers for all the concerns that parents may have about their children. As a result, in the conference an imbalance occurs that again effectively limits reflective interaction between parents and teachers. In discussing students at a teacher-parent conference, we should try to avoid assigning labels to children. Labeling students is often counterproductive because it does not help parents understand problems or arrive at possible solutions. Many of these labels may be unknown to parents and tend to confuse them. Perhaps teachers are sometimes their own worst enemies in conferences. Frequently, teachers have a tendency to just dominate a conference by talking too much and not listening enough. Even if you have a limited amount of time, give parents the opportunity to participate as active members of the conference. An effective teacher-parent conference should not focus on your perceptions of how difficult it is to be a teacher and how hard a job it is. This sends a message to the parents that you are not sympathetic to the needs of their children. A final pitfall to avoid is perhaps the most difficult for all of us, not just teachers. We must take special care not to form prejudicial opinions about any of our students. It is difficult not to be influenced by cumulative records, other teachers or administrators, and prior experiences with siblings and parents, but we must not allow ourselves to be negatively influenced by outside forces. Our responsibility is to treat every child with respect, to collaborate with all parents, and to provide for every child the most effective learning environment possible.

Parents as Partners

In exploring the topic of effective communication with parents, we have examined a number of vital issues; however, the issue of direct parental involvement in the classroom has not been examined. How do you feel about having parents as part of the instruction in your classroom? Perhaps you have never given this question much thought, or perhaps you are one of those teachers with experience in this area. Whether you are or are not directly involved in a program that integrates parents in the learning environment, it is an issue that warrants further exploration.

Tinajero and Nagel (1995) related their experiences in a large urban U.S. school with a diverse population from many cultural groups. One of their conclusions was that many parents did not know that the school needed or wanted them, but once the school decided to actively seek parental involvement, many parents became involved in various ways. Some of these parents became directly involved in the instructional process as partners. Some direct results of parental involvement in the classroom were that culturally and linguistically different children felt a sense of refuge and belonging that had not been present before. The presence of parents in the classrooms stimulated the use of oral language to tell stories and share ideas. Parents were also encouraged to tutor individual students, and were especially good at giving students praise, encouragement, and extra attention. A special section of the classroom was set aside for this purpose, so that children could feel secure and develop a sense of familiarity within this area. Parents were particularly adept at supporting written communication for those students who were still developing literacy in their primary language. Teachers involved parents in shared language experiences in which the parents and teacher collaborated in the same activity, for example, with the parent reading the Spanish version of a book while the teacher read the English version. Children then discussed the story in the language in which they felt the most comfortable. Another benefit of parental involvement in the instructional process was the promotion of after-school study groups offered in both Spanish and English to make sure that the children understood their assignments, and to share experiences between students and parents.

Parents also acted as resource persons in the classrooms. For example, they shared stories about personal experiences that were of great interest to the students, who were able to relate to the events and ideas. Other students were intrigued because they knew the speaker. Another activity that effectively involved parents was sharing literature that included oral reading, telling stories, and reciting poetry. Other parents shared information about events such as quinceanera, which is the Hispanic custom of celebrating a daughter's 15th birthday.

Once again, we have demonstrated the need for parental support in schools. The use of parents as partners in the instructional process is another valuable tool that is available to schools and teachers.

Developing a Parental Involvement Plan

In this chapter, we have discussed the importance of communicating with and involving parents in the schoolwide community. A number of different perspectives has been presented, including our own. Clearly, it is an undisputed fact that parental involvement is a critical component of an effective school. How, then, can we encourage and actively seek greater parental involvement in our schools?

The National PTA (1997) has outlined a process for initiating and maintaining a parental involvement plan that features seven steps.

The first step in this process requires the creation of an action team. Team members include parents, teachers, principal, other school staff members, and community members from within each school's population boundaries. This team's primary task is to reach a common understanding and to set mutual goals to which each person is committed.

The second step in this process is to review current practices regarding parental involvement. School staff and parents should be surveyed to ensure a consensus on the current status.

In the third step, first steps and priority issues, such as developing a parental involvement policy, should be identified. A comprehensive, well-balanced plan will include: what will be done; purpose of the activity; who will do this; when; materials/resources needed; and evidence of success.

Developing a written parental policy that establishes the vision, common mission, and foundation for future plans should comprise the fourth step.

Securing support is a crucial fifth component of any parental involvement plan. Stakeholders who are responsible for implementation, those who will be affected, and those outside the school community should be continuously informed and updated regarding the plan's progress. Financial needs should be determined and resources should be secured.

The primary focus of the sixth step in this process is to provide professional development opportunities for the school staff. Training models should encompass interaction with issues, ways to work together effectively, and appropriate monitoring and evaluation tools.

In order to ensure long-term success, the crucial seventh step requires continuous evaluation and revision.

Summary

The primary purpose of this chapter was to discuss the importance of communicating with parents. The first section dealt with a topic of particular concern for readers of this text: involving parents in the evaluation process. In the next section, we discussed the impact of parental involvement on schools. Included in this discussion were research findings related to the effect of parental involvement on student success, school quality, and a school's program design. Also, several indicators of successful communication between home and school were identified. Other topics discussed included conferencing with parents, parents as literacy partners, and developing a parental involvement plan.

CHAPTER 9

The Administrator's Role

The Principal as an Agent of Change

In examining the role of the principal in the implementation of an effective schoolwide instructional program, it is important to note that the principal is the instructional leader in the school and therefore the key to change. The principal, as instructional leader, affects faculty morale, grade level and schoolwide curriculum, instructional decisions, and assessment practices. Through this important leadership role, the principal is in the position to encourage the use of best teaching practices. Therefore, it is critical for principals to reflect on how their leadership decision-making has a significant impact on the decision-making of staff members, and how their priorities influence the instructional decision-making in their schools.

We believe that an effective principal with a vision for change can collaborate with teachers, students, and parents to develop the ingredients for a successful instructional program. Within this program, the following components should be evident. The connection of reading and writing should be the primary focus of successful literacy instruction. There should be focus on process as well as product in all instructional areas, and teachers should be involved in daily assessment to evaluate students' growth over time. Within the parameters of this program, we believe that rubrics used with other assessment procedures, both standardized and informal, should form the foundation for an effective and consistent evaluation process.

As a change agent, the principal should consider some very pertinent questions before attempting to implement changes in the school's instruction program. These questions include:

1. What type of school do I want for my students, staff, and parents?
2. What is important for my students to learn? How do I want them to learn?
3. How will the success of the students and staff be evaluated?
4. Which educational strategies, programs, and research studies pertain to my school?
5. If parents were able to choose their school, would they select my school? Would I send my own child to my school?
6. What is the purpose of our school and with what are we most concerned?
7. How can change be most successfully accomplished?

In addition, the administrator must consider the components of an effective school. Among these components are:

1. collaborative problem-solving and decision-making between staff and administration;
2. instructional leadership;
3. high expectations for students, staff, parents, and the community;
4. the development of a student-centered safe environment;
5. quality curriculum and research-based instructional practices;
6. assessment of student and teacher performance;
7. emphasis on parental involvement and communication within the community; and
8. a physical plant conducive to successful learning.

One School's Vision

We are pleased to present excerpts of an interview with the principal and a teacher from one of the most successful and highly decorated elementary schools in this country. Our purpose is to permit you to "listen in" on a conversation between a principal and teacher related to one component of an excellent instructional program—literacy. Through this interview, we will show some of the efforts that one principal and her staff have made to implement change in their instruction and assessment practices.

Dr. Kerry Laster and Ms. Martha Maple of Shreve Island Elementary School in Shreveport, Louisiana, were interviewed by Dr. Earl Cheek of Louisiana State University and A&M College in Tucson, Arizona, on October 31, 1997. Under Dr. Laster's leadership, Shreve Island Elementary has received the U.S. Department of Education's Blue Ribbon School Award presented in November 1997, in Washington, D.C. Other significant awards are the International Reading Association Exemplary Program Award presented in May 1996; the 1997 Council for Exceptional Children's Allyn and Bacon Exemplary Learning Disabilities Award; and the National Council of Teachers of English "Center of Excellence for At-Risk Students" Award presented for the 1989–1990 school year. Both Dr. Laster and Ms. Maple have given many presentations on their school program at state, regional, and international conferences of the International Reading Association and the Council for Exceptional Children. Dr. Laster was awarded a Fulbright Memorial Fund Teacher Program in 1997 for study in Japan and was named Louisiana Principal of the Year in 1992. In addition, Dr. Laster has been named the Louisiana Reading Association's Principal of the Year in 1989 and 1998, Louisiana Association of School Executives Educator of Distinction Award in 1997, and Northern Life Educational Unsung Heroes Award in 1997. Ms. Maple was a finalist for Louisiana Teacher of the Year in 1992, and in 1996 she was named the Special Education Teacher of the Year for Louisiana. Shreve Island and its staff have also been awarded many more regional and state awards in the past five years. We believe that Shreve Island represents the highest level of excellence in the development of a successful instructional program and are pleased to present the following interview related to one component of Shreve Island's program—literacy.

Dr. Cheek: What is your philosophy of literacy instruction?

Dr. Laster: My philosophy of literacy instruction is to develop readers and writers for lifelong literacy. I want children to consider reading and writing a valuable, vital part of their lives from now on, from the day they leave my school. That, to me, is literacy. Also, you must have teachers who are informed and knowledgeable and know how to teach reading, how to determine what to do when children are not being successful and then to help them be successful. So I think informed teachers have to be a big part of it, and I think assessment is a big part of it because you need to know where your students are, and you need to use various assessments to guide what you're doing. Again, I think my philosophy is that children must be good readers and good writers, which is the foundation for all literacy instruction.

Ms. Maple: And you're right, because you have to assume that the teacher is first; you must have a well informed, very dedicated teacher, committed to professional development. I just read something this morning that said teaching is a learning process, and that is exactly right. So if a teacher is not working and striving every day to know more about literacy instruction, good literacy instruction, then it's not going to happen.

Dr. Laster: And the principal still must be the person who is the motivator, who is extremely knowledgeable, who can guide those teachers by providing them with articles, opportunities for staff development, opportunities for conferences and then work alongside them to make sure they do have the knowledge that they need to expand the philosophy.

Dr. Cheek: How do you begin to develop that philosophy at your school? Describe the process.

Dr. Laster: I develop that philosophy by providing teachers with information about reading, providing many opportunities for teachers to go to conferences, to attend inservices, to visit among themselves, to share strategies and things that I have learned with them, and to help them develop ideas so that then they can take and use them in the classroom. I do not try to tell them this is what we're going to do and this is exactly how we're going to do it, but to fill them with ideas so they can take those ideas and implement them in their classrooms.

Ms. Maple: Another aspect of that, Kerry, is that it's the same process as a teacher with a class, with modeling as an essential component. As you know, I have been a teacher in your school for the last seven years, and one important component that I saw when I arrived, which I had never seen in another school in all the years I've been teaching, is a principal who first of all was a dedicated, committed educator, and who was continually striving to be better and to have a better school, and who modeled all of that. It made it easier for me, it made it less threatening for me, and I think that's what I see in my colleagues. If it's modeled in and around us, it's contagious. And that's what I see, the interaction with teachers on the staff where there is modeling done.

Dr. Laster: I do think interaction is a primary key, because at the school level it's critical to have that connection with the teachers.

Dr. Cheek: How do you involve teachers in this process? Also, central office staff, parents, etc.?

Dr. Laster: I guess it starts with our group interviews in which we interview several teachers because we want to make sure that they have the same philosophy we do before we take them on board.

Ms. Maple: As a teacher interviewing another teacher, I want make sure that the teacher understands what the philosophy is here in this school before deciding to come here. Do you understand what's happening here? Do you understand what the philosophy is here? Do you understand our belief system and if you do, do you want to become a part of that and are you willing to make a commitment to do that? It's not easy, and we try to make that clear. It helps them to know whether they want to be a part of our school community.

Dr. Laster: Martha and some of the other teachers have helped me to understand that taking a young teacher who is enthusiastic, who wants to learn, and to provide them with opportunities to grow and expand, is often more logical than to take someone who is already set and not really interested in change. There's always room to grow, and so we have hired a number of young teachers and also developed our own, through our own student teachers. So, the key is to involve the teachers from the very beginning.

Ms. Maple: Our school not only keeps central office personnel, but school board and people who are connected to the school board system, fully informed about what's happening. We are aggressive in letting them know what we're doing, so there's always an extreme awareness level on the part of people who are in the school community about what's happening at our school.

Dr. Laster: I send lots of notes to them, articles with little notes about something that I want them to be aware of, that I think is a key item that they need to know about, and the only way that I can be sure they know is if I send it to them. Also, with our PTA monthly newsletter, with our calendar, any event we have at our school, they're invited.

Dr. Cheek: How important is assessment to a literacy program?

Dr. Laster: I think it's the key. I want all of the teachers to know how our children are progressing, what our areas of weakness are, what our strengths are, but not only that, but to compare them to years past. But I also think that it's important that we meet by grade levels and really analyze our progress. It's important to examine the total assessment package to see how it fits together, so that all the teachers are working towards the same goals.

Ms. Maple: It has to be a united effort and a whole process because I can't as a fourth grade teacher just have tunnel vision about fourth grade. I'm not isolated. I'm responsible for the children coming up, I'm responsible for the ones going on, I need to know what the fifth grade is doing, I need to know what the third grade is doing, and be aware of that, because my instruction is affected by the entire assessment process.

Dr. Cheek: Can standardized tests and informal literacy assessment procedures coexist in a school?

Dr. Laster: Absolutely. I think that you need to have a balanced assessment program, which is what you have using standardized tests and informal kinds of literacy assessment. Standardized tests aren't going to go away. That's the bottom line on what's happening with my children and what I'm measured on and what my teachers are measured on and what my students are measured on. I don't like that, but just because I don't like it doesn't mean it's going to go away. So I've got to mesh together informal kinds of assessment, which we are doing with our means of assessing children, student portfolios, and standardized tests. Some of the grants we have involve pre- and post-testing so we can make sure we're documenting growth, not just with the California Achievement Test and the Iowa Test of Basic Skills, but with other instruments that we think will measure the kind of growth we want to assess.

Ms. Maple: And I couldn't agree more, because I think you've got to use all the tools for the literacy development of the child. You can't use just standardized testing, you can't use just authentic assessment, you have to use all these tools and mesh them all together.

Dr. Laster: And for teachers it is a growing process to learn how to do that. It's not something that when we first started using portfolios, I thought everyone should attempt. Every teacher is at a different level in the assessment process and in using this information to make judgments about what their children need. And I think everyone is using a form of portfolios even though we might not call it that. I think most good teachers have a portfolio and do some authentic kinds of assessment even though they may not think so. I believe that we need to do more of it. I just don't believe that giving children a little test with five or ten questions where they fill in the blank or they match items is really a true picture of their knowledge, and that is particularly true for some of these kids who learn in different ways. You're not measuring their knowledge in an accurate way.

Dr. Cheek: Do you believe portfolios should be an integral component of classroom literacy assessment?

Dr. Laster: Absolutely. But I do think that teachers are probably already doing some portfolio assessment and don't even realize that they're doing that. The most difficult aspect of portfolio assessment is the management of it, and they will have to educate the parents on that because I think that parents expect to see these ditto sheets with a grade on them sent home. And if you're really doing true, authentic kinds of assessment, you're not going to have as much of that. And you must help parents understand what you're doing and how you're assessing their children. But absolutely, I think that portfolios are an effective way to assess children and particularly to show growth over time, which is what I see as the purpose of assessment.

Dr. Cheek: What role does the use of rubrics play in the implementation of portfolio assessment?

Dr. Laster: I think rubrics are important, but I think it's unrealistic for teachers or for us to think that teachers are going to utilize rubrics for everything they do. I think teachers frequently develop criteria for projects and different activities that children have to do that really could be considered a rubric, but might not be written down on a piece of paper in a form that would be called a rubric. For instance, regarding projects that our children have, teachers tell them what the criteria are that you want them to meet and what's acceptable and what's not acceptable, but I'm not sure that my teachers truly call them rubrics. I want my teachers to examine whatever it is that they want their children to learn, to set up criteria, whether they call it a rubric or not, and then determine whether or not the children are meeting those criteria.

Ms. Maple: And I want students, through the use of whatever kind of rubric or criteria that I develop in a classroom setting, to know enough about that and be a part of the decision-making so that they feel some of the responsibility for their learning. This is an exciting thing to me about the use of rubrics as criteria for projects or homework or whatever a student is doing, because I ask my students to evaluate with me, through the use of a rubric or whatever criteria I've set.

Dr. Cheek: Do you believe that rubrics contribute to assessing students' growth over time?

Dr. Laster: Absolutely. I think that's the key to using rubrics. That you're going to give them some criteria, some standards, to really show growth from one period of time to another in the school year. I certainly believe that it is a better way of demonstrating growth over time than more traditional kinds of testing.

Dr. Cheek: Should rubrics be used as a stand-alone indicator of literacy growth or should they be integrated with other standardized measures and other informal tests?

Dr. Laster: They have to be integrated. You can take rubrics and relate them to making sound decisions about children's progress, and if you integrate that information with teacher-made tests, standardized testing, and other forms of literacy assessment, then I believe that together all of those things viewed as a whole interact to demonstrate literacy growth.

Ms. Maple: One of the reasons that education is criticized is because, when change occurs and something like authentic assessment or portfolios becomes trendy, suddenly we tend to throw everything else out and focus on that and say that's the one way to do it and then we discover that it isn't really the best way, which brings more criticism. Hopefully we're moving into a period where we are beginning to see and understand that it does take multiple ways of assessment, and it does take different views to provide effective instruction.

Lessons from Shreve Island Elementary

From this interview, we can see many ways that Dr. Laster has served as instructional leader at Shreve Island so that the school has a sound literacy program. Dr. Laster and Ms. Maple have given us a window into their literacy program, yet the lessons from Shreve Island apply to all aspects of a school's instructional program. Through our examination of one school, we can summarize several points about the role of the principal.

To stimulate the development of an excellent instructional program in which rubrics are one component of assessment, the principal should:

1. Stay informed about best teaching and assessment practices;
2. Keep teachers informed about best teaching and assessment practices by providing them with current journal articles and opportunities for staff development;
3. Provide opportunities for teachers to share ideas and insights;
4. Model dedication, commitment, enthusiasm, and personal growth;
5. Involve teachers in decisions about the hiring of staff;
6. Share accomplishments with the school board, central office staff, parents, and the community;

7. Promote continuous assessment of the schoolwide program, as well as assessment of individual student progress; and

8. Look for ways to integrate authentic assessment practices with the district's required grading policies and standardized testing.

Final Thoughts

In concluding this chapter and our text, we want to remind you that rubrics are only one aspect of an exceptional instructional program. Rubrics, however, provide a means of assessing student progress that differs greatly from traditional grading and even from other forms of authentic assessment. They are distinguished from other assessment tools by their carefully written criteria that delineate various levels of proficiency that may be found among students on a common skill or task. In addition, rubrics demonstrate to the students and their parents various levels of proficiency ranging from unsatisfactory to exemplary.

In this text, we have given you a framework for using rubrics in your classroom. The success of your effort will be determined by how well you have written your rubric's criteria, how thoroughly you have involved your students, and how thoughtfully you have integrated rubrics with other methods of assessment. We believe that, by using rubrics, your students will be better learners and you will become a better teacher. We encourage you to try to develop and refine rubrics as part of your instructional program.

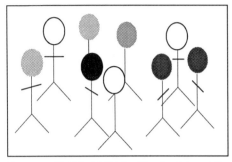

REFERENCES

Bower, E. M. (1960). *Early identification of emotionally handicapped children in the schools.* Springfield, IL: Charles C. Thomas.

Cheek, E. H., Flippo, R. F., & Lindsey, J. D. (1997). *Reading for success in elementary schools.* Madison, WI: Brown & Benchmark.

Clay, M. M. (1993). *An observation survey of early literacy achievement.* Portsmouth, NH: Heinemann.

Ebeling, D. G., Deschenes, C., & Sprague, J. (1994). *Adapting curriculum and instruction in inclusive classrooms: Staff development kit.* Bloomington, IN: Institute for the Study of Developmental Disabilities.

Fountas, I. C., & Pinnell, G. S. (1996). *Guided reading: Good first teaching for all children.* Portsmouth, NH: Heinemann.

Fredericks, A. D., & Rasinski, T. U. (1990). Involving parents in the assessment process. *The Reading Teacher, 44*(4), 346–349.

Grossman, H. J. (Ed.). (1983). *Classification in mental retardation.* Washington, DC: American Association on Mental Deficiency.

Henderson, A. T., & Berla, N. (1995). *A new generation of evidence: The family is critical to student achievement.* Washington, DC: Center for Law Education.

Losen, S., & Diament, B. (1978). *Parent conferences in the schools: Procedures for developing effective partnerships.* Boston: Allyn & Bacon.

National PTA. (1997). *National standards for parent / family involvement programs.* Chicago: Author.

North Carolina Department of Public Instruction. (1997, October). Try to make the most of your parent-teacher conferences. *The Parent Institute, 9* (2), 3.

Tinajero, J. V., & Nagel, G. (1995). "I never knew I was needed until you called!": Promoting parent involvement in schools. *The Reading Teacher, 48* (7), 614–617.

U. S. Office of Education. (1977). Procedures for evaluating specific learning disabilities. *Federal Register, 42,* 65082–65085.

Zemelman, S., Daniels, H., & Hyde, A. (1993). *Best practice: New standards for teaching and learning in America's schools.* Portsmouth, NH: Heinemann.

INDEX

ABOUT THE AUTHORS

EDUCATION RESOURCE CENTER
UNIVERSITY OF DELAWARE

Debbie Rickards is currently a second grade teacher at Boone Elementary School in the Alief Independent School District in Houston, Texas. She previously has taught first grade, fourth grade, elementary language arts enrichment classes, and special education. She received her Ph.D. from Louisiana State University in 1997.

Earl Cheek is Director of Graduate Studies and Professor of Education at Louisiana State University. He is the author of numerous articles and books, among them *Reading for Success in Elementary Schools* and *Diagnostic-Prescriptive Reading Instruction,* both published by McGraw-Hill.

ANTI-RACISM
IN U.S. HISTORY

Recent Titles in
Contributions in American History

The Fragmentation of New England: Comparative Perspectives on Economic, Political, and Social Divisions in the Eighteenth Century
Bruce C. Daniels

The Southern Frontiers, 1607–1860: The Agricultural Evolution of the Colonial and Antebellum South
John Solomon Otto

Progressivism at Risk: Electing a President in 1912
Francis L. Broderick

The New Deal and Its Legacy: Critique and Reappraisal
Robert Eden

Campaigning in America: A History of Election Practices
Robert J. Dinkin

Looking South: Chapters in the Story of an American Region
Winfred B. Moore, Jr., and Joseph F. Tripp, editors

News in the Mail: The Press, Post Office, and Public Information, 1700–1860s
Richard B. Kielbowicz

North from Mexico: The Spanish-Speaking People of the United States. New Edition. Updated by Matt S. Meier
Carey McWilliams

Reagan and the World
David E. Kyvig, editor

The American Consul: A History of the United States Consular Service, 1776–1914
Charles Stuart Kennedy

Reform and Reaction in Twentieth Century American Politics
John J. Broesamle

A Quest for Security: The Life of Samuel Parris, 1653–1720
Larry Gragg

ANTI-RACISM
IN U.S. HISTORY

The First Two Hundred Years

HERBERT APTHEKER

CONTRIBUTIONS IN AMERICAN HISTORY,
NUMBER 143

GREENWOOD PRESS
New York • Westport, Connecticut • London

Library of Congress Cataloging-in-Publication Data

Aptheker, Herbert.
　　Anti-racism in U.S. history : the first two hundred years /
Herbert Aptheker.
　　　　p. cm. — (Contributions in American history, ISSN 0084–9219
; no. 143)
　　Includes bibliographical references and index.
　　ISBN 0–313–28199–8 (alk. paper)
　　1. United States—Race relations.　2. Racism—United States—
History.　I. Title.　II. Series.
E185.61.A62　1992
305.8′00973—dc20　　　　91–24177

British Library Cataloguing in Publication Data is available.

Library of Congress Catalog Card Number: 91–24177
ISBN: 0–313–28199–8
ISSN: 0084–9219

First published in 1992

Greenwood Press, 88 Post Road West, Westport, CT　06881
An imprint of Greenwood Publishing Group, Inc.

Printed in the United States of America

The paper used in this book complies with the
Permanent Paper Standard issued by the National
Information Standards Organization (Z39.48–1984).

10　9　8　7　6　5　4　3　2　1

Copyright Acknowledgment

The publisher and author are grateful to the following for granting permission to
reprint copyrighted material: Excerpts from *Slaves without Masters* by Ira Berlin.
Copyright © 1974 by Ira Berlin. Reprinted by permission of Pantheon Books, a
division of Random House, Inc.

To the memory of
William L. Patterson

Contents

Contents

Acknowledgments

I have had considerable help in writing this book. David B. Davis, Mechal Sobel, Sidney Kaplan, Toby Terrar, Clarence Kailin, George Fishman, and Brad Artson generously responded to inquiries. Library assistance came from Daniel Spector, David Fathi, Iris Curtis, and the research staff of the law library of the University of California (Boalt Hall). Indispensable was the help, over a period of years, given by Elizabeth C. Rudd. Other assistance will be acknowledged in reference notes. Those notes also indicate my great indebtedness to many scholars. The influence of my mentors—Carter G. Woodson and W. E. B. Du Bois—was pervasive.

Fay P. Aptheker again read every word, raised important questions, and gently corrected errors. This has been true for over fifty years; the passage of time has intensified the indebtedness.

Abbreviations

AHR	American Historical Review
AQ	American Quarterly
FHQ	Florida Historical Quarterly
JAH	Journal of American History
JHI	Journal of the History of Ideas
JNH	Journal of Negro History
JSH	Journal of Southern History
Md. Hist. Mag.	Maryland Historical Magazine
MVHR	Mississippi Valley Historical Review
NCHR	North Carolina Historical Review
NEQ	New England Quarterly
NHB	Negro History Bulletin
Pa. Hist.	Pennsylvania History
PMHB	Pennsylvania Magazine of History and Biography
VMHB	Virginia Magazine of History and Biography
WMQ	William and Mary Quarterly

Introduction

In the early 1970s, after I had concluded a lecture on John Brown before African American youngsters, one among them came to me. He said: "Did I hear you right? Did you say that John Brown was white?" Since I had never been asked that question before, I was somewhat surprised. "Yes," I replied, "John Brown was white." "God," the child exclaimed, "that blows my mind!" I decided then to undertake a study of anti-racism in U.S. history, concentrating on the appearance of this view among white people, though not ignoring the contributions made to the idea by Black people themselves, both through their activity and their participation in the argument.[1] I found that there does exist a fairly extensive literature by scholars that deals with anti-racism to one degree or another; nevertheless, given the consequence of the subject, its treatment is insufficient. Furthermore, there is no single book devoted to the subject.

Anti-racism among white people in the United States (with influences from other lands) has been significant beginning in the colonial epoch and continuing through the twentieth century. The belief exists, however, that anti-racism has been rare and that racist thought has been well-nigh universal. A significant source of this view is prevailing historical literature that either omits or minimizes anti-racism or affirms racism's unchallenged acceptance. The truth, we repeat, is otherwise.

In rectifying errors, one must be careful to avoid exaggeration. This is a danger in all historical revisionist effort; the danger is intensified when subjective considerations are weighed. It is certain—indeed, painfully obvious—that racism has permeated U.S. history both as idea and practice. Nevertheless, it always has faced significant challenge.

Racism is not to be confused with ethnocentrism, nationalism, elitism, or male chauvinism. There are common ingredients in all, and no doubt this has played a part in racism's appearance, virulence, and persistence. But belief in the superiority of one's particular culture or nation or class or sex is not the same as belief in the inherent, immutable, and significant inferiority of an entire physically characterized people, particularly in mental capacity, but also in emotional and ethical features. That is racism. It has been applied especially, but not exclusively, in connection with people of African origin. Racist notions have been applied to other people—American Indians, for example—and have been rejected (this will be noticed in subsequent pages), but the central focus of racism in the United States has been upon African-derived people. This work will particularly deal with this focus of racism and its rejection.

My study has persuaded me that the following generalizations are valid: (1) anti-racism is more common among so-called lower classes than among the so-called upper class; (2) anti-racism especially appears among white people who have had significant experiences with people of African origin; and (3) anti-racism seems to be more common among women than men.

The impact of the prophetic quality in religion upon the history of anti-racism has been profound; this is, perhaps, of greater consequence than any other single influence. This reality will appear throughout the body of this work so far as Christianity is concerned. The concept of human oneness and equality is a tenet of both Catholic and Protestant teaching, especially of evangelical Catholicism, as Toby Ferrar has called it;[2] today it is called the theology of liberation. Similarly, the idea of the equality of humanity forms a central thread in Hebraic literature.[3]

The break with feudalism (and especially with its assumption of de-marked, permanent status), both in religious form (the Reformation and the rise of Protestantism) and the secular form culminating in the American, French, Haitian, and Latin American revolutions, was fundamental to the questioning of racism, as of other inhibiting and invidious outlooks. Related to this was the appearance of capitalism. Here a contradictory force appeared. On the one hand, capitalism supported concepts of elitism, "rugged individualism," colonialism, and the "survival of the fittest." It had an insatiable appetite for expansion and rested upon exploitation. In the absence within capitalism of the status-fixed features of feudalism, racism (and male supremacy) provided devices for defining place, thus helping to divide and therefore weaken those forced to labor. All this tended to help initiate, welcome, and intensify racism. On the other hand, necessities of mechanization, technical advance, market expansion, individual capacity, initiative, and motivation might conflict with racist requirements and help question racism itself. Another factor was capitalism's rejection of feudalism's static and hierarchical features. The various revolutions promulgated ideas—as expressed in the Declaration of Independence, the Preamble to the U.S. Constitution, and the Declaration of Human Rights—that served as very significant instruments in the questioning of racism.

Examining the literature convinces me that for many of the people of the sixteenth through the nineteenth centuries there was an inherent absurdity of racism. Thus the qualities of African-derived peoples—speech, sadness, joy, love, tenderness, ferocity, skill, arts, organization, attractiveness (both aesthetic and sexual), and the will and capacity of resistance—were evident in various degrees and at different times. Though all this tended to make racism absurd (especially in its more virulent forms), still racism's function as a bulwark of the status quo made questioning it difficult. Yet the literature does convey the feeling that racism's very absurdity was important in evoking the objection to it.

Recent scholarship has indicated that much of the pro-slavery propaganda was directed by the master class at persuading its own members and other white people within the slave system of the righteousness of slavery. I suggest that the intensity and pervasiveness of racist propaganda had a similar purpose, namely, to persuade white people that the basic rationalization for slavery—the slave's inhumanity or, at best, significant and indelible inferiority—was valid. As one slaveowner said to a visiting English author, Harriet Martineau, if this was not true, if they were enslaving people who were equal to them, then, of course, the game was up and emancipation was required.[4]

Of all invidious concepts, that of male chauvinism comes closest to racism. It involves the denigration of an entire people, this time on the basis of gender; justifications for this have included insistence on marked mental inferiority as well as decided temperamental inadequacies. Consequent persecution and deprivation also have been acute.

The idea reappears, also, that the poor are without merit as well as without wealth and that these absences are causally connected. Ideas of the inferiority of the peasant and even of different qualities of brains in rich and poor were not unknown. Eugenics, too, has made poverty a hallmark of innate incapacity. Roger-Henri Gaurrand, for example, wrote: "To the conquering bourgeois, the proletarian was a savage of the most dangerous variety, a member of an inferior race."[5] Roman Catholic teaching often attributed class differences—as between the nobility and commoners or between landlords and peasants—to an inherent superiority of the former compared with the latter, an elitism closely related to racism.[6]

Color distinction alone has not been present at all times where racism in fact exists. This is notably true in the approach of the English ruling class to the Irish people, whose subjugation and atrocious treatment were rationalized in terms that can only be called racial, though here religious differences also played a significant role. Still, color difference and racism normally do go together.

There is a common conception that racism is of very ancient vintage, if not coexistent with the human presence. Modern scholarly consensus, however, holds this to be false; ancient society generally seems to have been without racism.[7] Further, its absence or, at least, insignificance seems to

have marked medieval Europe and most Muslim civilizations. Racism, however, certainly has marked so-called Western civilizations from the sixteenth
century to the present. Literature detailing its history is abundant. But, for
the same period, rejection of and challenge to racism have been present and
significant. The literature on this has been relatively sparse. Let us, then,
attempt to correct this neglect.

1

Anti-Racism: Denial and Distortion

There is a marked diversity in the historical literature in its treatment of racism. Thus there has been a sharp, sometimes even heated, disagreement as to the source of racism.[1] But for the purposes of this work it is not necessary to enter this debate.

Several historians have made contributions to the history of anti-racism; almost always, however, this was done incidentally, as it were, in works that concentrated upon other subjects. The list of such authors is by now fairly lengthy; their contributions will be noted as this work progresses. Here, as in so many other cases, W. E. B. Du Bois was among the first, if not the first, to suggest that among people not at the top of the social order, especially in the colonial era, something approaching and even reaching mutuality and equality existed. The work of James Hugo Johnston also merits special notice in this connection.[2]

Historians who do note anti-racism among white people sometimes express sharp qualifications about it or even surprise at its existence. Some illustrations are in order.

James M. McPherson—whose writings have been of decisive consequence in depicting the struggle for equality—rather paradoxically accepted the view of U. B. Phillips and Allan Nevins that the determination to maintain white supremacy was fundamental to Southern and national history. Both Phillips and Nevins, in developing this position, presented racism as a universal attribute of white people in the United States. McPherson, on the other hand, knew that such universality did not exist, and much of his writing demonstrated this.

He wrote that the stridency of slaveowners' propaganda in support of slavery indicated that "the South's [that is, slaveowners'] conscience" was "troubled about slavery." He quoted approvingly William R. Taylor's 1961 book, *Cavalier and Yankee*, to this effect, as he did Charles G. Sellers's

work of the previous year. This view was persuasively set forth at some
length by Ralph E. Morrow in an essay published in 1961. Apparently the
idea did not occur to him (or others) that the even greater stridency—
hysterical fury, often—with which African American inferiority was affirmed might also have reflected profound doubts. Certainly the data, as
the bulk of this book will show, demonstrate very widespread questioning
among white people in all sections of the nation and in all periods of its
history of the myth of "Negro inferiority." Yet the position of Phillips and
Nevins on this question dominates the historical literature to this day and
was reaffirmed even by McPherson.[3]

Somewhat similarly, Winthrop D. Jordan in the preface to his *White over
Black* penned these words:

> During the Revolutionary era Americans suddenly came to question not only the
> rightness of slavery but also to realize for the first time that they had a racial problem
> on their hands, that the institution which their ideology condemned was founded
> on perceptions of physiological differences which they thought they could do little
> or nothing about.[4]

Much of the material in Jordan's own book refutes the assertion that Americans suddenly questioned slavery in the revolutionary era; by that time, on
the contrary, the institution had been seriously challenged for decades. But
the book itself is filled with insistence by many Americans that the perceptions were at least dubious and probably erroneous, and therefore they
urged a termination of the status rationalized by those perceptions.

Eric Foner, in the midst of a book examining the ideology of the Civil
War era, the central theme of which was to question the notion of racism's
unchallenged sway, nevertheless remarked, as if by rote: "In the United
States of the mid-nineteenth century, racial prejudice was all but universal."[5]
In a somewhat similar way, H. Shelton Smith, in a book subtitled *Racism
in Southern Religion*, wrote in its preface: "It is the purpose of this volume
to trace the growth of this anti-Negro movement between 1780 and 1910
and to indicate its impact upon human relations."[6] But the content of the
book is filled with denials of "Negro inferiority" and the insistence that
holding such a view is blasphemous. Some who denied inferiority did not
draw from this a condemnation of slavery, holding the latter to be a secular
condition that might accord with God's will; but Smith showed that even
where slavery was not attacked, racism often was.

Occasionally one gets the feeling that authors are startled by their own
findings and therefore offer some qualifying comment quite out of keeping
with those findings. James B. Stewart, for example, whose writings have
been models of care and perception, quoted from sermons in the 1820s that
offered "direct espousals of black equality." Others insisted that to enslave
"persons whom God had created equal to whites in every temporal and

spiritual way" was sinful indeed. Stewart added that all his witnesses "would have failed if judged by modern standards of racial equalitarianism." What standards are higher than "direct espousals of black equality" or insisting that African Americans were "equal to whites in every temporal and spiritual way"?[7]

Ira Berlin, in a powerful book effectively challenging conventional portrayals of the pre–Civil War South and especially of the position of its free Black population, offered a section on close Black-white relationships, particularly among the poor, in seven Southern states from 1840 to 1860. Nevertheless, he concluded lamely and inexplicably: "Although friendly, even equalitarian relations between whites and blacks continued to exist on the margins of Southern society, they never threatened white supremacy." But the preceding pages had not indicated what was "marginal" about the events described in seven Southern states during the pre–Civil War generation. Berlin wrote that they did not "threaten" white supremacy, but they certainly were part of the pattern that caused the slaveowners of a white supremacist society to feel threatened and, by 1861, to act out this fear. The book itself sustains that conclusion.[8]

With some regularity in the literature one finds authors arguing the pervasiveness of racism from data that suggest—or at least might be read to suggest—the opposite. Thus, in an article throwing doubt on conventional views concerning "the status of Blacks in 17th century Virginia," Warren Billings concluded: "Once white Virginians perceived free blacks and miscegenation as serious threats to the public weal and to their own private interests, they moved to circumscribe the African bondsmen's approach to liberty."[9] Clearly Billings had in mind not "white Virginians" but rather those few white Virginians who held office and passed laws. Miscegenation requires, of course, white participation; therefore some "white Virginians" did not view their acts as "serious threats." Further, it is difficult to understand how African bondsmen could be approaching liberty unless some "white Virginians" acquiesced in, if they did not encourage, such movement.

Indeed, the anti-miscegenation legislation of the seventeenth century suggests this kind of reading. In 1663 the Maryland legislature found it necessary to enact the following law:

And forasmuch as divers free born English women forgetful of their free condition and to the disgrace of our nation, do intermarry with Negro slaves, by which, also divers suits may arise, touching the issue of such women, and a great damage befall the master of such Negroes, for preservation whereof, [and] for deterring such free born women from such shameful matches, be it enacted, etc. that whatsoever free born woman shall intermarry with any slave, from and after the last day of the present assembly, shall serve the master of such slave during the life of her husband; and that all the issue of such free born women, so married, shall be slaves as their fathers were.[10]

Laws of this nature were repeated by Maryland in 1681, 1684, 1715, and 1717. Their passage confirms the racism of the rulers of Maryland. At the same time, both the existence and the repetition show that for some white people, not of an exalted level, there was an absence of, or even a resistance against, racism.

Again, Roger Fischer, treating "Racial Segregation in Ante-Bellum New Orleans," observed that laws in that city forbade Black people from "participating in white activities and using white facilities." Fischer continued that the legislators found themselves "powerless to prevent whites who so desired from mixing freely with Negroes in colored taverns, bawdy houses and dance halls."[11] As a result, in the 1850s regulations were passed in New Orleans outlawing all interracial activity. Those found guilty of violating such regulations faced fines—if they were slaves, lashes. Laws, enacted in December 1856, January 1857, and March 1857, provided increasingly heavy penalties.

Fischer concluded that this showed that "white New Orleanians grew increasingly suspicious of all activities that brought whites and Negroes together." Rather, the data showed that those whites in New Orleans who enacted laws were "increasingly suspicious," that other white people chose to socialize with Black people, that this was mutual, and that such behavior was common enough so that those who ruled felt obliged to restrain such choice by heavy penalties against both whites and African Americans and to do this repeatedly.

As a final illustration of what I think is a misinterpretation of data, consider the abundant literature dealing with the racism of white voters who refused to enfranchise Black men in the North and West during the years just before, during, and after the Civil War. The emphasis upon the existence of such racism is the theme of books by V. Jacque Voegeli, Eugene H. Berwanger, James A. Rawley, and Phyllis Field. These volumes present the overwhelming impact of racism as ubiquitous, decisive, and basically self-generating. As Field wrote: "It was the stereotype of the black man rather than slavery itself that served most effectively to condemn him."[12]

Certain problems may be noticed on the basis of the data offered by these authors themselves. Thus, on the question of whether or not Black men should have the suffrage—the main content of the books—one finds that in Minnesota in 1865 and 1867 the "yes" vote was 45.2 percent and 48.8 percent, respectively; in Wisconsin in 1865 the "yes" vote was 46 percent; in Connecticut that year, 44.6 percent; in Ohio in 1867, 45.9 percent; in Missouri in 1868, 42.7 percent. In New York the affirmative vote in 1846 was 28 percent, in 1860, 36 percent, and in 1869, 47 percent. In Iowa and in Minnesota, in 1869, suffrage for Black men was approved by over 56 percent in each case.

These percentages are of white men who voted to enfranchise Black men. They demonstrate that in the important question of political empowerment, a substantial percentage of white men favored an anti-racist position, exactly the opposite of the conclusions of the books mentioned. In later pages we shall return to this development.

Often the universality of racism is simply assumed; this occurs even at times when material is presented showing the absence of such universality. A typical example occurs in an essay by Alfred Kazin dealing with Abraham Lincoln.[13] Alluding to the Lincoln-Douglas debates, Kazin remarked that "the 'Negro' was the issue of the time, but remained a symbol to everyone, never an individual human being." He continued that, knowing this, Douglas, being "alert to the prejudices of the crowd," referred "scathingly" to a recent episode when Frederick Douglass had ridden in a carriage "with white women." One may suppose that a skillful politician like Stephen Douglas knew what he was doing; yet one must observe that Kazin, writing more than a century after Douglas's demagogy, seems to have missed the fact that Frederick Douglass was accompanied by white women. This would seem to reflect a rejection of racism by those women.

Another more explicit affirmation of the universality of racism appears in a fairly recent book by John S. Haller, Jr. Dealing with attitudes among scientists, Haller wrote: "The subject of race inferiority was beyond critical reach in the late nineteenth century. Having accepted science and its exalted doctrinaires, American society betrayed no statement, popular or otherwise, that looked to a remodeling of its social or political habits of race."[14]

This unequivocal statement is false; it is erroneous for any period of U.S. history and especially so for the late nineteenth century. That period was indeed the "nadir" of racism, as the late Rayford W. Logan put it, but it also was a period marking a decisive turning away from that nadir, as the second volume of this study will show. Even within the time limit of this volume, the statement is exaggerated. It is the overwhelming weight of this kind of writing and the absence of any systematic critique thereof that led Robert Moats Miller, for example, to ask: "Can we not agree that it is the consensus of recent scholarship that racism was an article of faith with almost all modern Europeans and their descendants in North America" and that this alleged consensus prevailed "almost until our generation?"[15]

Reality on the question of the history of challenge to or rejection of racism has also suffered because there are numerous instances wherein evidences of anti-racism have been turned into the opposite. Thomas Graham, for example, has pointed out that in the case of Harriet Beecher Stowe "the salient argument of her writings was for the full, equal brotherhood of all men."[16] Contrary to contemporary stereotype, she felt that in "general intelligence" all peoples were essentially alike. Despite some lapses, this was the thrust of her thought, but—as illustrated in J. C. Furness's *Goodbye to Uncle Tom* (1956)—her views are regularly misrepresented.

Perhaps even more grossly distorted have been the views of Horace Bushnell (1802–1876). Charles C. Cole, Jr., in 1950 made that distinguished minister a racist; this was copied by Barbara M. Cross in her biography of him (1958) and by George Fredrikson in his *The Black Image* (1971). The distortion of Bushnell occurred in making his references to gorillas and chimpanzees point to African Americans, when in fact Bushnell was insisting on the human character of all African-derived peoples; they were made by God in His image, and unless they were enfranchised another Civil War might be required. Indeed, Bushnell anticipated much of contemporary racial egalitarianism and even suggested that the future might well see Africa at the apex of world culture.[17]

During the revolutionary era a considerable literature appeared treating the pros and cons of slavery. Important in this connection was Benjamin Rush's *Address upon Slave-Keeping* (1773) sharply attacking the practice. Shortly thereafter came Richard Nisbet's attack upon Rush with *Slavery Not Forbidden by Scripture* (1773). Both these works will be examined hereafter, but here note is to be taken of the appearance later in 1773 of an anonymous pamphlet issued in Philadelphia entitled *Personal Slavery Established*. The latter has been widely accepted in historical literature as a defense of slavery, but as Lester B. Scherer demonstrated,[18] it actually was a strong, if satirical, attack upon slavery specifically directed against Nisbet; further, this pamphlet contained a section entitled "Capacities of Africans" that ridiculed the idea of their inferiority.

At times, people whose central contribution was opposing racist practices are presented in a contrary guise or in strange company. Even in John Hope Franklin's *Racial Equality in America*, where he pointed out that "the re-markable thing about the problem of racial equality is the way it has endured and remained topical," he at times slipped into one-sidedness in presenting his argument. Thus, writing that "this sense of racial inequality [was] as pervasive as slavery itself" in the eighteenth century, he cited remarks at a Harvard commencement in 1773 where the speaker insisted that slavery accorded with the Blacks' inferiority and was salutary for all. It was absurd for anyone "to interfere with the beneficent social order, just to pursue some mystical primeval equality." The problem here, however, is that this Harvard student was participating in a debate on the propriety of slavery and that there was an opponent whose views were contrary to those of the benighted one quoted. The fact that slavery and the nature of the slaves was a matter of debate in prerevolutionary Massachusetts is as consequential as the ideas of an advocate of a "beneficent social order."

Further, in this same book, Franklin wrote that "the position of the Abolitionists themselves in the matter of racial equality was, at best am-bivalent." Had this read "at worst," it would have been more accurate. Again, in noting that slaveholders "were not alone in insisting that blacks were not the equals of whites," Franklin correctly called attention to figures like Louis Agassiz and Francis Lieber, but then added Lydia Maria Child to this list.[19] But Child was as principled and courageous an anti-racist as white America can show, belonging not in the company of Agassiz and Lieber but rather in that of the Grimké sisters and of John Brown—the figure, next only to Jesus, most admired by her.

The endurance and devastating impact of racism in the United States certainly is a fact and one that merits the most profound attack. This basic thesis of John Hope Franklin's book is true, and racism's condemnation is vital. In condemning racism, however, it is not helpful to deny, minimize, or obscure evidence of the repudiation of this barbarism. Anti-racism has persisted in this nation's history and is an important, though grossly neglected, aspect of that history.

2

Questioning Racism's Pervasiveness

There have been historians whose findings have led them to suggest doubts about the prevailing concept of the largely unchallenged domination of racism in the thought of white people in the United States. Significant in this regard has been Jeffrey Brooke Allen. In one article Allen examined the question "Were Southern White Critics of Slavery Racists?" Here he limited himself to Kentucky and the upper South from 1791 to 1814. In another article he examined "The Racial Thoughts of White North Carolina Opponents of Slavery." In the first article Allen stated that his purpose was to challenge "the generally accepted notion that the majority of white anti-slavery Southerners were racists." In the second he concluded that "virtually all" of the North Carolina white opponents of slavery "denounced not only slavery but also the racist ideology which so frequently served as its justi-fication."[1] While Allen's work has considerable value and will be used in subsequent pages, it is possible, I think, that the findings reported by him do not fully sustain the somewhat sweeping language he has used.

Gary B. Mills, in a very careful study dealing with antebellum Alabama, summarized:

Wherever whites and free blacks met each other on a one-to-one basis, toleration and often friendship resulted. Nothing has emerged so far to support the theory that whites in Alabama hated or feared free blacks; they did not fear the widow next door who was a founding member of their church or hate the barber with whom they hunted. Instead, it was the vague and theoretical mass of black freedmen that troubled them—the one popularized by political demagogues who built careers by swaying the emotions of voters, the one condemned by social malcontents who habitually penned the hate-filled and anonymous "letters to the editor" that are quoted today as measures of public sentiment.

Mills's concluding sentence is substantiated by his very important article:

"In view of the degree to which this study suggests a re-interpretation of southern race relations, a similar re-evaluation of other southern states on an unprecedented, comprehensive, grassroots basis is also mandated."[2]

In a study, some of which moved past the time limits of this volume, Michael C. Coleman found an absence of racism among missionaries to American Indians. Coleman examined the correspondence of four hundred such missionaries writing to the Board of Foreign Missions of the Presbyterian church. He reported that the letters showed ethnocentrism but were not racist. Where failings seemed to be present among the missionaries' charges, they were considered "the product of circumstances, not race." These men felt that "racism was outrageously anti-scientific"; they believed that the "Indians were human beings of full spiritual, intellectual, and social potential." Coleman found a "nearly total absence of explicit or even implicit racism in tens of thousands of pages of correspondence and published literature."[3]

Finally, I think it appropriate to call attention to the stimulating book by David Edwin Harrell, Jr., chairman of the history department at the University of Alabama, Birmingham, although it is entirely beyond the time scope of the present volume.[4] This study of contemporary Southern religious sects showed that some, which may be described as right-wing fundamentalists, issue propaganda similar to that of the most rabid advocates of slavery. But Harrell emphasized that this is true only of the most publicized elements in Southern religious sects. Much of the teaching of other such sects, however, insists upon human equality, specifically and strenuously denounces racism, and expresses admiration for Dr. Martin Luther King, Jr. In many instances the sects in practice are integrated from top to bottom.

Harrell rightly lamented that "the social views of the churches of the poor have generally been ignored by scholars"; and not only their churches, one should add. The book must be studied by all who believe that racism is all-pervasive in the past and present of U.S. history and society. Harrell observed correctly that earlier sociologists, such as Leonard W. Doob, writing in 1937, and Mary Gardner, Allison Davis, and Burleigh B. Gardner in *Deep South*, published four years later, reported a notable absence of racism among many of the poorer whites. Indeed, James McBride Dabbs insisted over thirty years ago that racial violence in the South was attributable basically to the propertied, not the poor, and that the latter "have been charged with a degree of racial animosity they do not really feel."[5] As the twentieth century approaches its end, the time surely has come for the historical profession as a whole to take seriously the findings of keen sociologists fifty and sixty years ago and the observation of so knowledgeable a contemporary as Dabbs in the 1950s and to notice the racist-rejecting, integration-practicing poor Southern white folks who have been living in Christian fellowship with their Black neighbors for generations.

Several historians have produced books that contribute significantly to a

historiography of anti-racism in the United States. Outstanding in this regard, in addition to Du Bois's *Black Reconstruction* and the entire commitment of Carter G. Woodson, was the remarkable work of James Hugo
Johnston noted earlier. Though written with great, even extreme, restraint
because of its period of creation and its subject matter, it is an extraordinary
account not only of racist practice and belief but also of the rejection of
both, a fact somewhat obscured in Winthrop D. Jordan's brief foreword to
the published version, which finally appeared in 1970. Confined to pre-
Civil War years and largely to Virginia, Johnston's work challenged the
stereotype of a rigidly racist society.[6] Certainly, those who ruled sought
such a society, but just as certainly they did not succeed.

Johnston offered many examples of petitions to the Virginia legislature
from owners seeking to manumit slaves. He showed that such petitions
frequently offered reasons for the actions that affirmed admiration for the
one to be benefitted in terms at least implying the denial of inferiority. Thus
an owner requested such permission in Dinwiddie County in December
1810. He wished "to see liberated" James, his miller for over seventeen
years. During that period, stated the petitioner, "he has conducted himself
with respect to honesty, sobriety, and every other virtue generally found in
human nature with so much zeal, that he has obtained not only my most
unlimited confidence, but so far as I can judge that of all others that are
acquainted with him." Another, writing in 1830, insisted that his slave "is
as honest a man as ever lived in the state of Virginia," and so he wanted
that person to be free.

Johnston, citing the work of another African American pioneering historian, Luther P. Jackson, observed that the latter had shown, back in 1927,
that "certain white men [in Virginia] made a practice of assisting Negroes
to buy their freedom." Others, as is well known, assisted slaves to flee.
Johnston called special attention to one such, a James Allen, who "gave his
life to make possible the escape of a slave" in Virginia in 1802. In this case,
the slave, Charles, had made good his escape; suspicion fastened on Allen
as one who had assisted the fugitive. Allen was lashed and told that the
beating would stop when he revealed Charles's whereabouts. Allen chose
silence and was beaten to death.

The egalitarian beliefs and habits of eighteenth-century Methodists and
Baptists are well documented, and reference will be made to this later. Here
it is to be noted that Johnston called attention to a complaint to the governor
of Virginia in 1789 denouncing these "disorderly People" who "under the
cloak of religion" held meetings of Blacks and whites as often as three times
a week and even resisted patrols ordering them to disperse. In particular,
concern was expressed about the behavior of "Mr. Charles Neale," who
held such meetings in his home and physically evicted law-enforcement
personnel who tried to prevent such subversion.

Johnston remarked: "Unfortunately little is known of the social attitude of poor white men in this period"—anticipating by almost forty years a similar observation by Herbert Gutman.[7] He continued, however, "There is evidence that among this class were to be found those whose hatred of the upper classes made them allies and aids to the Negro conspirators." Johnston cited the slave conspiracy in Virginia in 1816 in which a white man, George Boxley, was jailed for being a participant and a sympathizer.[8] He called attention also to a letter of 1821 to the governor accusing an unnamed white man of similar subversion.

Johnston's work is vital, too, because it refers to many petitions to the legislature seeking an end to slavery. Some were very numerously signed and often conveyed rejection of the idea of Black inferiority. Thus one from an unspecified number of white men from Frederick and Hampshire counties in 1786 stated that the signers were "fully persuaded that liberty is the birthright of all mankind, the right of every rational creature without exception ... that the body of negroes in this state have been robbed of that right ... and therefore ought in justice to have that right restored." Indeed, these petitioners insisted—as did David Walker in 1829 and William Lloyd Garrison in 1831—that if the grievances producing the late Revolution justified that effort, then surely the same principle "doth plead with greater force for the emancipation of our slaves in proportion as the oppression exercised over them exceed" that which the colonists had formerly suffered.

Johnston called attention also to two petitions, one signed by 422 and the other by 115 citizens, both dated 1795. These Virginians united in calling slavery "an outrageous violation and an odious degradation of human nature." This, said these hundreds of white Virginians, was all the more reprehensible at the time they were petitioning, for it was a time "when the living spirit of liberty seems to be diffusing itself through the world." They continued that they knew that objection to emancipation flowed not only "from interested motives" but also from allegations of the "unfitness of individuals for freedom." But one must, they insisted, be "sensible of the effect of custom and prejudice arising from a habit of looking upon the African race as an inferior species of mankind and regarding them only as property." The petitioners rejected such "prejudice" and insisted that they were believers in the teaching of Jesus. Hence they urged the legislature to pass regulations that would "restrain the holders from inhuman treatment" of slaves. In addition, they called on the lawmakers to ensure that the children of those then enslaved would become free when "of proper ages" and would receive instruction so that they might become literate and to "invest them with suitable privileges as an incitement to become useful citizens."

Johnston also suggested that in the colonial period, when indenture of white workers was common, the latter may well "have lacked much of the 'natural race prejudice' that is attributed to the governing aristocrat."[9] Considerable confirmatory evidence has since accumulated. In this connection, observe the remarkable book by Mechal Sobel, *The World They Made Together: Black and White Values in Eighteenth-Century Virginia*.[10] Her main point was not, as one reviewer thought, that "blacks and whites in eighteenth century Virginia formed a common cultural world."[11] What she did mean to convey, as she emphasized to this writer,[12] was that the African American and the white Virginian worker "shared values," "shared experiences," and "shared lives," but that "their world views were *not* identical, although organically related to each other." She continued, "Indeed, the sharing was what I emphasized, and still want to, but the difference is I think significant." A main contribution of this path-breaking book is its emphasis on African influences upon white people rather than the reverse; it demonstrated how great that influence was in outlook, habits, and, especially, worship.

For present purposes, the Sobel book makes the point—obvious enough once stated—that in colonial Virginia the laboring population, African and white, played, lived, labored, and worshipped together and that one result was the emergence of "a new culture...a mix of African and English values." Sobel emphasized the ruling class's effort at division through propaganda, social pressure, and legislation, for example, laws against miscegenation (1691, 1705), prohibiting Black testimony against whites (1705), and forbidding free Blacks to vote (1723). She wrote of "marked separation in the nineteenth century" but believed that "the attempt to separate the two races was not as successful as early as has been assumed." Much of the body of her book showed that in personal behavior and in common labor, worship, and resistance such separation was hardly successful in the colonial period.[13]

Earlier, in an article to which not enough attention has been paid, T. H. Breen had concluded after studying the late seventeenth- and early eighteenth-century history of this colony: "But the story of Virginia's labor force between 1660 and 1710 was more than a dreary narrative of suffering and oppression. For a few decades, it had been possible to overlook racial differences, a time when a common experience of desperate poverty and broken dreams brought some whites and blacks together."[14] It is my belief, for which the remainder of this book will seek to bring forward confirmatory evidence, that the separation of Black and white peoples and the acceptance of racism upon which that separation so heavily depended never were as successful as the bulk of the historical literature and the dominant belief pattern of the nation would suggest.

3

Anti-Racism's Presence: Examples from the Literature

The pervasive quality of racist thought and practice throughout the history of the United States is clear, but it has never been without substantial challenge. Consider these observations by two keen English visitors in the pre–Civil War years. In the closing years of the 1820s, Basil Hall wrote concerning the South: "Generally speaking, though by no means always, I found the most sensible planters of opinion, that there was not naturally and essentially any intellectual difference between the races."[1] Some dozen years later, in 1840, James S. Buckingham found himself at what he called a cotton factory near Athens, Georgia. He wrote: There is no difficulty among them [the workers] on account of color, the white girls working in the same room and at the same loom with the black girls, and boys of each color, as well as men and women, working together without apparent repugnance or objection."[2] Similarly challenging dominant conceptions is this comment by Carl Bridenbaugh: "The only blacksmith near Staunton [Virginia] in 1753 was a free Negro who had come with a Scottish wife from Lancaster and who understood and read German very well."[3]

Other examples of such circumstances are frequent; they recur in different generations and in every region. Consider the family that produced the renowned African American, Benjamin Banneker. So far as the Western Hemisphere is concerned, the story began with Mary Welsh, who came to Maryland in the early 1680s as an indentured servant. Her indenture ended in 1690; she soon was able to acquire some land and in 1692 purchased two male slaves. She manumitted both soon thereafter, and one, named Bannaka, became her husband in 1696. A daughter from that marriage, named Mary, married a slave, Robert. Both lived with the Bannekers (as the name now was spelled). Benjamin was the son of this Mary and Robert.

Benjamin, free, himself inherited some land. As a child in colonial Maryland, he and at least three other Black children attended school with white youngsters. All this went on while Maryland legislators in 1661, 1684, 1715, and 1717 were somewhat frantically passing laws providing various discouragements, fines, and even prison for—quoting the 1717 enactment— "any white man or woman who cohabited with a Negro, free or slave."

As subsequent pages will show, such cohabitation was common not only in Maryland but throughout the United States and especially in the South. Banneker's accomplishments as mathematician, clockmaker, surveyor, and almanac author led some contemporaries to question concepts of the inferiority of African-derived people. That which was true for him was true, as we shall see, for many other Black people of comparable stature. In Banneker's case, a local contemporary paper, the *Georgetown Weekly Ledger*, suggested that he proved that the idea of the African as being "void of mental endowment was without foundation." His accomplishments were cited similarly by both the Pennsylvania and Maryland societies then concerned with a gradual ending a slavery as proof of the equality of peoples.[4]

Banneker himself was quite aggressive on this question. Thus he wrote to Jefferson (enclosing a copy in manuscript of his forthcoming almanac) that he was aware that prejudices against African peoples were "so prevalent," but, counting on his expectation that Jefferson would be "less inflexible in sentiments of this nature" than many others, he was bold enough to let him see a sample of his scientific work. Banneker hoped that Jefferson's "sentiments are concurrent with mine, which are, that one universal Father hath given being to us all; and that he hath not only made us of one flesh, but that he hath also, without partiality, afforded us all the same sensations and endowed us all with the same faculties; and that however variable we may be in society or religion, however diversified in situation or color, we are all in the same family and stand in the same relation to him." Alas, while Jefferson did courteously acknowledge this letter, did express his hope that Banneker might be correct, and did send a copy to his friend, the philosopher Condorcet, in France, the sad fact is that Banneker was too advanced for Jefferson.

On Jefferson, however, it is to be noted that in a letter to Francois Jean, Marquis de Chastellux in Paris, June 7, 1785, he had written: "I believe the Indian to be in body and mind equal to the whiteman. I have supposed the blackman in his present state, might not be so. But it would be hazardous to affirm that, equally cultivated for a few generations, he would not become so." Most regrettably, however, as Fawn Brodie pointed out, Jefferson did not include this suggestion in his very influential *Notes on Virginia*, which conveyed a contrary impression.[5]

Perhaps reflecting the resistance of dominant mythology to effective challenge is the fact that it prevails notwithstanding the appearance of what is by now a fairly considerable body of contrary literature. A reason for the survival—apart from its usefulness to those who dominate the present order—may lie in the fact that the literature often expresses surprise at its findings, as has been noted earlier; or the literature sometimes asserts the allegedly marginal or exceptional quality of the evidence it presents.

When, however, the body of that literature is assembled, it does not suggest marginality or exceptionalness. It conveys, rather, how dubious is the mythology of an all-pervasive and well-nigh unchallenged racism. Confining ourselves now to some of the most important recent studies of the slave era, let us see what emerges.

Among established professional historians, an early effort at an overall view of slavery, breaking with the by-then weakened hegemony of U. B. Phillips, was that by Kenneth M. Stampp, first issued in 1956.[6] In that work Stampp emphasized the care with which Southern lawmakers strove to maintain separation between Blacks and whites. They took great pains to assure that Southern white people "were not to do or say anything which might destroy," as a Louisiana law put it, "that line of distinction established between the several classes"—meaning races.

Illustrating the concern, Stampp culled from a Virginia newspaper of 1853 the story of a Richmond policeman who apprehended a Black man and a white man "walking arm-in-arm." The question was "the why and wherefore of such a cheek by jowl business." Both were arrested; luckily for the white man involved, "he could produce witnesses who testified that he was a person of 'general good character, who happened to be on a spree at the time he was found in company with the negro.' " The white man, thus vouched for, was released "with an admonition"; what happened to his companion does not appear. Actually, as we shall see, the record of the slave South is filled with evidences of this kind of seditious joviality and fellowship.

Stampp also observed the abundance of slave artisans—a phenomenon widely referred to as contradicting racist assumptions, as, again, later pages will show. Stampp noted that this skill "often won great admiration." He called attention to an English visitor's comment that the reality should "encourage every philanthropist who has had misgivings in regard to the progressive power of the race." By no means unknown was the condition in which the African American was the white man's teacher in mechanical skills; Stampp, for example, noted the case in Louisiana in 1831 where a white worker had asked permission of the slaveowner to work with his Black carpenters "for the sake of Instruction."

Prior to the discouraging or outright banning of manumission, there occurred, as already noted, numerous cases of such action, at times accompanied by explanations filled with a sense of the humanity of those being freed. Characteristic was the example from North Carolina wherein a master willed his slaves' emancipation. This was done, said the master, because he believed that "every human being, be his or her colour what it may, is entitled to freedom." His conscience condemned him for acting contrary to this belief. Slavery, he knew, violated "the golden rule [that] directs us to do unto every human creature, as we would wish to be done unto," and he wished "to die with a clear conscience." This repentant slaveowner urged everyone "seriously to deliberate on my reasons."

James M. McPherson's numerous and significant publications have offered evidence of the reality of anti-racism in U.S. history. Especially important for present purposes is his 1964 volume, *The Struggle for Equality*.[7] He observed that the idea of inferiority was central to the defense of slavery; Frederick Douglass had stated that "this question is at the bottom of the whole controversy." McPherson emphasized that the basic arguments of the Abolitionists (Black and white), taken from their understanding of science and history and their reading of the Bible, was "the essential unity and equality of races"; adverse environment was a basic explanation, they believed, for deficiencies in human conduct. The influence of some outstanding European scientists—Alexander von Humboldt, in particular—was important in helping combat racism.

Arguments from relevant portions of ancient history, especially Egyptian, and notice of outstanding figures of African derivation, like Banneker and Toussaint L'Ouverture, were important in the Abolitionists' literature as part of their anti-racist agitation. Here the writings of William Wells Brown, Wendell Phillips, and Mary Putnam (the sister of James Russell Lowell) were especially significant. Phillips had reached the point where he could insist in public speeches in 1863 before tens of thousands of sympathetic listeners: "I despise an empire resting its claims on the blood of a single race. My pride is in the banner that welcomes every race and every blood, and under whose shelter all races stand up equal."

John L. Thomas, in introducing a noteworthy collection of Abolitionist writing, offered a view in refreshing contrast to the rather cynical attitude that for a time dominated the field.[8] He was sound, I think, when he wrote that the Abolitionists' opposition to the colonization scheme was based on their rejection of the scheme's "sweeping assumption of inferiority and unfitness." The argument of the Abolitionists, he correctly insisted, was "devastatingly simple": "Slavery was a sin and a crime, a sin because it denied to the Negro the status of a human being, a crime because it violated the natural right to life, liberty and the pursuit of happiness guaranteed in the Declaration of Independence." Thomas continued: "These two beliefs in the spiritual equality of all believers and the political equality of all Americans served as the chief moral weapons in the attacks on slavery."

The generous size of Winthrop Jordan's *White over Black: American Attitudes toward the Negro* is matched by its importance. However, it would have been fairer to the volume's contents if its subtitle (with its use of the plural) had served as its actual title, for the fact is that Jordan's book contains important and copious material showing that attitudes were indeed plural, contrary to the notion conveyed by the title.

Early on, Jordan quoted an English master of a slaving vessel, writing in

1694, who found it difficult to understand why his cargo "should be despised for their colour, being what they cannot help, and the effect of the climate it has pleased God to appoint them." The master continued: "I can't think there is any intrinsic value in one colour more than another, nor that white is better than black, only we think it is so because we are so, as well as the blacks, who in odium of the colour, say, the devil is white, and so paint him." Jordan commented that this "was surely a remarkable complaint" from one occupied as he was.[9]

Emphasizing the occupation of the complainant perhaps does make the complaint remarkable; but the main point is that the content of his remarks was not remarkable. In fact, his views may even be called commonplace at the time. Thus Richard Baxter, who served as chaplain to Cromwell's army from 1654 to 1657, had warned slaveowners in 1673 that while "their sin [may] have enslaved them to you," still they must not forget "that they are of as good a kind as you; and born to as much natural liberty." Indeed, Baxter insisted that whatever their earthly situation might be, "yet Nature made them your equals." Particularly, warned the minister, it was necessary to remember that "they have immortal souls, and are equally capable of salvation with yourselves."[10]

Baxter's insistence on the basic unity and equality of humanity was traditional seventeenth-century theology. In 1614 the Reverend Samuel Purchas preached that "the tawny Moore, black Negro, duskie Libyan, ash-coloured Indian, olive-coloured American should with the white European become one sheep-fold, under one great Sheepheard . . . all may be One in him that is One, and onely blessed for ever."

It is this traditional outlook that explains why the Georgia merchant, James Habersham, wrote in 1770 (a year before he became Georgia's acting governor) that he knew of the Africans' "unimproved capacities," but he rejected the notion of "some ignorant people [who] would foolishly insinuate, that they are scarcely reasonable Creatures, and are not capable of being instructed in the divine Truths of Christianity." Such an idea, wrote Habersham, is "an absurdity too obvious to deserve any refutation." Indeed, as Jordan remarked in connection with similar statements by William Fleetwood, bishop of London, in 1711, ideas of this nature "had become almost commonplace" by the mid-eighteenth century.[11]

Before the close of the eighteenth century, as future pages will confirm, the specific denial of inferiority and denunciation of racial prejudice came from a long list of outstanding figures, among whom may be named the Reverend Samuel Davies (speaking shortly before he became president of the College of New Jersey, that is, Princeton), James Otis, Benjamin Franklin, John Jay, Benjamin Rush, Alexander Hamilton, John Wesley, James McHenry, Samuel Hopkins, Nathaniel Appleton, William Pinkney, Robert Pleasants, Moses Brown, and Jeremy Belknap—hardly obscure or marginal figures in the history of the United States. State anti-slavery societies in several states late in the eighteenth and early in the nineteenth centuries insisted, to quote from a 1795 statement of the society of Pennsylvania, that African-derived peoples were "in no wise inferior to the more fortunate inhabitants of Europe and America."

Earlier, we remarked that H. Shelton Smith's study of Southern religion was presented by the author as an examination of the "anti-Negro movement" from 1780 to 1910, and we commented that paradoxically much of the book's content brought forward ideas attacking, not upholding, racism. Here are some illustrations from Smith's volume. The Reverend Samuel Willard of Boston's South Church suggested in 1703 that slavery began in sin, and he was not urging its abolition; rather, he thought that it was a condition that, like other tribulations, should be endured. But the minister did enjoin kindliness upon the slaveowner because it was necessary to understand the humanity of the slave, who had a soul "of as much worth, as the Soul of his Master, having the same Faculties and Powers . . . and being alike Precious to Christ."

Earlier, Cotton Mather (1689) had denounced masters who denied knowledge of the gospel to their slaves. Many among them insisted on the "dullness" of the African, but this, Mather asserted, was nothing but rationalization. If they kept the gospel from their slaves, he warned, "You deny your Master in Heaven." Here, as with Willard, Mather—himself the owner of slaves—was not attacking slavery but was rejecting the idea of the slaves' inferiority as a justification for it.

Bishop Fleetwood was brought forward by Smith, as he was by Jordan. Again, his attack was not upon slavery, but in a 1711 sermon he did insist that Africans were "equally the workmanship of God" as were their owners and that they were "endowed with the same Faculties and intellectual Powers" as white people.

Upon returning from the mainland colonies, Dean George Berkeley (later bishop) stated in 1732 in a sermon before the Society for the Propagation of the Gospel that he had found resistance to converting slaves because some masters insisted that they were "creatures of another species." This, said the very distinguished theologian, was really "an irrational concept" that required the society's vigorous opposition.

In the South during the 1740s, the famous George Whitefield attacked harsh treatment of slaves while rejecting the idea that religious instruction was dangerous to the stability of a slave society. Whitefield did not call for an end to slavery but did insist that the Africans in the New World "were naturally as capable of improvement as whites."

Some divines combined a rejection of racism with an attack upon slavery. This was true, for example, of Samuel Hopkins, a Congregational minister in Rhode Island. He remarked in 1776 that zealousness in attacking slavery would follow if whites could understand that the African people were "as by nature and by right on a level" with themselves.

On the question of the alleged stupidity of the slaves and the assertion that this justifies their condition, Methodism's founder, John Wesley, declared in his *Thoughts on Slavery* (1774):

Allowing them to be stupid as you say, to whom is that stupidity owing? Without question it lies altogether at the door of their inhuman masters, who give them no means, no opportunity of improving their understanding.... The inhabitants of Africa where they have equal motives and equal means of improvement, are not inferior to the inhabitants of Europe.... Their stupidity therefore in our plantations is not natural; otherwise than it is the natural effect of their condition. Consequently, it is not their fault, but yours; you must answer for it, before God and man.

Smith's book continued with other illustrations reflecting the opposite of his title and prefatory remarks. Some examples, such as those of David Rice of Kentucky, will be elaborated on in later pages. Here one more citation will do, that of David Barrow's 1808 essay on *Slavery Examined*, also published in Kentucky. Like Wesley, Barrow insisted that the slaves' "pinched situation" was sufficient explanation "for any observed limits in their capacity." Indeed, he wrote that considering their "situation," "I believe I may venture to say, their talents or natural abilities, are not inferior to the whites in any respect." Barrow's work, like that of Rice, will be discussed at greater length in later pages.[12]

Note was made earlier of Ira Berlin's important study of the pre–Civil War Southern free African American population. The book is rich with material countering the idea of a monolithically racist white Southern population. The egalitarian beliefs and practices of several Protestant denominations, particularly early in the slave era, are fairly well known. Berlin observed that "some evangelicals made no apology for slavery and frankly preached equality of blacks." Again, later pages will illustrate that fact. As to egalitarian behavior, Berlin called attention to an advertisement in a Maryland newspaper of 1793 for a fugitive slave, Sam, who "was raised in a family of religious persons, commonly called Methodists, and has lived with some of them for years past, on terms of perfect equality." The advertiser continued: "The refusal to continue him on these terms, has given him offense, and is the sole cause of his absconding."

Southern white people assisting slaves in their flight were not uncommon. The joint flight of slave and white indentured servant (sometimes interracial couples with children) also recurred; examples from Georgia, the Carolinas, and Virginia in the late eighteenth century were cited by Berlin and will be noted later in this book.

In religious practice, the breakdown of the color line was common; Berlin's work is notable for illustrations of this. Blacks ministered to mixed congregations in the South, especially in the last decades of the eighteenth century, as is attested by the lives of such Black preachers as Henry Evans,

William Lemon, John Chavis, David George, Jesse Peters, Jacob Bishop, George Liele, and Andrew Bryan in Virginia, North Carolina, and Georgia. Berlin added other examples, less well known, especially in Maryland, continuing into the nineteenth century.

This occurred also, of course, in the North; Richard Allen's African Church in Philadelphia, for example, had white as well as Black members. The case of the extraordinary Lemuel Haynes (1753–1833) has at last been told with some fullness through the work of Helen McLam and Richard Newman. Probably the first African American ordained in the United States—in November 1785 by the Association of Congregational Ministers of Litchfield County, Connecticut—Haynes was pastor of white churches in several communities in Massachusetts, Connecticut, and New York and, for thirty years, in Rutland, Vermont.

On this matter of church practice and anti-racism, Berlin wrote a paragraph meriting full quotation:

The pressure of Christian equalitarianism forged new racial modes and brought whites and blacks together in places where previously they had never met. It was not unusual for black churchmen to attend synods and association-meetings with whites. Several free Negroes represented their churches in meetings of regional Baptist associations. In 1794, when one Virginia church called this practice into question, the Portsmouth Association firmly announced that it saw "nothing in the Word of God, nor anything contrary to decency to prohibit a church from sending as a delegate any male member they shall choose." Four years later, the association accepted Jacob Bishop as its first black delegate.

Somewhat less widespread, but noteworthy, was the appearance of schools for educating Black and white children together in the South in the late eighteenth and early nineteenth centuries. This occurred in Maryland and Virginia, the Virginia Quaker, Robert Pleasants, being especially prominent in such work. Berlin suggested that this equalitarianism was less common in schools than in evangelical churches, for the former, unlike the latter, "were middle-class and upper-class institutions, and class distinctions alone excluded most Negro freemen."

Nevertheless, this practice of integrated education did exist and did persist, law or no law, well into the final decade prior to secession in the South. It existed, too, not without difficulty, in the North, and later pages will treat this. Berlin quoted a Richmond newspaper in 1855 that there was "good reason to believe that there are schools in this city in which negroes are taught by white persons to read and write." The case of Mrs. Margaret Douglas, sentenced to jail in 1853 for this "crime," is illustrative.

The widespread, indeed, institutionalized, ignoring of the color line in formerly French and Spanish Southern areas, especially New Orleans, Mobile, and Pensacola, was illuminated by Berlin and by several other historians. Berlin observed that the 1818 Louisiana law prohibiting free Negroes from keeping white indentured servants reflected "the freemen's continued high status"; their employment as soldiers further emphasized this reality. Later, when manumission was legally barred in much of the South, "freedom by courtesy" became fairly common. Southern whites, impelled by various motives—usually kinship—managed emancipation despite the law and sometimes even made public record of this.

Berlin remarked that "despite the dense wall of racial antagonism . . . close living conditions and the common pattern of their daily lives frequently pushed the races together." He continued: "They lived together, worked together, inevitably slept together, hopelessly blurring the color line." This was especially true in "working-class districts of Southern cities," where "the same easy intimacy between free Negroes and whites" often developed. This "fraternization between whites and free Negroes extended to all corners of working-class life"; "warm friendship between free Negroes and whites also flourished at the other end of the social spectrum," but there, naturally, this was rare. However, among the poor, "whites and free blacks turned away from the hard life of scratching at the soil and hunted and fished together."[13]

Berlin concentrated upon the nineteenth century. Mechal Sobel, as we have seen, found that "in the eighteenth century South, blacks and whites lived together in great intimacy, affecting each other in both small and large ways." What existed, she found, was "a biracial society" in which whites "worked with blacks, played with blacks, lived with blacks, and eventually prayed with blacks."

Sobel thought that "ultimately, an ideology based on white superiority did divide poor whites from blacks; however, a very long history of black-white interaction preceded the marked separation of the nineteenth century."[14] But, as observed, Berlin's earlier work had already shown how partial that separation was, especially among those who labored and did not rule.

A final book to be commented upon, as a whole offering data of value for a history of anti-racism, is by Carl Degler.[15] One of Degler's main points, he wrote, was to show "that the South is not and never has been a monolith." He meant the white South, and there certainly is no quarrel with that statement from the present writer. When, however, Degler wrote that "most [white] Southerners were never torn by the wrong of slavery," he was offering an opinion that is widely accepted but can neither be substantiated nor refuted. Certainly, as his book helped show, the questioning of slavery's propriety by white Southerners in the nineteenth century was quite widespread; this appears from those articulate and literate enough to have left record of their opinions on this matter. Since slavery dominated the South, to express misgivings about it, not to speak of opposition, was not the way to "get ahead." One may, therefore, suggest the existence in the South of significant inhibition against expressing such views.

Degler stated that he thought that his book was not contrary to the Phillipsian view of the very near universality of agreement among white people as to white supremacy. Rather, he wrote that "in an important sense, this book is an illustration of his [Phillips's] central theme," namely, that the South "shall be and remain a white man's country." But Phillips did not present this as a contest as to whether or not it was to be such a country; on the contrary, his point was that it was such a country. His emphasis was on unanimity, on the acceptance of such a condition, and on placidity as characterizing prewar Southern society.

There is no doubt that those who ruled that South were committed to the creation and preservation of a white supremacist South. The point is, however, that the effort to create and to maintain such a society was onerous, that challenges to it were continuous and serious, and that the history of that white South is not of a placidly existing white male supremacist society but rather of a society constantly facing challenge, protest, and dissent, both individual and collective. The history of that pre–Civil War South is one of a social order dominated by white male slaveowners constantly engaged in defending what they had created and finally going down to military defeat caused, in considerable part, exactly because the South was far from a monolithic society—quite apart from the 35 percent of its population that was African American. One may now assert without fear of contradiction that this considerable proportion of the South was not the docile inferiors Phillips postulated.

Degler also remarked in substantiation of his acceptance of the Phillipsian approach that "in a sense this book is a study in the way class has been subordinate to race in the life of nineteenth century Southerners." Insofar as his book ignored the realities of class-based differentiation on questions of both slavery and racism, it displayed a significant weakness. Earlier pages have already shown how important class cleavage was on this matter. Ensuing pages will add other evidence.

The main content of most of Degler's book shows something of the opposition among Southern whites to slavery, a subject by no means unknown by 1974; but the work does contain useful additions and summaries. Also, in doing this, Degler's work offers material relevant to an inquiry into anti-racism in the pre– and post–Civil War South. This will be noted in appropriate sections of my investigation.

4

Sexual Relations

The centrality of sexual relations showed itself in the contact between European and African people. Sexual attraction was immediately apparent. It made difficult adherence to the idea of the bestiality of the African, which gave way, for this and other reasons, to the idea of the Africans' immutable, inherent, and significant inferiority to the European—in the latter's opinion, of course. The urgency to abandon the idea of bestiality was intensified because copulation between a white and a Black often led to offspring— that is, an infant who, presumably, was human.

Still, this idea of bestiality, though abandoned fairly early and quite generally, did have lingering impact. A person of Jefferson's intelligence, for example, could believe aspects of this nonsense. In 1900 a Christian minister could write and a St. Louis religious press could issue a book entitled *The Mystery Solved: The Negro A Beast*, which, by the way, throws some light on Du Bois's choice of a title for his 1903 classic, *The Souls of Black Folk*. The idea that Africans and African Americans had tails resulted in strange behavior among some European people not only in World War I but even in World War II.

Still, it was not the beasts of Africa who were enslaved by the Europeans; they were discerning enough to know that fruitful labor could come only from the African who had this capacity—as well as the power of sexual attraction. This sexual attraction not only helped destroy concepts of bestiality; it also had the capacity to help undercut concepts of inferiority, particularly when sexual activity became part of a human relationship rather than a momentary encounter.

The latter form of contact was common—in slavery, institutionalized— and might well serve to intensify rather than reduce ideas of inferiority. But human relationships did develop; that they might develop, all slaveholding societies realized. Moreover, the issue from such intercourse—especially if the mother was white—might well present upsetting ideological and practical challenges to the status quo.

The data demonstrate that sexual relationships between whites and Blacks were common. This was true not only of white men with Black women but also—probably with less frequency—of white women with Black men. These data show, also, that while much of this was casual (and often carried through forcibly by the white male) or mercenary, a considerable portion of such behavior reflected mutual respect and quite often devotion. When the latter existed, anti-racism also existed.

Racism was a basic rationalization for modern slavery; as Montesquieu pointed out, if the slave was the equal of the owner, slavery would be difficult to justify—therefore it was decided that the slave was not equal. Action questioning racism had to be made anti-social, indeed, seditious.[1] This is the point of the well-known cases, in early English America, of the public shaming and punishing of white people found guilty of having intercourse with Black people. Well known, too, is the fact alluded to in earlier pages that Southern colonies found it necessary in the seventeenth and eighteenth centuries to pass law after law—with increasing penalties—punishing those involved in such sexual relationships. As already suggested, the need for such laws showed the legislators' concern; it showed also the existence of the practice. That such laws were often repeated, with punishment intensified, shows not only the persistence of the concern but also of the "crime," despite the penalties entailed.

The study of Alabama by Gary B. Mills, alluded to earlier, is of very great consequence on this question. Mills, in a three-year project, went beyond traditional historical technique by approaching "the free Negro on an individual basis." This entailed a "name-by-name" examination of the lives of over 5,600 people from birth to death.[2] Mills was careful to note some exceptional qualities in Alabama's history; thus he observed that while Virginia outlawed intermarriage in 1705, Louisiana (as a French colony) in 1724, and North Carolina only in 1838, Alabama never prohibited it. While an 1852 law in Alabama did declare that any person solemnizing a marriage between a white and a Black was guilty of a misdemeanor, it did not declare such a union void, nor did it impose any penalty upon the people entering such a marriage.

Mills determined from the 1860 census returns that 78 percent of Alabama's free Black population was characterized as "mulatto," making it second only to Louisiana in this regard. However, while a considerable section of the Mobile region of Alabama, like Louisiana, had much Latin influence, assigning this as a reason for the high percentage does not reflect the realities of Mills's study, for it found "little difference" between Anglo and Latin societies. Mills, nevertheless, decided to restrict his report "to the Anglo portion of the state."

Mills did not find that the free Negro population owed its origins, to a very significant degree, to manumissions by planters of their offspring. Of course, this occurred; indeed, 32 percent of manumissions were probably due to this circumstance, but 68 percent were not.

Striking was Mills's finding that of the free Negro population where parentage could be identified, almost all—94 percent—were "offspring of a recognized, long-term and apparently stable marital relationship." His study also persuaded him that even in those cases where parents could not be identified by name, there existed "considerable evidence of marital stability among free mulattoes."

Mills found that "of the 83 open and stable interracial alliances" in Anglo Alabama, 51 percent involved white women, data very wide of the stereotype. Further, over 20 percent of clandestine interracial alliances had "identifiable white mothers." Indeed, when all known factors were tabulated, "the extant records of Alabama's free mulattoes identify . . . a white mother in 156 percent more cases than a white father."

In the interracial cases of which public record exists, no upper-class white women were involved; but such cases "frequently did" become a matter of public record among "the yeomen class and among the poor whites." Mills was careful to underline the fact that the white women in these interracial alliances must not "be relegated to the role" of reprobate. They were of the lower rungs economically, but the data showed their relationships to have been "extended." Only 7 percent of these women bore white illegitimate children.

Especially important is Mills's insistence that while it is widely alleged that white Southerners "despised miscegenation," he was unable to find any evidence "within Anglo-Alabama of any community action, overt or covert, taken against whites" who entered such relationships, most of which lasted about two years. Records that do exist, which Mills called "numerous," on the contrary "indicate public tolerance and respect for the individuals involved."

The concluding remarks of Mills have been quoted earlier in this work; certainly he was correct in observing that his study "suggests a reinterpretation of southern race relations" and that the kind of detailed study he made is "mandated" for "other southern states." Actually there does exist at least one other such detailed study, which Mills apparently did not know. This examined Edgefield County, South Carolina.[3] It confirmed (or, rather, anticipated) Mills's findings. Its author, Orville V. Burton, concluded that "the antebellum free blacks who remained in Edgefield County compared favorably in wealth and occupational status to a large group of whites." Burton found "that interaction of blacks and whites before the Civil War [but not after 1877] occurred much more often, and more easily than has usually been assumed." This study found that census returns revealed that sixty black people lived in thirty "mixed households." It reported "clear evidence of mixed marriages" and other evidences of "close associations" between the races. Further, "Assimilation of mulattoes who could pass as whites was accepted by the community." In general, in this South Carolina county prior to the Civil War (and for some years thereafter), Burton found "frequent examples of familial connections as well as evidence of daily contact between free blacks and whites, particularly less affluent whites, through the arrangement of their households, neighborhoods, and occupations."

Decades before Burton and Mills, the African American scholar James Hugo Johnston produced a study that anticipated many of their findings.[4] It was not possible for Johnston, then at the beginning of his career and a Black man in the pre–World War II United States, to undertake the kind of intensive work done by Burton and Mills. Nevertheless, despite these restraints, his work constituted a significant challenge to what was then a blatantly racist historical establishment.

Johnston's book is very rich in evidence of interracial sexual activity. He emphasized the fact—as Carter G. Woodson had done back in 1918[5]—that such relationships frequently involved white women; he related accounts of trials of several white women for this "crime" in seventeenth-century Virginia and in North Carolina and Pennsylvania in the next century. He observed that contemporaries in North Carolina in 1835 offered the opinion "that almost all of the free Negroes of that state before the Revolution were the mulatto children of white mothers." He cited also instances of this in South Carolina and Maryland. Indeed, Johnston affirmed of this prerevolutionary era that "the records of the time, letters and memoirs give testimony to indiscriminate mingling of the races, the white, the Indian and the Negro."

It may be noted that Alan Watson very recently has called attention to numerous instances in law reports from South Carolina, in the pre–Civil War generation, of manumissions by will, with the testator directing the freedom of a slave woman and the children she had borne him. At times, the executor was directed to take the woman and children north and thus make their freedom secure. Watson added: "It seems reasonable to believe that the cases which reached the law reports represent but a small proportion of the attempted manumissions and that many more manumissions would have occurred but for the legislation against freeing slaves."[6]

Johnston observed that legal racial intermarriages rarely occurred among the upper classes, but nevertheless "some of the men of this class maintained permanent relations with Negro women to a more or less open extent." He reiterated that especially in the Colonial era "there was much miscegenation." He called attention to a petition "of George Ivie and others" in May 1699 urging that the Virginia Council repeal the law prohibiting the marriage of English people with Indian and Black peoples. Johnston remarked "that an element of that colony was not in sympathy with the planter policy on the question of race mixture."

In an entire chapter ("The White Man and Race Relations"), Johnston cited case after case of white men, in their wills, referring with affection and gratitude to African American women with whom they had spent years—often a lifetime—together. These instances came from Virginia, North Carolina, Tennessee, Georgia, Alabama, Mississippi, and especially Louisiana, of which more later. In these wills provision of inheritances was common, and language such as "my bosom friend" in reference to the Black woman involved, together with acknowledgments of, for example, "my natural colored daughter," recurred.

Another chapter ("The Status of White Women in Slave States") abounds in records of divorce proceedings instituted by white women because their husbands practiced what was called "flagrant infidelity" with Black women. In many cases these complaints make clear that the Black-white relationship was long-lasting. The documents themselves refer to "great affection" between such couples. Complaints occasionally specified that the husband insisted on disregarding racist practices—demanding, for example, that the Black woman dine with other members of the household. Most of Johnston's examples came from Virginia—more accessible to him then than other states—but he did cite evidence of similar cases in Alabama and Louisiana.

Johnston noted several cases of white families torn apart because the male insisted on living openly with a Black woman. Numerous wills leaving estates to Black women were contested by white family members; again Johnston cited evidence mainly from Virginia, but he did refer to similar instances in Mississippi and Alabama as late as 1859 and 1860.

Notable are the pages (250–57) Johnston devoted to recounting some details of twenty-two divorce proceedings brought by husbands against wives because the women persisted in sexual relations with Black men. These were not momentary affairs; rather, in one case, the woman "lived in open adultery with a free man of color" and bore his child. Another white woman chose to live with a slave for over six years, and together they had two children. Such cases were documented from various counties in Virginia from 1802 to 1849; occasional cases were cited from elsewhere, as in North Carolina in 1829.

These instances concerned Black-white relations where the women were married. Johnston noted that "evidence is found that makes it clear that unmarried white women were concerned in similar relations with Negro men." In this connection Johnston called attention to the sixty cases of reported rape by Black slaves upon white women in Virginia from 1789 to 1833. He was "astonished at the number of cases in which white citizens of the communities in which these events transpired testify for the Negro and against the white woman and declare that the case is not a matter of rape, for the woman encouraged and consented to the act of the Negro." Johnston found that of the sixty cases tried, twenty-seven showed such testimony.

Johnston's work brought forward significant additional evidence of black men and white women living together. He noted, for example, that the 1830 Virginia census returns often fell one short in specific household enumerations. "The explanation," he wrote, "seems to be that the additional family member was the white wife of the free Negro head of the family." This suggestion is supported because in the case of Nansemond County the 1830 census taker, unlike others, decided on his own initiative to state "and white wife" following the name of the free Negro head of the family. In that county, in that year, this census taker noted nine such cases. In 1844, in a count taken of a part of Southampton County, note was made of five cases of a "white mother" in a household composed otherwise of Black people.

Johnston added that his examination of the correspondence of pre–Civil War Virginia governors showed "many references to the relations of white women and the Negro"; at times this appeared because white women were accomplices in the flight of slaves. One white woman undergoing criminal investigation because of her husband's charge of infidelity was quoted this way in a case in Powhatan County in 1815: "She had not been the first nor would she be the last guilty of such conduct." She added: "She saw no more harm in a white woman's having been the mother of a black child than in a white man's having one, though the latter case was more frequent."

Johnston included a chapter on "Indian Relations" that showed that sexual connections between Indians and African Americans and Indians and whites were common. Indeed, the advocacy by white men, including such notables as William Byrd, Patrick Henry, John Marshall, and William Crawford, of Indian-white intermarriage was by no means unknown, and as late as 1824 an effort in Congress to legalize such marriages was narrowly defeated. However, while this is related to the rejection of racism in general, it moves away from the focus of the present work on Black-white relationships and the racism related to the African American.

Johnston published as an appendix the report of the Special Committee (chaired by George Bradburn) of the House of Representatives of Massachusetts that urged the House, early in 1841, to respond favorably to the petition presented by William E. Channing and forty-two other Bostonians "and many other petitions of a similar character" praying for the repeal of the state's anti-miscegenation law. In this report note was taken of the fact that no such law existed in Vermont, New Hampshire, and Connecticut; that in any case, law or no law in Massachusetts, "such connections" did occur. For this reason and the view that the law "encourages licentiousness," was simply unjust, and often victimized women and children, its repeal was urged. While such cases of Black-white relationships were not common in the state, noted the report, they did occur, sometimes involving "distinguished examples," but the committee avoided particulars. In any case, it unanimously held that the anti-miscegenation law "ought to be obliterated from the statute book of this Commonwealth, as contrary to the principles of Christianity and Republicanism." In 1843 the law was repealed, and Black and white people—especially women—by their courageous public denunciation of this manifestation of racism—were decisive in bringing this about.

Edmund S. Morgan observed in his study of colonial Virginia that sexual relations between Blacks and whites were far from uncommon. In this connection he enumerated cases of mulatto offspring in several counties and commented: "It would appear that black men were competing all too successfully for white women, even in the face of severe penalties."[7]

On the other hand, Allan Kulikoff in a more recent work dealing with the same general area and about the same period suggested that only "a tiny number of white women slept with slave men." He called attention to one such case, that of an indentured servant, Mary Wedge, who "persisted in a common-law marriage to a slave on a nearby plantation and bore seven children"; Kulikoff added that "the uniqueness of her case points to the limits of miscegenation in the Chesapeake." It is not quite clear whether this "uniqueness" consisted in the relationship or the abundance of offspring. In any case, just after referring to the "tiny number," Kulikoff reported that in Prince George County in Maryland in the 1720s and 1730s "sixteen white women were convicted of bearing twenty-five mulatto bastards."[8] Is "tiny" the correct word for this? Furthermore, miscegenation was not the result simply of the activities of white women.

Herbert Gutman paid slight attention to miscegenation. He wrote: "Not all sexual ties between slave women and white men were exploitative, and not all interracial contacts between slaves, ex-slaves, or free persons involved black women and white men. The wartime and early post-war records [he referred to the Civil War] detail isolated but nevertheless significant instances of slave women and white owners deeply attached to one another."[9] This, however, hardly conveys accurately the scope, time sweep, and consequence of interracial sexual relations, particularly in a volume ranging from the prerevolutionary to the post–World War I periods and concentrating on the history of the Black family.

Kenneth Stampp gave fairly extensive treatment to interracial sexual relations. His main emphasis was upon their long-lasting quality and, by inference, their refutation of concepts of a racist monolith. Certainly, in slavery the sexual victimization of the black woman was institutionalized; yet Stampp expressed the opinion that the evidence suggested "that sexual contacts between the races were not the rare aberration of a small group of depraved whites but a frequent occurrence involving whites of all social and cultural levels." He thought that white women were less involved in this than white men but believed that, especially in the colonial period, sexual interrelationship "when slaves and indentured servants worked on the same estates, was never entirely negligible"—a careful choice of words probably minimizing reality.

Stampp also called attention to cases of white women and Black men sustaining relationships for prolonged periods. He believed, probably correctly, that "most miscegenation, however, involved white males and female slaves." He remarked, again, that such relations quite often were prolonged rather than casual. Stampp thought that this conduct was especially prevalent in Louisiana, but he observed that it was not rare in South Carolina, Kentucky, and Virginia. He confirmed, as do many other sources, that it was not uncommon for one's "colored mistress and their mulatto children" to live "as a family upon terms of equality, and not as a master with his slaves."[10]

James M. McPherson is among the few historians to emphasize the commitment of the Abolitionist movement not only to end slavery but also to combat racism. On miscegenation, in particular, he called attention to the often-neglected reality that some among the Abolitionists defended it; he named Louisa May Alcott, Lydia Maria Child, Anna Dickinson, Gilbert Haven, Moncure Conway, and Wendell Phillips.[11]

One can name others with this attitude. Lewis Tappan, for example, had a positive attitude toward miscegenation, though he did add that it would be wise for partners to have similar religious convictions. William Lloyd Garrison in the pages of the *Liberator* very early (May 7, 1831) expressed his view on this and never altered it: "If he has 'made of one blood all nations of men on the face of the earth', then they are of one species, and stand on a perfect equality: their intermarriage is neither unnatural nor repugnant to nature, but obviously proper and salutary.... By the blissful operation of this divine institution, the earth is evidently to become one neighborhood or family." Myrtilla Miner, the remarkable white woman devoted to the education of African American people (of whom more later), felt that racial intermarriage was in no way objectionable; indeed, she thought that it was a way to resolve the racial problem, as she stated in an 1853 letter.[12]

Winthrop Jordan's *White over Black* tends to be contradictory on the question of miscegenation. At one point he wrote that "no one thought intermixture was a good thing"; later, while noting that some colonists "were willing to allow, even advocate intermarriage with the Indians," he wrote that this was "an unheard of proposition concerning Negroes." Yet at another point he observed that "community feeling was of course not monolithically arrayed against interracial union." Here he cited, as Johnston had reported, the fact that in 1699 some Virginians had urged the repeal of a law prohibiting intermarriage and that in 1755 the North Carolina Assembly had favored a petition from the "inhabitants of several counties asking repeal of the laws in which free Negroes or Mulattoes intermarrying with white women are obliged to pay taxes for their wives and families." Indeed, at another point Jordan called attention to a poem defending miscegenation published in a South Carolina newspaper in 1737.

Jordan presented the colonial legislation prohibiting miscegenation as demonstrating that "public feeling about miscegenation was strong enough to force itself over the hurdles of the legislative process into the statute books of many English continental colonies." He noted especially such legislation in the 1660s in Maryland and Virginia.

Another and contrary interpretation of this legislation is possible and has been suggested by this writer and others, including Johnston. It is far from clear that colonial legislatures were as sensitive to "public feeling" as Jordan's remark would indicate. On the contrary, the public had little to do with the legislatures, at least "public" as defined in the present.

It was because such interracial behavior occurred and recurred that the elite who made the laws moved to prevent it. Their language was, as Jordan reported, "dripping with distaste and indignation"; but the distaste and indignation were theirs and not of the so-called common people—the actual public—which seems to have paid a minimum of attention to matters of color. Hence the need, for those who ruled a society reared on a color line, to enact this legislation and to do so repeatedly, with ever-increasing penalties, as we have seen. Actually, Jordan's book, despite its title, is filled with evidence of the rejection of racism by many white people in the period it covers; we have already noted some examples of this and will note more before this volume closes.[13]

Ira Berlin's already-cited work, while showing the institutionalized subordination of the free African American population, at the same time may be viewed as an extended presentation of the hollowness of its rationalization on grounds of innate inferiority. Not least does this appear in the volume's material on sexual relations between whites and Blacks.

In the seventeenth century, as Berlin showed, sexual relations of a lasting character (as well as those of a fleeting nature) were quite common. Various kinds of laws were found to be necessary by those who ruled to discourage or to prohibit such relationships, but they were largely unsuccessful. Such relationships of a prolonged character usually involved the poor, especially indentured whites and free or enslaved Afro-Americans.

In French and Spanish Louisiana such relationships were especially common. In Mobile and Pensacola one had societies in which "free Negroes [enjoyed] a measure of equality with whites." In these areas cohabitation of Black and white was common—by the late eighteenth century, institutionalized.

Particularly among the working population of the pre–Civil War South there existed "easy intimacy" between free Negroes and whites, "hopelessly blurring the color line." The general sense of Berlin's findings on miscegenation is in these lines:

The pattern of interracial sexual unions reveals the full range of relationships between whites and blacks. Although these illicit sexual liaisons bespoke exploitation as well as intimacy, their circumstances sometimes suggest the close, friendly ties between whites and blacks. Perhaps nowhere were these relations more frequent than in the working-class districts of Southern cities. Although the taboo on interracial sex was the strictest rule of the Southern racial code and laws forbidding sexual relations between whites and blacks littered the statute books, violations were commonplace.

Open racial unions, mostly among the poor but by no means unknown among the well-to-do, in fact flourished throughout the South and throughout the antebellum era. Not infrequently, as Berlin observed, there existed "strong bonds of affection" that "steeled whites and blacks to challenge racial standards and establish open, stable relationships."[14]

It will not be amiss to illustrate interracial sexual relationships of a lasting character among upper-class pre–Civil War Southerners by citing the example of George J. F. Clarke (1774–1836). Clarke was an outstanding figure in Florida during the period of its Spanish possession; his distinction was great even under U.S. ownership. In the latter period his eminence diminished, however, perhaps because of his interracial relationship. But this continued to his death. Indeed, Clarke "never sought to conceal" what his biographer called "his irregularly established family." He gave his children from this relationship the first names of his father and brothers and his own surname and "openly acknowledged his paternity." His will, dated 1834, provided an "extensive inheritance" to the eight children resulting from his relationship with the African American woman who predeceased him.[15]

Joel Williamson, in his study of *New People* (what Edwin Embree fifty years earlier had called *Brown America*), also suggested, as the literature generally affirms, that in the early colonial period the propertyless white people "took their lovers from the class most readily available, black or white and without great regard for color." Somewhat invidiously, however, he added: "These laboring people themselves had in a sense been aliens at home, they were aliens in America and they were not so deeply steeped in the color line as were their betters. They were more likely to respond to the body than to the mind, and the result was the first wave of mulatto offspring in the new land."[16]

There is no evidence concerning the relative attractiveness of "the mind" to the slaveowners as compared with the laborers; and those owners had quite easy access to "the body," which they were not loathe to employ. But there is evidence that among those whose class ties were close, relationships between Blacks and whites often were quite lasting, as we have seen, and did ignore the color line so dear to the dominators of a slave society in which only the colored were to be slaves.

Williamson called attention to the fact that in South Carolina—which in the era of slavery never did prohibit interracial marriage—early in the eighteenth century there was an exchange of letters published in a newspaper, the gist of which defended miscegenation. This attitude persisted until well into the nineteenth century. One historian studying carefully the Edgefield District found that in 1850 some 250 African Americans lived quite undisturbed among several thousand white neighbors. This led him to conclude that "the barriers in Edgefield District between whites and free blacks were not so formidable as historians have thought," a report strikingly similar to that about Alabama by Gary B. Mills previously noted.[17]

In the immediate post–Civil War period a Union officer observed in Greenfield County, South Carolina, that it was not uncommon for poorer white women to be married to African American men and that this met no display of anger or resentment from white neighbors.[18] Confirming evidence from two other historians may be offered in conclusion on this point. Peter Wood in his probing study of colonial South Carolina suggested that interracial relationships were more frequent and "perhaps more open" than in later decades. He affirmed that Black men "had relationships with white servants and free women"; he observed that an English visitor at this time was struck by the fact that "the whites mix with the blacks and the blacks with the whites."[19]

A careful study of the situation of African Americans in seventeenth-century Massachusetts revealed a similar situation. Their legal rights were the same as those of others; racial intermarriage was not illegalized until 1705. Colorphobia seemed absent, and "a certain amount of fraternization between races in the lower classes" existed.[20]

Of the colonial period the evidence demonstrates that Mechal Sobel was correct when she concluded that these decades showed "a very long history of white and black interaction";[21] such interaction notably included long-term sexual relationships. The preceding pages have summarized the more significant evidences of this; other confirmatory data are quite abundant. Much of it is by no means limited to the colonial period; later pages will note some of this.

In the most personal and private components of human existence, evidence exists to deny the universality of racism in the United States.[22] That such evidence does exist in this area, despite recurrent legislation making miscegenation criminal and despite persistent racist propaganda that permeated every social avenue and institution, points to the artificiality of racism and makes absurd notions of racism's "instinctual" quality.

5

Rejecting Racism by Joint Struggle

Joint resistance to joint oppression often occurred, involving not only white indentured servants and Black slaves but also, with some frequency, Indian slaves. The serious conspiracy in Virginia in 1663 involved both slaves and indentured servants. There was Black-white participation in Nathaniel Bacon's uprising of 1676.[1]

Joint flight was frequent; also, assistance to fleeing slaves by whites who were not indentured occurred often enough to be strongly condemned repeatedly by masters. The presence of servant and slave together in maroon communities was not unknown. All such activities persisted throughout the era of slavery, but it is likely that most were more marked in the earlier period of that institution.

Studies of flight from servitude in the United States have been numerous; several are noteworthy. Their findings point to the high incidence of Black-white unity. Peter Wood, in his already-cited study, observed that in South Carolina Blacks and whites were together from time to time in maroon groupings and that in flight they were also "occasionally thrown together." At times, flight involved a Black man and a white woman; more common were men of both colors fleeing together; Wood also noticed complaints against white people who encouraged or assisted slaves to flee.[2]

In an earlier work Gerald W. Mullin had called attention to similar joint activity in eighteenth-century Virginia.[3] He reported that "instances of slaves and free men running off together ... were not infrequent"; less common were Black men and white women absconding together. Widespread were complaints from slaveowners against whites who assisted slaves to run away. Further, some fugitive slaves lived more or less openly among white people— unharmed and sometimes unreported for prolonged periods.

The fullest record of fugitive slaves is that compiled by Lathan A. Windley in four volumes, dealing with the South from 1730 through 1790.[4] The materials in these volumes show that flight together of Blacks and whites recurred fairly often. Illustrations with specific page references are offered here. Volume 1 treats of Virginia. In 1737 a white servant and a Black male slave fled (3); in 1737, the same (4); in 1738, one white and two Black men (7); in 1739, white and Black (8); in 1739 again, three whites and one Black (9); yet again in 1739, one white and one Black (9); and a fourth time in 1739, one white and one Black (10); in 1751, two white women, one white man, and one Black man together (20); again in 1751 a Black man fled, and according to the advertisement, "He is supposed to be in company with one Mary Marshall, an Irish woman" (23); in 1752, one white man and one Black man—"they took a gun with them" (28); in 1771, again a white man and a Black slave fled together (97); in 1774 a Black woman "went off with a white man" (144); in 1775 a Black man fled, and "it is probable there is a white servant with him" (171); in 1774 a Black woman "went off with a white man" (148); in 1768, males, two white and one Black (286); in 1768, the same situation but different people (289); in 1775, again two white men and one Black man took off together (333); in 1783, one Black man "with a white woman named Pat Channeler" (349); again in 1783 one Black man fled "in company with a white man," and they had a gun (388).

Volume 2 treats of Maryland, and on page 14 is advertised the flight in 1755 (from Virginia but apparently to Maryland) of one Black man and one white man together; in 1755 again, a Black and a white together (22); three Blacks and one white in 1765 (58); again that year a Black man fled, and the advertiser stated: "I imagine he has got a forged pass, as he had been concerned with some white people of the same stamp" (63); in 1775, Tom, a Black slave shoemaker, had fled; perhaps, said the owner, he was concealed and was employed "by some white people, who make so familiar with my slaves to my great prejudice" (112); the owner of David announced his flight in 1789 and added: "From his connection with a certain Nell Hazellep . . . I have every reason to believe she has induced him to take this step, and think it probable he is now secreted by her" (180); in 1775 two white indentured servants and a Black slave fled together (192–93); in 1781 an ad was placed for "one white mulatto slave"; he was a carpenter and took off with his tools, and, the owner said, he was persuaded to do so by Rachel Dorsey, a white woman with whom he fathered two children; furthermore, the owner added that he "supposed they will pass for man and wife and make for Virginia" (245); in 1783 appeared an ad for a fugitive who was "a tawny woman"; the owner continued, "it is suspected she will be carried off, or concealed, by a white man, who has been very intimate with her for some years" (335); a 1790 ad told of two brothers who played the fiddle "exceedingly well" who had fled; the master continued that they "may be harboured by free Negroes, or by white persons, who are enemies to slavery, and may think such a conduct warrantable" (411).

Volume 3 treats of South Carolina. Here are some relevant advertisements: in 1736 "a white servant boy named Peter... has enticed an Angola Negro to go along with him, named Dick" (21); in 1754 six Black slaves, two men and four women, one of whom was pregnant, fled; "it is supposed they have been decoyed by a white man" who was short, talked "very broad Scotch," had red hair, had a horse, and was a carpenter (155); in 1761 a slave named Hannah fled, probably with a white man named Joseph Johnson, headed, the owner thought, for Georgia (198); in 1762 three slaves, described as an elderly woman, a man of twenty-three, and a boy of twelve, fled in a canoe accompanied by "a free Indian wench" who was described as the wife of the male slave. It was added that "a white man was also seen in the canoe with them" (212). In 1763 an ad was placed for four slaves who had fled at different times. This told of "a pernicious custom" that had developed among "back-settlers" acting in concert with magistrates to "keep them at work for themselves"—presumably as free workers and perhaps here indicating the chronic labor shortage that afflicted such areas. The advertiser promised a reward for any informer who would expose "any white man" involved in this conduct (227–28). In 1790 an advertiser lamented the flight of four slaves and added that he would pay twenty pounds to a white informer and ten pounds to a Black informer, because he "has some reason to suspect that there are certain despicable characters in the city [Charleston] who harbour and encourage the desertion of negroes from their owners, and by furnishing them with tickets in their masters' names, render their recovery extremely difficult" (410–11). In 1766 five male slaves fled and were seen "going up Savannah River in a boat with some white men" (417); in 1767 "an Irish man" named Jonathan MacConnell, who was six feet tall and "well made," helped three slaves flee from Thomas Fuller, the advertiser, and also three other slaves from other owners—"all of them being armed." In this very ominous case a handsome reward (one hundred pounds) was offered for MacConnell's capture and lesser sums for the slave fugitives (421). References to fugitives being "harboured" and employed by those sheltering them recur. An ad in 1766 from an owner who had suffered the flight of three slaves stated that "as it is a customary thing for the back settlers of this province to keep them employed, privately and in order to bring such offenders to justice" a reward of fifty pounds would be paid if the culprit was white and ten pounds if the culprit was Black (604).

Volume 4 contains ads from Georgia. In 1772 and 1773 Henry Laurens, a leading South Carolina politician, placed an ad in a Georgia newspaper telling of the loss of several slaves. In one case, said Laurens, the slave was "harboured by some evil-minded person"; in the other the slave was "supposed to be enticed away and harboured by some white person" (46). In 1781 a male slave fled "in company with a white man driving a cart" (85); in 1788 a slave named Isaac, a butcher by trade and well known in Savannah, fled; "it is supposed he is harboured by some white person, as he has been encouraged in making his escape by one Clark, a waggoner or barber" (162).

Letitia Woods Brown observed that in the eighteenth century "little distinction was made between servants and slaves in the work performed and in day-to-day living" in the District of Columbia. She added that they not only worked together "but consorted to escape their employees as well." As a typical example she cited an advertisement in a Virginia newspaper of 1806 where one Spencer Ball sought the return of his slave Emanuel, stating that the slave had "a number of friends and associates among the lower class of whites."[5] Carter G. Woodson, back in 1918, had called attention to the joint flight of male slaves and white female servants in prerevolutionary Pennsylvania.[6]

In addition to the evidence of Black-white collaboration present in advertisements for fugitive slaves, other aspects of the slave experience are dotted with the records of white people who put their liberty and even their lives on the line to render assistance to slaves. Reference here is to such activity inside the South; analogous activity elsewhere will be considered at another point.

In earlier work I called attention to such behavior; there references were offered to contemporary sources—letters, petitions, court records, governors' papers, newspaper and travel accounts, and the like. These will be summarized herewith, and specific documentation will be found in the cited works.

A striking fact in the voluminous record of slave discontent and protest is the recurrence of white sympathy for, and even participation in, such slave activity. Confining the area now considered to the South, one finds white people accused of resisting slave patrols in Virginia in 1798. In North Carolina in 1851 Adam Crooks and Jesse McBride were driven out for antislavery activity of an unspecified character. Jarvis C. Bacon was arrested several times in the 1850s in Virginia on similar but undetailed charges.

In the paroxysms of fear and hysteria that swept the rulers of the South in 1856 and 1860, charges of provocative behavior by whites accused of sympathy for the slaves—usually called "traitors" or "incendiaries"—were quite common. How valid these charges were, given the panic and obvious political motivations, one cannot know, but that there were painful results is clear. Thus in 1856 accused whites were compelled to flee for their lives from Florida and Mississippi; in Texas at this time a white man named Davidson, described as an "Ohio abolitionist," was implicated in a slave plot and suffered one hundred lashes.[7]

In 1795 a series of conspiracies culminated previous years of major slave unrest in Louisiana. At that time three white people, Joseph Rayado, George Roekemburg, and John Sarge, were convicted as accomplices of the slaves and sentenced to imprisonment for seven years.[8] In the Gabriel conspiracy in Virginia in 1800, contemporaries implicated white people as being sympathetic. I tended, in my treatment of this, to express serious doubts that the charges were valid since they seemed to fit so neatly with political propaganda aimed at Jefferson during that election year. A very recent study, however, suggested that the involvement of some whites in the slaves' plans was real.[9]

Whites were implicated in a similar event in Virginia in 1802. In this case one of the slaves arrested stated—according to papers reaching the governor—that he had "joined with both black and white which is the common man or poor white people"; he was prepared "to lose my life in this way." There were charges of white implication in slave disturbances in Louisiana in 1805 and in Virginia six years later. In 1812 Louisiana authorities were seriously troubled by what they felt was a major slave conspiracy; especially bothersome was white involvement. One of the whites was named Macarty; his fate is not known. Another, however, named Joseph Wood, was hanged.

In 1816 in Virginia a white man of very modest circumstances named George Boxley was arrested and convicted on the charge of leading a slave insurrection. This Boxley anticipated John Brown; contemporaries charged that he "declared that the distinction between the rich and the poor was too great, that offices were given rather to wealth than to merit; and [he] seemed to be an advocate for a more leveling system of government." In particular, "For many years he had avowed his disapprobation of the slavery of the negroes, and wished they were free." Boxley was jailed—the plot was betrayed—but with the help of his wife he escaped; neither was ever apprehended. Six of the Black rebels in this case were hanged; six others were banished.

In Georgia in 1819 a white man named Alexander Russell was killed by a guard for implication in a slave disturbance. The next year, in Virginia, an unspecified number of white men were arrested together with several suspected slave rebels; the results in this instance seem not to be available.

Involved in the great Denmark Vesey slave conspiracy in South Carolina in 1822 were four white men. These were Andrew S. Rhodes, William Allen, Jacob Danders, and John Igneshias. All were tried, convicted, and sentenced to fine and imprisonment. According to contemporary reportage, Jacob Danders insisted that the slaves "had as much right to fight for their liberty as white people."

In the generation of the Nat Turner cataclysm of 1831, reports of white involvement in slave unrest were fairly common, but certitude is not possible. Still, Governor John Floyd of Virginia remarked in his legislative message of December 1831 that unrest was "not confined to slaves." The same is true of North Carolina in this period, with contemporaries blaming slave unrest upon "some rascally whites."

In the very complicated events in Mississippi in 1835 there is evidence of white sympathy with rebellious slaves; similar suspicions appeared that year in other Southern states. A white man named Robinson was hanged at that time near Lynchburg, Virginia. That same year a white man named Brady was jailed in South Carolina for similar sedition. In that state and in Georgia that year three white men were lynched because they were believed to have Abolitionist sympathies. Another white man that year was driven out of Twigg County, Georgia, because of suspicions of undue sympathy for slaves.

Contemporaries believed that two whites—unnamed—were involved in what appears to have been a considerable slave disturbance in Louisiana late in 1835. A number of slaves and three free Black people were executed in Louisiana in 1837. In this instance about fifty slaves were arrested; one report stated that two white people were implicated and that one of them had been killed. In 1838 slave conspiracies were reported from the District of Columbia and from Kentucky; in both instances some whites were held to be implicated.

Unrest among slaves in the District of Columbia surfaced again in 1840; the local press then announced the arrest of a few whites described as "vagrants" and suspected of implication. A large number of slaves—several hundred—were implicated in planned insurrections in a few parishes of Louisiana in 1840. Many were executed; several committed suicide. A few whites—the exact number is not certain—also were apprehended; some were denounced as "white abolition rascals" by the press. At least two were lashed by a lynch mob and driven from the state.

At least one slave rebel was executed in Georgia in 1841; a white man, described as a young teacher named Hawes, was implicated, but his fate is not known. An uprising of about seventy-five slaves occurred in Fayette County, Kentucky, in 1848; there was a pitched battle with pursuing slave-owners and an unreported number of casualties. All or nearly all of the slave rebels apparently were captured. Three among them, held to have been leaders, were hanged. A young white man, a student named Patrick Doyle from Centre College in Danville, Kentucky, participated with the slaves in this outbreak. He was convicted and sentenced to imprisonment for twenty years.[10]

Lawrence D. Reddick devoted several pages of his 1939 dissertation to supporting his opinion that "from the documents of this study it is clear that there must have been more Negro sympathizers among the white population than is generally assumed." He quoted an 1860 newspaper advising: "Sleepless vigilance is necessary—not so much over the deluded Negro, as over suspicious white men in our midst." Reddick noted the great excitement in New Orleans in 1853 because of allegations of a slave conspiracy involving white allies. He cited contemporary Southern press reports in the late 1850s and in 1860 from several states implicating white people in slave unrest. One, named Edward Chandler, was implicated in Mississippi; another, named Benjamin Hunt, in Virginia. Others, unnamed, according to such reports, insisted that "John Brown was a good man and was fighting in a good cause, and did nothing but what any other honest man would do."[11]

A conspiracy involving as many as two hundred slaves distressed those who ruled Colorado County, Texas, in 1856. The press charged that several Mexicans were involved. One paper said: "The lower class of the Mexican population are incendiaries in any country where slaves are held." Many were driven from the state "under the penalty of death"; a white man named William Mehrman—obviously not Mexican—was similarly treated.

In this year of major unrest touching the entire South, whites were implicated several times; sometimes names appeared. Thus in Alabama a James Hancock was charged as subversive; in Tennessee someone named Williams. In Texas a Reverend Thomas Donegan was named. Those severely lashed included a man named Hurd in Arkansas and another named Davidson in Texas.

In the generalized panic over slave discontent (alleged and real) that swept the South in 1860—stimulated by the John Brown effort and the elections—white men were often held to be implicated. Reports recur of their being arrested and lashed and even executed. This was true, for example, in Texas, Alabama, Georgia, Mississippi, and Virginia. In Mississippi the white man executed was named Harrington; in Virginia, Flynn.

In Alabama, where the press reported that the seditious ones had in mind the redistribution of property, it was declared that "the instigators of the insurrection were found to be low-down, or poor, whites of the country." In this instance, among the twenty-nine people executed, four were white men; two were named—Rollo and Williamson.

A white person, described as a stonecutter of German descent, was involved in a plot of slaves uncovered in January 1861 in Columbia, South Carolina. In July 1861 five white men were implicated with seditious slaves in Mississippi. In August 1864 three slaves and one white man were hanged in Georgia at the order of an investigating committee; white men, described as "deserters and escaped Yankee prisoners," were accused of being prominent in a slave plot uncovered near Troy, Alabama, late in 1864. The latter was the last reported slave conspiracy so far found. The following year, of course, witnessed the passage of the Thirteenth Amendment, abolishing slavery. That ended slave insurrections—nothing else could.

It should be observed, also, that communities of outlying fugitive slaves—maroons—existed in the swamps, fastnesses, and mountains of the South. From time to time, contemporaries reported the presence of white people in these settlements. Examples include cases in Virginia in 1782 and 1818, North Carolina in 1830 and 1864, Alabama in 1860 and 1863, Louisiana in 1861, and Florida in 1862 and 1864.

David Walker's impassioned call for slave rebellion, issued in Boston in 1829, was distributed mainly by Black people in the South. Its existence led to panic among the slaveholders, whose representatives called special sessions of several state legislatures to deal with the menace. Among those found guilty of distributing this fiercely seditious pamphlet were some white people. These included Elijah H. Burritt, a printer in Milledgeville, Georgia, who was forced to flee a lynch mob and successfully reached the North; Edward Smith, a seaman out of Boston, discovered in South Carolina, who was sentenced to a fine and a year in prison; another seaman, named James Smith, arrested in New Orleans and also jailed for a year; and two missionaries to Indians in Georgia, known only as Worcester and Butler. Both, said a contemporary, were "maltreated and imprisoned" for this offense.[12]

Other pieces of information point to militantly anti-slavery expression carrying evidences of a rejection of racism by Southern whites that provoked official retaliation. Examples include the case of James Hall Mumford, forced to leave Virginia in 1802 on the grounds that he encouraged slave unrest. Another instance, in 1804, involved a judge in Georgia, Jabez Brown, Jr., who created a sensation with what contemporaries called an "inflammatory" charge to a grand jury. The actual charge seems not to have been printed, but the members of the grand jury publicly denounced this unusual judge. There is evidence that he had criticized slavery in the severest manner and allegedly believed that slaves would be justified if they rebelled. He was jailed—apparently briefly—for "inciting insurrection"; upon release he was required to leave the state and seems to have settled in Rhode Island.

Elsewhere attention was called to the considerable number of white people who, at great risk, assisted slaves to flee. Of course, African American people undertook this activity in great numbers. Among the white people who participated in such efforts inside the South were Calvin Fairbank, James Allen, John Fairfield, Alexander M. Ross, David Nelson, Delia Webster, Amos Dresser, Reuben Crandall, John B. Mahan, James E. Burr, George Thompson, Charles T. Torrey, Edward Sayres, Daniel Drayton, Jonathan Walker, Seth Conklin, John Hunn, Thomas Garrett, C. W. Robinson, Samuel A. Smith, Thomas Brown, William L. Chaplin, Elijah Harris, John Cornutt, Nathan B. Watson, and Lewis Paine. Some—Fairfield, Allen, Torrey, and Conklin—lost their lives in this work. The personification of revolutionary commitment by a white person who burned racism out of himself, who identified with the slave, and who gave his life in the effort to destroy both slavery and racism was, of course, John Brown. He and his comrades— of whom sixteen were white—sealed in selfless effort and in blood this sense of solidarity, this supreme manifestation of anti-racism in U.S. history.[13]

Certain other evidences of noteworthy commitment to human emancipation that showed no racist distinctions may be offered. A study of "The Fugitive Slave of Maryland" noted that between 1800 and 1860 four white Marylanders were convicted of assisting fugitive slaves. The author in reporting this added that "just" four were convicted.[14] Remembering, however, the nature of the "crime" and the great difficulty in obtaining convictions of native whites in a state forbidding Black testimony, the use of "just" would seem to be questionable.

The name of William Shreve Bailey belongs among the honor roll of Southern white people whose commitment to Black emancipation was total. Bailey was a mechanic of Newport, Kentucky. In 1849 a local paper began publishing articles from him attacking slavery. The next year Bailey established his own little paper, the *Newport News*, with an anti-slavery orientation. A slaveholders' mob burned its office in October 1851. Workers associated with Bailey and his wife brought out a paper with a very provocative title, the *Free South*. Bailey was arrested, charged with incendiarism, and jailed. Granted bail, he left the state and went to England, where he gave anti-slavery lectures. He decided to return to Kentucky to stand trial, but the outbreak of the Civil War intervened.

In the same period and area as Bailey's efforts were those of the better-known John G. Fee of Bracken County, Kentucky. In that county in the 1850s members of two churches voted to admit African Americans on terms of equality with white people. Fee, Wiley Fisk, and John A. R. Rogers—through the American Missionary Association—founded Berea as an inter-racial school in Kentucky in 1855. Despite severe harassment, this school maintained its integrated character; immediately after the Civil War it became a college and remained integrated until the terror of post-Reconstruction, abetted by the U.S. Supreme Court, forced, for a time, a lily-white Berea—but this phase of its history and resistance to racism belongs in a subsequent volume.[15]

Noteworthy also is the case of James L. Bowers of Kent County, Maryland.[16] Bowers was notorious in his state for his anti-slavery convictions. In the early 1850s he had been tried for helping slaves flee, but proof was insufficient and he was released. He continued to express his hatred of slavery. As a result, in 1858 a posse tarred and feathered him and gave him twenty-four hours to leave Maryland. On the same occasion, these heroic ones flogged a free Black man whose last name only—Butler—is known. The mob also tarred and feathered a Black woman known only as Tillison.

Very significant, however, is the fact that white people friendly to Bowers twice attacked members of the posse and in each instance had the better of the encounter. While the elite of the area held a meeting addressed by members of Congress, justifying the posse's act and decrying attacks upon its members, surely they were not calmed by a report in the press that "at least three quarters of the people are on Bowers's side; nearly all the laboring class or non-slaveholders, with a part of the slaveholders themselves."

Finally, in the invaluable collection edited by Helen T. Catterall of judicial cases involving slavery, there are several notices of white people involved in efforts to assist slaves. These include an 1836 case in Virginia where a white man was convicted of aiding a slave to escape and was fined $200 and sentenced to six months in jail. Two years later a group of three white men—Peter M. Garner, Mordecai Thomas, and Crayton Loraine of Ohio—were apprehended in Ohio for assisting six slaves to flee. Five of the slaves were retaken, but the whites were released, for they were intercepted in Ohio. In 1848 a white man named James Cole was sent to jail for two years, having been found guilty of advising slaves in Virginia to flee; other cases with jail as punishment in Virginia involved whites named Blevin, Smith, and Sherman who were sentenced to five years, four and a half years, and six years, respectively, for assisting or advising slaves to "abscond." In 1827 a white man named Prout was fined in the District of Columbia for "enticing slaves to flee." There were also several cases of free Black people convicted of this crime.[17]

6

Grégoire, Banneker, and Jeffersonianism

In the House of Delegates of a Virginia shaken by the Turner slave rebellion, William Preston said on January 6, 1832: "If those who are slaves here, were not what they are, if, Mr. Speaker, they were white men in oppression and bondage, I would rejoice in a revolution here."[1] Similarly, a young slaveholder in South Carolina admitted to an English visitor that "if it would be proved that negroes are more than a link between man and brute, the rest follows of course and he must liberate all his."[2]

Here was made explicit the decisive nature of racism as a bulwark of slavery in the United States. Material offered to this point certainly would seem to be sufficient to convince the Virginian and the Carolinian; however, the essential reason for holding on to this peculiar property was suggested by Patrick Henry, who, unable to defend the damned thing, said simply that he held to it because of its convenience.

One of the most dramatic "proofs" demanded by the South Carolinian came in the words of the slaveowners themselves when placing advertisements for their fleeing chattel. The sharp contradiction between the descriptions there given and concepts of racism—of "links between man and brute"—was commented upon by Abolitionists and other contemporaries. That such descriptive language could be used decade after decade by people depending upon the rationalization quoted shows how decisive "convenience" can be in shaping behavior.

Notice must be taken of this contradiction, for it did impact upon racism's hold in the time of slavery. Lorenzo J. Greene many years ago commented on this in an article treating of fugitive-slave advertisements in New England newspapers.[3] Since then a considerable body of literature building on Greene's suggestion has appeared. Michael P. Johnson, for example, in a helpful presentation of data culled from two South Carolina newspapers from 1799 to 1830, though not concentrating upon the description of the slaves, nevertheless did call attention to the skills many of them possessed, as described by their owners—carpenters and blacksmiths, bricklayers, and so on—who were "excellent," "very artful," "very sensible," or "very sensible and artful."[4]

On this point the collection of advertisements by Lathan Windley is again most illuminating. In these advertisements many fugitives are described as skilled artisans—carpenters, coopers, shoemakers, and so on. Others could read and write or "can read very well"; another spoke Portuguese as well as English and played both the fiddle and the French horn; another—advertised for by Thomas Jefferson—was a shoemaker and carpenter and "something of a horse jockey"; another read and wrote, knew "something of figures," had the habit of preparing certificates of freedom for comrades, and knew something about healing, wherefore he was commonly called doctor; another played the fiddle "exceedingly well"; another spoke Spanish and French as well as English; another also spoke three languages, not specified; and still another "played the violin" on formal occasions.[5]

Gerald W. Mullin remarked how numerous were the accounts of highly skilled slaves, with advertisers lauding their aptness with expressions such as "remarkably smart and sensible," "very well qualified," and "very ingenious at any work." Similarly, Peter Wood in his study of early South Carolina emphasized the varied skills of the slaves; they "dominated the cooper's art"; "skill and intuition" of a high order existed among many of them; often they were "accomplished artisans" in every imaginable endeavor. In brief, they "understood most handycrafts," as a resident wrote in 1744. Even earlier, in 1688, masters were urged to permit the Africans to be "smiths, shoemakers, carpenters, bricklayers," for "they are capable of learning anything." Of course, as Wood pointed out, skills with metal and wood were not unfamiliar to Africans at home.[6]

Pioneering on this matter of the highly skilled character of much slave labor was Marcus W. Jernegan's book *Laboring and Dependent Classes in Colonial America*, published in 1931. Additional material was provided soon after World War II by Leonard P. Stavisky.[7]

The contemporary awareness of the capacities of many of the slaves was in glaring contrast to concepts of inferiority. Sometimes the language chosen to describe these skilled ones itself manifested the repudiation or, at least, the contradiction. At other times observers, foreign and domestic, Northern and Southern, slaveowners and nonslaveowners, made explicit an awareness of how this reality collided with racist mythology.

Furthermore, from time to time, some person of African descent would display such extraordinary capacity that his or her role cut the heart out of the racist stereotype. Indeed, early anti-slavery societies, like those of Pennsylvania and Maryland in the 1790s, had as one of their objectives the collection of such evidence to refute the idea of the African as, at best, an inferior human being.

This reality of especially noteworthy people of African descent as ammunition against racism was often referred to before (and after) the Civil War. Several people played a role in this aspect of the anti-racist drama, but none was more important than the French revolutionary, Henri Grégoire (1750–1831).

Grégoire's work was pioneering, full, and very influential.[8] He was a central figure in revolutionary France and was extraordinary in his time for the principled manner in which he opposed all forms of discrimination, including that against Jews, the English oppression of the Irish, and especially the European and American practice of enslaving those of African origin.

He insisted on the equality of all peoples and particularly denounced allegations of African inferiority. Charles Sumner's 1870 eulogy was not off the mark: "In all history, no hero of humanity stands forth more conspicuous for instinctive sympathy for the Rights of Man and constancy in their support."

Grégoire provided funds for a prize contest on the subject: "What is the best way to erase the white man's unjust and barbaric prejudice against African and mulatto skin color?" His own writings against the slave trade, slavery, and racism were voluminous and were translated into English by Thomas Clarkson in England and David B. Warden in the United States. The latter effort was published in 1810 and was often reprinted. It was dedicated to those who had argued in favor of the African people; Grégoire listed forty-seven from France, eighty-six from England, fourteen from the United States, four from Germany, three each from Denmark, Sweden, and Italy, two each from Holland and Poland, and one from Spain.

Grégoire was forthright; he insisted that "Negroes being of the same nature as the whites, have the same rights as they to exercise; the same duties to fulfill." He added: "We may consider it as a truth well ascertained that cupidity will always find pretexts to justify their slavery."

There will be occasion later to refer to other aspects of this full-length book. Here it may be noted that in its original French it was sent by Grégoire to Jefferson some time after the latter had completed his second presidential term. Jefferson in his *Notes on the State of Virginia* (1785) had excoriated slavery in language by now well known, but never exceeded in severity. "The whole commerce between master and slave," said this slaveowner, "is a perpetual exercise of the most boisterous passions, the most unremitting despotism on the one part, and degrading submission on the other." Jefferson emphasized the harmful effects of such a relationship upon the master's character and upon that of his children; they, he thought, "cannot but be stamped by it with odious peculiarities." He thought that statesmen who permit such a social order must be stamped with "execration." Jefferson "trembled" for his country when he considered that God was just and that "his justice cannot sleep forever." The Almighty, he thought, "has no attribute which can take side with us" should the day come—as it would—when a contest between slave and master should ensue. This was an idea Jefferson repeated in a private letter to James Monroe in 1800, when the latter, as governor of Virginia, faced the problems induced by the major slave conspiracy led by Gabriel.

In later correspondence with Benjamin Banneker, Jefferson had been respectful, but when he wrote to Condorcet in Paris about Banneker, he affirmed his doubts as to the intellectual capacity of African people. The impact of ensuing years and of Grégoire's work perhaps induced a positive change in Jefferson, for he wrote the Frenchman from Washington on February 25, 1809, acknowledging receipt of the latter's work, published in Paris in 1808, dealing with the literature of Negroes. Here Jefferson stated:

Be assured that no person living wishes more sincerely than I do to see a complete refutation of the doubts I have myself entertained and expressed on the grade of understanding allowed them by nature, and to find that in this respect they are on a par with ourselves. My doubts were the result of personal observation on the limited sphere of my own State, where the opportunities for the development of their genius were not favorable, and those of exercising it still less so. I expressed them therefore with great hesitation; but whatever be their degree of talent it is no measure of their rights. Because Sir Isaac Newton was superior to others in understanding, he was not therefore lord of the person or property of others. On this subject they are gaining daily in the opinions of nations, and hopeful advances are making towards their re-establishment on an equal footing with the other colors of the human family. I pray you therefore to accept my thanks for the many instances you have enabled me to observe of respectable intelligence in that race of men which cannot fail to have effect in hastening the day of their relief, and to be assured of the sentiments of high and just esteem and consideration which I tender to yourself with all sincerity.

The evidence does not permit one to declare with confidence what Jefferson's final view on this question was. It is certain, however, that George Wythe (1728–1806), his teacher, friend, and neighbor, had a quite enlightened view. His biographer stated that Wythe undertook the education of a young slave in his household and that "unlike Jefferson . . . Wythe proved through experiment that color had no bearing on the capacity of a mind to learn."[9] Perhaps this experience of Wythe's also influenced Jefferson's apparent modification of the opinion expressed, with some diffidence, in his *Notes on the State of Virginia.*

Jefferson's views on slavery and the African American are relatively well known. Less well known are the views on these subjects of two of his most distinguished contemporaries and fellow slaveowners. James Madison lamented the fact that "we have seen the mere distinction of colour made in the most enlightened period of time, a ground of the most oppressive dominion ever exercised by man over man." George Mason—of Bill of Rights fame—said that slavery "discouraged arts and manufactures" and produced "the most pernicious effect on manners." In language reminiscent of Jefferson's and also as denunciatory of slavery as anything ever written in English, Mason went on:

Every master of slaves is born a petty tyrant. They bring the judgment of heaven on a country. As nations cannot be rewarded or punished in the next world they must be in this. By an inevitable chain of causes and effects providence punishes national sins, by national calamities.[10]

7

"Inferiority" and Poets, Preachers, and Teachers

Among the African American people whose accomplishments challenged racist stereotypes, none was better known than Phyllis Wheatley (c. 1753–1784); the literature concerning her is abundant. Her poetry—the equal of anything produced in her time and place—was very widely published, was on the whole admired, and resulted in her achieving fame in the United States and in England.[1]

Typical of the impact her work had was the remark by Benjamin Rush in his 1773 *Address to the Inhabitants of the British Settlements in America upon Slave-Keeping* that her "singular genius and accomplishments are such as not only do honor to her sex, but to human nature." Another example of contemporary respect for her work—this from a fellow poet—is in Charles Crawford's 1794 work. It contains a lengthy note about her; Crawford concluded that her career "offered evidence that Negroes are not by nature inferior."[2]

In 1788 the Philadelphia Abolition Society received a request from London emancipationists for information about outstanding Black people that might be useful "to contradict those who assert, that the intellectual faculties of the negroes are not capable of improvement equal to the rest of mankind." Again, Benjamin Rush came forward to challenge racist stereotypes, for it was he who responded with accounts of an African American physician, James Derham, and a mathematical genius, Thomas Fuller (called "Blind Tom" in the contemporary press), a slave living in Virginia.[3]

Rush, the leading physician in the United States, testified to the marked proficiency of James Derham in a communication to the society, which caused it to be published in the *American Museum* (Philadelphia) in January 1789. Rush stated that he had personally ascertained that Derham, then in his twenties, was "perfectly acquainted" with treating several diseases, that though young he had had considerable experience, and that, in general, his competence as a physician was clear. Rush's account of the seventy-year-old Fuller also was published in the same issue of this widely read monthly. It emphasized that the African American possessed extraordinary mathematical ability. When Fuller died in 1790, the Boston *Columbian Centinel* called attention to this and concluded its obituary this way: "Had his opportunities of improvement been equal to those of thousands of his fellow-men, neither the Royal Society of London, the Academy of Sciences at Paris, nor even a Newton himself, need have been ashamed to acknowledge him a Brother in Science."

Similarly, Fuller's death was commented upon by the *General Advertiser* in Philadelphia (December 28, 1790). This paper said that Fuller offered an example of "the genius, capacity and talents of our ill-fated brethren." It was added reason, the paper said, to deplore prejudice against African-derived people on the basis of "a supposed inferiority of their intellectual faculties; sentiments as ill founded in fact, as they are inhuman in tendency."

It was in this same period that the abilities of Benjamin Banneker attracted national attention. Newspapers noted his talents; the *Georgetown Weekly* thought that they showed that Jefferson's doubts on the capacities of the African were "without foundation" in the light of a Banneker. Banneker's accomplishments and his *Almanac* led James McHenry—a former Maryland senator and a future secretary of war—to write in the *Philadelphia Advertiser* that these offered "fresh proof that the powers of the mind are disconnected with the colour of the skin." Banneker's work, McHenry added, was a "striking contradiction" to concepts that "the Negroes are naturally inferior to the whites."[4]

The Banneker almanacs were known internationally: six annuals from 1792 to 1797 were issued in twenty-eight editions, with printings made in Baltimore, Philadelphia, Trenton, Petersburg, Richmond, and Wilmington. His work attracted the attention of the influential Quaker James Pemberton, president of the Pennsylvania Abolition Society (1790–1803), and of David Rittenhouse, president of the American Philosophical Society.

Pemberton sent Rittenhouse examples of Banneker's work. The latter on August 6, 1791, returned these to Pemberton, writing that he thought them "a very extraordinary performance, considering the Colour of the Author." He believed that "the Calculations" made by Banneker were "sufficiently accurate." He closed with this sentence: "Every Instance of genious amongst the Negroes is worthy of attention, because their oppressors seem to lay great stress on their supposed inferior mental abilities."

Near his seventy-fifth birthday, Banneker passed away in 1806. The obituary in the *Federal Gazette and Baltimore Daily Advertiser* (October 28, 1806) closed: "Mr. Banneker is a prominent instance to prove that a descendant of Africa is susceptible of as great mental improvement and deep knowledge of the mysteries of nature as that of any other man."[5]

Recurrent in the literature rejecting racism is reflection on the talents of the many African American people who played outstanding roles in the anti-slavery struggle. Repeatedly, figures like Frederick Douglass, Theodore S. Wright, Charles Lenox Remond, John S. Rock, Sojourner Truth, Robert Purvis, Harriet Tubman, William Wells Brown, and dozens more were brought forward as living refutations of racism. Examples permeate the literature; one may be offered.

Parker Pillsbury of New Hampshire, a pioneer and staunch Abolitionist, was especially militant in opposing both slavery and racism. In his memoirs he called particular attention to the impact of such figures as those named here. He asked, having in mind Douglass and Remond, "When, or where in all the historic or traditionary years of the past, shall the self-made man be found to measure with such a phenomenon as this?" Referring to them and others like Sarah P. Remond and Sojourner Truth, he not only noted their living refutation of racism, but added, "It was my pleasure and privilege to meet as best of friends, as well as co-workers," with them and others.[6] The significance of this kind of experience—of course continuing into the twentieth century—is of the most profound consequence in the effort to cleanse the United States of racism.

Some African American preachers and teachers of the late eighteenth and early nineteenth centuries had remarkable careers in both the North and the South. Some among them serviced largely white people, though at times their listeners or students were both Black and white. The very fact of such practice demonstrates a repudiation of racism; at times, moreover, the repudiation was made explicit.

A notable example of such a career in the North is that of Lemuel Haynes (1753–1833). Biographical accounts of Haynes are now fairly abundant, so that extensive summary is not necessary.[7] For present purposes, the point is that this Black man was encouraged by a white Connecticut clergyman to master Latin and Greek. Haynes preached his first sermon in 1780 before a white congregation in Granville, Vermont. In 1783 he married Elizabeth Babbit, a white schoolteacher of that town. The marriage lasted until his death, and there were ten children.

In response to the urging of the Granville congregation, Haynes was officially ordained in 1785. He then preached for two years in Torrington, Connecticut. John Brown's parents were among his flock. Thereafter he served a mixed congregation in Rutland, Vermont; several of his sermons were printed, and some were widely distributed. His views on religion were orthodox; his politics were Federalist. On occasion, he made clear his detestation of slavery. There were some racist incidents in his life; apparently, they were not very frequent.

In 1804 Middlebury College conferred on Haynes an honorary master of arts degree—unprecedented at the time. Haynes preached also in Massachusetts and New York, but most of his efforts were in Vermont. Here, then, was a Black man serving as a minister of mostly white people, living with a white wife and numerous offspring, being honored by a college, and being a widely read author, all this during forty-five years of the young Republic's existence.

Haynes was not unique, even for Vermont. Alexander Lucas Twilight (1795–1857) was the son of Ichabod and Mary Twilight, who gave birth to him in Corinth, Vermont. He was indentured to a neighboring farmer and at the age of twenty enrolled at Randolph Academy near Bradford. Earning his own way, in six years he managed to complete elementary studies and go on to two years of college work. In 1821 he enrolled at Middlebury College and received his bachelor's degree there in August 1823, thus becoming the first African American college graduate.

Twilight taught for four years in Peru, New York, where he married Mercy Ladd Merrill; whether or not they had children is not known. In addition to teaching, Twilight studied theology and in 1827 was licensed to preach by the presbytery in Plattsburgh, New York.

At the age of thirty-four he was asked to supervise a grammar school in Brownington, Vermont. From 1829 to 1834 Twilight was a minister of the local church as well as principal of the school. The latter increased in enrollment; Twilight was responsible for the erection of what was in its day perhaps the largest academy building in the state. Twilight was elected to the state legislature and served in Montpelier one term (1836–37)—probably the first Black man holding such office.

Brownington Academy prospered under Twilight; perhaps 3,200 students passed through its halls during his stewardship. Some were of distinction, like James W. Strong, the first president of Carleton College. After Twilight's death, the academy declined and closed in 1859. In 1986 Twilight Hall opened its doors at Middlebury College.[8]

To the examples of Haynes and Twilight is to be added the better-known career of James W. C. Pennington (1807–1870). Pennington escaped from slavery in Maryland about 1828; he taught at schools for Black children in New York and in Connecticut in the 1830s and was licensed to preach in 1838, serving as pastor at a Congregational church in Hartford (1840–47). In Hartford he twice served as president of the otherwise all-white Central Association of Congregational Ministers and frequently exchanged pulpits with white ministers whose congregations, said one contemporary, were "sometimes astonished ... by seeing one of the blackest men in the pulpit."

Pennington was a militant leader of his people and in 1855 organized an early civil-rights organization called the New York Legal Rights Association; this launched suits against discrimination in public conveyances. After the 1850 Fugitive Slave Act, Pennington went to Europe and was effective in England, France, and Germany in exposing American slavery and racism. The University of Heidelberg awarded Pennington a doctor of divinity degree, and in doing so it announced that "the University of Heidelberg thus pronounces the universal brotherhood of humanity."[9]

Such activity on the part of African American people was by no means confined to the North. On the contrary, one has the similarly remarkable career of John Chavis (c. 1763–1838). Chavis's work was done in North Carolina, Virginia, and Maryland; he was both preacher and teacher. In these occupations he serviced both white and Black people. His outlook, like that of Haynes, was conservative; unlike Haynes, however, he seems never to have permitted anti-slavery feelings to reach his lips or pen. Chavis's career surely undercuts the idea of a uniformly racist white South. This free person of color was classically educated and served as a teacher of the children of prominent Southern families, including future governors and senators.

Like Haynes, Chavis had served in the revolutionary army. He was ordained as a Presbyterian minister and maintained an active ministry for the first thirty years of the nineteenth century. Earlier he had conducted a school for both white and Black children in Fayetteville, North Carolina—at about the time, by the way, that David Walker was growing up in that town.

While licensed as a missionary to slaves, Chavis preached to more whites than Blacks. This was especially true in Virginia, where he reached thousands of auditors. By 1805 some church officials found his popularity among whites troublesome and urged him to confine his efforts to his own people. The fact is, however, that he preached to both peoples in Maryland, Virginia, and North Carolina until the panic induced by Nat Turner's rebellion in 1831 terminated this practice and eroded his status.

In these last years, wrote Margaret Burr Des Champs, "paternalism replaced the spirit of equalitarianism which had earlier characterized the Presbyterians' relationship with Chavis." Impoverished in his old age, Chavis was supported with a fifty-dollar annual grant from the Orange Presbytery until his death in 1838.[10]

It is an arresting fact that especially in the late eighteenth and early nineteenth centuries there were quite a few Black preachers to whom whites and Blacks looked for spiritual sustenance and guidance. Carter G. Woodson, W. H. Brooks, and other pioneers in Afro-American history called attention to this soon after World War I.

Brooks, for example, observed that in 1792, a Black man, Jacob Bishop, served as the pastor of a white church in Portsmouth, Virginia. In the same period Walter Lemon was the pastor for several years of a white church in Gloucester County, Virginia. Early in the nineteenth century Joseph Willis was prominent in the Baptist church in Mississippi and Louisiana; he was indeed the pioneer moderator of the (white) Louisiana Baptist Association formed in 1818.[11]

In the 1790s it was not unusual for free Black preachers to participate with whites in the South in synods and other religious gatherings. When this practice was questioned in 1794 by a Virginia church, the challenge was rejected by the Portsmouth Association as noted earlier. In 1798 this association accepted Jacob Bishop as a delegate. Evidence of this rejection of racist behavior in this same period recurs in other areas of Virginia and in South Carolina and Tennessee. Said a Baptist church in the latter state in 1806: "The Black Brethren . . . enjoy the same liberty of Exercising public gifts as white members have or do enjoy."[12]

A careful study of this subject in Virginia reported: "Ecclesiastical relations between black and white members of the Baptist Church in Virginia were on a more equalitarian basis than at any time in the denomination's history." In the late eighteenth and early nineteenth centuries "Black and white Baptists worshipped together, and apparently there were no segregated seating arrangements within the sanctuaries." Separation was reported in Alexandria in 1808, but generally, "Negroes were accepted for church membership in the same manner as whites."[13] Not exceptional was the selection of an African American, Israel Decoudry, by the Davenport Baptist Church in Prince George County as one of its representatives at a region wide association; this occurred in 1797, 1800, and 1801. Of Black preachers at this time, white parishioners in Virginia, for example, said that they had "gifts [that] exceeded many white preachers" (1787); another was a "most wonderful preacher," and a third was "much admired" (1789).

During the era of postrevolutionary exuberance, Black-white worship was not uncommon in the North also. Thus, during a revival in 1798, Richard Allen's African Church in Philadelphia had, according to him, "nearly as many whites as Black" in attendance. This egalitarian behavior did evoke some concern; a Maryland newspaper in 1793 noted that Methodists conducted themselves "on terms of perfect equality" and suggested that this was exaggerating, perhaps, the teachings of Jesus. But others, hearing Black preachers, thought that their gifts "exceeded" those shown by "many white preachers"; some were thought to be "ordained of God to preach the gospel." Estimates of this nature were offered of Black preachers like Henry Evans, who organized the first Methodist church in Fayetteville, North Carolina, and Walter Lemon, who served for decades as the pastor of a church in Gloucester, Virginia, until his death in the early 1800s.[14]

Mississippi was witness, in its early years, to Black-white unity and mutual respect that only now are being discovered. A study of race and religion in Mississippi reported that "unpublished church records reveal that before 1830, blacks and whites received equal treatment in the churches." Further, "white evangelicals welcomed slaves into the churches, often opposed slavery, and defended slaves' religious freedom." This study found that "white evangelicals recognized blacks as their spiritual brothers and sisters with souls equal to their own"—an attitude that "shook the foundations of the slave system." Blacks worshipped together with whites, were baptized in the same waters, and even were licensed to preach; indeed, "blacks and whites interacted and together shaped the character of worship services."

But by 1830 the economy of slavery conquered Mississippi, and with that conquest, persistence in egalitarian behavior became impossible.[15]

Kenneth K. Bailey has argued persuasively that "the southern churches were not so comfortably aligned with the racial mores of their region during the slavery era as now seems to be believed." Evidence of this has been offered in preceding pages, but Bailey emphasized that "southern Protestantism persistently proclaimed the common origin of all mankind." This was acted upon frequently in many parts of South Carolina, Georgia, and Mississippi well into the years prior to secession. Bailey called special attention to the remarkable career of Andrew Marshall, pastor of the First African Baptist Church in Savannah. While Marshall's work was largely confined to Savannah, he did preach elsewhere in Georgia and also in Charleston, New Orleans, and New York; indeed, he once preached before the Georgia legislature. He died at the age of 101 in 1856; the cortege was a mile long and contained fifty-eight carriages. Mourners were Black and white, numbered hundreds, and came to pay final tribute to "our aged and venerable 'Father of Israel,' " as a leading Baptist association put it. He was, said the (white) Georgia State Baptist Convention, "a strong man, both in body and mind," whose life had been "abundantly useful."[16]

Egalitarian behavior, often accompanied by explicit rejection of racism, was by no means confined to religious aspects of life, and much of it persisted to the years just before the Civil War. Illustrations abound. Thus the operator of a ferry crossing the Potomac in the 1830s placed two of his slaves, Ned and Jupe, in the position of "foremen." As such, "They determined rates, collected receipts, hired extra labor, including local whites, and were allowed to spend ferriage receipts without specific authorization."[17]

John Hebron Moore has called attention to the elevated position of numerous slaves working in the cypress lumber industry in the lower Mississippi Valley in the generation before the Civil War. Whether in sawmills, in logging operations, or as crewmen on rafts and flatboats, these Black men labored side by side with white workers, "performing the same duties as the whites." Especially in the transportation aspects of this industry, owners "tended to allow wide latitude to skilled slaves who had proved themselves trustworthy." Indeed, some were placed "in sole charge" of various vessels, and these "could scarcely be distinguished in their daily lives from free men."

An outstanding example of such an African American was Simon Gray of Natchez, owned by a merchant but hired by the senior partner of a major lumbering firm. Gray began work in 1835, and by 1838 he was in charge of a rafting crew; here he oversaw the dispensing of money for the crew's expenses and for the purchase of lumber. Gray's expertise led to his promotion "to the rank of flatboat captain, a position he held until the Civil

War." As captain, Gray was in charge of crews sometimes as numerous as twenty men, Black and white. It was he who kept all records, and he was the person who actually paid the white workers their wages.

By 1853 Gray "became free in all but the legal sense of the word." He was then receiving cash bonuses and "a salary of eight dollars per month." Later he was paid twenty dollars per month—the same wages then paid white workers. Gray was saving money, and sometime before the outbreak of war he apparently purchased his own son, though because of Mississippi law the "ownership" was hidden and therefore formally the son was not free. The Yankee capture of New Orleans in July 1863 "evidently brought the Negro flatboat captain the freedom he desired," and records of Simon Gray disappear.

Moore remarked that other slave employees of this firm, while not holding the positions Gray did, nevertheless "enjoyed unusual status." Some were literate; at least one, William Thompson, used that skill to forge a pass and escape to Canada. Another source cited by Moore disclosed that the Weldon brothers in the construction business in Mississippi employed many slaves, including highly skilled craftsmen, in building bridges, factories, and court-houses. Indeed, their architect was a Black man, John Jackson; it was Jackson who designed the courthouse in Vicksburg that remains to this day.

Moore referred to the data he assembled as being "isolated instances"— certainly in prewar Mississippi they were not common. Still, such cases existed even in that state right down to the Civil War; these instances, isolated though they may be, point to behavior among some whites in Mississippi that contradicts racist notions.[18]

Somewhat similar was the experience of Abram, slave of David Ross, one of whose extensive holdings was that of the Oxford Iron Works in Virginia. All workers at this plant were slaves; Abram was its manager. Ross was a fairly severe slave master, but he did refuse to separate families, and he did harbor secret doubts about the justice of slavery; he even allowed himself to hope that its end was foreseeable. Abram was his right hand; he was in actual charge of the overall operation of the mill. Ross, in a letter dated February 7, 1818, described him as a person of "unblemished character . . . integrity, great understanding, and talents"—hardly descriptive of a racist outlook.[19]

This same David Ross owned a general store in Petersburg, Virginia; serving as a clerk for him was Christopher McPherson, then a slave but actually in charge of several white employees. Ross manumitted McPherson in 1792. McPherson then moved to Norfolk, later served as a clerk in the House of Representatives in Washington, and thereafter clerked for the leading Virginia attorney, W. H. Hening, in Charlottesville. He also served for a few years as a clerk in Virginia's High Court of Chancery. Meanwhile, he had become convinced—as had quite a few of his contemporaries—of the impending end of the world and tried to persuade others, including John Adams and James Madison, of the reality of this vision.

Having accumulated some wealth, McPherson opened a school for the instruction of Black people, free and slave (for the latter, of course, the permission of their owners was required), in Richmond in 1811. This operated in the early evening, and its master, hired by McPherson, was a white teacher named Herbert H. Hughes. Instruction was in arithmetic, English, geography, and astronomy; the monthly charge was $1.25. At its opening twenty-five students were present.

The enrollment increased, and with it so did McPherson's enthusiasm. Hence he published a letter in the Richmond *Virginia Argus* (March 12, 1811) urging "the people of colour throughout the United States...to establish similar institutions in their neighborhoods." Some residents of Richmond complained to the paper's editor, Samuel Pleasants, and urged the school's closing. Hughes opposed this, and Pleasants published two letters from him in which he affirmed his intention to continue teaching. Police harassment now ensued, and it appears that the somewhat mysterious Mr. Hughes decided to leave town. When McPherson showed that he meant to find another teacher and to reopen his school, he was arrested. McPherson was declared insane and was confined to an asylum in Williamsburg. This internment seems to have been quite brief. McPherson left the South at an undetermined date and died in New York City in 1818.

McPherson's life shows the reality of racism; it also shows, however, that this reality was not simple and not monolithic. On the contrary, his positions, his efforts, and his connections with Hughes and with Pleasants— editor of a leading Virginia newspaper—show how complex was that reality and how significant was its questioning.[20]

In the North cases of anti-racist behavior were numerous. A well-known example is that of the African American pioneer opponent of slavery, James Forten of Philadelphia (1766–1842). Forten was an inventor and a fairly wealthy sail maker; by 1807 he employed a racially mixed group of thirty workers.[21] In the instance of Forten and others cited earlier—and to be cited later—there is no contemporary evidence of any difficulty among these Black and white coworkers.

In this region rejection of racist behavior patterns before the Civil War was more common than dominant historical generalizations indicate. Of course, nothing negates the reality of the overwhelmingly racist essence of that area at that time; on the contrary, a man like Forten, for example, devoted his own life not only to the fight against slavery but also to the battle against discrimination. At the same time, the fact that Forten owned and conducted a business with a fairly considerable integrated work force is not to be ignored.

Other examples must become part of the general historical consciousness.

Macon B. Allen (1816–1894), as an illustration, seems to have been born free in Indiana. At an unknown date he moved to Portland, Maine, and managed to gain some economic success. Encouraged by white friends, he studied law and sought admission to the bar in 1844. His sponsor was William Pitt Fessenden, then leader of the Maine bar and later a congressman, member of Lincoln's cabinet, and U.S. senator. An early chronicler of the legal profession in Maine remarked of Fessenden: "He received colored persons into his house, he took them to church, he visited them in their families, and encouraged them in every way to give them self-respect and a place in society."[22] Despite that sponsorship, Allen's first effort was rejected; it was alleged that since he was Black he was not a citizen and therefore could not be an attorney. Allen and his friends persevered, however; Allen was successful and seems to have been the earliest licensed African American attorney in the United States. Allen later was active in Reconstruction efforts in South Carolina, served as a judge in that state, and thereafter continued his law practice. He died in Washington in 1894.[23]

Better known is the career of John Mercer Langston (1829–1897). Relevant is the initiative of Philemon Bliss, attorney, newspaper publisher, judge, and member of Congress, who met Langston in connection with joint anti-slavery work in Ohio. Langston, being rejected at a law school in Cincinnati because of his color, was trained for the law by Bliss, who insisted that Langston's "intellectual worth and liberal education [at Oberlin] would do honour to any one, white or black." Studying and working with Bliss (and taking meals with the Bliss family), Langston was admitted to the bar in September 1854 and went on to a distinguished law practice (with mostly white clients) and a historic political career in Ohio and in postwar Virginia.[24]

Somewhat similar is the instance of Robert Morris (1823–1882), befriended by Ellis Gray Loring, a leading Boston attorney and Abolitionist. Morris lived as a servant in the Loring home, then became a clerk in Loring's law office, studied law, and was admitted to the bar in February 1847. He went on to a significant law practice and an influential role in the anti-slavery and anti-racist struggles of the pre– and post–Civil War periods.[25]

Quite extraordinary in their national impact were the musical capabilities of the Lucas family. Its founder was Alexander Lucas, born near Milford, Connecticut, in 1805. He began work as a shoemaker but early displayed great musical talent. He, his sister-in-law, Dinah Lewis, and, with the family's growth, Simeon, Alexander, Jr., Cleveland, and John gained renown as a group. Their debut together was in New York City in 1853; five thousand people jammed the hall at their recital sponsored by the Anti-Slavery Society. The press generally was enthusiastic in its reception of this family and did not fail to notice the anti-racist influence of their performance; one newspaper in upstate New York commented that the Lucas family was doing "more to secure position for the colored man than all the theorists and speculators about the rights of man have got accomplished in America."

Toward the end of the 1850s the Lucas family joined the renowned (white) Hutchinson family of anti-slavery singers. This Black-white traveling group of talented people raised the hackles of some racist newspaper editors; but tens of thousands of people of both colors enthusiastically responded to their artistry, and they did travel together. Of this experience, Asa B. Hutchinson recalled in 1875 that the families faced hostility at times but did this together; he added, "We never formed an alliance with any musical people with whom we fraternized so pleasantly and loved so well."

Elizabeth Taylor Greenfield, born in Natchez, Mississippi, in 1809, was reared from early age by a Quaker woman (a Mrs. Greenfield) of Philadelphia. By the 1850s she was known as "the Black Swan," and her voice was captivating audiences in New England, New York, the Midwest, and Canada. Newspaper notices were very positive. She died in England in 1876.

Thomas J. Bowers (1836–1885), born in Philadelphia, also achieved fame as a concert vocalist. In the 1850s he performed with the "Black Swan" several times. Unlike her, however, Bowers publicly protested against racism; still, his audiences were numerous and press notices favorable.[26]

8

"Inferiority" and Entrepreneurs, Seamen, and Cowboys

A considerable number of African American people—some slave, more free—achieved significant degrees of success in various economic undertakings. In all, or nearly all, such cases there were white people (sometimes related biologically) who played helpful roles. In doing so, these whites often explicitly attacked racist stereotypes and practices. An example is the case of John C. Stanley of North Carolina, who became free in 1798, prospered as a farmer and a barber, and devoted much of his wealth to purchasing the freedom of others—from 1808 through 1818 he brought to freedom in this way twenty-three people.[1]

James Thomas (1827–1913) of Missouri and Tennessee had a highly successful career, again starting as a barber and then accumulating considerable wealth, largely in real estate. Aspects of his life, such as the employment of whites to serve his business and domestic needs, contradicted racist stereotypes; his autobiography is filled with evidences of this.[2]

The finest hotel in Charleston before the war was owned by a free man of color, John Jones. The best study of free Black people in South Carolina showed that despite "strenuous efforts...to restrain free intercourse between black and white," such intermingling, including marriage, was not uncommon. While "association between free blacks and whites of the upper class was by no means rare," it was particularly marked among poorer people. Here, indeed, "Unhampered by social conventions and considerations of caste, a truer fraternity existed between black and white. The lower-class free black did not need to carve a niche for himself in white society; he was merely a confrere in a fellowship of have-nots."[3]

Louisiana, especially New Orleans, was noteworthy for the cracking of racist barriers and stereotypes. This has already been noted in another connection and will again be noted in future pages; it is to be remembered that even in the professions African Americans sometimes broke through segregation. Notable was Alexander Chaumette, a native of New Orleans and winner of a medical doctorate from Paris. In Louisiana he passed the state's qualifying examinations and practiced his profession as a respected member of the medical fraternity. One finds also, in New Orleans, several instances of free Black people employed in supervisory positions over white laborers—bricklayers in 1858, for instance. Again, there appears to be no evidence of difficulties in this connection.[4]

Another illustration of the porous quality of antebellum Southern racism is offered in the career of Frank McWhorter, who preferred to be known as "Free Frank" (1777–1854). Born in South Carolina and taken as a slave-child to Kentucky, by 1810 he was hiring his own time and managing to save money. He bought his wife's freedom in 1817, his own two years later, and during the next forty years, at a cost of $15,000, purchased the freedom of fourteen other family members.

A farmer, stock raiser, and manufacturer (of saltpeter), he moved to Illinois in 1830 and there lived out his years. In his will, Free Frank provided for buying the freedom of four grandchildren. In pre–Civil War Illinois, far from unmarked by racism, Free Frank did have the assistance or the friendship of several white people; one, Abraham Scholl of Kentucky, was a particularly warm and thoughtful friend.[5]

The life of free African American people in Missouri also shows wide variation in condition, wealth, educational opportunities, and relationships with white people. The latter not infrequently manifested respect and rejected racism in practice.[6]

Ira Berlin suggested that antebellum Southern whites "believed free Negroes to be men and women like themselves." He observed that in the 1850s a leading Richmond newspaper, while stating that many among the free Black population were not models in behavior, went on to ask: "What else could be expected of a people barred from education and proscribed from all areas of gentility?" This paper, still, insisted that "they number among them men of the highest character and respectability—men of piety—men of substance—men of considerable intelligence." This is the language of a Virginia newspaper eight years prior to secession and the creation of a government founded, according to its vice president, on the proposition that the African American was an inferior species of humanity.[7]

This brings to mind a strikingly similar statement in a book published in London at about this time—and one not unknown in the United States. An English businessman of wealth admitted in 1849 that racism certainly existed in his own country "among good society." But he went on: "Yet men whom business or colonial connection has brought into familiar intercourse with the black or coloured races, know well that the educated among them are not inferior to whites in any of those qualities which acquire esteem for the gentleman or confidence for the merchant."[8]

A recent study has shown the existence of several hundred free African

American families of considerable wealth in the South. Many of them—especially in the deep South—had white family relationships. One finds in 1860 several leading South Carolina officeholders and slaveowners referring to such Black people, who were not too distant from them in property terms (and perhaps in other connections), as people who "command the respect of all respectable men." They were, said this public statement, "good citizens" (no matter what the Supreme Court had found three years before) and showed "patterns of industry, sobriety, and irreproachable conduct."[9]

Among those without great wealth, as these pages have insisted, close relationships between whites and Blacks prior to the Civil War were not uncommon. Another who observed this was Robert S. Starobin. He wrote that in antebellum Southern enterprises, "to a striking extent, whites often worked alongside or in close physical proximity to slaves who were laboring at similar tasks." His study persuaded him that "historians have exaggerated ... racial hostility," for, as he found, "many white and black workers labored together without friction." His conclusion was: "Racial hostilities occurred, of course, but they were much less significant than the striking extent of interracial cooperation among workers at most integrated industries." He thought that "the absence of racial conflict is surprising considering the racist foundation upon which slavery existed."[10] This absence is not "surprising" if one places it in the context of behavior especially among the "plain people" of the South in their day-to-day lives and activities.

There was one particular kind of employment of African American men in the pre–Civil War United States that tended especially to challenge racist ideology and practice. This was maritime pursuit, which, as I wrote many years ago, "had always been [of] importance." Indeed, I then added, Black men had "traditionally followed the sea." Attention then was called to the fact that in the colonial period, African Americans, slave and free, were employed on privateers, trading vessels, and fishing boats. Some of the leading figures in Black history, at some point in their lives, followed maritime occupations. Among these, for example, were Crispus Attucks, Paul Cuffee, Prince Hall, Denmark Vesey, Frederick Douglass, James Forten, and Henry Highland Garnet.

Black men were fairly common in the Continental and state navies during the Revolution and played a conspicuous part in the navy in the War of 1812 and in the Civil War. During the War of 1812 and for years thereafter, according to a distinguished contemporary, Black men formed from 10 to 20 percent of the crews, and racism seems to have been notable by its absence. Then, we are told, "The white and colored seamen messed together. ... There seemed to be an entire absence of prejudice against the blacks as messmates among the crew." It is clear that in the decades prior to the Civil War there not only were mixed crews but also some masters of merchant vessels who were Black.[11]

A recent study commented that "seafaring [was] one of the few jobs readily available" to Black men in the late eighteenth and early nineteenth centuries. There was a high proportion of Black men aboard ships during this period in Philadelphia and Providence and in leading port cities of Connecticut, Massachusetts, and New York. This occupation was characterized by "egalitarian impulses" that "frequently confounded shoreside racial etiquette." Sometimes in this work white men were subordinate to Blacks. There were, in fact, "innumerable Yankee ships on which black men before the mast ranked higher and earned more than white co-workers." Thus it was logical for Melville in his *Billy Budd* to make a Black seaman "the center of a company of his shipmates," for he was "on every suitable occasion always foremost."

Racism was present even aboard ships during this period, but a careful student concluded, "Overtly racist actions by other sailors were often subordinated to the requirements of shipboard order, and the unprecedented toleration that existed at sea afforded black men a virtually unknown degree of equality with white co-workers." Data already presented would question how "unknown" this behavior was, but aboard ships certainly the equality was real, not formal, and "black sailors received pay equal to that of whites in the same position."[12]

The prominence of Black men in the naval fighting of the War of 1812 was emphasized many years ago by Lorenzo J. Greene.[13] He observed that in the 1813 engagement between U.S. and British ships on Lake Erie, Captain Oliver Perry was upset by what he described as "a motley crew of blacks" as well as others. Perry complained of this to his commanding officer, Commodore Isaac Chauncey. The latter replied that he had "fifty blacks" on his own ship and that "many of them are among my best men." Moreover, he told Perry: "I have yet to learn that the color of a man's skin or the cut and trimmings of his coat can affect a man's qualifications or usefulness." Of Perry's four hundred men, one hundred were Black; together they destroyed the British fleet and assured Perry his immortality.

Another pursuit, like that tied to the sea, was relatively free of racism; though this was followed in the post—Civil War United States, it belongs here. This was the Western cattle industry. Kenneth W. Porter made a careful study of the several thousand Black men—perhaps a quarter of the total of trail drivers. He found that "many of them were especially well-qualified top-hands, riders, ropers, and cooks." Porter wrote:

> That a degree of discrimination and segregation existed in the cattle country should not obscure the fact that, during the halcyon days of the cattle range, Negroes there frequently enjoyed greater opportunity for a dignified life than anywhere else in the United States. They worked, slept, played, and on occasion fought side by side with their white comrades, and their ability and courage won respect, even admiration. They were often paid the same wages as white cowboys and, in the case of certain horse-breakers, ropers, and cooks, occupied positions of considerable prestige.[14]

9

From Egypt to Philosophes to Quakers

That Egypt exemplified one of the most enduring of civilizations and that its arts and sciences were of the highest order, exerting decisive influence upon other societies, is not questioned. What was denied for many years, however, was the significant role of Africans—meaning Blacks—in Egyptian history. The importance of this denial to racists is clear; its refutation also clearly was very consequential for those rejecting racism. This Egypt question recurred in the nineteenth-century discussion of racism and colonialism. The work of W.E.B. Du Bois here, as in other areas, pioneered in advancing the position now accepted—that is, the basic African role in Egyptian civilization.[1]

With the epochal developments of the fifteenth century—especially the European interventions in western Africa and the Western Hemisphere— questions as to the nature and abilities of the inhabitants of these regions became matters of vital concern. Since the object of such intervention was conquest and exploitation, finding such inhabitants to be either not human or, if human, significantly and ineradicably inferior to the interlopers was of great psychological, religious, and political consequence. But such a conclusion nevertheless was not easily reached and was not unanimously assented to even in the early period.

Study of the rejection of concepts of the bestiality or deeply inferior nature of the original inhabitants of these vast areas was led, in the case of Spain, by Lewis Hanke and, in the case of Portugal, by A.J.R. Russell-Wood. Both scholars brought forward evidence of the vigor with which racist concepts were combatted, beginning in the fifteenth century.[2]

In practice, the opponents of racism were overcome, though sometimes both church and state did yield, if reluctantly, to their arguments. The tradition and the content of their egalitarian position influenced later and more successful efforts.

In Spain a leading writer of its golden age was Francisco Gomez de Quevedo y Villegas (1580–1645). This satirist, poet, novelist, and revolutionary attacked concepts of racism in a 1640 essay issued in English in 1798. Here he had an African spokesman insist that "there is no cause for our slavery but our colour, and colour is an accident, not a crime. Yet certain it is that those who lord it over us have no colour for their tyranny but our colour, which is produced by the presence and nearness of the great beauty—to wit the sun." The African, through Quevedo, continued: "Why do not the whites consider, that if we look like blots among them, one of them looks like a stain among us?" The enslavement of the Black was held to be inexcusable by this African, who added: "In all ages there have been men of our complexion famous for martial exploits, learning, virtue, and sanctity; it is needless for me to repeat a catalogue of them, for they are sufficiently known."[3]

Forced labor—by indenture and chattel slavery—was a fundamental component of the history of the United States from its colonial roots to the latter part of the nineteenth century and, with some modification, well into the twentieth century. Concepts of elitism and racism were basic rationalizations for such oppression and exploitation. From the beginning, however, the idea of the nonhumanity or the innate inferiority of the African peoples was rejected by a significant number of white people within the present boundaries of the United States. We refer not to those who rejected slavery, but to those who rejected racism. Some who did not argue for the termination of slavery did affirm their rejection of racism, but in the overwhelming majority of cases, denouncing racism meant attacking slavery, and defending slavery meant accepting racism.

The dominant view of the historical profession was bluntly stated by a distinguished English member. He referred matter-of-factly to the Elizabethan English person's "belief in the eternal, God-given inferiority of the Negro" and the belief that "hence the proper status of Negroes was slavery."[4] This, the writer continued, was "in essence" the argument of Winthrop Jordan's *White over Black*. We have stated that Jordan's title and much of his data do emphasize the prevalent and virulent racism marking the period of his concern from the late sixteenth to the early nineteenth centuries. As has been shown, however, a substantial component of that book brings forth evidence of the questioning and often the rejection of racism.

This is true even though, I think, Jordan does underplay or minimize such anti-racist evidence. Illustrating this—in addition to what I believe is his unfortunate introduction to James Hugo Johnston's book, alluded to earlier—is the way in which he dealt with the influential English philosopher and physician, Sir Thomas Browne, whose dates (1605–1682) are barely later than those of Elizabeth. Browne's "Of the Blackness of Negroes" was noted because in it the color of the African was not attributed to climate (as was then commonly done) but was held to be a permanent condition transmitted biologically. This position, quite advanced for its time, was then placed by Jordan within the context of blackness as a mark of a people considered "radically defective in religion."[5]

This, however, is inaccurate. It misses the point that Browne was drawing contrary conclusions. Having rejected both the idea of climate and the "curse of Ham" as causes of the Africans' blackness, and having made the observation of its biological source, Browne went on to declare that he failed to understand why blackness was considered a curse—he could not "make out the propriety" of such an estimate. He insisted that there was nothing more beautiful in one color as compared with another. Beauty, he thought, might be conceived in connection with symmetry and harmony but not with color. Do people, Browne asked, when they consider animals, object to black as compared with white, or with another color? Furthermore, he wrote, "And by this consideration of Beauty, the Moors also are not excluded, but hold a common share with all mankind." Indeed Browne made his point explicitly: "To infer this [being black] as a curse, or to reason it as a deformity is in no way reasonable."[6] This was a rather advanced position for its time; Jordan's omission in summarizing Browne perhaps helped mislead Plumb.

An important and neglected dissertation is "The English View of Negro Slavery to 1780." Its author, William D. Stump, summarized his work with these words: "Prior to 1780 opinion in England definitely favored the Negro as an individual and condemned the institution of slavery." He found that in the century prior to 1780 there was available in England considerable information on Africa and its inhabitants, that the physical description of the continent was favorable, and that its inhabitants were "highly regarded" as being "possessed [of] quick perception," "very humane and hospitable," and excellent craftsmen and artisans. Morgan Godwyn's *The Negro's and Indian's Advocate* had been published in England by 1680. It had rejected concepts of the nonhumanity of the African and had pointed out that among them some held that "a white complexion denoted inferiority." A Frenchman of the time, engaged in the slave trade, reported similar feelings among the Africans and made clear that he himself found nothing to substantiate the idea of African inferiority. Concluding his study, Stump found that "prior to 1780 various influences molded England thinking into an undeniable anti-slavery bias"; he affirmed this even though, he correctly added, "most authorities state the contrary."[7]

Egalitarianism was central to the thought of the seventeenth-century English revolutionaries, and a feeling of equality carried over into later reflections concerning the enslavement of Africans. By the early eighteenth century denunciations of both the slave trade and slavery were not rare in Great Britain. Sometimes these contained the denial of racism itself.

William Fleetwood, bishop of St. Asaph, for example, in a sermon preached in February 1711 before the Society for the Propagation of the

Gospel, denied African inferiority. He insisted that the Black person was "equally the Workmanship of God with themselves [meaning the planters]; endowed with the same Faculties and intellectual Powers; Bodies of the same Flesh and Blood, and Souls as certainly immortal."[8] Other bishops of the Church of England at this time, including George Berkeley and Joseph Butler in 1729 and 1739, while not attacking slavery itself, did insist upon the African's equality with white people.[9]

There is good evidence, also, that England's Board of Trade found colonial legislation aimed at free Black people questionable since it was apparently based—to quote the secretary of the board, writing in 1735—"merely upon Account of their Complection"; the governor's reply to the secretary's query made clear that not color but possible involvement in social unrest was the source of the questioned law.[10]

The noted Scottish jurist, George Wallace, in his first volume of *A System of Principles of the Law of Scotland* (1760), denounced slavery and insisted—indeed, held it to be axiomatic—that "all that inequality, which is to be found among the individuals of human race, is derived from political and arbitrary institutions alone." In the same year in London, under the pseudonym J. Philmore, appeared *Two Dialogues on the Man Trade*, which, like Wallace, called for the immediate abolition of slavery and assumed equality of Black and white people. Philmore also justified slave rebellion and even war upon England by the international community if it persisted in carrying on such an abomination as the slave trade.[11] Both works were used by Anthony Benezet in the second edition (Philadelphia, 1762) of his *Short Account of Africa.*

The *philosophes* of prerevolutionary France strongly affirmed both anti-slavery and anti-racist positions, though much later commentary denies or minimizes this.[12] In this connection even Montesquieu's exquisite satirical attack on the rationalizations for "The Slavery of Negroes" was misinterpreted as late as 1914 as an argument favoring slavery. One finds in the *philosophes'* writings from 1748 to 1765 excoriations of slavery, denials of African inferiority, and even justification for slave rebellion. Voltaire, a principled pacifist, thought that of all wars, one carried out by slaves for freedom was "perhaps the only just one."

In the colonies that were to become the United States, attacks upon slavery and doubts about African inferiority recurred, beginning in the sixteenth century. Among the many admirable features of Roger Williams (c. 1603–1683) was his fraternal regard for Indians and his sharp protest when, after the Pequot War of 1637, Puritans sold Indians into slavery. In 1652 his own colony of Rhode Island provided Africans with the same legal status as white indentured servants, but this enactment seemed to have lacked enforcement.

George Fox (1624–1691), founder of the Quaker persuasion and repeatedly a political prisoner, cautioned the addressees of *Friends beyond*

Sea, That Have Blacks and Indian Slaves (1657), written in England, to remember the fundamental teaching of Jesus—the equality of all people in the eyes of God—though he never quite called for the abolition of slavery. He did declare, after visiting the West Indies and the mainland in the 1670s, that slaves were to be taught the gospel, for Christ "shed his blood for them as for you" and "hath enlightened them as well as he hath enlightened you." This is from his *Gospel Family Order* (1676); here he suggested that the Africans might be set free, as were bondsmen in the so-called Old Testament, "after a considerable term of years, if they have served them faithfully."

In the Dutch colony founded in 1663 by the Mennonite Pieter C. Plockhoy in what is today Delaware, slavery was forbidden, but in 1664 when this area was taken over by the British, the Plockhoy effort was obliterated.[13]

Richard Baxter (1615–1691), the English nonconformist clergyman whose writings were numerous and influential, in his *Chapters from a Christian Directory* (1673) denounced slave traders as "enemies of mankind"; his attack upon slavery was equally vehement. He did, however, like Fox, urge obedience on the part of the slaves—their position reflected, he thought, God's will. Still, his powerful assault upon the slave trade and slavery is part of a strong militant tradition. Moreover, when he cautioned slave-owners to guard their own behavior toward those they held as slaves, he told them to "remember that they are as good as you; That is they are reasonable creatures as well as you, and born to as much natural ability."[14]

Perhaps the first questioning of the holding of slaves in the mainland came from an Irish Quaker, William Edmundson. Preaching in Newport, Rhode Island, in 1676, Edmundson called slavery "an aggravation and an oppression upon the mind." He urged his listeners to consider that the African slave could "feel, see and partake" of Christ's gospel even as they. In a footnote he asked the momentous question: "And many of you count it unlawful to make slaves of the Indians: and if so, then why the Negroes?"

All questioning of the enslavement of the African, even when this did not suggest emancipation, posited the equality of the slave in the eyes of the Creator. Milton Cantor was correct when he declared that "articulate clerical opinion" in this period "often stressed Negro-white equality, at least when it came to their respective spiritual natures." Thus he noted that Cotton Mather "refused to accept the doctrine of racial categorization and affirmed the basic unity of all men before God."[15]

Illustrative of this great force was the renowned Germantown Protest drawn up by four Friends of that Pennsylvania town on February 18, 1688.[16] The signers were "Garret henderich, Derick up de graeff, Frances daniel Pastorius, and Abraham up de graeff." Five arguments were mustered to support this unequivocal call for slavery's abolition: It violated the Golden Rule; it was wicked, for it traded in human beings with immortal souls and separated families and encouraged adultery; it was based on thievery and the purchase of the booty of thieves; it besmirched the name of Pennsylvania;

and it was dangerous. As to the last consideration, uprisings among slaves had already occurred, said the four. If and when these outbreaks again occurred and the slaves "fight for their freedom," would masters in this New World "take the sword at hand and war against these poor slaves, licke, we are able to believe, some will not refuse to doe; or have these negers not as much right to fight for their freedom, as you have to keep them slaves?" It is difficult to create a rejection of racism more positive than that thundering question. This appeal was lost in the labyrinth of Committees and Meetings; its plea even within the Quaker community was not implemented for a century. But it was the beginning of a very long journey.[17]

What appears to have been the first published anti-slavery work in the colonies came from another Quaker, George Keith of Pennsylvania. This was *An Exhortation and Caution to Friends Concerning Buying or Keeping of Negroes*; it was written in August 1693 and published, as a fifteen-page pamphlet, later that year in Philadelphia by William Bradford. Being printed, it could more easily have lasting impact; it was commented upon, for example, by Benjamin Franklin in a letter dated November 4, 1789. Its arguments are essentially those of the Germantown Protest. Emphasized by Keith was the idea of the equality of all human beings: "*Negroes, Blacks* and *Tawnies* are a real part of Mankind for whom Christ hath shed his precious blood, and are capable of salvation, as well as *White Men*."[18]

Henry J. Cadbury published the text of another strong Quaker denunciation of slavery presented by Robert Pyle to the Concord, Pennsylvania, Monthly Meeting ten years after the Germantown Protest.[19] It repeated many of the arguments of that document and particularly emphasized the danger of slave rebellion. Should such break out, Pyle said, "we might have let them alone." The essential point, again, was slavery's violation of the Golden Rule. Pyle urged a program of education of the slaves with the objective of emancipation; he suggested, too, that slaves so freed ought to be compensated for their unpaid labor. Pyle did not suggest compensating the owners. The argument and the plan clearly rejected racism.

There is evidence of strong anti-slavery action by other Quakers—William Southby and John Farmer—in the early years of the eighteenth century. Neither effort was successful at the time, but both reflected a deep revulsion at Christians enslaving human beings, thus again projecting a fundamental source of anti-racism.[20]

The first printed attack upon slavery in Massachusetts was a three-page broadside issued by Green and Allen in Boston in June 1700. This was *The Selling of Joseph* by Samuel Sewall (1652–1730). At the time Sewall was a judge of the Massachusetts superior court; in the last decade of his life he was chief justice.[21] The leaflet grew out of a legal battle with John Suffin, who sought to extend an African's servitude beyond the term of the indenture; this ended with the latter being declared free in 1703.

Sewall argued that "uneasiness" caused by the slaves had led to the questioning of slavery. It was well to question it, he went on, for man-stealing was denounced in the Bible; moreover, it was clear, he added, that they were "unwilling servants." They were the descendants of Adam, as all men were. Hence they were the equals of other men; they were, indeed, "the Offspring of God; they ought to be treated with a respect agreeable." True, Sewall thought that their differences were so great that "they can never embody with us." Yes, the differences were great, he said, but they were the children of God and therefore were in no way inferior to other men.

The insistence on the humanity of the African, on his being the work of God, on Christ's blood having been shed for him as for all people, on the Golden Rule as a basic guide for believers and enslavement as a gross violation thereof, and on slavery as evil's embodiment, separating families, encouraging adultery, buying and selling human beings, and practicing cruelty fills the early anti-slavery literature, like that produced by John Hepburn (1715), a Quaker tailor in New Jersey, and by Ralph Sandiford of Philadelphia in 1729. Elihu Coleman, a Quaker from Massachusetts, has the distinction of publishing a pamphlet in 1733, *Testimony against Making Slaves of Men*, which was approved by the Monthly Meeting of Nantucket. Coleman not only based his argument on the ideas already summarized; he added that the idea that Africans should be slaves because they seemed ignorant need not apply only to them: "If that plea would do, I do believe they need not go so far for slaves as now they do." Moreover, if the slaves were ignorant, who kept them so?

The most remarkable of the earliest anti-slavery agitators surely was Benjamin Lay.[22] Like his friend Sandiford, Lay was born in England (in 1677). He seems to have been disowned by Quakers early in his adult life; precisely why is not clear. He continued, however, to consider himself a Friend. Beginning in 1718, he lived in Barbados for about a decade, and when the authorities again found him unpleasant, he moved to Philadelphia in 1731.

Here Lay began his very vigorous anti-slavery (and anti-penal) work; he was befriended by both Anthony Benezet and Benjamin Franklin. It was the latter who, in 1737, published his long book (of 272 pages, with a title beginning *All Slave Keepers That Keep the Innocent in Bondage* that goes on for another 106 words, ending with *in America*). This book excoriated slavery and slave keepers; it posited the quality of all persons before God their creator and Jesus their savior and therefore demanded an immediate end to the sin of slavery.

It was as rambling and eccentric as its author. Lay was four feet seven inches tall, was a pronounced hunchback, and wore a long white beard that tended to accentuate a very large head. But it was his practice, not his book or his person, that left the deepest imprint upon contemporaries.

Once, for example, he stood barefoot in the snow before a Quaker meeting house. This evoked remonstrances from the Friends, who expressed concern for his health. He replied that while they showed solicitude for him, they were without mercy in contemplating the infinitely worse conditions of the African slaves. Again, he seems to have actually kidnapped a neighbor's child, and when the parents appealed to him for aid, he turned the boy over to them and asked that they consider how the parents of those held in bondage must feel when their offspring were torn from them.

One of Lay's most spectacular exploits occurred within a Friends' meeting house. He entered clad, apparently, in normal attire, but under his Quaker garb he wore a military uniform and sword and tied to his belt a bladder filled with a red fluid. In the course of the Friends' contemplation, Lay arose, denounced slaveholding, tore aside his cloak, and said that owners of slaves were men of war and—piercing the bladder—men of blood.[23]

Part of the unsuccessful effort to reject slavery for Georgia presented arguments not unlike those in the Germantown Protest. Thus, when some settlers petitioned the proprietors of the new colony in 1738 to permit the introduction of slaves, settlers in Salzburg countered with their own petition. "It is shocking to human nature," they said, "that any Race of Mankind and their Posterity, should be sentenced to perpetual slavery; nor in Justice can we think otherwise of it, than they are thrown among us to be our Scourge one Day or another for our Sins; and as Freedom to them must be as dear as to us, What a Scene of Horror it must bring about."[24]

In the record of anti-slavery and anti-racism no one is more consequential than John Woolman, whose impact prior to the Revolution in this regard is rivaled only by that of Anthony Benezet. Before dealing with these two remarkable figures, note should be taken of Samuel Davies (1723–1761), a Presbyterian minister, who served in Virginia and in his last years was president of the College of New Jersey (Princeton University). In Virginia, as a significant force in the Great Awakening, Davies preached to, baptized, and instructed several African slaves. While he seems never to have advocated an end to slavery, he did write a friend in England in 1755 that "a considerable number" among the Black people had "given credible evidences, not only of their acquaintances with important doctrines of the Christian religion, but also a deep sense of them upon their minds, attended by a life of strict piety and holiness." He was persuaded of their stature as human beings, which led him to urge benevolence upon the masters, though, as stated, he seems never to have reached the point of advocating their freedom.[25]

John Woolman (1720–1772), a New Jersey tailor, farmer, and Quaker, devoted his life to serving the values of Jesus as he understood them. As a Quaker minister he traveled widely in the mainland colonies, particularly in the South, combatting all evidences of injustice, violence, and oppression. Slavery especially affronted him; his experience led him to urge its termination and also persuaded him that ideas of the inferiority of African-derived peoples were as false as they were pernicious. His first publication—written in 1746, soon after his original major journey through Maryland, Virginia, and North Carolina—was *Some Considerations on the Keeping of Negroes. Recommended to the Professors of Christianity of Every Denomination.* This was a twenty-four-page pamphlet, several times reprinted in changed—usually enlarged—form. It was widely read and quite influential.[26]

Following a brief introduction and preceding the text of his work, Woolman italicized *"Forasmuch as ye did it to the least of my brethren, ye did it to me."* He continued that common joys and troubles came to all and that death and judgment also awaited all people. This, he suggested, taught "an idea of general brotherhood." If, however, he went on, attention was focused upon "outward circumstances" and these were found to be superior to those surrounding others, men faced the danger of becoming enamored of "fond notions of superiority." The past suggested, Woolman wrote, "that men under high favours have been apt to err in their opinions concerning others." But, he believed, "To consider mankind otherwise than as brethren, to think favours are peculiar to one nation and exclude others, plainly supposes a darkness in the understanding."

Woolman returned to the idea that

when self-love presides in our minds our opinions are biased in our own favour. In this condition, being concerned with a people so situated that they have no voice to plead their own cause, there's danger of rising ourselves to an undisturbed particularity till, by long custom, the mind becomes reconciled with it and judgment itself infected.

Though there existed, he thought, "different degrees and a variety of qualifications and abilities" among peoples, still all were dependent upon each other. If men understood this, conceit might be abandoned and all might be treated as having one Father. That enslavement existed before now, Woolman stated, did not relieve men of its present existence and their benefitting from it now; it was no remedy to simply go along with things as they were, for as they were, they were not just.

Woolman especially emphasized the harmful effect of slavery upon the children of slaveowners, as Jefferson and Mason were to do. So circumstanced, such children "will be possessed with thoughts too high for them." This, continuing, would intensify its baleful effects, thus "gradually separating them from (or keeping from acquaintance with) that humility and meekness in which alone lasting happiness can be enjoyed." He added: "Whoever rightly advocates the cause of some, thereby promotes the good of all." "Duty and interest are one," Woolman thought, and the path of fraternity is the way to peace.

Perhaps Woolman's essence is in the paragraph where he suggested that thinking favors were peculiar to one people as contrasted with another darkened one's understanding, as previously quoted; the paragraph continued,

For as God's love is universal, so where the mind is sufficiently influenced by it, it begets a likeness of itself and the heart is enlarged towards all men. Again, to conclude a people froward, perverse, and worse by nature than others (who ungratefully receive favours and apply them to bad ends), this will excite a behaviour toward them unbecoming the excellence of true religion.

In a *Journal* entry for 1757, Woolman said of the slaves he saw laboring in Virginia:

These are the people by whose labour the other inhabitants are in a great measure supported, and many of them in the luxuries of life. These are a people who have made no agreement to serve us, and who have not forfeited their liberty that we know of. These are the souls for whom Christ died, and for our conduct towards them we must answer before that Almighty Being who is no respecter of persons. They who know the only true God, and Jesus Christ whom he hath sent, and are thus acquainted with the merciful, benevolent, Gospel Spirit, will therein perceive that the indignation of God is kindled against oppression and cruelty, and in beholding the great distress of so numerous a people will find cause for mourning.

Mary Stoughton Locke, in a monograph that remains indispensable though it was first published in 1901, wrote: "There is probably no other man in the period of gradual abolition who did so much for the anti-slavery movement in America as Anthony Benezet."[27] This is a valid claim; it should be added that no one has been a clearer and more fervent opponent of racism than this Pennsylvania Quaker.

The evidence indicates that Benezet (1713–1784) was moved to his opinions and activities by close contact with the African-derived peoples themselves. His letters and printed works abound in references to their ability, fortitude, unhappiness, and abuse; he felt that eliminating the last condition would end the third and bring into proper play the first two attributes. His own experience with Black people, as a friend and as a teacher, was considerable. Because of this, he discovered, as he wrote, "amongst the Negroes as great a variety of talents as amongst a like number of whites; and I am bold to assert, that the notion entertained by some, that the blacks are inferior in their capacity, is a vulgar prejudice, founded in pride or ignorance of their lordly masters, who have kept the slaves at such a distance as to be unable to form a right judgment of them."[28]

Benezet was opposed, however, to immediate emancipation. He concentrated his demands on ending the slave trade, believing that with this achieved, gradual manumission (with colonization in the West) might be accomplished. Nevertheless, he fiercely denounced slavery. His *Short Ac-*

count of That Part of Africa Inhabited by the Negroes, first published in 1762, and his *A Caution and Warning to Great Britain* (1766) were frequently reprinted well into the nineteenth century. Benezet corresponded with Benjamin Rush, Benjamin Franklin, Moses Brown, John Wesley, Thomas Clarkson, and Granville Sharp, among many others. His influence was very great.

Benezet's central significance was his conviction and insistence that the idea of African American inferiority was false. His educational work with Black and white children of both sexes was intensive and prolonged. It persuaded him of the fundamental equality of Black and white people, and he was indefatigable in spreading that view. It is clear, for example, that Benezet's work was important in moving Franklin to a more enlightened position on these questions. To convey something of the forcefulness of his conviction in this regard, one may quote a paragraph in which he wrote of himself:

A. Benezet, teacher of a school established by private subscription, in Philadelphia, for the instruction of the Black Children and others of that people, has for many years, had opportunity of knowing the temper and genius of the Africans; particularly of those under his tuition, who have been many, of different ages, and he can with Truth and Sincerity declare, that he has found amongst them as great variety of Talents, equally capable of improvement, as among a like numbers of Whites.[29]

Benezet is also noteworthy as a pioneer in bringing forward evidence from a wide variety of sources—not only English but also French and Dutch—refuting the prevalent notions of Africa as a continent bereft of significant social development. In this regard Benezet anticipated modern anthropological and historical scholarship.

By the time of the decade prior to the American Revolution, there appeared people on both sides of the Atlantic who expressed surprise that anyone could seriously believe in the inferiority of fellow human beings because of a difference of color, or that anyone would employ such an idea as justification for slavery. Thus Benezet, in a pamphlet published just before the Battle of Lexington, quoted the bishop of Gloucester in England as having exclaimed in a sermon delivered in February 1766:

Gracious God! to talk (as in herds of cattle) of property in rational creatures! Creatures endowed with all our faculties, possessing all our qualities but that of colour; our brethren both by nature and grace, shocks all our feelings of humanity and the dictates of common sense.... Nature created man free, and grace invites him to assert his freedom.[30]

Two years earlier, James Otis in his seminal work, *The Rights of the British Colonies Asserted and Proved* (Boston, 1764) had insisted that "the colonists are by the law of nature freeborn, as indeed all men are, white or black." Continuing by citing Montesquieu's sardonic justification of slavery, Otis asked:

> Does it follow that it is right to enslave a man because he is black? Will short curled hair like wool instead of Christian hair, as 'tis called by those whose hearts are as hard as the nether millstone, help the argument? Can any logical inference in favor of slavery be drawn from a flat nose, a long or short one?

The same argument is in *Letters from a Farmer in Pennsylvania*, which appeared originally in 1767 and 1768 in a Philadelphia newspaper and later as a pamphlet entitled *Serious Address to the Rulers of America*. This was by John Dickinson (1732–1808), one among the decisive founders of the nation. He urged his fellow colonists that they not confine their demands for liberty to themselves, but that with equal vehemence they ought to denounce "the crying crime of holding your fellow men, as much entitled to freedom as yourselves, the subjects of your undisputed will and pleasure."[31]

It is noteworthy that in the 1760s influential Quaker Monthly Meetings were ready to accept teaching of Friends like Benezet. In 1765 the Philadelphia Monthly Meeting asserted that the African-derived slaves had been "unjustly deprived of the common Priviledges of Mankind"; three years later the New York Monthly Meeting endorsed this view and added: "We are ... fully of the mind that Negroes as rational creatures are by Nature born free." With this it followed that Friends would set up schools for freed African Americans; that established in 1770 in Philadelphia had "the purpose of proving that Negroes had the 'Capability and Inclination for receiving Instruction.' "[32]

The Reverend Charles Chauncey was an early opponent of slavery among the New England clergy. In his *Appeal to the Public*, published in Boston in 1768, he lamented the fact that slaves, "as good by nature as their masters, were bought and sold as though they were an inferior order of dogs!"[33]

This questioning of the propriety of slavery that appeared in the colonies in the prerevolutionary generation is part of the same intellectual development in the home country of Great Britain. David B. Davis noted what he called "a growing Anglo-American consensus" during this period in opposition to slavery. Among the "enormously influential" figures—to use his words—cited by Davis in this connection was James Beattie.[34] But Davis did not observe that this consensus not only decried slavery but also denied its racist underpinning. This was notably true of Beattie.

James Beattie (1735–1803), a poet and philosopher—for many years professor of moral philosophy at the University of Aberdeen—in his two-volume *Elements of Moral Philosophy* stated that "slavery is inconsistent with the dearest and most essential rights of Man's nature ... that it seeks to degrade into brutes, beings whom the Lord of heaven and earth endowed with rational souls, and created for immortality." He continued:

That a man, a rational and immortal being, should be treated on the same footing with a beast or a piece of wood, and bought and sold, and entirely subjected to the will of another man whose equal he is by nature, and whose superior he may be in virtue and understanding, and all for no crime, but merely because he was born in a certain country, or of certain parents, or because he differs from us in the shape of his nose, the colour of his skin, or the size of his lips;—if this be equitable, or excusable, or pardonable, it is vain to talk any longer of the eternal distinctions of right and wrong, truth and falsehood, good and evil.

Beattie did not think immediate emancipation practical, but he hoped that exposure of slavery's evil "may have a tendency to alleviate" it and might even, perhaps, "contribute something, however little, to its final abolition." Beattie then examined arguments in favor of slavery and refuted them. In doing so, he insisted that the African "is not deficient in sensibility" and that "in love and in friendship he has sometimes given proof of such generosity as would do honour to any hero of romance." He felt that all evidence showed that the Africans "inherit from nature a constitution of mind very capable of improvement."

Turning to the notion that the African was not really human, Beattie rejected this as absurd and added that the slaveowners "know [the slaves] too well to have any doubt of their being men." Developing this idea at some length, Beattie added that the African "has frequently given proof of an elevated and generous mind, and of great ingenuity in those arts and manufactures to which he has been accustomed to attend." Indeed, reality showed, said Beattie, that either "his soul is human, or that ours is not human."

Concluding his rather lengthy examination of this subject, Beattie wrote "that all men upon earth, whatever their colour, are our brethren and neighbours; and if so, both reason and Scripture declare, that it is our duty to love them, and to do unto them as we would that they should do unto us." In the last section of the volume Beattie ended abruptly by affirming the humanity of the American Indian, as he had done of the African.[35]

10

The American and French Revolutions

One might well expect that the generation witnessing the American and French revolutions, with their insistence upon "self-evident" truths, the propriety of pursuing happiness on earth, and the duty to resist oppression, would be one in which questioning slavery—and its accompanying racism— would proliferate. The record supports this expectation.

Notable, for instance, is the essay *Thoughts upon Slavery* by John Wesley (1703–1791), Methodism's founder. This was published in 1774 and included the following statement:

Give liberty to whom liberty is due, that is, to every child of man, to every partaker of human nature. Let none serve you but by his own act and deed, by his own voluntary choice. Away with all whips, all chains, all compulsion! Be gentle toward all men, and see that you invariably do unto every one as you would he should do unto you.

In his final year Wesley wrote to the English leader of anti-slavery efforts, William Wilberforce, on February 24, 1791: "O be not weary of well doing! Go on, in the name of God and in the power of his might, till even American slavery (the vilest that ever saw the sun) shall vanish away before it."[1] With these views from Methodism's founder, no wonder his followers in the United States were so troublesome to slaveowners for many years, as future pages will show.

One of the foremost American revolutionaries was Benjamin Rush (1745–1813), eminent physician and pioneer psychiatrist (to use the modern term), surgeon general of Washington's army and a signer of the Declaration of Independence. Rush also was one of the founders in Philadelphia in 1775 of a very early anti-slavery society. Among his publications was *An Address to the Inhabitants of the British Settlements in America upon Slave-Keeping*, first issued in 1773 and written at the suggestion of Anthony Benezet.

Rush began by declaring that he intended "to combat the principal arguments" used to justify slavery. In doing so he met head-on the idea that "the Intellects of Negroes, or their capacities for virtue and happiness" were somehow inferior to those of white people. False, Rush declared; on the contrary, he insisted that the African was in every respect "equal to the European." Then Rush went on to excoriate the cruelty basic to slavery, citing the reports of eyewitnesses, especially in the West Indies.[2]

Rush's assault quickly aroused one West Indian planter, Richard Nisbet, to publish a counterblast; Rush responded immediately with an *Answer*, also published in 1773. Nisbet's response was largely an insistence upon the inferiority, if not the inhumanity, of the African. Accordingly, Rush's reply was devoted to demolishing Nisbet's racism. In the course of this effort, Rush insisted that different areas, histories, and conditions produced different customs and life-styles. But difference was exactly that—it was not inferiority. "To a Mind divested of those Prejudices with which Custom leads us to view objects," this reality would become plain. Rush added: "But supposing our Author had proved the Africans to be inferior in every thing to the Inhabitants of other quarters of the Globe will his Cause derive any strength from it? Would it avail a man to plead in a Court of Justice that he defrauded his Neighbour, because he was inferior to him in Genius of Knowledge?"

Rush closed with vigor: "You have thrown a Veil over the true Causes which destroy so many thousands of your fellow Creatures every year.... You have attempted to sink Creatures formed like yourself in the Image of God, and equally capable of Happiness both here and hereafter, below the rank of 'Monsters and Barbarians' [quoting Nisbet], or even Brutes themselves." Mercifully (and, as it turned out, somewhat prophetically), Rush concluded, "I hope you will not fail immediately to ask forgiveness of your Maker, and your Country, for the attack you have made upon the Rights of Mankind."[3]

This Rush-Nisbet exchange is only one piece of evidence (many others will be offered) belying the view expressed by one historian—a view offered without substantiation as though it was self-evident—that "the tension between Revolutionary belief and practice of slavery produced a distinctive view of the character of the Negro, to the extent that it seemed to many to be the very nexus of the problem. That distinctive view is an unkind one and the debasement of the Negro's character is an essential element in the story."[4]

Benjamin Rush was by no means alone during the revolutionary generation. Many then viewed the Revolution's premises as not only hostile to slavery but also to the racist rationalization of it. John Trumbull (1750–1831) is another instance. He was one of the so-called Connecticut Wits. He was a prodigy, passing Yale's examinations at the age of seven and matriculating at the age of thirteen. In the early 1770s he was a tutor at

Yale and later served in the law office of John Adams. Trumbull's own politics, like those of the other Wits, were Federalist; his satirical poetry was a favorite of his generation.

Reflective of the significant and growing anti-slavery feeling that accompanied the revolutionary atmosphere, Trumbull, at the age of twenty, contributed a series of essays, using a pen name, to a leading Connecticut paper; one, published on July 6, 1770, was a devastating assault, via satire, upon the pro-slavery argument.

Trumbull began:

It is strange that any person should be so infatuated, as to deny the right of enslaving the black inhabitants of Africa. I cannot look on silently and see this inestimable privilege, which hath been handed down inviolable from our ancestors, wrenched out of our hands, by a few men of squeamish consciences, that will not allow them or others to peaceably to enjoy it. I therefore engage in the dispute and make no doubt of proving to every unprejudiced mind, that we have a natural, moral, and divine right of enslaving the Africans.

After ridiculing some of the pro-slavery arguments—that Africans were children of Ham, for example—he devoted more space to spoofing those who expounded the good done the Africans by enslaving them. Here he noticed some of the characteristics of the Africans, such as their freedom from luxury and from idleness; these were "wholly monopolized by their masters." The Africans were noted, too, for their "forebearance, justice and forgiving temper." These traits, of course, showed their inferiority, that is, their particular fitness for slavery. Equally certain was it that their "dullness of intellect," which the enslavers claimed to see, showed this same aptitude for enslavement.

Trumbull observed that a main defense of slavery for the Africans was that it brought them into contact with the delights of Protestantism; therefore, he urged that steps be undertaken at once to enslave "the Chinese, the Tartars, or the Laplanders," as well as "the Turks and the Papists." In fact, he thought that it would be well if slave-catching flotillas left at once from Republican shores for Constantinople and Rome on missions of benevolence and enlightenment.[5]

Some of the content of the revolutionary generation's ideology influenced individuals who themselves refused participation in the Revolution. An example of this occurred in 1771 when an extraordinary charge was made to a grand jury in North Carolina by the chief justice of that colony, Martin Howard, who had been reared in Rhode Island and appointed to his North Carolina post in 1767. (As a Tory, Howard retired to Great Britain during the Revolution.)

Howard was himself a slaveholder, but on this occasion he bitterly attacked the inherent brutality of enslavement, though he did not call for its abolition. He did, however, attribute its source to "avarice" and said that it "produces the worst effect upon our manners." But, more to the present purpose, Judge Howard added: "The souls and bodies of negroes are of the same quality with ours—they are our own fellow-creatures, tho' in humbler circumstances, and are capable of the same happiness and misery." The text of this charge was published in the press of North Carolina and—since Howard had come from Rhode Island—in the *Mercury* of Newport in May 1772.[6]

Much of the very influential work of Benezet appeared in the early 1770s. Especially important was his *Some Historical Account of Guinea* (1771), which had decisive influence upon Thomas Clarkson, among others. This book examined the history of the African slave trade and the impact of that trade upon Africa itself and reprinted the findings of many travelers in Africa. It included also the views of Granville Sharp on the slave trade.

Benezet placed this effort within the context of its time, "when," as he wrote, "the liberties of mankind are becoming so much the subject of general attention." This work emphasized the finding of numerous observers as to the "natural capacity and good disposition" of the Africans. It explicitly rejected concepts of inferiority and urged, as a matter of equity and Christian behavior, an end to the slave trade and serious efforts toward the elimination of slavery in the Western Hemisphere.[7]

In 1772 Thomas Swan, a British merchant visiting Boston, published there a lengthy pamphlet entitled *A Dissuasion to Great Britain and the Colonies from the Slave Trade*. Swan's argument was cast in religious, economic, and political terms.[8] He appealed especially to those who had not taken a stand against the slave trade and concluded that "if you have not lost all sense of benevolence, all sympathy and compassion towards those of your Brethren who have the same capacities, understanding and souls, and who were born to inherit the same salvation with you; I say, if you are not callous to every Christian, human and manly sensibility, you certainly must feel compassion for these extremely oppressed people."

A forthright attack upon slavery and racism appeared in 1772 from a prominent New Jersey Quaker, David Cooper.[9] In denouncing slavery—he quoted Wesley's "sum of villainies"—Cooper scornfully rejected ideas of African inferiority. He wrote: "The power of prejudice over the minds of mankind is very extraordinary; hardly any extremes too distant, or absurdities too glaring for it to unite or reconcile, if it tends to promote or justify a favourable result." It was this, Cooper insisted, that accounted "for the fallacious reasonings and absurd sentiments used and entertained concerning negroes, and the lawfulness of keeping them slaves." The heart of Cooper's argument is in this paragraph:

Justice abhors punishing an innocent person, and if they are innocent why should they not enjoy their natural rights as fully and absolutely as the rest of mankind?

Or is it their being born of a different colour from ourselves that gives us this prerogative of dealing with them as we please; making natural justice quite another thing when apply'd to negroes from what it is when apply'd to those of our own colour. However, this simple circumstance may have prejudiced our minds, it may be well for all who are concerned with this people to remember, that they are equally the work of an Almighty hand, with a soul to save or loose, as themselves, and being so, doubtless will avenge their cause, altho' in his mercy he forbears long, the time of retribution will come; justice is as much his attribute as mercy.

Winthrop Jordan called attention to a letter from an opponent of slavery that appeared in the *Virginia Gazette* (August 20, 1772).[10] Again satire was resorted to: "If Negroes are to be Slaves Account of Colour, the next Step will be to enslave every Mulatto in the Kingdom, then all the Portuguese, next the French, then the brown-complexioned English, and so on till there be only one free Man left, which will be the Man of the palest Complexion in the three Kingdoms."

By 1773 the propriety of enslaving African people had become so significant a question that it formed the matter of a debate held as part of the Harvard commencement.[11] Two graduates, Theodore Parsons and Eliphalet Pearson, were the participants. Parsons opposed enslavement; Pearson favored it. The latter did so on the grounds that social organization required rule, and that meant rulers. The rulers exercised authority on the basis of greater competence as compared with those ruled; Pearson cited God's rule over the universe and parents' rule over children. The propriety of domination arose, Pearson thought, from the fact that some "are actually found so far to excel others both in respect of wisdom and benevolence" that this was proper, whether the superiority resulted from "nature or education."

Warming up to his task, and prodded by Parsons's argumentation, Pearson finally exploded that "these miserable Africans" had characters compounded of the capacity of children or idiots or madmen. Being so constituted, they were "altogether incapable" of self-government; hence their enslavement was both proper and necessary.

Parsons countered by dismissing the analogy of God and parents as irrelevant. He added that sufficient authority existed to doubt the Africans' savagery. Indeed, Parsons added that if "modern writers of the best reputation are to be credited" (and here he had the benefit of Benezet's work), then "their manners [and] conveniences and enjoyments" or "in a word their manner of life [is] much more agreeable than has been heretofore represented." Parsons labelled "ridiculous" efforts to equate Africans with some "brute creation." "It is well known," he insisted, "that stupidity is by no means the natural characteristic of these people." If one considered the oppression to which they were subjected in this part of the world, one ought, he thought, "to admire that there are any the least appearances of sensibility remaining in them."

Parsons had already heaped ridicule on what "could hardly be imagined," that anyone would justify one people enslaving another because of a difference in complexion or the structure of one's hair or nose—"for if man is to be led and governed by a nose, it may well be questioned whether a nose of a different figure would not be better adopted to the purpose." He concluded by declaring that Pearson's insistence that the slavery of some enhanced humanity's happiness "must, I think, allow, that the direct way to increase their happiness is by every possible means to increase their misery." Pearson lamely brought the debate to a close by saying that he would allow its resolution "to be determined by the judgment of others." The substance of the debate of 1773 formed much of U.S. history until a civil war almost destroyed it; in essence, the debate has continued to the present.

It should be noted that while Benjamin Franklin became a vigorous foe of slavery and opponent of the ideas of inequality only after the Revolution, he had stated in a letter to Condorcet in March 1774 that while the free Blacks in Philadelphia generally were poor people, "I think they are not deficient in natural understanding, but they have not the advantage of education." Franklin added, "They make good musicians."[12]

Levi Hart in Pennsylvania in 1775 cried out that it was "high time for this colony to wake up and put an effectual stop to the cruel business of stealing and selling our fellow men." He went on, "What inconsistency and self-contradiction is this!" "When," he asked, "O when shall the happy day come that Americans shall be *consistently* engaged in the cause of liberty?"[13]

That same year, Thomas Paine devoted his first published essay to the question of slavery. Paine (1737–1809), the son of a poor English Quaker farmer, was dismissed from a civil service job because he led efforts to increase wages. He gained the friendship of Franklin, then in England, and migrated to the mainland colonies in 1774 with a letter of introduction from him. Very soon after he settled in Philadelphia, Paine published in the *Pennsylvania Journal and Weekly Advocate* (March 8, 1775) an essay on "African Slavery in America."

With characteristic vigor, Paine began: "That some desperate wretches should be willing to steal and enslave men by violence and murder for gain, is rather lamentable than strange." Still, he found it extraordinary that people who thought of themselves as Christians would tolerate it, given the considerable body of literature showing its vile character and harmful consequences.

The Africans themselves, Paine continued, were "industrious farmers" and bothered no one, but by "wicked and inhuman ways" they had been enslaved. Paine appealed to the Golden Rule as reason enough to detest slavery; he summarized the atrocities basic to the institution. However, he said, his purpose was not so much to condemn slavery as to entreat Americans to end it. For this purpose, Paine suggested a careful process of emancipation with steps to ensure that the freed people might live "like other men." Their capacity to do so was never questioned by Paine.[14]

Soon after this article was published, there was founded on April 14, 1775, in Philadelphia the Society for the Relief of Free Negroes, Unlawfully Held in Bondage, the first of its kind. Paine was a charter member, and soon men like Benjamin Rush and Benjamin Franklin joined him. He later helped draft and, as clerk of the Pennsylvania Assembly, signed the act abolishing slavery, passed on March 1, 1780. This act in its first section stated that the Creator had shown no preference as to the complexion of humans. The legislators, believing themselves "weaned by a long course of experience from these narrow prejudices" hitherto existing, now felt it right to pass this law. It was hoped, said this section, that thus might be taken "one more step to universal civilization" by restoring to the African people "the common blessings that they were by nature entitled to."

Earlier, on January 12, 1775, residents in Georgia, also stirred by the revolutionary movement, drew up a protest against slavery that posited the humanity of the slaves among them.[15] The statement came from residents of St. Andrews Parish; its moving spirit was Lachlan McIntosh. The signers wanted to show "to the world that we are not influenced by any contracted or interested motives" in throwing their support to the movement opposing the king's tyranny. On the contrary, they possessed "a general philanthropy for all mankind of whatever climate, language or complexion." Hence "we hereby declare our disapprobation and abhorrence of the unnatural practice of slavery in America (however the uncultivated state of our country or other specious argument may plead for it) a practice founded on injustice and cruelty, and highly dangerous to our liberties (as well as our lives), debasing part of our fellow-creatures below men, and corrupting the virtues and morals of the rest and laying the basis of that liberty we contend for (and which we pray the Almighty to continue to the latest posterity) upon a very wrong foundation."

Samuel Hopkins, minister of the First Congregational Church in Newport, Connecticut, in the spring of 1776 issued *A Dialogue Concerning the Slavery of Africans*. This was directed to the members of the Continental Congress because it was felt that the fate of half a million slaves should be considered by them. The Africans, said Hopkins, were "under such a degree of oppression and tyranny as to be wholly deprived of all civil and personal liberty." There was no "just cause" for this; on the contrary, it was monstrous and cried out for prompt remedy. That remedy was emancipation; they should then be subject "to the same restraints and laws with other freemen." There should be no "peculiar disadvantages" as now burdened Blacks among those who were not slaves. No, let them be put "in a way to provide for themselves" so that they might live "comfortably."

Hopkins said that some suggested that he exhibited "too much zeal," but—in language anticipating Garrison by some fifty years—he was combatting "a sin of crimson dye," and opposition to that could not be "urged with too much zeal." They were taught, said Hopkins, to think of Africans as though they were beasts rather than humans; this was vicious nonsense. This inculcation of prejudice led many among them "not to be sensible of the abuses they suffer." Did they but shed their prejudices, such abuses "would appear terrible in our sight." Hopkins's impassioned prose is filled not only with detestation of slavery but also with an insistence upon the slaves' humanity and upon the equality of all people no matter what their color.[16]

Hopkins persisted in maintaining these positions after the Revolution. When he moved to Rhode Island, he contributed essays to local newspapers in the 1780s insisting that Black people were "as much included in the assertions as ourselves," by which he meant the assertions in the Declaration of Independence.[17]

Somewhat after Hopkins issued his *Dialogue*, James Oglethorpe (1696–1785), Georgia's founder, wrote to Granville Sharp on October 13, 1776, that his experience had taught him that the philosopher David Hume was wrong when he affirmed African inferiority. Oglethorpe thought that on the contrary, the African was inferior to no other human being and, indeed, was capable of establishing a high form of civilization.[18]

Manumission of slaves by owners moved by the spirit of the Revolution multiplied in the final generation of the eighteenth century. One of the slaveowners so moved was Freeborn Garretson of Maryland. He emancipated his slaves in 1775 and, as a Methodist minister, devoted much of his remaining years, until his death in 1827, to preaching against slavery and bringing the good news of the gospel to slaves in Virginia and North Carolina as well as his native Maryland. In the latter place he was severely beaten in 1775 by a planter who said that Garretson "would spoil his negroes." Garretson, however, persisted in his ministry of emancipation and benevolence. He was persuaded by his experience of the full capacity of African Americans; one among them, he wrote in 1777, "exceeded all the youths I had ever seen for a gift and power of prayer."[19]

The requirement of waging the revolutionary struggle at times evoked opinions rejecting racist notions. The involvement of African Americans in the fighting, on land and sea, was notable during that contest. At times, to bring this about, concepts of the inferiority of Black people had to be combatted. A notable instance of this came when Alexander Hamilton urged—unsuccessfully, as it turned out—their enlistment in South Carolina.

In this connection Hamilton on March 14, 1779, wrote to John Jay, the president of the Congress, that he thought that the slaves, if offered freedom in exchange for enlistment, would fight well. Their lack of education would not militate against this, Hamilton thought. He knew that property considerations would oppose this, but he thought that the crisis required it. In any case, Hamilton suggested, the British might use them, if the revolutionaries did not. Hamilton went on that he believed that "their natural faculties are as good as ours," although "the contempt we have been taught to entertain for the blacks, makes us fancy many things that are founded neither in reason nor experience." Hamilton added that he favored enlistment also because it might "open the door to emancipation," and that would serve both "the dictates of humanity and true policy."[20]

No white American was more forthright in his opposition to racist discrimination than John Jay, who, after his distinguished role in the Revolution, went on to become the first chief justice of the U.S. Supreme Court and a two-term governor of New York. In 1785 Jay said: "I wish to see all unjust and unnecessary discrimination everywhere abolished, and that the time may soon come, when all our inhabitants, of every color and denomination, shall be free and equal partakers of our political liberty."[21]

The significant case of *Brom and Bett v. John Ashley*, decided by the Court of Common Pleas in Great Barrington, Massachusetts, in August 1781, produced an expression repudiating racism. Mum Bett, as Elizabeth Freeman was called, had been the slave of a Colonel Ashley of Sheffield. Outraged at mistreatment, she absconded and resisted Ashley's extralegal and legal efforts to get her to return. She persuaded another Ashley slave, named Brom, to join her in a suit for freedom. The effort was conducted in court by Theodore Sedgewick, then a young Stockbridge attorney and later a U.S. senator. A jury found in favor of the two African Americans and ordered the colonel not only to pay legal fees but also to pay each of them thirty shillings as damages.

Elizabeth Freeman worked for the Sedgewicks for a few years and then, with a daughter, set up her own home nearby. She died in 1829. Two years later Sedgewick, part of the budding anti-slavery movement, spoke at the Stockbridge Lyceum on "The Cause of Man." Here Sedgewick reminded his audience of Elizabeth Freeman: "She claimed no distinction," he said, "but it was yielded to her from her superior experience, energy, skill and sagacity." Sedgewick continued: "If there could be a practical refutation of the imagined superiority of our race to hers, the life and character of this woman would afford its refutation."[22]

The final nail on slavery's coffin in Massachusetts was driven in two years after the Elizabeth Freeman case; this also originated in the freedom efforts of an African, here named Quack Walker. In *Commonwealth v. Jennison*, Chief Justice William Cushing made it clear that if slavery ever had existed in Massachusetts—and never by statute—it certainly had no existence any longer, for by 1783, he said, "a different idea has taken place with the people of America, more favorable to the natural rights of mankind and to that natural, innate desire of Liberty, with which Heaven (without regard to color, complexion or shape of noses) has inspired all the human race."[23]

A Methodist-sponsored anti-slavery petition, numerously signed, was presented to the Virginia legislature in 1785. In their plea, rejected by the legislature in November, the petitioners remarked "that the arguments [for slavery] drawn from the difference in Hair, Features, and Colour, are so beneath the Man of Sense, much more the Christian, that we would not insult the Honourable Assembly by enlarging upon them."[24]

Statements attacking the idea of the inferiority of particular peoples recurred in documents from emancipationist societies that multiplied in this revolutionary generation. Among the earliest of these was the New York Manumission Society, which was formally organized in 1785. Among its officers were figures like John Jay and Alexander Hamilton; others of national reputation who helped found this organization included Cadwallader Colden, Daniel D. Tompkins, and James Duane. The society's purposes are given in the preamble of its constitution:

The benevolent Creator and Father of Men having given to them all an equal right to Life, Liberty and Property, no Sovereign Power on Earth can justly deprive them of either; but in conformity to *impartial* Government and laws to which they have expressly or tacitly consented.

It is our duty, therefore, both as free Citizens and as Christians, not only to regard, with compassion, the Injustice done to those among us who are held as Slaves, but to endeavour by lawful ways and means, to enable them to Share, equally with us, in that civil and religious Liberty with which our indulgent Providence has blessed these States, and to which these, our Brethren, are by nature, as much entitled as ourselves.[25]

Similarly, the constitution of the Pennsylvania Society for Promoting the Abolition of Slavery, adopted in April 1787 in Philadelphia, stated: "It having pleased the Creator of the World, to make of one flesh all the children of men—it becomes them to consult and promote each other's happiness, as members of the same family, however diversified they may be by colour, situation, religion, or different states of society." Among its members, in addition to Franklin, Rush, and Paine, were Robert Morris and James Pemberton.

Annual sermons before analogous societies in other states included in their attacks upon slavery and the slave trade clear denials of the inferiority of Africans and insistence upon natural equality as characterizing all human beings. This was true of the discourse delivered in September 1790 before the Connecticut Society for the Promotion of Freedom by the Reverend James Dana of the First Congregational Church in New Haven and in May 1791 under the same auspices by Zaphaniah Swift.[26]

It was at about this time that the Shaker religious movement—the Millennial Church—led by Anna Lee made its appearance in the United States. Its first settlement actually dated from 1776 in what is now upstate New York. By the early nineteenth century there were perhaps nineteen such communities, peaking to a total membership of about five thousand. This celibate religious organization with collective property ownership and gender equality also rejected any racist practice. One of its centers was in Kentucky, but the remainder were in New England and the Midwest. A historian of the movement has written: "The Shakers were always opposed to race discrimination and to human slavery. Some of their early converts in the South were slave owners but before joining the Shakers they freed their slaves.[27] In particular, one Matthew Houston, of Kentucky, when joining, emancipated forty slaves. There was apparently no thought of segregation in so doing, for colored Shakers were found mixed in with white members in many societies.

Jacques Pierre Brissot de Warville (1754–1793), a leading French journalist and revolutionary, visited the United States in 1788. His resulting journal was soon translated and published in several editions and languages before the close of the eighteenth century. Brissot sought out Benezet and visited his Philadelphia school, where, he wrote, he could find "no difference" in the mental capacity of the Black children and white children. He found good reading capacity among the former as well as significant mathematical accomplishment, high memory retention, and, in the case of one "young Negro," an excellent talent for painting. Brissot commented upon the widespread discriminatory practices he encountered in the United States generally, but he found some African Americans who cultivated excellent farms. His observation led him to conclude: "Negroes by their virtue and diligence, disprove slanderous lies which their oppressors utter about them."[28]

The *American Museum*, a leading magazine of the time, in Philadelphia in 1788 published an essay whose author was called "Man" and was identified by the publication as an African. The piece condemned slavery and the slave trade and specifically denied racist allegations of inferiority. Indeed, the writer said, having Africans in mind: "Give them a Locke or a Newton for teachers, and you will soon see one African at the head of your academies." The next year, in "A Letter on Slavery by a Negro," this magazine published another essay by one who announced himself to be a former slave. The author flatly insisted, "We are men not of an inferior species"; the essay added that to retain slavery in a republic boasting of liberty was immense hypocrisy. This author declared: "If treated like other men, and admitted to a participation of their rights, we should differ from them in nothing perhaps but in our possessing stronger passions, nicer sensibility and more enthusiastic virtue."[29] That such essays were published in such a journal confirms the fact that the rejection of racism was widespread in this immediate postrevolutionary era.

11

The Republic's Early Years

The adoption of the U.S. Constitution and the early meetings of Congress afforded opportunities for intensified agitation of the subject of slavery and the position of the African American people. The beginnings of the French Revolution also stimulated such activity. The Société des Amis des Noirs was formed in 1789; it immediately entered into correspondence with kindred organizations and individuals in New York and Philadelphia, as well as London. Simultaneously, in Great Britain the struggle against the slave trade and denunciations of slavery intensified with Thomas Clarkson, Granville Sharp, and William Wilberforce coming to the fore; Grégoire in France had a similar effect.

In the last two decades of the eighteenth century, reflecting and bolstering this international movement, frequent and often vehement denunciations of racism appeared in the United States. The year 1789 was a banner one; some of the material reflecting this has been offered earlier in this volume.

Another person whose work reached print in that year was the Reverend John O'Kelly; he was born in Virginia and engaged in ministerial efforts there as well as in North Carolina. Slavery affronted him. In his *Essay on Negro Slavery*, published in 1789 in Philadelphia by Prichard and Hall, he especially denounced assertions of Black inferiority and criminality. The ignorance of the slaves was pointed to by defenders of slavery, yet the slaveowners imposed the ignorance. Further, many white people suffered from profound ignorance, but their enslavement was not advocated. Racism justified slavery; slavery was an abomination. End slavery, and the racism that rationalized it would disappear.[1]

Even Richard Nisbet, who, as we have seen, attacked Benjamin Rush and defended slavery with the most blatantly racist language in 1775, had second thoughts. In 1789 he published in London a pamphlet, *The Capacity of Negroes for Religious and Moral Improvement*, in which he made clear that he no longer doubted that capacity. "Every prejudice against this unfortunate people," wrote Nisbet in 1789, "is mere illusion proceeding from the natural but pernicious abuses which follow an unlimited power of tyrannizing over our fellow creatures."[2]

William Pinkney, a member of the Maryland legislature, asked in its hall in 1789 of "Gracious God" if it were possible that the Lord had "intended to proscribe these victims of fraud and power, from the pale of society, because thou hast denied them the delicacy of an European complexion!" Was it possible, asked the Marylander, that "darkness of skin, the flatness of a nose, or the wideness of a mouth, which are only deformities or beauties as the undulating tribunal of taste shall determine," were to define the status of human beings? People not blinded by arrogance and position must know that African people "are in all respects our equals in nature" and that they possess fully "equal facilities of mind and body."[3]

In 1789 the Maryland Society for Promoting the Abolition of Slavery was formed. Its constitution declared: "The common Father of Mankind created all Men free and equal, and his great command is, that we love our Neighbors as ourselves, doing unto all Men as we would they should do unto us. ...The human race, however varied in Colour or Intellect, are all justly entitled to Liberty."[4]

Similar statements were made by similar societies in several other states in the 1790s. They appeared also in the statements adopted at joint meetings of these societies. For example, at the third convention in 1796, it was emphasized that "among the great discoveries" announced in the Scriptures was "the precious record of the original equality of mankind and of the obligations of universal justice and benevolence which are derived from the relation of the human race to each other in a common Father."[5]

Winthrop Jordan noted the appearance in the 1780s and 1790s of writings rejecting ideas of racial inferiority, though the evidence will not support his assertion that these appeared with "remarkable suddenness." Jordan called attention to the 1790 work of Charles Crawford that, differing from its 1784 edition, insisted upon the equality of Africans and therefore affirmed their right to all civil functions and, Crawford added, the right to marry whomever they wished. Jordan noted also that Hannah More (1745–1833), the influential English writer and reformer, devoted a poem to slavery (published in New York City in 1788) that vehemently denied any mental deficiency on the part of the African.[6]

Betty Fladeland recently called attention to poetry attacking ideas of racism that was published in London in the late 1780s. One poem, in a volume entitled *The Wrongs of Africa* by William Roscoe (1753–1831), contains these lines:

> Formed with the same capacity for pain,
> The same desire of pleasure and of ease,
> Why feels not man for man?

Another work of this period, entitled "American Independency," was by Edward Rushton (1758–1814); it contained these lines:

And pronounce the immortal decree,
Whate'er be man's TENETS, his FORTUNE, his HUE,
He is man and shall therefore be free![7]

The same ideas appeared regularly in the pronouncements of Quakers, including those in the South until persecution led many of them to leave the slave area and others to close their mouths. Characteristic was the anti-slavery plea sent by the Yearly Meeting of the Society of Friends of North Carolina to that state's General Assembly in 1796. "God," said the memorial, "is no respecter of persons, having 'made of one blood all nations of men' and sent his Son into the world that all might be saved, for he tasted death for every man so that all people, whatever their complexion may be, are objects of his mercy."[8]

With the material already presented, one is not surprised to find in the *Maryland Journal and Baltimore Advertiser* of March 31, 1789, a letter, signed "Benevolus," applauding a slaveowner who had recently freed seventy-five slaves as a matter of conscience and then asking: "Why has the pride of American youth been immolated on the altar of Liberty [in the late Revolution] if her sons are not to taste her blessings?"[9] The conscience that moved this Maryland slaveowner to divest himself of his human property led Richard Randolph (father of John Randolph of Roanoke) to emancipate two hundred slaves in his will in 1797. He did this, he wrote

to make retribution as far as I am able, to an unfortunate race of bondmen, over whom my ancestors have usurped and exercised the most lawless and monstrous tyranny, and in whom my countrymen (by their iniquitous laws, in contradiction of their own declaration of rights, and in violation of every sacred law of nature, of the inherent, inalienable rights of man, and of every principle of moral and political honesty) have vested me with absolute property.

In this will Randolph referred to his slaves as "fellow-creatures, equally entitled with ourselves to the enjoyment of liberty and happiness." He "humbly begs their forgiveness for the manifold injuries that he too often inhumanely, unjustly, and mercilessly inflicted on them."[10]

This humanistic response to the quality of the revolutions then shaking the globe worried those in power in the slave regions. Thus in North Carolina, where manumissions multiplied in the dozen years following 1776, the legislature directed in 1787 that this practice was to cease. The act began: "Whereas divers persons from religious motives, in violation of the law that slaves are to be set free for meritorious services only continue to liberate their slaves." Having ordered the practice to stop, the legislature also directed sheriffs to apprehend such newly freed ones because, it stated, they "are now going at large to the terror of the people of this State."[11]

This revolutionary generation witnessed invigoration of women's assertion of their humanity and equality and demand for dignity and freedom. At this time one finds in England, for example, the work of Mary Wollstonecraft and in the United States the prodding of Abigail Adams and the writings of Judith Sargent Murray ("Constantia"). Murray's "On the Equality of the Sexes," apparently drafted in 1779, was published in the *Massachusetts Magazine* in the spring of 1790. While the essay never mentioned chattel slavery or the African American people, it shouted relevance to both with its insistence upon equality regardless of sex, its decrying of the subordination of half the human race, and its announcement that lack of education and opportunity sufficiently explained any alleged deficiencies in performance. In the case of Abigail Adams, one finds not only affirmation of the need for the emancipation of women but also, as she wrote her husband in September 1774, an abhorrence of slavery: "It always appeared a most iniquitous scheme to me to fight ourselves for what we are daily robbing and plundering from those who have as good a right to freedom as we have."[12]

In other writing I observed that the years of the Haitian Revolution produced in the United States a number of speeches and essays justifying the uprising on the grounds of the immutable right of all human beings to their freedom. This assumed the essential equality of all peoples. One finds, for example, such expressions from Dr. George Buchanan in a speech on July 4, 1791, delivered before the Maryland Society for Promoting the Abolition of Slavery, and like thoughts were given prominent display in the *American Museum* of Philadelphia and the Hartford *Connecticut Courant* in the 1790s. Well-known figures like David Rice of Kentucky (who will be noticed again) and Theodore Dwight of Connecticut offered similar views. Dwight, in fact, in 1794 asked the question, if and when slaves rebelled in the United States, "What American will not admire their exertions, to accomplish their own deliverance?" Indeed, earlier James Madison himself was sorely puzzled as to how or whether to punish a captured runaway slave from his own estate. The future father of the Constitution said in 1783 that he "cannot think of punishing him by transportation merely for coveting that liberty for which we have paid the price of so much blood, and have proclaimed so often to be the right and worthy pursuit of every human being."[13]

In 1790, then, it was not unusual to find a Baptist minister in North Carolina publicly condemning slavery as a "violation of the rights of nature, and inconsistent with a Republican government." Black people, said Reverend John Asplund, "have as good a right as we, both to civil and religious liberty."[14]

The year 1790 marked the appearance of a long and bitter satire denouncing slavery from Benjamin Franklin. While Franklin had printed the writings of Benjamin Lay in 1729 and Ralph Sandiford in 1739 and had been influenced by Benezet's work, his commitment to active anti-slavery work came after the Revolution.[15] As president of the Pennsylvania Society for Promoting the Abolition of Slavery, Franklin issued a public appeal in November 1789 for funds to establish a school where black people of all ages might be educated in order to prepare themselves for a fruitful life as citizens.

Franklin's final public act was the signing of a memorial presented to Congress on February 3, 1790, on behalf of the society. This memorial posited itself on the equality of all human beings—"all formed by the same almighty Being, alike objects of his care, and equally designed for the enjoyment of happiness." Quoting from the Preamble of the Constitution he had helped to produce, Franklin's petition said that "these blessings ought rightfully to be administered without distinction of color, to all descriptions of people." Hence, the petition concluded, end slavery and "promote the general enjoyment of the blessings of freedom."

A day before Franklin's petition reached the House, a similar one from Quakers had come before it. That had been attacked with venom by several members. Franklin's petition met equal hostility; a representative from South Carolina, indeed, suggested that Franklin as a signer of the Constitution "ought to have known it better" and not bothered the House with such a document. The petition was killed; the final word on it in the House was uttered on March 23, 1790.

Two days later, and twenty days before he died, Franklin sent to the Philadelphia *Federal Gazette*, under the name Historicus, a long communication that began by noting objections from congressmen to "meddling with the affairs of slavery." He continued by remarking that these objections reminded him of a speech made a century earlier by Sidi Mehemet Ibrahim, "a member of the Divan of Algiers," denouncing a petition from "a Sect called Erika" urging "the Abolition of Piracy and Slavery as being unjust."

Before presenting further details of this "petition," it is necessary to remind the reader that Franklin was writing at a time when the difficulties with the so-called Barbary pirates off the coast of Algiers were seriously troubling West European countries and the United States. The demands of these African-based seamen for tribute, if not met, often resulted in the enslavement of European and American crews. Tribute was paid by the countries involved, including the United States, but when the cost finally became too great, the United States chose forcible resistance. The result was the Tripolitanian War, which began in 1800 and ended only in 1815 with satisfaction to Washington and the release of some white slaves, including citizens of the United States.

Franklin began his essay by asking on behalf of the African official whether "these Erika considered the Consequences of granting their Petition." Those consequences, in their hot climate where labor was especially difficult, would be disastrous if these "Christian dogs" were not available to labor. In any case, they were well provided for in accordance with the humanitarianism of Islam; further, Islam's sacred text said nothing against slavery. On the contrary, if one looked, he would find there justification for the enslavement of others, especially nonbelievers. Further, their slaves were well treated; indeed, their lives were better, by all reports, than their lives had been in their benighted homes. Further, there were thousands of these slaves among them, and if they were not in their care, what would become of them?

"Let us then hear no more of this detestable Proposition, the Manumission of Christian Slaves, the adoption of which would be depreciating our Lands and Houses, and thereby depriving so many good Citizens of their Properties, create universal Discontent, and provoke Insurrections, to the endangering of Government and producing general Confusion." Hence the Divan, hearing such arguments, "came to this Resolution: 'The Doctrine, that Plundering and Enslaving the Christian is unjust, is at best problematical; but that it is in the interest of this State to continue the practice, is clear, therefore let the Petition be rejected."

Franklin concluded by suggesting that "like motive" produced like result; hence he thought it likely that the legislatures considering the slave trade would act with the wisdom of the Divan. Franklin thought, too, that American statesmen in rejecting the petition's "meddling" with slavery might be very interested in examining the penetrating reasoning shown in "the African's Speech."[16]

Jedidiah Morse (1761–1826) was minister of a congregation in Charlestown, Massachusetts, for thirty years. He was an early opponent of the genocidal treatment of the American Indians. He is best known as the "father of American geography," for his books on that subject were widely used. In one, first published in 1789, there is a sharp attack upon slavery with a paragraph contrasting Black and white people, which certainly did not favor the latter:

The Africans are said to be inferior in point of sense, understanding, sentiment and feeling to white people. Hence the one infers a right to enslave the other. The African labours night and day to collect a small pittance to purchase the freedom of his child. The white man begets his likeness, and with much indifference and indignity of soul, sees his offspring in bondage and misery, and makes not one effort to redeem his own blood. Choice food for satire! Wide field for burlesque! Noble game for wit! Sad cause for pity to bleed, and for humanity to weep![17]

In *The American Museum* for the issues from January through December 1791 appeared an essay in the form of an autobiography of an African, entitled "The Negro Equalled by Few Europeans." The magazine stated that this was translated from the French but identified neither translator nor author. The work commented that in the face of the greed and cruelty characterizing the slave trade, "in vain would it have been, to have talked of the virtues of negroes." Those who attacked them were "consumed" by the "thirst for gold." Of this metal "we had but little to give them; and soon they hoped to draw from our bodily strength, a more precious merchandise." It concluded: "Break down the walls of brass which prejudice has reared! Sweep it from your sight! It conceals men, it conceals brethren from you."[18]

Among the most devoted and effective of early opponents of slavery—rivaling Benezet in this respect—was Warner Mifflin (1745–1798). He was raised in a slaveholding family in Virginia, but was persuaded, when only a lad of fourteen, of the wrongfulness of slavery by one of his father's slaves. When he inherited the estate, he freed nearly one hundred slaves in 1775; he did this, stated the act of manumission, because he "believed Freedom to be their Natural and just right." As a Quaker minister, Mifflin devoted his life to the anti-slavery effort. This took him to North Carolina, Maryland, and Delaware as well as throughout his native Virginia. He carried on this work when he moved in his last years to Pennsylvania.

Mifflin often appeared before state legislatures to plead for an end to slavery; he was instrumental in persuading Virginia, in 1782, to permit manumission. In November 1791 he presented a mildly worded emancipationist petition to Congress. This was rejected after fierce denunciation by Southern representatives, one of whom, William Smith of South Carolina, anticipated the logic of the "gag rule" instituted by the House a generation later. Smith said that the right of petition was perverted when it was used to present documents threatening the stability of the nation. He added that the petition represented the "mere rant and rhapsody of a meddling fanatic."

Assaults of this character led Mifflin to publish his *Defence of Warner Mifflin* in 1796 in Philadelphia. This book not only attacked slavery as sinful but also rejected ideas of Negro inferiority. Thus, as to their alleged "thievishness," Mifflin wrote that the slaves produced all and were denied all; hence "in equity" they might take what they needed. In this way he refuted other components of racist mythology.

Referring to the enslavement of whites "by the Algerines," he asked if assisting a fugitive slave in such a case would be judged "criminal." Why was such an act in the United States called criminal among "professors of Christianity in a similar case, towards a people who differ from us by a few darker shades of skin?" Did this not violate the Scriptures, which teach that God "is no respector of persons" but "hath created of one blood all nations of men"? Two years later this devoted and courageous participant in the effort to promote equality and freedom died as a victim of the epidemics that then regularly swept cities.[19]

David Rice, after a twenty-year ministry serving Presbyterians in Virginia, moved in 1783 to the frontier area of the state that soon would become

Kentucky. He and three colleagues organized the Presbytery of Transylvania in 1786 and founded an elementary school—the seed of Transylvania University.

Rice detested slavery. When preparations were under way for the 1792 convention that would launch Kentucky, he authored a thirty-two-page pamphlet, under the pseudonym Philanthropos, *Slavery Inconsistent with Justice and Good Policy*, published in Lexington that year. Rice was elected a delegate to the convention and fought there to make Kentucky a nonslave state. A major speech he then delivered—based upon his pamphlet—was published in Philadelphia in 1792, the next year in London, and several times thereafter (for example, in New York City, 1804 and 1812).

Rice pleaded at the convention that slavery was Virginia's sin; let the delegates now choose to make Kentucky "innocent of it." His essential point was the equality of all peoples; hence each human being had a God-given right to freedom. Slavery inflated the ego of white people, it violated Republican principles, it fostered licentiousness, and it induced social discord. Slavery could not be legal because it was robbery.

Let the state, he urged, forbid the importation of slaves, let it provide at once for the gradual emancipation of those few then enslaved within its borders, and let it develop an educational program to prepare the African American to exercise the rights of citizenship. Rice never doubted the full capacity of the African American, given opportunities equal to those provided for white people, to function well in every personal and civil capacity. Alas, however, by a vote of twenty-six to sixteen, slavery was written into Kentucky's constitution.[20]

Albert Gallatin (1761–1849), a member of the cabinets of Jefferson and Madison and minister to France and to Great Britain, was also noteworthy for his abomination of racism in connection with both the American Indian and the African American. As a member of the Pennsylvania legislature in the early 1790s he denounced slavery. In a letter written in February 1794, Gallatin remarked apropos of the Haitian Revolution that in it, "I see nothing but the natural consequence of slavery." He went on, "Can we help acknowledging"—in words anticipating Lincoln's Second Inaugural Address—"that calamity to be the just punishment of the crimes of so many generations of slave-traders and slave-hunters?"

In 1847, pleading for "peace with Mexico," he asked rhetorically, "Is it compatible with the principle of democracy, which rejects every hereditary claim of individuals, to admit an hereditary superiority of races?" He believed that such claims were "but a pretext for covering and justifying usurpation and unbounded ambition." To the year of his death, Gallatin insisted that "all these allegations of race and destiny neither require nor deserve any answer; they are but pretenses under which to disguise ambition, cupidity, or silly vanity." Not long before he passed away, Gallatin publicly affirmed his emancipationist views—and for them was actually hooted down by a racist mob.[21]

The emancipationist societies of several states were part of the American Convention for Promoting the Abolition of Slavery and Improving the Condition of the African Race, which was of consequence in the 1790s. In the memorial adopted by the 1794 meeting of the convention, directed to slave states, it complained that Black people were treated as "objects of plunder" and were in despair. It urged the adoption of legal protection for the human rights of the slaves until "a radical abolition of slavery itself, by exploding the general opinion, that the colour of a man is evidence of his deprivation of the rights of man, shall afford more effectual security."

In that year the London society opposed to the slave trade, being encouraged by a recently enacted U.S. law banning the use of ports within the nation for building or supplying African slave-trading ships, wrote the Pennsylvania Abolition Society that, hopefully, this might herald "the Dawn of the Day . . . when Skin shall no longer afford a handle for Injury and a seat of prejudice, but that black and white then shall be seen living together throughout the United States as Friends and Brothers." In the 1796 Address to Blacks from the third meeting of the convention, the African Americans were assured that the Societies of the Convention viewed them "as Friends and Brethren."[22]

Benjamin Rush maintained his concern about slavery and the condition of the African American until his death in 1813. As president of the convention, for example, he signed a significant communication from it to the Pennsylvania Abolition Society in January 1795, in which the idea was expressed that even after emancipation, when "the African" had been "restored to the enjoyment of his rights," still the "great work of justice and benevolence is not accomplished." For when African Americans were citizens, it must be made certain that they have access to "the higher branches of science and in all the useful parts of learning." No doubt was expressed as to their capabilities; on the contrary, this program, it was confidently affirmed, would "confound the enemies of truth by evincing that the unhappy sons of Africa, in spite of the degrading influence of slavery, are in no wise inferior to the more fortunate inhabitants of Europe and America."[23]

On the same day, in the same capacity, Rush wrote to the South Carolina legislature. Here he emphasized the danger to the state of having in its midst "a numerous class of Men . . . deprived of their natural rights, and forcibly held in bondage." In order to eradicate this evil, "as a first step," he urged that the trade in slaves be banned. Ultimately, he added, steps to freedom must be taken, but presently, "when the minds of our citizens are debased, and their hearts hardened, by contemplating these people only through the medium of avarice and prejudice (a necessary consequence of the traffic of

Man)," the petition was confined to banning the trade and thus stopping the increase in slaves.[24]

A moving affirmation of egalitarianism came from Joseph Drinker, a cooper, who described himself as a "simple Quaker." This "simple" person made a plea in January 1795 "for the admission of Colored People to the Society of Friends." He told his Philadelphia coreligionists:

It has frequently been a trouble to me to find many of my friends, whom I highly Esteem, let Prejudices prevail with them So far on account of Externals. [This, he thought, violates] our Fundamental Principles, viz—that God is no respecter of Persons... that what God hath cleansed no man should call common or unclean. Christ died for all men... now if we say one thing and practice another, shall we not be charged with Hipocricy?... Let us examine our hearts and see if Pride is not the Bottom [of] those Prejudices so that some are ready to say to these poor despised Blacks, Stand off I am more holy than thou art.... All people should come and partake with us.... [This is the] sincere desire of an obscure brother known by the name of Joseph Drinker.

Thomas E. Drake, who published this communication, noted that in 1796 the Philadelphia Friends adopted a rule accepting all "without respect of persons or color" and suggested that this "obscure brother's" plea may have helped bring about that wholesome result.[25]

An important example illustrating the significance of the opposition to slavery and the rejection of racism in late eighteenth-century American thought is the *Circular Letter* issued early in 1798 by David Barrow. It was written by this Baptist minister in order to explain to his congregation in Southampton County, Virginia, why he had decided to move to Kentucky.

Like so many others at the time, Barrow had freed his slaves (in 1784). Not prospering, and finding the continuation of the institution in his native state objectionable, he decided in the 1790s to go to Kentucky, where, at the time, it appeared possible that slavery would not gain a foothold. He was mistaken about Kentucky's future; he maintained, however, his anti-slavery views, and this resulted in the 1798 publication.

In it, Barrow referred to slavery "with all the horrors attending it" as so monstrous that "it is impossible for language to dress it in colours too dark." Barrow, in summarizing "my political creed," explicitly rejected racism. He opened by declaring, "I believe the natural equality of man, except in some monstrous cases." He went on, "Liberty, with a right to a good character, of acquiring and possessing property, with the enjoyment of life and members, and the means of defending them, is the unalienable privilege of all complexions, shapes, and sizes of man, who have not forfeited those blessings by their own personal misdemeanors."

Further, he believed "that no man can be bound in person, or property, but by the laws of his own making, or that of his representatives, fairly chosen." All men of proper age should have the franchise; none should be excluded from any public office. In sum, Barrow desired "the downfall of all despots and despotism; and that the *great trump of Jubilee may be shortly sounded from pole to pole*; that all oppressed, in all countries, may enjoy the sweets of liberty, and *every man*, of all complexions, *return to his inheritance.*"[26]

To further illustrate the approach to racism that was common at this time, it may be noted that when the English surgeon Charles White (1728–1813) published *An Account of the Regular Gradation in Man* in London in 1799 and suggested that the African, Indian, Asian, and European "seem evidently to be different species," he received objections from some engaged in efforts to end slavery and the slave trade. They suggested that his view might support those defending slavery. White responded by assuring his correspondents of his own sympathy with their cause; he added, "The negroes are, at least, equal to thousands of Europeans in capacity and responsibility; and ought, therefore, to be equally entitled to freedom and protection." White made the point, as others had done and were to do again, that, in any case, there was no reason to afford a Newton greater rights than any other person.[27]

Having an awareness of how widespread was the rejection of racist postulates by the close of the eighteenth century makes it possible to sympathize with the exclamation from the Abbé Grégoire in December 1798, when he was faced with a defense of slavery on the grounds of the alleged inferiority of its victims: "I swear," he then wrote, "that I am a bit ashamed to fight such an objection at the end of the eighteenth century."[28]

12

The New Century's Youth

The first three decades of the nineteenth century witnessed an extraordinary outburst of slave militancy in Latin America and in the United States. Within the United States, peaks were represented by the Gabriel conspiracy in Virginia in 1800, the uprising among slaves in Louisiana in 1811, the serious ferment in and around New Orleans in 1812, the plots in Virginia in 1816, in Camden, South Carolina, that same year, and in Augusta, Georgia, in 1819, and the vast slave conspiracy led by Denmark Vesey in South Carolina in 1822.

Significant in connection with these events were the alleged involvement of white men, the hanging of one white man and the jailing of another in 1812 events, the leading role of a white man, George Boxley, in the 1816 Virginia plot, and the jailing of three white men convicted of implication in the Vesey effort. Other forms of slave unrest, particularly maroon activity (again, white people were said to have been involved in some instances), especially marked these years.[1]

In the North among Afro-Americans the period witnessed the appearance of their first newspaper (in 1827)—and a militant one it was—and two revolutionary pamphlets, the mysterious *Ethiopian Manifesto* by Robert Alexander Young published in New York City in February 1829 and the extraordinary and very influential *Appeal to the Colored Citizens of the World* published in September 1829 by David Walker in Boston, which went into its third printing by 1830. The latter, justifying slave insurrection, was distributed in the South by free Black people and by several white men, all of whom suffered for their subversiveness.

The 1820s saw the seeding of what soon became the national movement committed to the immediate abolition of slavery and associated especially with the name of William Lloyd Garrison. The latter's mentor was Benjamin Lundy; both men were uncompromising opponents of racism as well as of slavery. By 1830 appeared also the convention movement among African Americans with its message of militant struggle and denunciation of racism—a message to which Garrison had the good sense to listen.

James Monroe, as governor of Virginia, interviewed Gabriel and other rebels in the Virginia conspiracy of 1800 (which Monroe believed involved thousands of slaves). Monroe sought information, but, as he wrote to Jefferson, these people were revolutionists and would provide him with none. Monroe, one-time revolutionist and now governor, asked the author of the Declaration of Independence, soon to be president, for advice on punishing these black revolutionaries. Jefferson urged the governor to exercise as much mercy as his office would allow. He wrote that the world knew who was right and who was wrong on the present occasion; this was, he suggested, another reason for the exercise of mercy. At least thirty-five rebels were hanged; but Jefferson's suggestion of mercy perhaps accounts for the fact that ten among them were spared hanging and suffered banishment to the West Indies slave market—possibly a preferable fate. Still, the point here is to observe Jefferson's remark that the world knew who was right and who was wrong in this encounter—were those who were right the inferior ones?[2]

The condemnation of racism in the United States in this generation took less private and elliptical forms than the Monroe-Jefferson exchange. St. George Tucker, a Virginian, who moved in the same circles as Jefferson and Monroe, had urged slavery's "gradual abolition" in a book of 106 pages, A Dissertation on Slavery, published by the well-known Matthew Carey in Philadelphia in 1796. Later, moved by Gabriel's plot, he published a pamphlet, reiterating his opposition to slavery but adding now: "It may be fairly inferred that the negroes, if once emancipated, would never be satisfied with anything short of perfect equality"—certainly a remarkable prophecy, not unlike Du Bois's challenge in his 1906 Niagara Address to the people of the United States. Tucker and Du Bois certainly did not project such demands on the basis of any concept of the inferiority of the African American. Tucker in this 1801 effort was not reconciled to living with the African Americans in "perfect equality" and therefore suggested, as the title of his pamphlet said, "a proposal for their colonization."[3]

In England, as feeling opposed to the slave trade and to slavery intensified, rejections of ideas of African inferiority multiplied. In this connection one may cite the anti-racist views of William Wilberforce, Thomas Fulwell Buxton, Thomas Clarkson, and Henry Peter Brougham (1778–1868), founder in 1802 of the influential Edinburgh Review. In that publication Brougham argued in 1805 against racial attacks upon Africans; he insisted that "they have the same propensity to improve their conditions, their faculties and their virtues, which forms so prominent a feature of the human character over all the rest of the world." The great impact of such figures upon the United States need not be argued.[4]

In the early years of the nineteenth century, the person from abroad with the greatest influence in combatting concepts of African inferiority was Henri Grégoire, mentioned earlier. His major work was published in English translation by David B. Warden (1778–1845), then secretary to the United States Legation in Paris. This book of over 250 pages dealt directly with "the intellectual and moral faculties and literature of Negroes" and brought forward examples of the work of fifteen Africans.

Grégoire here and in other writings denounced all racist persecution, specifically against the "untouchables" of India, the Irish, and the Jews. But his main concern was the enslavement of the African. The myth propagated as to their inferiority demonstrated, he wrote, "that cupidity will always find pretexts to justify their slavery." But the Africans, he insisted, "being of the same nature as the whites, have the same rights as they to exercise, and the same duties to fulfill." Three chapters were devoted to documenting African skills in pottery, leather, ivory, wood, and other materials, and in conducting civil and social affairs in Africa. Their militancy was alluded to and their successes in struggle, as evidenced by the maroons in Jamaica and Brazil, were described. Grégoire cited his experiences at schools for Africans established by Wilberforce as also vindicating his rejection of racism. He brought forth numerous testimonies to the same effect; his main effort, indeed, consisted of marshaling the facts concerning fifteen outstanding African personalities in various endeavors.

Concluding, Grégoire suggested that "we may say, in general, that virtue and vice, wisdom and foolishness, genius and stupidity, belong to all countries, nations, heads and complexions." His final paragraph merits quotation:

May European nations at last expiate their crimes against Africans. May Africans, raising their humiliated front, give spring to all their faculties, and rival the whites in talents and virtues only; avenging themselves by benefits and effusions of fraternal kindness, at last enjoy liberty and happiness. Although these advantages be but the dream of an individual, it is at least consoling to carry to the tomb the conviction, that we have done everything in our power to procure them for others.[5]

Philip D. Curtin has brought together important information relevant to an inquiry into anti-racist thought. Such thought, he showed, was not uncommon in English writing during the eighteenth century. Adam Smith himself had asked in 1757: "What different ideas are formed in the different nations concerning the beauty of the human shape and countenance?" He suggested that "a fair complexion is a shocking deformity in the coast of Guinea. Thick lips and flat nose are a beauty."

J. F. Blumenbach, the celebrated German scientist, affirmed African equality. For this purpose he, like Grégoire, gathered biographies of outstanding Africans in science, literature, and government, which he offered in an essay published in 1799 in the *Philosophical Magazine* of London. Blumenbach's influence was strong far into the nineteenth century.

Another figure of consequence in this connection was the Reverend James Ramsay, who spent two decades in the West Indies. Upon his return, in his main work, *Essays on the Treatment and Conversion of African Slaves in the British Sugar Colonies* (1784), Ramsay took an anti-racist position.

Curtin noted that in 1841 an official of the Crown, Richard R. Madden, questioned several people involved in African settlement if they thought that Africa's population was inferior to the European; five out of seven did not think so. Nine teachers in this area also were questioned; eight said that they found no difference in learning ability between whites and Africans.[6]

Alexander von Humboldt (1769–1859), a decisive force in science in the nineteenth century, strongly attacked slavery and made clear his rejection of racist ideas. Illustrative of his egalitarian approach was his widely cited *Political Essay on the Kingdom of New Spain*. This examined with respect the Spanish American populations and offered the opinion that the "mixture of the European and the negro" tended to produce an especially "active [and] industrious" human being.[7] Humboldt's influence upon Charles Sumner was considerable; the two men met in Berlin in 1840. In a letter to Richard Cobden written from Boston, July 9, 1850, Sumner urged that Humboldt be elected president of the World Peace Congress to meet in Frankfurt.[8]

In his last years Humboldt was vigorous in his attacks upon slavery. He had been friendly with Jefferson, Madison, and, especially, Gallatin.[9] Many leading Russian writers of the late eighteenth and the nineteenth centuries published views similar to those of Humboldt. Included were Nikolai Novikov (1784), Vassili Popugayev (1804), Michael Lunin (1839), Nikolai Nikrasov (1857), and Vladimir Obruchev (1861). N. G. Chernyshevsky (1828–1889) and Karl von Baer (1792–1876), the latter a founder of modern embryology and a pioneer anthropologist, specifically rejected racism. The renowned explorer and ethnographer, N. Miklouku-Maclay (1846–1888), came to anti-racist conclusions on the basis of wide experience; his views influenced Tolstoy.[10]

The development of radical views on labor, property, government, slavery, and racism appeared in England early in the nineteenth century. This influenced the better-known English anti-slavery movement associated with figures like Elizabeth Heyrick, a pioneer advocate of immediate emancipation, whose writings deeply moved Garrison. Important work has been done in this area by James Malvin and Iain McCalman. The latter, in particular, has stressed the central role of West Indian Black people and their significant impact upon English working-class militants in the pre-Chartist period. The repudiation of racism was fervent in this movement and within these circles. All this was not without influence upon Wilberforce and other anti-slavery pioneers.[11]

Repudiation of racism by white people, especially those living in the South, was not unusual in the first two decades of the nineteenth century. We earlier noted the appearance of David Barrow at the conclusion of the preceding century. After Barrow came to Kentucky, he joined other radical Baptist ministers in a long and bitter struggle within church circles on the slavery question.

In 1807 Barrow and others like him, involving nine churches, formed the Baptized Licking-Locust Association, Friends of Humanity. For this association, Barrow produced a fifty-page pamphlet with the long and forthright title *Involuntary, Unmerited, Perpetual, Absolute, Hereditary Slavery Examined; On the Principles of Nature, Reason, Justice, Policy, and Scripture.* This was published in 1808 in Lexington; on its title page appears: "This pamphlet is not to be sold, but given away." Associated with Barrow were ministers like Carter Tarrant and David Benedict; similar movements appeared at about the same period in Illinois, where James Lemen and other small farmers also adopted the name "Friends of Humanity." In Tennessee at this time Elihu Embree founded his pioneer newspaper, *The Emancipator.*

In the same year as the publication of Barrow's pamphlet, the Kentucky Abolition Society was formed. It seems to have had about two hundred members and to have lasted about fifteen years.

Barrow's work was unequivocal in its rejection of the idea of innate inferiority of African-derived people. Time was, he wrote, that equality of humanity was "a favorite *theme* amongst us," but no longer. How could that be defended "if 'God made of one blood all nations of men' "? If "our former declarations were founded on truth, how unrighteous must that policy be, that deprives a very considerable part of the inhabitants of these states of their equal share in those rights their nature entitles them to?" Barrow went on:

Slavery with all the mortifying degradations it involves, does not, nor indeed cannot, divest MAN, the noble image of his adorable Creator, here below, of the sensations and powers it has pleased his kind benefactor to endow him with. Deprived of his *birth right*, FREEDOM, he still sees, hears, feels, tastes and smells— and above all,—thinks, reasons, reflects and draws conclusions, *independent* of all the TYRANTS on earth.

Barrow did not flinch from the alarm at the prospect of "amalgamation." "It has long been my contention," he wrote, "that any woman who is good enough to make a man a concubine, etc., ought to serve him as a wife." The "main objection," he declared, to slavery's termination was rarely "brought in sight"; it was, he said, "the love of money...covetousness, self-aggrandizement and self-ease." Barrow insisted that the Africans in "their talents or natural abilities are not inferior to the whites in any respect; and evidences are not wanting to prove, where opportunity has been afforded them, that they are equal to any other people in arts etc." No, the defense of slavery, Barrow reiterated, rested ultimately on "love of money."

That was the root of the acquiescence in, even advocacy of, the damnable sin of slavery. But remember, he warned, slavery was defended and practiced at peril to one's character and one's soul in the hereafter.[12] No more forthright blasting of slavery and of racism ever came from a white person than that written in Kentucky in 1807 by a refugee from slave-bound Virginia.

Barrow's vehement anti-slavery and egalitarian positions led to severe trials for him within his traditional church and produced schism. Very similar was the experience of the Quaker, Elias Hicks, and for the same reasons. Hicks (1748–1830), born in Long Island, New York (Hicksville in Long Island recalls his memory), was an itinerant preacher of great power. His principled stand against slavery and racism induced a split in the Society of Friends in 1825. Important in Hicks's development were extended tours in 1798 and 1813 of Virginia and Maryland. He not only detested slavery but also denounced excessive wealth and even suggested that communal ownership of property would be healthier than private.

In 1811 he published his *Observation of the Slavery of the Africans.* Hicks insisted that African-derived people "possessed the same inalienable rights of life, liberty and the pursuit of happiness" as any other human beings. The claim by apologists for slavery that they were "a different and inferior race of mankind" was nonsense and a cover for oppression. This pamphlet was widely circulated in the United States and in England.

Hicks was an early advocate of the nonuse of slave-grown products, a movement of greater consequence than its scant discussion in historical literature would suggest. Hicks urged also that upon emancipation, the Black people be given land in the West and that when legal requirements were met, their settlement be admitted into the Union as a state.[13] This idea, in various forms, also has a long and fairly important history, though, again, accounts of it are rare.

The early emancipationist societies, as in Delaware and North Carolina, from the late 1790s to the end of the 1820s maintained an active propaganda against slavery, offered legal advice to the free Blacks, helped rescue those illegally enslaved, freed some from kidnappers, maintained schools for the children of free Black people, and "frequently disputed [ideas of] the natural inferiority of Negroes." Many such emancipationists, finding slavery intolerable and their own efforts not successful, migrated from the South, especially into Ohio, Illinois, and Indiana. Numbers among them became significant participants in subsequent anti-slavery efforts.[14]

One such migrant, a woman "of humble origins," in leaving the slave area and settling in Salem, Ohio, put her thoughts about this move in an old schoolbook. The historian who has rescued this stated that it was written in 1812 by Mary Hamlin.[15] It blasted not only slavery, but the pretensions of racism used to justify the sin:

> Here no domineering
> No cursing or swearing

Nor nocking poor negroes about....
Ohios fine stream
Has the foremost claim
Of Liberty here upon earth
All colours are free
In Equality
All equal all free from birth....
Poor African tribe
How shall I describe
The hardship that they undergo
In supporting our pride
And debauch us beside.

It was in this period and in Ohio that there appeared the fundamental contribution of Benjamin Lundy to the struggle against slavery and racism—and he always combined the two. Lundy (1789–1839), born in New Jersey of Quaker parentage, happily has found an excellent biographer.[16]

By the early 1800s the widely traveled Lundy was in Ohio and there was a main founder, in Mount Pleasant in 1815, of the Union Humane Society. He shortly gave up his saddlery occupation and devoted all his time to the effort to end slavery and racism. This involved his founding a paper, the *Philanthropist*, and in 1821 the *Genius of Universal Emancipation*; Garrison joined this paper eight years later as its associate editor. The *Genius* ceased in 1835; the next year Lundy founded in Philadelphia the *National Enquirer*. Shortly after Lundy's death this was taken over by John Greenleaf Whittier and issued under the title *Pennsylvania Freeman*.

The Union Humane Society's constitution (drafted by Charles Hamilton) was adopted in April 1816. Its outlook was based upon the Golden Rule and the Declaration of Independence. Merton Dillon summarized:

It would try to end racial prejudice by seeking to repeal legal disqualifications and to remove other impediments to civil rights, help Negroes already freed to become useful members of society.... Clearly, though the society hoped to see slavery ended, its chief activity would be to aid free Negroes and to eliminate racial prejudice and legal discrimination.

Typical of the views propagated by this society were those expressed by a newcomer to the area from New York City, a young lawyer, Thomas Hedges Genin. In May 1818 Genin—then twenty-two years old—addressed the society's semiannual meeting. He advocated emancipation and attacked the recently formed American Colonization Society because, he said, its program and the rationalization for that program would serve to "perpetuate and extend" racism. What was required, said this Humane Society speaker, were efforts to enhance the rights and condition of free Black people and not to project idle and prejudiced notions of deportation. Genin insisted that the African American "is not inferior to the rest of mankind." He added that Africa had been a center of highly advanced civilizations. Emancipation and an egalitarian America—in his words, "a biracial America"—were Genin's vision; in projecting it he summed up the society's outlook.

Dillon chose a contribution to the *Genius* in November 1821 by one signed "Humanitas" as "neatly summing up both the secular and religious aspects" of its message:

If "life, liberty, and the pursuit of happiness" are undeniable rights of man, if "all the nations of men who dwell upon the earth are created of one blood"; if all are sons of one common father, and equally objects of a Redeemer's love, let the professors of Christianity arise from their thoughtless lethargy.

Commenting on Lundy's outlook, Dillon observed that "even some confirmed opponents of slavery" found it difficult—in some cases, impossible—to give up racist concepts. But Lundy was firm on this; he had burned out such ideas. In a letter written in 1825 he insisted: "The odious distinctions between white and black, etc., have all been created by tyrants and their co-adjutors for the express purpose of acquiring and preserving their *usurped authority*. This is the Alpha and Omega of it." Dillon aptly concluded his study of Lundy:

He never veered from his faith in human equality and that view of the source of prejudice. All other true Abolitionists agreed with him that the conditions imposed by slavery were responsible for the apparent inferiority of American Negroes. Free the slaves, educate them, cease oppressing them, and they would prove as capable of achievement as other men.

Substantially similar views appeared from other sources at this time. For example, the idea, already expressed, as we noted, in the seventeenth century, reappeared that if slavery continued, slave insurrections would occur. When they did, it was asked, who would deny the justness of the rebels' cause? This was, for example, the argument of Jesse Torrey in 1816, John Kenrick in 1817, and John Rankin (another émigré from Virginia to Kentucky) in 1823. Also, they expressed belief in the equality of all humanity. Rankin, for example, demanded: "What people have ever given stronger marks of genius than are exhibited by the enslaved Africans in America?"[17]

Sarah Wentworth Morton (1759–1846) was a prominent member of Boston's literary circle in the early nineteenth century. Her *My Mind and Its Thoughts* was published in 1823—a year after Denmark Vesey was executed. Particularly catching the eye of contemporaries was her poem, "The African Chief," in that work. Its theme was the justice of the chief's seeking freedom by force—that freedom that had been taken from him by force. Its most severe condemnation was for "the hard race of pallid hue. Unpracticed in the power to feel."[18]

The schools for Black children established by the New York Manumission Society conducted "public exhibitions" of the accomplishments of their students. These evoked serious doubts as to the validity of concepts of African American inferiority. The historian of that society observed that these exhibitions "admirably succeeded in dispelling reservations in the minds of many as to the practicality of educating Negro children." He cited as an example of this impact an 1817 letter published in the New York *Monthly Magazine*, written by one who had attended such an exhibition. It had convinced him, he wrote, "that Negroes are abundantly endowed by nature with every moral and intellectual faculty and were capable of repaying the most assiduous culture."

At the exercises conducted by this school in 1824, one of its students reminded guests that "God hath made of one blood all nations of men"; where, he asked, "is the advocate of our cause that dares to lift the voice of truth, and shake a continent with its admonitions?" No wonder the editors of the New York *Commercial Advertiser*, having attended these exercises, stated (May 12, 1824) that their level was as high as that of any other school they had ever witnessed. They concluded: "Those who believe, or affect to believe, that the African race are so far inferior to the whites, as to be incapable of any considerable degree of mental improvement, would not require any stronger testimony of the unsoundness of their opinions."[19]

Far from Virginia and Philadelphia, New York and Ohio, the Reformed Presbyterian Church in Ryegate, Vermont, through its minister, the Reverend James Milligan (who was born in Scotland in 1785 and came to the United States in 1802), was precipitating controversy in 1819 by not only demanding the immediate end of slavery but also calling for "full integration of Afro-Americans into American society."[20]

The North Carolina Manumission Society (1816–1834) consisted mostly of Quakers; the society's top membership seems to have been some two thousand. They did not agree as to how manumission was to proceed, but they did agree that somehow it had to be accomplished. According to one of its chroniclers, they were "unanimous in their opposition to ideological racism." One member, writing from Stokes County in 1824, insisted that the idea of Black inferiority was false and that "when the shackles of slavery are out of the question [African Americans] exhibit as bright talents as persons of a lighter complexion," if given proper educational opportunities. They would then, he thought, be "fit examples of imitation even for the whites in the seminaries of the United States." Two years later, Nancy D. Hunt of Guilford County, warning of the likelihood of slave insurrections, declared the argument of inferiority "a position as remarkable for its selfishness as for its absurdity and villany."[21]

This North Carolina society published in 1830 *An Address to the People* that insisted that "Negroes are *human beings*, and are capable of loving, of being endeared to each other.... liberty is the *unalienable right* of every human being.... God has made no difference in this respect between the *white* and *black*." The *Address* urged, therefore, that measures be adopted for gradual emancipation and that provision be made for the education of the African American population.[22]

The question of slavery agitated the membership of the Presbyterian church in Kentucky and Tennessee in the 1820s and early 1830s. Thomas T. Skillman, editor of the *Western Seminary* from its founding in 1823 to his death ten years later, made of his Lexington, Kentucky, paper so vigorous an opponent of slavery that on his death Garrison penned a glowing tribute.

Robert J. Breckinridge walked out of the Kentucky Synod in 1833 because it was not as vigorously anti-slavery as he desired. In a church periodical, the *Biblical Repertory*, in July 1835, he declared that slavery was "utterly abhorrent from every word of God." He insisted: "The man who cannot see that involuntary domestic slavery, as it exists among us, is founded on the principle of taking by force that which is another's has simply no moral sense."

The anti-slavery of others in Kentucky and Tennessee at this time—including Hugh Bass, James C. Barnes, and Will Breckinridge—exuded contempt for the idea of the inhumanity of those enslaved. The Manumission Society of Tennessee published in 1823 an address whose point was that God had created all people as equal in every essential respect, temporal as well as spiritual. The address specifically rejected the idea that Africans "are a stupid kind of people" and urged, therefore, that they "be placed on the common footing of humanity."[23]

Numerous essays appeared in the 1820s in the upper South denying African inferiority. These ridiculed apologists for slavery who oppressed the slaves and then used the results of that oppression as justification for their criminal behavior. James B. Stewart, who brought together many such essays, concluded that in several cases their authors considered slavery to be "an unvarnished sin." They believed, Stewart added, that "those enslaved were fully equal to whites."[24]

One of the most explicit attacks upon racist ideas was contained in a pamphlet published in 1820. This was a sermon by Josephus Wheaton, pastor of the church of Holliston, Massachusetts. Wheaton, expressing traditional Christian views, insisted upon the equality of all human beings: equality in mental endowment, in moral quality, in proneness to sin, in immortality of soul, and in possession of inalienable rights that may be restricted or obliterated by evil acts but cannot be denied in essence. These were indeed, Wheaton insisted, part of the quality of any human being, and, of course, they were enunciated in the Declaration of Independence. One could not be, he continued, a Republican and a slaveholder; a slaveowning republic was a contradiction in terms.

Wheaton insisted that evidence abounded of the splendid qualities of the African and of civilizations in Africa. In any case, however, he went on, the

Africans' right to freedom and to all civil rights was indubitable; withholding them was wicked. Such wickedness surely would incur the wrath of the Lord; if persisted in, it would produce a fearful calamity, an awful punishment from an outraged Creator.

Immediate emancipation might not be practical, said Wheaton, but measures must be instituted at once with the clear object of the speedy termination of the abomination. Terribly distressing were congressional actions just taken (what are now called the Missouri Compromise) because these assured the expansion of slavery. They projected not its termination but rather its enhanced stability.

Wheaton closed with a plea for prayers that the Lord might delay his judgment and that the path of righteousness would be followed in time to prevent disaster. Here is a sampling from this sermon, whose author remains obscure:

> Thus it appears that notwithstanding the variety of peculiarities by which mankind are distinguished from each other, they not only belong to the same species, but are all equal in respect to their natural faculties, their moral agency, their original characters, their immortality, and their native rights....
>
> But let us remember that all mankind are naturally equal. The negro is equal in many respects, especially in his natural rights, with those who enslave him. His life, liberty and happiness, are as valuable to him as ours are to us....
>
> The slaves are men and naturally equal with those who hold them in bondage.
> ...
>
> Yes, strange as it may seem, in these United States there are not less than *twelve hundred thousand slaves*. Such a number of our fellow men, whose native rights are equal, and whose civil privileges ought to be equal with our own, are held in unwilling and perpetual servitude among us.[25]

It was common for those who condemned slavery to charge the defenders of it on the basis of the alleged inferiority of its victims with gross hypocrisy. Typical, for example, was the remark of Joseph Doddridge, an Episcopal minister in western Virginia, made in 1824, that "we debase them [the slaves] to the condition of brutes and then use that debasement as an argument for perpetuating their slavery." Carl Degler, in calling attention to this, found it quite "remarkable" for "condemning the racial defense of the institution."[26] On the contrary, such argumentation was frequent. Rather than being remarkable, in its time and place it was far from unusual.

We may continue the display of such evidence. John Finley Crow, a Presbyterian minister, was a leader of the Kentucky Abolition Society. In the May–June 1822 issue of the *Abolition Intelligencer and Missionary Magazine*, published in Shelbyville, Kentucky, he cited the Bible's teaching that blacks were "not an inferior race, fit, from the constitution of their nature, only to serve." No, he insisted, they "are men of the same [human] race, possessing the same original power" as those who owned them.[27]

In the 1820s were composed the *Letters on American Slavery* by John Rankin, another émigré from the slave South, at this time pastor of the Presbyterian Church in Ripley, Ohio. These letters to the author's brother, Thomas Rankin, a slaveholder in Virginia, contain powerful attacks upon slavery. They are particularly marked by repeated insistence upon the equality of the African American. Among them, Rankin wrote, "are many who possess the strongest powers of mind." All humans, he held, had a common origin, "and consequently possess precisely the same nature." The Africans "possess all the original properties of human nature, and consequently are capacitated for freedom"; they were, in fact, "created for freedom." In mental endowment "they are naturally equal to the rest of mankind." Rankin called special attention to the activities of the Union Presbytery of East Tennessee, which had manifested its opposition to slavery and its confidence in the capacity of the African by making possible the emancipation of several. Some, said Rankin, had already demonstrated how able they were; he cited especially the Reverend John Gloucester in Philadelphia.[28]

James Duncan's *A Treatise on Slavery* is still another publication of the 1820s (it was first published in 1824). It was a fierce assault upon slavery and upon its rationalization, the alleged inferiority of the Black people. Again, Duncan's point was the scriptural and secular objections to slavery; the institution violated the Golden Rule and denied the equality of human beings, a basic teaching of Christianity.[29]

Alice D. Adams called attention to the appearance in 1825 and 1826 in the *Boston Recorder* of essays denouncing slavery and insisting upon the common humanity of all races.[30] These essays urged not only a policy of emancipation but also that such a policy should be accompanied by assistance and provision of education for the victims of oppression.

The colonization movement, begun in December 1816, was the creation of slaveowners and was subsidized by some slave states; its basic purpose was to further the removal of free Blacks from the United States in order to make slavery more secure. It did attract, however, some people who favored slavery's demise. Its propaganda reflected these opposite positions. Most of it was devoted to affirming Black racial inferiority as requiring colonization; some of the essays its organ published, however, insisted that with an altered environment Black people would be able to build an adequate, even an admirable, civilization.

One finds, therefore, an occasional essay in the organ of the American Colonization Society praising early African civilizations, suggesting that Haiti's independence affirmed the African's competence, and citing outstanding personalities of African descent and educational successes by African people; illustrated by reference, for example, to the work of Anthony Benezet. These, while rare coming out of such a source, did constitute another strand challenging dominant racist ideology; from time to time they were noticed by genuine fighters for African American liberation.[31] By 1829

Henry Clay, the Kentucky slaveowner (then secretary of state), privately affirmed his belief that the African Americans were "rational human beings, like ourselves capable of feeling, of reflection, and of judging what naturally belongs to them as a portion of the human race."[32]

13

Lane Rebels and Black Rebels

What Henry Clay was thinking in 1829 was what another Kentuckian bearing a name as distinguished in his state's history as that of Clay published in 1830 in the *Kentucky Reporter*. This was from Robert J. Breckenridge:

Men will not always remain slaves. No kindness can soothe the spirit of the slave. No ignorance, however abysmal, can obliterate the indelible stamp of nature, whereby she decreed man free. No cruelty of bondage, however rigorous, can suppress forever the deep yearnings for freedom.[1]

The thoughts of Clay and Breckenridge reflect their class's awareness, as the 1820s closed, that something electrical and fearful was throbbing in their society. This is why, beginning in the late 1820s and reaching a crescendo shortly before the Nat Turner cataclysm of August 1831, Southern states passed new laws further restricting the rights of free Blacks and further inhibiting the activities of slaves. This is why, also, federal reinforcements were sent in this same period to forts in North Carolina, Virginia, and Louisiana.

Never were the slaves in the United States more restless—so many flights, so much maroon activity, so many plots and uprisings, so much slave-created arson and poisoning. Furthermore, in the 1820s, with increasing frequency as the decade waned, reports reached the Southern press of serious slave unrest in Martinique, Puerto Rico, Cuba, Antigua, Tortola, Demerara, Barbardos, St. Lucia, Grenada, Dominica, Trinidad, and Jamaica.

Not unrelated to the 1829 and 1830 statements from Clay and Breckenridge were the efforts in Kentucky in the closing months of 1829 to hold a constitutional convention, one of the purposes of which, some insisted, was the adoption of measures pointing to the termination of slavery. The effort to convene such a convention failed, but news of it was broadcast. Further, in 1830 a bill aimed against slavery was introduced in Kentucky's legislature. True, its consideration was postponed indefinitely—that is, it was killed—but the vote to postpone showed eleven opposed to eighteen in favor. It was this Kentucky activity that moved Hezekiah Niles to remark in his influential periodical: "We have no desire to meddle with the general question of slavery—it *must* be met sometime, though probably not in our day."[2]

Very important, indeed, in creating among slaveowners a feeling that something new and threatening was in the air was the publication in 1829 of David Walker's *Appeal to the Colored Citizens of the World*, which reached its third printing by 1830. The literature on this astonishing work with its amazing title is by now abundant, and its sensational impact upon the South has been elucidated. Walker's work itself reflected the mounting organizational activity of the Northern African American population, for example, the appearance in 1827 of *Freedom's Journal* in New York City (for which Walker served as an agent) and the beginning of the Black people's convention movement.

This period witnessed the rising impact of Lundy's work, Garrison's joining him, the jailing of Garrison, and the great effectiveness with which Garrison turned his cell into a fount of agitation against slavery. All this—and much more, of course—eventuated in the appearance of the national crusade for the abolition of slavery. This crusade was led by professional revolutionists, men and women, Black and white, with most classes of society represented but with the greatest numbers coming from the poorer farmers, the artisans, and the budding urban working class. This, again, was part of a great international movement to end slavery, a movement with important strength in England, Scotland, Ireland, France, and Germany.

Fundamental to this organized assault upon slavery was an intensified attack upon racism. Here, again, the direct victims, the African American people, played the pioneering and decisive role. Yet here, too, success could come only with Black-white effort. Just as in the movement against slavery, women of both colors played a key role, so in the attack upon racism, women were outstanding. The special meaning of slavery for women is plain. Of great consequence in the related but not identical struggle against racism was the fact that the content of racist slanders against people of African origin was nearly indistinguishable from the male-chauvinist characterization of women.

The organized Abolitionist movement had three goals: (1) to end slavery; (2) to improve the condition of the free Black population; (3) to extirpate racism. In an earlier work I paid some attention to the anti-racism component within the Abolitionist movement. Now I will bring forward the argumentation against racism that was part of abolitionism more fully than was possible before.[3] While white participants in abolitionism often did suffer from racist failings—especially in showing paternalism—the main point is that they were participants, often at very great hazard, in a vital emancipation effort with anti-racism central to its character.

Just as the argument against the participation of women in abolitionism was held by some to be diversionary and therefore harmful, so it was argued at times that fighting against slavery was difficult enough, that resisting racism was something else and indeed diversionary to the main purpose. Particularly illustrative of this latter view were the well-known Lane Seminary debates on slavery early in the 1830s. As a result of that exhausting event, the students not only organized an anti-slavery society but also set themselves the task of discovering the reality of the situation of Black people where they were and notably in Cincinnati. They opened schools and Bible classes and earned the friendship of Black people while seeking to combat actively the discriminatory reality that marked that city.[4]

Especially active in the Lane Rebels' attack upon racism were Augustus Wattles and Marius Robinson. They were convinced, as their comrade, Henry B. Stanton, wrote, that "prejudice was vincible; that being a sin it could be repented of, being a folly it could be cured." Wattles finally directed four schools with five teachers servicing two hundred African American students in Cincinnati.

Theodore Weld, a leader of the student rebellion, wrote to Arthur Tappan in New York City on April 12, 1833: "We have formed a large and efficient organization for elevating the colored people in Cincinnati." Lyman Beecher, the head of Lane, found the insistence upon discussing slavery on the campus distressing enough, but this activity of meeting directly with and learning from the African American population was simply impermissible. Hence he wrote Weld: "You are taking just the course to defeat your own objects. If you want to teach colored schools I can fill your pockets with money, but if you will visit in colored families, and walk with them in the streets, you will be overwhelmed."[5]

Relevant at this point, though interrupting for a moment the continuity of this narrative, is an earlier experience of Beecher.[6] He had helped established the Cornwall Foreign Missions School in Litchfield, Connecticut, in 1819. Youths from Polynesia, China, and Japan, as well as American Indians, were students. In 1823 a former student, John Ridge, an Indian, and Sarah Northup, daughter of the school's steward, were married. This aroused some opposition; the editor of the local paper suggested that the bride's mother deserved drowning, the groom hanging, and the bride a lashing. This seems not to have transpired. Soon, however, Harriet Gold also chose to marry an Indian, Elias Boudinet. The bride was burned in effigy, and Beecher publicly denounced the marriage as an insult to the community. The couple remained "unrepentant." The school closed in 1826.

The Lane Rebels (they included Blacks and whites, and several among the latter were from the South) would have none of their principal's advice. On the contrary, one of the several white women in Cincinnati, Mrs. Phebe Matthews Weed, attracted to the Lane Rebellion, "perfectly identified herself with the scorned and persecuted class.... She lived in their families, made them her companions, linked herself to their lot, shared with them their burdens and their bonds."[7] Mrs. Weed wrote to Weld in March 1838 of her experiences teaching Black people: "I cannot conscientiously acknowledge that in point of intellect they are in the least inferior to the whites."[8] Weld's own behavior was the same as that of Mrs. Weed. In 1836 he wrote:

> If I ate in the city [Cincinnati] it was at their Tables. If I slept in the City it was in their homes. If I attended parties, *It was theirs—weddings—theirs—Funerals— theirs—Religious meetings—theirs—Sabbath schools—theirs—Bible classes—theirs.* During the 18 months that I spent at Lane Seminary, *I did not attend Dr. Beecher's church once.* Nor did I ever attend any other of the Presbyterian Churches in the city except Asa Mahan's and did not attend there more than half a dozen times.[9]

Lane's student rebellion led to the invigoration of Oberlin, which was thenceforward to be committed to the rejection of racism. In practice for most of its history this commitment was real and pervasive in its teaching. If a student found this lesson indigestible, that student was expelled. As one of the teachers, the Reverend Henry Cowles, put it: "Our great business here is to educate mind and heart, and we should deem ourselves to have small cause to be proud of our success if we should fail to eradicate, in no long time, the notion that 'nature' has made any such difference between the colored and the white 'classes' that it would be wrong for either to associate with the other."

Presidents Asa Mahan and James H. Fairchild exemplified anti-racist commitment. The same was true of such teachers as John Morgan, Henry E. Peck, James Monroe, and Norton S. Townshend. Certain students like Edward Daniels and the women admitted to Oberlin as part of its revolutionary practice, especially Lucy Stone and Antoinette Brown (the latter, in theology, admitted only as an auditor) also actively combatted racism. African American students were few in the pre–Civil War period, but those who did attend—John Mercer Langston is an outstanding example—found such faculty and such students genuine companions in a common teaching and learning experience. It must be added, however, that except for Fanny Jackson, hired in 1864 to teach preparatory students, there were no African Americans on the Oberlin faculty until 1948.[10]

The Tappan brothers, Arthur and Lewis, were effective Abolitionists; it is probably true, however, that it was their commitment to fighting racism, more than that against slavery, that was the main cause of the vehemence with which they were attacked. Even the leading evangelist Charles G.

Finney (1792–1875) wrote Arthur Tappan in 1836 that his insistence upon fighting against the separation of the races was harmful. "Abolition," he wrote, "is a question of flagrant and unblushing wrong. A direct and outrageous violation of fundamental right. The other is a question of prejudice that does not necessarily deprive any man of any positive right."

The significance of Finney's objection is illuminated when it is borne in mind that he was a leader of the Ohio Anti-Slavery Society in the 1830s. In his *Lectures on Systematic Theology* (1846) Finney affirmed what came to be called the "higher law" doctrine: "No human constitution," he wrote, "or enactment can, by any possibility, be law that recognizes the right of one human being to enslave another."[11] Finney served as president of Oberlin College from 1851 to 1865. He favored separation of Black and white students, but this was not instituted, with objection coming especially from the Tappan brothers.[12] The question of Black-white and male-female education at Oberlin illuminates the matter of racism even among white people who rejected slavery.

It was agreed that anti-slavery was the correct posture, but the admission of Black students, especially men, was another matter. When a questionnaire was presented in 1834 to the students "as to the practicality of admitting persons of color," the vote went in opposition, thirty-two to twenty-six. But leaders behind Oberlin's drive for integration, like Asa Mahan, John Morgan, and John Jay Shipherd, fought this question through together with sympathetic students, male and female. Early in 1835 it was agreed that Oberlin would be coed and Black-white, a decision that, at the time, made Oberlin "odious" to many. Yet the policy was maintained. By 1846 a leading figure at the institution explained: "The white and colored students associate together in this college very much as they choose. Our doctrine is that *mind* and *heart* not *color*, make a man and a woman too. We hold that neither men nor women are much the better or much the worse for their *skin*."[13]

As to the position of Finney that combatting racism detracted from the anti-slavery effort, the Abolitionist movement as a whole, and especially the African American component thereof, argued precisely the opposite. They held that the "prejudice" grew out of and sustained slavery. To attack slavery effectively, they insisted, required attacking its basic rationalization. Attacking that rationalization went to the root of attacking slavery and seeking an egalitarian society. Of fundamental force in the argument was the insistence that the teaching of Jesus and the commitment of the Declaration of Independence and of the Constitution's Preamble posited the rejection not only of slavery but also of racism.[14]

This was at the heart of the historic debate on slavery held in Virginia's legislature in 1831–32, hard on the heels of the Turner uprising and the repression and terror that followed. While the emancipationist intent of this Virginia debate has been somewhat exaggerated, the content of the debate was profound. Descriptions of the merciless nature of slavery were offered that were never surpassed, and these were cited repeatedly in the anti-slavery movement.[15]

While later historians have commented upon this debate quite extensively, they have generally ignored its anti-racist qualities and have concentrated rather upon objections to slavery. The fact is that in this debate by members of the Virginia legislature there were many expressions affirming the humanity of the slaves, and some were directed clearly against the dominant racist position. These appeared in the Virginia press of the time and were widely used as part of the anti-slavery effort in ensuing years.

The debate as a whole reflected the division between western counties, where slavery was a relatively minor factor and anti-slavery expressions were not uncommon, and the central and eastern counties, where the opposite was true.[16] Here attention will be called to those remarks that undercut the racist basis of the slaveholders' social order. Thus Samuel M. Moore of Rockbridge County on January 11, 1832, spoke of the evils of slavery and thought that none could deny that slavery "is an act of injustice, tyranny and oppression," for "to hold any part of the human race in bondage against their consent" could only thus be characterized. The right "to the enjoyment of liberty," he said, "is one of those perfect, inherent and inalienable rights which pertain to the whole human race." Twelve days later, Moore again turned to the Declaration of Independence and noted that when it said men it did not say white men. Further, he could not believe that anyone could reconcile slavery with the basic teachings of Christianity, which insisted upon the equality of all humans and the vitality of the Golden Rule.

William Preston of Montgomery County on January 16, 1832, implicitly justified the insurrection that had sparked the debate when he said: "The love of liberty is the ruling passion of man, it has been implanted in his bosom by the voice of God, and he cannot be happy if deprived of it." The next day, Preston made clear his quite subversive beliefs by the disingenuous device of denying his own utterances:

I will not advert to the great principles of eternal justice, which demand at our hands the release of these people—I will not examine, here, the authority upon which one part of the human family assumes the right to enslave the other—I will not open the great volume of nature's laws, to ascertain if it is written there that all men are alike in the sight of Him, who must regard with equal beneficence, the creatures of his hands, without distinction of color or condition.

Philip A. Bolling of Buckingham County on January 25, 1832, thought that if a person of some decency might possibly justify slavery, surely such a one could not justify the trade in slaves: "Dividing husbands and wives, parents and children, as they would cut asunder a piece of cotton cloth. They have hearts and feelings like other men. How many a broken heart— how many a Rachel mourns because her house is left unto her desolate."

Other delegates repeated this idea of the humanity of the African American and that because they were human, nothing could or would extinguish their craving for freedom—and this was enunciated on the heels of an uprising of slaves. In the course of insisting on these points, George L. Williams of Harrison County on January 19, 1832, denied assertions that the slaves were content. Such assertions, he insisted, could not be true because "the poorest tattered negro... feels within him that spark which emanates from the deity—the innate longing for liberty.... No human being was ever born without the wish for liberty implanted in his soul."

James McDowell of Rockbridge County, two days later, agreed with his colleague from Harrison County. The slaves, he said, were human beings. That meant, he went on, that no matter how oppressed one among them might be, still, "the idea that he was born to be free will survive it all." Then using an image that had to distress those who had just witnessed the wrath of Nat Turner and his comrades, McDowell said that this indelible yearning to be free "is a torch that [is] lit up in his [the slave's] soul by the hand of the Deity and [is] never meant to be extinguished by the hand of man."

Basic to the defense of slavery was the fact that slaves were legally sanctioned property. Surely no one was so fanatical as to question the sanctity of property rights. While this idea was asserted in the debate, even it was contested—indirectly, it is true, but contested. The argument again rested precisely upon the humanity of the slave, this ineradicable peculiarity of the "peculiar institution."

Thus John A. Chandler of Norfolk, arguing on January 17, 1832, in favor of colonization so that Virginia might not be overwhelmed by the increasing number of Africans, noted that the gentleman from Brunswick County had demanded, "Are not our slaves our property?" Others, Chandler observed, had agreed with this. Chandler went on: "As a Virginian, I do not question the master's title to his slave; but I put it to the gentleman, as a man, as a moral man, as a Christian man, whether he has not some doubt, of his claim being as absolute and unqualified as that of other property?"

Here was put the issue to which a later legal scholar referred in the title of his book *Justice Accused: Antislavery and the Judicial Process.*[17] While that process, being pragmatic, had adopted as its defense what Justice John McLean had said when sending a fugitive back to slavery, "The law is our only guide," nevertheless he had added, "It is admitted, by almost all who have examined the subject, to be founded in wrong, in oppression, in power against right." In the words of John Chandler of Virginia and of Justice McLean doing his duty, one hears the cry of Nat Turner when a court-appointed interrogator had demanded of the doomed one an admission that what he had done was wrong: "I do not feel guilty, I have not done wrong." Then Turner hurled this at his questioner: "Was not Christ crucified?"

Henry Berry of Jefferson County on January 20, 1832, assured his colleagues that he had no fears "from any efforts at insurrection" because he was confident that "we have the power to crush any such effort." Still, he went on—as though driven—with all their power and with the fact that they had just enacted very "severe laws" for repression, everything seemed to be in vain. Why in vain? Because, he said, nothing "can extinguish that spark of intellect which God has given them." Yes, they kept their slaves in ignorance, said Berry of the county called Jefferson; perhaps light still penetrated their brains? Maybe the slaveowners could keep out that light, he wondered, by gouging out the slaves' eyes? No, he feared that, too, would be in vain, for "can a man be in the midst of freemen, and not know what freedom is? Can he feel that he has the power to assert his liberty and will not do it?"

What a dilemma! At its heart was the knowledge of the humanity of the slave; that knowledge tormented the slaveowner. As Jefferson the slaveowner had written, he trembled "for my county when I reflect that God is just and that his justice cannot sleep forever." Should a conflict come between slaves and those who owned them, "The Almighty has no attribute which can take side with us in such a contest."

14

Abolitionism and Racism

There is no doubt that even among a portion of the white people who were part of the Abolitionist movement, racist attitudes persisted. Black Abolitionists in particular, like Frederick Douglass, Theodore S. Wright, John S. Rock, and others pointed this out and struggled against it.[1] The tendency, however, in historical literature is to focus on this reality and to neglect the consequential fact that abolitionism as a movement was committed to struggle against racism. This commitment was understood to be an indispensable component of the anti-slavery effort.

The American Anti-Slavery Society in its beginnings in 1833 was a Black-white organization, from officers to members. So fundamental an instrument as the *Liberator* was a Black-white one, with most of its circulation, by far, in its crucial early period among Black people and most of its funds then also coming from them. Many of its writers and distribution agents were African American people. The third article of the 1833 society stated:

This Society shall aim to elevate the character and condition of the people of color, by encouraging their intellectual, moral and religious improvement, and by removing public prejudice; that they thus may, according to their intellectual and moral worth, share an equality with the whites, of civil and religious privileges; but the Society will never in anyway, countenance the oppressed in vindicating their rights by resorting to physical force.

The pacifist position enunciated in the final section of this article remained the position of the society and of Garrison, but as the power of the slaveholding class grew and its exercise became increasingly threatening to the political, moral, and economic viability of other components of the nation, a militant abolitionism, symbolized by John Brown, became more and more consequential.[2] Even Garrison wavered in his pacifism when civil war became a reality.

The major content of that article, however—namely, its announced purpose of "removing public prejudice" against the African American population—never was diluted. On the contrary, as the movement grew and the societal crisis intensified, the need to combat racism became more urgent. The urgency was understood and was acted upon so that anti-racism became an integral part of abolitionism.

The anti-racist commitment of the American Anti-Slavery Society reappeared in state societies. For example, here is the beginning of the stated purpose of the Maine Anti-Slavery Society organized in Augusta in October 1834: "The most high, God, hath made of one blood all the families of men." From this axiom it proceeded to urge "immediate and entire emancipation" of the slaves and added that the society "by correcting prevailing and wicked prejudices [will] endeavor to obtain for them [the free Black people] as well as the enslaved an equality with the whites, in civil, intellectual and religious privileges."[3]

In the past a few historians have called attention to this aspect of abolitionism, though the contrary view has dominated the literature. Among those in the minority has been the late Louis Ruchames. In a splendid, but largely ignored, article, he wrote: "Abolition was far more than an anti-slavery movement; among its most important efforts were those which sought to improve the social, economic and legal status of the free Negroes of the North before the Civil War, and to secure for them equal rights and opportunities."[4]

Ronald Walters was somewhat ambiguous on this point. He did write that in defining an Abolitionist one must include a "commitment to the creation of a society in which blacks would have civil equality with whites." On the other hand, he also wrote that "abolitionists generally, rank as racists," though he added, "significantly less malignantly racist than white contemporaries." In noting those who were racists in this sense, Walters referred to Wendell Phillips and Theodore Parker, but this equation is erroneous.[5] Reading Parker, one is struck by his adherence to Anglo-Saxon superiority, which manifested anti-Black and anti-Semitic features;[6] but this is not true of Phillips, whose commitment to equality and rejection of racial inferiority was unequivocal.

Abolitionists, including Phillips, did hold to divergences as marking different peoples, but this is quite different from ideas of racism. Walters did not make that distinction, but he did see that those in the movement "had to convince whites that black people were indeed men and women like themselves." They did, Walters declared, insist that "prejudice ... was not natural" but was, rather, concocted by slaveowners whose system induced the conditions among Black people that were used to rationalize racism.

John L. Thomas had earlier pointed out, in explaining the vigor with which Abolitionists rejected proposals coming from the American Colonization Society, that these proposals rested upon racist beliefs. It was, as

Thomas observed, "precisely the sweeping assumption of inferiority which the pioneer [white] Abolitionists rejected."[7] When, on February 20, 1834, Arthur Tappan and Elizur Wright, Jr., on behalf of the American Anti-Slavery Society, appointed Theodore D. Weld its agent, they provided him with "Particular Instructions" that included: "We also reprobate all plans of expatriation, by whatever specious pretenses covered, as a remedy for slavery, for they all proceed from prejudices against color; and we hold that the duty of the whites in regard to this cruel prejudice is not to indulge it but to repent and overcome it."[8]

Noteworthy in the historical literature is the rather generous space Carleton Mabee provided to an examination of "Direct Action against Discrimination" in his study of what he called "nonviolent abolitionists."[9] Illustrative was Lewis Tappan's appeal, made at an anti-slavery meeting in 1836. He urged that white comrades remember that very important in combatting racism was their own conduct: "We must eat, walk, travel, worship with people of color and show to slaveholders and their abettors at the North, that we will recognize them as brethren."[10]

White Abolitionists, alone or with African American friends, protested discrimination in public facilities by boycotts, by court suits, by petitions to government authorities, or by what a later age called "sit-ins." Black Americans had been doing these things for years and had faced assault and arrest. After a time, whites joined them—examples were Garrison, Phillips, Nathaniel Rogers, and John Collins—sometimes being physically assaulted along with Blacks, as was Collins with Douglass in combatting Jim Crow cars in Massachusetts. People like Ralph Waldo Emerson and Charles Sumner regularly rejected invitations to lectures when they learned that Jim Crow arrangements were practiced by those doing the inviting.

Sumner dramatically illustrates the shift of opinion on racism that often marked the careers of white people. In 1834, when he first saw slaves in Washington, he wrote his parents that they seemed "unendowed with anything of intelligence above ye brutes." But by 1843 he wrote Congressman Robert C. Winthrop that color should in no way determine citizenship. That same year he thanked John Jay (1817–1894), grandson of the statesman and chief justice John Jay, for sending him a pamphlet attacking caste and slavery. He wrote that racism practiced by churches calling themselves Christian was "irrational." He continued, "Professing the religion of Christ, they disaffirm that equality which he recognizes in all his presence." He added that in Rome, at a convent, he had observed an African monk who was treated with no show of prejudice; he suggested that this indicated that the Catholic church was "wiser and more Christian" than others.[11]

A similar development is apparent in Henry Wilson (1812–1875), another leading Massachusetts politician. As a young man, in the 1830s, he was a member of a twelve-man debating society in Natick. In 1836 he argued before its members that the African was mentally inferior to white people, a position with which ten others agreed, but one, identified only as Fiske, disagreed and was called a "negrophilist." But by the early 1840s, as a member of the state legislature, Wilson insisted on the equality of Black people before the law and supported an end to laws banning intermarriage and segregating the militia and the schools. By this time Wilson, who had begun life as an apprenticed cobbler, was identifying racism with class distinctions that had "so long enabled the few to oppress the many." Garrison's *Liberator* (February 25, 1842) called attention to Wilson's "honorable arguments."[12]

In the summer of 1834 a racist mob attacked a service being held in the Fourth Presbyterian Church in Newark, New Jersey. This was done not only because of the anti-slavery views of its minister, the Reverend Dr. William R. Weeks, but also because his congregation, while predominantly white, did contain Black worshippers. The minister defended his anti-slavery views and insisted that the foundation stone of the Republic was the idea of human equality. He thought it especially ironic that in a Christian church, the presence of Black and white people worshipping together should be condemned; he confessed himself unable to understand such logic or morality.[13]

Indeed, the Abolitionist movement emphasized the scandal of a segregated church. For example, the *American Anti-Slavery Almanac* for 1840, published by the society in Boston and in New York, contained this paragraph:

That hue and features, which the churches publicly deride and blasphemously criticize and scout by compelling all those who have them to act *apart, because* they have them—God approves, they are his own hand-writing upon their forms, pronounced by himself 'very good'—and to convert them into a *Badge of Degradation*, is monstrous impiety.[14]

Abolitionists vehemently and explicitly rejected racism from the beginning to the end of their effort. Garrison in the second issue of the *Liberator* (January 8, 1831) helped launch a campaign against the Massachusetts law banning marriage between white and Black people. This was part of the effort—successful in a dozen years—that took the form not only of argumentation but also demonstrations by white and Black people together (men and women). Garrison insisted that "intermarriage is neither unnatural nor repugnant to nature, but designed to unite people of different tribes and nations." The law banning intermarriage was repealed on February 24, 1843. Garrison in a letter to his English friend Richard D. Webb, written four days later, hailed this as "another staggering blow...to the monster prejudice." It would help, he thought, "establish justice and vindicate the equality of the human race."[15]

Garrison, in deliberately trying to overcome racism, sought out African American people, listened to their debates, and expressed himself as honored when asked to address one of their organizations. This was important to his education. In 1832, for example, an organization of Black people, the Female Literary Society of Philadelphia, asked him to share his views with them. After this experience, Garrison remarked: "If the traducers of the Negro race could be acquainted with the moral worth, just refinement, and large intelligence of this association their mouths would be hereafter dumb."[16]

Despite all that has been written about Garrison, I believe that insufficient attention has been paid to the direct, consistent, and vehement manner in which he attacked racism. Du Bois once noted of Florence Kelley that the insults she often faced may have arisen more from her commitment to equality in American life than to her advocacy of socialism.[17] I suggest, in a similar way, that the fierce attacks upon Garrison during and even after his lifetime may also have arisen not only because of the vehemence with which he attacked slavery but also with which he attacked racism.

Garrison attacked racism when it was manifested against the American Indian and the Irish in the United States; he especially, however, attacked ideas of African inferiority. His attack upon colonization ideas and the American Colonization Society was based primarily upon his belief that the movement and the society were permeated with racism. Characteristic is this remark from Garrison in August 1837:

Every slaveholder is a man-stealer ... [he believed] that immediate emancipation, without compensation or expatriation, is the duty of the master and the right of the slave, that prejudice against men on account of their complexion is sinful; and that the cord of caste between the white and black man ought to be burned out with fire.

In January 1838 he wrote of those who applauded the use of force by America's revolutionary fathers but drew the line on such use by the slaves: "They know that it is nothing but the sable hue of the skin, and the crisped hair of the victims, that make all the difference between the propriety of our conduct as abolitionists and that of our revolutionary fathers, which they applaud."[18]

Characteristic of Garrison was his reportage of an anti-slavery fair—those events conducted especially by women and serving as important forums for education and the raising of funds. Here is a report in the *Liberator*, January 2, 1837:

A cradle quilt was made of patchwork in small stars, and on the central star was written:

> Mother! when around your child
> You clasp your arms in love,
> And when with grateful joy you raise
> Your eyes to God above—

Think of the Negro-mother
When *her* child is torn away—
Sold for a little slave—oh then,
For *that* poor mother pray!

Of consequence in the early years of the Abolitionist movement were the writings of Charles Stuart, an English army officer. His widely circulated pamphlets were published in full in the *Liberator* (March 30, 1833; April 19, 1834). They attacked slavery, but they were noteworthy for their vehement rejection of racist notions.[19]

Among the most influential figures in the anti-slavery crusade was Lydia Maria Child; she was outstanding also for the vigor with which she rejected racism. Already a well-known author, Child chose to cast her lot with the subversive Abolitionists; especially resented by the establishment was her denunciation of ideas of African inferiority. While she was prolific, nothing had a greater impact than her first work on these subjects, *An Appeal in Favor of That Class of Americans Called Africans*, published originally in 1833.[20] James McPherson, in an introduction to a 1968 edition of that book, pointed out: "Two of its most important features are a defense of innate racial equality and an indictment of white racism in both the North and the South."[21]

In this work Child especially emphasized: "There is certainly no law of nature which makes a *dark color* repugnant to our feelings." She wondered, "Ought we to be called Christians if we allow a prejudice so absurd to prevent the improvement of a large portion of the human race?"

With great optimism she thought, "It cannot be that my enlightened and generous countrymen will sanction anything so narrow-minded and selfish." She devoted a chapter to the "Intellect of Negroes" and here offered evidence from ancient times to the present to refute concepts of racial inferiority. She dealt with reports going back to the sixteenth century from English, Spanish, French, and Portuguese observers denying its reality. She brought forward the careers of William Anthony Amo, James Derham, Thomas Fuller, Gustavus Vasa, Ignatius Sancho, Phyllis Wheatley, and others. "If we are willing to see and believe," she insisted, "we have full opportunity to convince ourselves that the colored population are highly susceptible of cultivation."

"We first crush people to the earth," she observed, "and then claim the right of trampling on them forever, because they are prostrate. Truly, human selfishness never invented a rule, which worked so charmingly both ways."

Child was among the earliest white people to observe that "by the thousands and thousands, these poor people have died for freedom." She continued: "But they have been hung, and burned, and shot—and their tyrants have been their historians! When Africans have writers of their own," she wisely prophesied, "we shall have their efforts for liberty called by the true title of heroism in a glorious cause."

She labelled racism a "ridiculous prejudice." She demanded that all civil rights be held by Black people; she insisted they should be free to marry whomever they wished. She paid tribute to pioneers in the anti-racist struggle, some, like Anthony Benezet, well known, and others, like John Kenrick of Newton, Massachusetts, still obscure. Kenrick, Child wrote, "aroused many minds to think and act upon the subject"; he contributed to local newspapers on questions of slavery and race and "gave liberal donations and circulated pamphlets at his own expense." It is clear that when Child was writing in 1833, Kenrick by then was not living.[22]

The connection between British and French personalities and organizations in these early years of the anti-slavery movement is relatively well known. Statements contesting ideas of racism also came from South Africa and were published in Massachusetts. Dr. John Philip, a Scotsman, had gone to South Africa in 1819 and very soon battled there for the equality of people of color. One of his findings was published in the *Missionary Herald* of Boston in October 1833. Here American readers learned from Dr. Philip: "So far as my observation extends, it appears to me that the natural capacity of the African is nothing inferior to that of the European . . . the people at our missionary stations are in many instances superior in intelligence to those who look down upon them as belonging to an inferior caste."[23]

Earlier, note was taken of the prominence of women in combatting racism. Among the women pioneers in this effort was Laura S. Haviland. She did produce an autobiography, but she deserves a careful modern biography. In her book Haviland argued passionately against racial (and religious) prejudices. In addition to her heroic work in assisting fugitive slaves (and helping the fabulous Calvin Fairbank), she opened a school for Black and white boys and girls in the little town of Raisin, Michigan, in 1830. She noted that prejudice manifested itself against this educational effort, but with no elaboration simply stated that it was overcome. This coeducational and integrated school carried on for some years in frontier Michigan under the dauntless Laura Haviland.[24]

One of the best-known Abolitionists—a participant from the early 1830s to the end of the Civil War—was the Reverend Samuel J. May of Massachusetts. In his memoirs he paid particular attention to what he called, in a separate chapter, "Prejudice against Color." Earlier in the book he recalled his contact with Garrison, beginning in 1830, and remarked: "He only, I believe, had had his ears so completely unstopped of prejudice against color that the cries of enslaved black men and black women sounded to him as if they came from brothers and sisters."

May recalled the powerful impact of Child's *Appeal*, especially on the matter of racism. His own church resisted segregationist practices; there were some protests, but the church held firm and overcame them. May's church served all people. May recalled the work of one Nathaniel Barney of Nantucket—like Kenrick a nearly forgotten fighter for equality. Barney,

described by May as one of the earliest Abolitionists, "denounced the prejudice against color as opposed to every precept and principle of God."
Barney boycotted means of transportation that discriminated due to color
and wrote letters to local papers denouncing the practice. Barney in fact
refused dividends from one company in which he held shares because it
practiced racial discrimination.

May pointed out that after the breaking of Jim Crow in Boston's schools
"a fair proportion of them [Black children] have shown themselves to be
fully equal to white children in their aptness to learn." Particularly important, he wrote, in combatting racism were the example and the lectures of
African Americans like J. W. Loguen, William Wells Brown, Samuel R.
Ward, Charles L. Remond, Henry H. Garnet, Frederick Douglass, "and
many more men and women who have been our faithful and able fellow-
laborers in the anti-slavery cause." He was certain that none "will presume
to speak of the inferiority" of Black people who had had the privilege of
hearing such advocates of freedom and equality.[25]

A widely circulated book issued by the American Anti-Slavery Society in
1837, compiled by Julius R. Ames, was filled with material denying the
inferiority of African Americans. Anthony Benezet was quoted to this effect,
for example. So, too, was an 1833 address by Alexander H. Everett ex-
patiating upon the absurdity of racism and adding important material on
the significance of earlier African civilizations.[26]

Another Abolitionist publication particularly strong in anti-racist argumentation was the work of Charles Olcott of Ohio. This is also of interest
since it denied the inferiority not only of African peoples but also of the
"lower classes of society." The relevant paragraph reads:

The truth is, there is no natural difference of mental capacity and ability, between
the upper and lower classes of society, nor between the different races of mankind,
as is sometimes falsely pretended. The natural abilities of the one are as good as
those of the other. Education and other means of improvement, have made all the
difference. The black race is in no respect naturally inferior, to the white or any
other race. The difference in the *condition* of the two races in this country has been
produced wholly by wicked artificial means.

This work is so extraordinary that further extensive quotation is merited:

And this pretense of inferiority is directly contradicted, by all the *recommendations*
contained in advertisements of negro sales, auctions, etc. The slaves are usually
described in such advertisements, as possessing uncommonly superior human qualities as, "likely," "smart," "very intelligent," "honest," "skillful," "experienced,"
"ingenious," "excellent," "first-rate" field-hands, cooks, grooms, coachmen, team-
sters, nurses, seamstresses, mechanics, engineers, etc., etc. No higher recommendations of the kind can be given to white persons.

Olcott, writing in 1838, expressed ideas still to be appreciated by many as the twentieth century ends. Thus: "It is my long-settled opinion, that all the physiological differences among the different races, are entirely the effect of differences in climate. But however or whatever the real causes may be, it is demonstrably certain that there is not the slightest difference in human identity or capacity, in any of the races."

Interest in this early anti-slavery work is enhanced by its explicit rejection of any idea of compensating the owners of slaves when (not if) emancipation came. On the contrary:

> In plain justice, the compensation should come *from*, not *to* the guilty slaveholder. He should pay the innocent victims of his barbarous oppressions, the wages he had robbed him of, and damages for the stripes and other cruelties he has inflicted on them. He has no *just* claim whatever to compensation for property he never *justly* owned, and the ownership of which was a continual crime of the first magnitude.

Beneath the title of this work appeared this sentence: "Compiled for the special use of Anti-Slavery lecturers and debaters and intended for public reading." Possibly the extraordinary views of Charles Olcott help account for his obscurity so far as later literature is concerned.[27]

In the year that Olcott was printing these sentiments in Ohio, Nathaniel Peabody Rogers (1794–1846), a lawyer, poet, and editor of the *Herald of Freedom*, was publishing in that organ of the New Hampshire Anti-Slavery Society, under the heading "Color-Phobia," these words: "Our people have got it.... They will die of it. It will be a mercy, if the nation does not. What a dignified philosophic malady!... Anti-slavery *drives it out* and after a while cures it. But it is a base, low, vulgar ailment."[28]

Influential in the Abolitionist movement was William Jay, son of John Jay, the first chief justice of the U.S. Supreme Court and himself hostile to slavery. The son not only rejected slavery but consistently attacked the idea of the inferiority of the African American. He was impressed with the activity and argumentation of the free Black population, especially its rejection of the program of the American Colonization Society. Writing in 1835 in a widely circulating volume, he stressed that the Colonization Society posited its program upon the alleged inherent inferiority of the Black population. This, Jay insisted, was quite false. He demanded of members of that society, many of them wearers of the cloth: "When have colonizationists warned Christians that the negro is created by the same Almighty Being, descended from the same parent, redeemed by the same Saviour, and made an heir to the same immortality as themselves?"[29]

Words from Southern missionaries to slaves sometimes rang with this same subversive note of a common humanity. Donald G. Mathews called attention to the Methodist mission to slaves; he concluded that "as a great moral cause, the mission was a noble effort to give men new life; but it was

also an ignoble effort to keep other men in bondage." He noted that the
slaves were fully aware of this paradox and told of the missionary who
asked congregated slaves, "What did God make you for?" and was taken
aback at the shouted reply: "To make a crop!" Still, as Mathews pointed
out, one found in the organ of this mission, the *Southern Christian Advocate*
(March 10, 1838), this admonition to the slaveholders, having in mind their
slaves: "They are human beings, and have the feelings of human beings—
feelings, too, with many of them as delicate and sensitive as your own, and
which demand to be respected, and carefully preserved from outrage." No
wonder Mathews wrote "of the grotesque mixture of ethics and exploitation."[30]

The anti-racist effort of many of the white women Abolitionists has been
emphasized by Gerda Lerner in her indispensable biography of Angelina
and Sarah Grimké. The essence of this was conveyed in the remarks by
Angelina Grimké to the Anti-Slavery Convention of American Women, held
in New York City in May 1837. Speaking of racism, she demanded: "Who
ever heard of a more wicked absurdity in a Republican country?" She
continued, "Women ought to feel a particular sympathy in the colored man's
wrong, for, like him, she had been accused of mental inferiority, and denied
the privileges of a liberal education."

At the next year's Anti-Slavery Convention of American Women—held
in the schoolroom of the African American teacher, Sarah Pugh, after ar-
sonists had destroyed the designated hall—a resolution was offered by Sarah
Grimké that affirmed that racial prejudice was the spirit of slavery and that
therefore it was "the duty of abolitionists to identify themselves with these
oppressed Americans, by sitting with them in places of worship, by appearing with them in our streets, by giving them our countenance in steam-
boats and stages, by visiting them at their homes and encouraging them to
visit us, receiving them as we do our white fellow-citizens."[31] This was
adopted, although not unanimously, and might well meet difficulty being
introduced, let alone adopted, even now that eighteen decades have passed.

Two years earlier, Angelina Grimké had asked in a pamphlet that attracted
wide attention, entitled *Appeal to the Christian Women of the South*: "Now
I ask *you*, is it right, is it generous to refuse the colored people in this country
the advantages of education and the privilege, or rather the *right*, to follow
honest trades and callings merely because they are colored? . . . Prejudice
against color, is the most powerful enemy we have to fight with at the
North."[32]

Lucretia Mott and Lydia Maria Child were other white women whose
denunciation of racism was as vigorous as that of the Grimké sisters. Child,
for instance, as noted earlier attacked concepts of African inferiority from
the 1830s on and never wavered in this commitment until her death in 1880.
In her *Anti-Slavery Catechism* (1839) she first remarked that if Africans
were inferior to others, that would be no reason to enslave them but rather

to offer them special assistance. In any case, she wrote, would any "consistent Republican" hold "that a strong-minded man has a right to oppress those less gifted than himself?" Further, if the slaveowners believed their own propaganda as to inferiority, why were they so careful to forbid any effort at providing learning for Black people? Did anybody think it necessary to pass laws forbidding the education of monkeys? Let those who doubted the intellectual and moral capacities of Black people, she went on, acquaint themselves with Toussaint L'Ouverture or listen to the sermons of Black ministers like Peter Williams of New York City or Robert Douglas of Philadelphia. The fact was, said Child in 1839,

> One great reason why the people of this country have not thought and felt right on this subject, is that all our books, newspapers, almanacs and periodicals, have combined to represent the colored race as an inferior and degraded class, who never could be made good and useful citizens. Ridicule and reproach have been abundantly heaped upon them; but their virtues and their sufferings have found few historians.[33]

While Child identified herself with the Abolitionist movement, one will find powerful attacks upon racism coming from others who thought it better not to so identify themselves. A notable example of this type of person was William Ellery Channing (1780–1842), who for almost forty years was minister of the Federal Street Congregational Church in Boston. In the 1820s Channing was instrumental in organizing Unitarianism; he also deeply influenced Emerson and William Cullen Bryant.

In December 1836, moved by mob assaults upon James G. Birney's Abolitionist paper, the *Philanthropist*, Channing praised Abolitionists for their heroic commitment, which made them, he said, defenders of "the most sacred rights of the white man." In this same essay Channing insisted that "he who cannot see a brother, a child of God, a man possessing all the rights of humanity under a skin darker than his own, wants the vision of a Christian."

Channing noted that some had lately discarded the concept of human equality, "so venerable in the eyes of our fathers." But he was not among them. On the contrary, Channing insisted: "All men have the same rational nature and the same power of conscience ... the diversities of the race vanish before them." The central fact, he said, was this: "He [man] cannot be property in the sight of God and justice, because he is a rational, moral, immortal being; because created in God's image, and therefore in the highest sense his child."[34]

By the late 1830s rejection of racism—sometimes not as sweeping as that by Channing—appeared fairly often, occasionally in rather surprising places. Often these statements were accompanied by considerations of class. Illustrative were the arguments in the 1837 Pennsylvania Constitutional Convention, where the question of barring Black men from the vote was debated and passed.[35] Several delegates argued against this, noting that there were Black citizens in the state "who were well educated and wealthy and who had a vested interest in the affairs of government." They pleaded that "withholding the basic right of citizenship from an entire class of people for no other reason than color was both immoral and unjust."

Actually, the first vote in the 1837 convention on limiting Black suffrage was in opposition, 61 to 49. The question arose again that fall at the reconvened convention. Petitions pro and con were presented, and newspaper comment also was about equally divided. Prominent in opposition to limiting the suffrage were James Merrill, William P. McClay, and especially Thomas Earle of Philadelphia (in 1840, the vice presidential candidate of the Liberty party). Earle insisted that "blacks were not inferior to whites." The restricted franchise was approved by the convention, 87 to 27. The constitutional changes, including that on the franchise, were approved narrowly in a popular vote of 113,971 to 112,759.

In North Carolina, two years earlier, a constitutional convention approved disfranchisement of the "free colored" population by a vote of 64 to 55. Leading the opposition was William Gaston, then on the state's Supreme Court (and earlier in Congress). Gaston's argument here anticipated that offered in Pennsylvania. Speaking of the free Black population, Judge Gaston said: "A person of that class, who possesses a freehold, is an honest man and perhaps a Christian, and I do think he should not be politically excommunicated and have an additional mark of degradation fixed upon him solely on account of his color." Gaston's biographer observed that though a slaveholder, he attacked the institution when speaking to his peers. He felt that "the Negro was a man with human feelings and passions, and with the soul and mind and every other attribute that made a man. Not only did the slave have human rights, but the freed negro, as a citizen, had civil rights."[36]

By the 1840s the crusade against slavery was of worldwide proportions and had become a dominant issue in the United States. The development of significantly different economic systems in their slave and nonslave areas, the consequent fragmenting of traditional political alignments, and the continual projection of the slavery question upon center stage assured the mounting importance of abolitionism.

The Abolitionist movement grew rapidly with hundreds of societies and thousands of members. Abolitionist lecturers addressed tens of thousands, their publications reached like numbers, and anti-slavery petitions (in some cases, anti-racist also) attracted hundreds of thousands of signatures from women and men.

A result of this—and furthering it—was widespread questioning of white supremacist thought. This built upon the not-insignificant foundation running back several generations, but now it took on a new dimension. With growing frequency in these years specific events—dramatic slave escapes and other displays of slave militancy and discontent—added to the doubts about African American inferiority.

An illustration appeared in 1839 with the *Amistad* uprising of slaves and the prolonged and rather sensational struggle that ensued to free the rebellious ones. The character of some of the *Amistad* mutineers impressed contemporaries. Thus a member of the Yale Divinity School, A. F. Williams, volunteered to be a teacher among them. Having done this, Williams wrote to Lewis Tappan, a leader of the defense effort, "that the Ethiopians are indeed a people not far below if not equal or even superior in intellect to most nations of the earth."[37]

By the early 1840s within the Abolitionist movement it had become common to emphasize the crucial importance of combatting racism. Such awareness and action existed in the earlier years, as we have shown, but in the 1840s and thereafter the anti-racist component of the movement gained a new consequence.

Illustrative are the proceedings of the Plymouth County (Massachusetts) Anti-Slavery Society meeting in 1841, reported very fully in the *Liberator* (December 10, 1841). Here Edmund Quincy—whose own private writings show that not all Abolitionists were cleansed of racism—offered the opinion that nothing could eliminate prejudice but the elimination of slavery; that "men hate those they injure."

This posture seemed to minimize the need for the struggle against racism itself, particularly in the North. When Frederick Douglass (then in his midtwenties) took the floor, he agreed that the main task was the ending of slavery, but he chose to emphasize, speaking here in the North, the poison of racism. He excoriated Jim Crow churches, for example, and he related the story of a white woman who had dreamed of being in heaven; when asked if she found Black people there, she had responded, "*Oh, I didn't go into the kitchen!*"

Douglass was forthright, knowing that his audience would listen (they had asked him to speak) and might learn. White people in the North, he went on, "say they like the colored man as well as any other, but *in their proper place*," and "they assign us that place.... They treat us not as men, but as dogs." Douglass concluded that nothing was worse, of course, than slavery—that damnable system "that sold my four sisters and my brother in bondage." That was the ultimate wrong, but racism was also wrong, and it stemmed from slavery and held it up.

Garrison followed soon after; he strongly concurred on the sinfulness of racism and its service in sustaining slavery. A resolution condemning racist prejudice and conduct was offered for a vote; some anonymous voices seemed to be opposed, but when they were called upon to come forward and explain their objections, none did. The resolution was put to a vote, and no negative one was offered. Certainly chauvinism existed, even here among partisans of abolitionism, but this was an exercise, and a powerful one, in excising it. The episode shows the deeply anti-racism commitment of the movement.[38]

Reflecting this concern with combatting racism was the fact that a widely dispersed publication of the American Anti-Slavery Society contained a section, "The African Character." This went back to Herodotus and forward to the British explorer Mungo Park (1771–1806) with a quotation from the latter: "I was fully convinced that whatever difference there is between the negro and the European, in the conformation of the nose, and the color of the skin, there is none in the genuine sympathies and characteristic feelings of our common nature." Repudiation of racism is the essence of this volume.[39]

Important in the anti-racist emphasis in this stage of the anti-slavery movement was the work of the Englishman Wilson Armistead. In 1848 his *A Tribute for the Negro* was published and thereafter often used in the United States.[40] Armistead edited *Five Hundred Thousand Strokes for Freedom: A Series of Anti-Slavery Tracts*, which first appeared in 1853. Several of the tracts had been published in the earlier decade and were reprinted; some were devoted largely to anti-racism, like number 13, a poem "The Negro Our Brother Man," and number 79, "Intellect and Capabilities of the Negro Race," which affirmed equality and brought forward examples of outstanding African American figures like Banneker.

William Jay, earlier referred to, continued to his death in 1858 to attack racism. He insisted, for instance, in an 1846 work, that while some might find slavery in the Bible and draw conclusions excusing it, none could possibly find in the Scriptures or in Christ's teaching any justification "of CASTE in the Church." No, the "injustice and cruelty" connected with it were based "simply and frankly on pecuniary interest, personal antipathy and popular prejudice." This practice stood condemned, Jay insisted, by that religion that "commands to do good unto all men and to honor all men."[41]

While much historical literature has focused upon the racist writings of those such as Charles Caldwell, Samuel E. Morton, Josiah Nott, George R. Glidden, and George Combe working in scientific areas from the 1830s to the Civil War, anti-racist opinions from others who labored in such areas in the same period are slighted. By the 1840s and 1850s scientists like Isaac McCoy, Thomas McKinney, Henry R. Schoolcraft, and Lewis H. Morgan were denying racist opinions, having in mind African Americans and American Indians and—after the War of 1848—Mexicans, too.[42] The views of Albert Gallatin on the Mexicans and his vigorous denunciations of racism in general have been noticed earlier.

Another scientist of the antebellum period who questioned the postulates of racist colleagues—and finds scant space in relevant literature—was J. Peter Lesley (1819–1903), an outstanding geologist and a founding member of the National Academy of Sciences. In an 1849 letter he declared the end of slavery certain; he added that racism was false, since the "world was made...for an endless movement and mingling of races, and the gradual improvement of the whole." Some day, Lesley then prophesized, with words that seem less extraordinary with every passing day, we might yet see "a black man governor of Georgia."[43]

Jeffries Wyman (1814–1874), of Harvard, an outstanding anatomist, rejected in 1847 the then fairly widespread idea of the kinship between the orang and the African. He emphasized "the vast difference between the conformation of the same parts [of the body] in the Negro and the Orang"— this when others (like those named earlier) were insisting on similarities to bolster their notion of the separate species of the African.[44]

In England the first half of the nineteenth century witnessed the publication of James Cowles Prichard's work; especially notable was his *Natural History of Man* in two volumes, which reached its third edition by 1848. Prichard emphasized the monogenesis of humanity. His impact within the United States was considerable and helped to counteract the racist argumentation of Josiah Nott and George R. Glidden.[45]

By the 1840s significant breakthroughs had been made against racist thought and against racist regulations and laws. This was true not only in Massachusetts and Vermont, to which reference has already been made. In Ohio, for example, despite its Black Laws and the fact that its school system normally was segregated, some towns in the Western Reserve defied this practice and integrated their schools. David A. Gerber, indeed, has written that in some of these schools "blacks were actually welcomed." By the late 1840s a sympathetic board of education in Cleveland "began to admit blacks to the schools...resisting all segregationist efforts to create a dual school system." Within another few years "the board began the almost unheard of practice of hiring Black teachers for the city's integrated classrooms."

In Oberlin at this time, despite some reluctant trustees, the student body was mixed, and the town became a goal for African Americans seeking educational opportunities. As Gerber observed: "Under the influence of abolitionist radicalism, the races mingled in town and college with an ease rare in ante-bellum America." Occasionally letters decrying racism began to appear in non-Abolitionist papers. Thus the *Cleveland Herald*, for example, in its issue of April 19, 1845, contained a letter from H.M.T. urging the repeal of discriminatory laws, for "men of dark complexion are endowed with the same properties as the fairest race."[46]

It was in this decade that the American Missionary Association made its appearance. Formed late in 1846 "as a protest against the silence of other missionary agencies regarding slavery," its gospel was to be "free of complicity with slavery and caste." Prominent among its founders were Lewis Tappan, Simeon S. Jocelyn, Gerrit Smith, Joshua Levitt, George Whipple, and William Jackson.

Anti-slavery churches were established by the association in the South as well as in the North. Its workers were harassed by legal and extralegal forces in Missouri, North Carolina, Kansas, and Kentucky. In the latter state, one agent was seriously injured by a vicious whipping and another, John G. Fee (1816–1901), finally was driven from the state.

Fee, one of the Lane Rebels, had been disinherited by his slaveholding father because of his views. He returned to Kentucky and, on land given him by his fellow Kentuckian, Cassius M. Clay, established his home, a church, and a school and called the settlement Berea. The church and school recognized no color line. Though Fee, prior to the war, was often physically abused, he was not daunted. Thus was planted the seed of Berea College, which, from 1855 to the present—with an interruption for a few years early in the twentieth century—persisted as an oasis of equality. While Fee was forced out of Kentucky in 1859 as a victim of that year's terror, he returned in 1863 and remained a pastor of Berea's church and a trustee of the college until his death.[47]

Fee was author of *An Anti-Slavery Manual* (1848), which denounced slavery and referred to racism as an "unholy prejudice" and as "woefully defective in logic." He insisted that circumstances were decisive in determining intellectual development and pointed to the careers of many Africans as scholars, poets, philosophers, and artists as proof of their intellectual capacities.[48]

The literature on the Underground Railroad is abundant, and much of it is excellent. It sprang out of the activities of the African American people in the first place, and white assistance existed in the South and in the North from an early period—certainly by the end of the eighteenth century. In many ways it was an arm of the Abolitionist movement, yet it was considerably broader. In its often-dangerous and always-illegal work many white women and men with no particular organizational ties were involved. This is a significant part of the anti-racist tradition in the United States.

One locale, well chronicled, will be examined. Its work was duplicated in towns and villages up and down the country. In 1844 a twenty-seven-year-old slave, known later as John W. Jones, together with five comrades, fled a Virginia plantation and finally made it to the town of Elmira in New York. On the way, they had stopped, exhausted and famished, in Bradford County, Pennsylvania, a few miles south of Elmira. Hiding in a barn, they were discovered by Mrs. Nathaniel Smith; she fed them and cared for them for several days and then sent them on north.

In Elmira they separated; none was retaken. The fugitive later known as John W. Jones worked as a handyman for a Mrs. Culp. She tried but failed in efforts to get him into a school. But a neighbor, one Judge Ariel S. Thurston, was impressed with "Jones," made him a member of his family, and did get him into school.

Shortly, John W. Jones became a respected member of the Elmira community, sexton of the First Baptist Church, and custodian of the town's two cemeteries. Jones soon owned his own home; it became a haven for many fugitive slaves, with much of the money for their care coming from white neighbors. Before Jones's fruitful life came to an end, he was director of the work of eleven white men in this town that had befriended him.[49]

The unity between African American people and white people in Underground Railroad activities is illuminated in the work of Thomas Garrett (1789–1871) of Delaware. Garrett assisted many slaves—numbering in the hundreds—to reach freedom. Garrett's home in Wilmington was one of the main bases used by the legendary Harriet Tubman; their paths crossed at least eight times. Garrett suffered persecution, including arrest, heavy fines, and near financial ruin, but nothing deterred him from what he insisted was the clear duty of a Christian.

Garrett worked together with William Still, the Black director of the Philadelphia center of the Underground Railroad, as well as with Harriet Tubman and several other Black men and women and with white people like John Hunn of Delaware. Garrett, a Quaker, was not satisfied with the lack of Friends' commitment to active anti-slavery work. As a result, he and like-minded Friends organized the Progressive Friends Meeting in 1852. This Meeting invited all to join who recognized "the equal brotherhood of the human family without regard to sex, color, or condition." Working with Garrett also were ship captains, especially a James Fountain and another known only as Captain Lambson; the latter was jailed in Norfolk, Virginia, for his part in assisting fugitives. Garrett's funeral brought an outpouring of thousands of mourners, Black and white. Leading the mourners were the venerable Lucretia Mott and William Still; letters were read from Garrison and Phillips and other immortals of the anti-slavery and anti-racist battle.[50]

The end of the 1830s marked the beginning of the remarkable educational work of Myrtilla Miner. She attended the Young Ladies Domestic Seminary in Clinton, New York, beginning in 1839. That school, established in 1821 by the Reverend Hiram H. Kellogg—a "work-study" institution—pioneered the admission of Black young women. Kellogg stated that he "chose to regard and treat them as *pupils*, not as colored pupils"; he added that his "confidence was not misplaced."

Here Miner had her first contact with Black people. For a few years she taught school in Mississippi—for whites only, of course—but in the 1840s she was teaching in upstate New York. In about 1850 she decided to open a school for Black children in Washington, D.C., and asked Frederick Douglass for help. He offered some, but he told Miner that he thought her chances for success were slim. She persisted. Believing, as she said, that African Americans were "decidedly intelligent and possessed of much talent," she wanted them to have the possibility of a broad education. Particularly, she wanted them exposed to "scientific intelligence."

This indefatigable Myrtilla Miner did establish a school for Black girls in Washington late in 1851. She declared in 1854 that having been a teacher for some twenty years, she did "unequivocally assert, that I find no difference of native talent, where similar advantages are enjoyed, between Anglo-Saxons and Africo-Americans." When a friend raised the "spectre of amalgamation," Miner responded with no alarm about such an eventuality; indeed, she thought that intermarriage would be quite common in future years.[51]

15

Immortals of Literature and Martyrs for Freedom

The two decades preceding the Civil War witnessed a profound questioning of racism as part of the flowering of American literature. The immortals, with the exception of Poe, generally expressed varying levels of contempt for concepts of the nonhumanity or the innate inferiority of colored people. All displayed disgust when faced by slavery itself. This was true of Whitman and Melville, of Thoreau and Stowe, of Lowell and Emerson. There is now a fairly considerable literature documenting this, and their own collected works and letters illuminate it.[1]

Herman Melville, criticizing Francis Parkman's racism, insisted in 1849 that treating other peoples with "disdain and contempt... is not defensible, and it is wholly wrong."[2] In his own *Omoo* (1847) Melville found it "a curious fact, that the more ignorant and degraded men are, the more contemptuously they look upon those whom they deem their inferior." In *Typee* (1846) Melville made clear that those people who were Black had a "claim to humanity and normal equality." His fascinating "Benito Cereno," published in 1855, has been variously interpreted; my own reading persuades me that Jean Fagan Yellin was correct when she concluded that in it Melville "used the standard literary versions of slavery and the black man, displayed their falseness, and destroyed them." The story shows, she wrote, "the stereotyped faces worn by black characters in our fiction to be masks."[3] It also shows that the racist idea of the superiority of the white man is nonsense; Yellin did not go that far, but I think that Melville's "Benito Cereno" does. Others, notably Sidney Kaplan, disagree.

With all the patronizing that so limits Harriet Beecher Stowe's *Uncle Tom's Cabin*, it is a fact that a basic component of that book was to show the contradiction between the concept of the slave as a thing, a commodity, and the reality of the slave as a man or a woman, as human. Hence, when the Southerner, Mr. Wilson, meets George, the runaway slave, and is faced with the human being, he decides against turning him in, as the law requires: "I s'pose, perhaps, I ain't following my judgment; hang it, I won't follow my judgment."

In a penetrating essay, Severn Duvall concluded: "Establishing the slave as a unique and human personality, reinforcing concrete characterization by angle of vision, she [Mrs. Stowe] then goes on to trap the white man into admitting it in word and deed. Inescapably, the Thing turns out to be a Man." In the United States of 1852 that was a blow against racism as well as against slavery.[4]

This is a good place to remark that the Fugitive Slave Law of 1850 created more opponents of slavery—if not Abolitionists—than the agitation of Garrison, Douglass, and Phillips combined. It did so for the reason indicated in Stowe's *Uncle Tom's Cabin* and Mark Twain's *Huckleberry Finn*. That law was posited upon the denial of the humanity of the African American, and that denial was at the root of the slaveowner's ideology.

Characteristic of very widespread response to that enactment was the resolution of farmers in Middlefield, Connecticut, soon after its adoption. Called together by William Lyman, one of their own, they agreed on the following public announcement:

The Fugitive Slave Law commands all good citizens to be slave-catchers; good citizens cannot be slave-catchers any more than light can be darkness. You tell us, the Union will be endangered if we oppose this law. We reply that greater things than the Union will be endangered if we submit to it. Conscience, Humanity, Self-Respect are greater than the Union, and these must be pursued at all hazards. This pretended law commands us to withhold food and raiment and shelter from the most needy—we cannot obey.[5]

Ralph Waldo Emerson, in his actions and words—in the latter case, especially his 1854 essay devastating Daniel Webster—showed his contempt for chauvinism. Thoreau, having in mind Parkman, wrote in his *Journal*: "it frequently happens that the historian, though he professes more humanity than the trapper, mountain man, or gold digger, who shoots one [Indian] as a wild beast, really exhibits and practices a similar inhumanity to him, wielding a pen instead of a rifle."

Thoreau went on to suggest that the religion of the Indian people—so defamed by many in the United States—was in no way inferior to that even of a Henry Ward Beecher. He concluded: "It is the spirit of humanity, that which animates so-called savages and civilized nations, working through a man, and not the man expressing himself, that interests us most. The thought of a so-called savage tribe is generally far more just than that of a single civilized man."[6]

Thoreau's views on the oneness of humanity help explain the passion with which he embraced John Brown—that latter-day Jesus, as he called him. The slavery and racism that polluted the nation, Thoreau believed, made it necessary for those in power to hang a John Brown.

The writings of James Russell Lowell in this pre–Civil War generation also were fiercely anti-racist. His essay "The Prejudice of Color" (1845) and his marvelous "Fanaticism in the Navy" (1848) are witnesses, as is his biting comment on "The Election in November," which appeared in the *Atlantic* (October 1860 VI: 492–502). There he insisted that "we shall continue to think the negro a man" and went on to excoriate the pretentions of racists in and out of Congress.

A quotation or two will convey the force of Lowell's feeling. In "The Prejudice of Color" he stated: "There is nothing more sadly and pitiably ludicrous in the motley face of our social system than the prejudice of color." That prejudice was "absurd" and "wicked." The revolutionary year 1848 added fuel to Lowell's condemnations of rationalization for oppression.[7] His writings then took on the character of condemnations of both class and racist oppression: of the oppression of the poor, whatever their color, reminding one of John Brown's statement to the Virginia court that was soon to condemn him to the gallows.

Referring to Lowell brings to mind the impact in the 1840s and 1850s of anti-racist works from English scientists, especially Brodie Crukshank and James C. Prichard. Prichard's *Natural History of Man* was noted earlier in this work; here it may be added that Prichard's views were popularized in such publications as the *Edinburgh Review*, read in the United States by many and commented upon at length by Lowell. The anti-racist writings of other British Africanists formed the body of *Record of an Obscure Man*, authored by Mary Putnam (Lowell's elder sister), published anonymously in 1861, and widely commented upon, especially by the Abolitionist and the African American press.[8]

Charles Sumner in the Senate in the 1850s was on the alert for evidence refuting racist notions. In this connection he wrote to Theodore Parker in 1854 for help on relevant printed sources (and got it). In 1858 Longfellow called to Sumner's attention the work of David Livingstone; Sumner wrote the poet, April 12, 1858, that "Livingstone's book puts a new gloss on the African character, and gives new scorn to the slaveholder." The book was Livingstone's *Missionary Travels and Researches in South Africa*. In it Livingstone wrote of the Africans with appreciation, commenting especially upon their artistry and skill, particularly in ironwork. Livingstone referred also to "the stupid prejudice against color."[9]

The fiction and nonfiction writing of Richard Hildreth has been expertly analyzed by Jean Fagan Yellin. His book *The Slave, or Memoirs of Archy Moore*, first published in two volumes in Boston in 1836, was reprinted in the 1850s (London, 1852; New York, 1857) and had its greatest impact in the latter period. It was an extraordinary account of an African American life written in the first person by a white man; this was done so well that it was widely assumed that the author was indeed a Black man. The book sought to undercut racism as well as to attack slavery; in both its success was notable. Hildreth's nonfiction work, *Despotism in America*, first published in 1840, also had this dual target and had some influence.[10]

At times, the reality of the humanity of the African American cut through racist mythology even in judgments from courts in slave states. Of such states, two—Tennessee and Louisiana—endowed slaves with the power of entering into contracts for the purchase of their freedom. From time to time, suits involving such laws reached the courts in those states; their validity was always upheld. Judge Green of Tennessee's Supreme Court, in rendering such a decision, said in 1846:

A slave is not in the condition of a horse. He has mental capacities, and an immortal principle in his nature, that constitute him equal to his owners, but for the accidental condition in which fortune has placed him.... the laws cannot extinguish his high-born nature, nor deprive him of many rights which are inherent in man.... he can make a contract for his nature, which our laws recognize, and he can take a bequest of his freedom, and by the same will he can take personal or real estate.[11]

Something of the passion hinted at in Judge Green's words in conveyed more dramatically in the diary of another member of the slaveholding elite, Mary Berkeley Minor Blackford (1802–1896) of Virginia. She despised slavery and put her hopes in colonization. Here she was not very unusual. But the thoughts she confided to this secret place reflect warm feelings toward slaves as human beings, with a high estimate of African Americans as people. She compared them favorably with white people. It is this feeling, this rejection of racism, so vital to the acceptance of slavery, that perhaps accounts for the passion of this paragraph penned about 1840 in her journal:

Think of what it is to be a Slave!!! To be treated not as a man but as a personal chattel, a thing that may be *bought* and *sold*, to have *no right* to your own wife and children, liable at any moment to be separated at the arbitrary will of another from all that is dearest to you upon earth and whom it is your duty to love and cherish. Deprived by the law of learning to read the Bible, compelled to know that the purity of your wife and daughters is exposed without protection of law to assault of a brutal white man! Think of this, and all the nameless horrors that are concentrated in the one word *Slavery*.[12]

If one knows that there were opinions such as these in the highest circles of Tennessee and Virginia, the hysteria that characterized decisive components of the slave-holding class as the life of its system approached termination is more easily understood.

In the pre–Civil War South, after the rulers had adopted a policy of defending slavery as a positive good and imposing severe restrictions upon expressions of an opposite view, there nevertheless persisted islands where this policy was defied. Breaking with the policy and ideology of the Bourbons meant not only objection but also, from time to time, vigorous rejection of both policy and ideology; the latter included challenges to the idea of African American inferiority.

Thus, writing about Louisiana, Charles B. Roussève declared: "When, before the Civil War, the Scottish Rite Masons in New Orleans, many of whom were Frenchmen, avowed abolitionists, and enemies of the Roman Church, adopted a resolution to admit free Negroes as members on terms of absolute equality and brotherhood, a number of free men of color forsook Catholicism for free Masonry."[13] Other facts about pre–Civil War Louisiana are relevant. Integration was the rule in the great St. Louis Cathedral in New Orleans before the war; the annual dinner of veterans of the Battle of New Orleans was integrated; a few wealthy free Black people in that city employed white servants; and it was not unknown for Black people to serve as tutors and music teachers for the children of wealthy white families.[14]

North Carolina also was home to white people who vigorously denounced slavery and questioned concepts of the inferiority of Black people. In the late 1820s and 1830s, as we have seen, this was not unique at all; William Swain, editor of the *Patriot* in Guilford County (1820–1835), is an example of such anti-slavery advocates. Later, in Jamestown, the Mendenhall family—Richard, his brother, George, and George's wife, Delphina—did not hide their abhorrence of slavery. Delphina Mendenhall, in particular, assisted Black people to get to the North; she seems to have persisted in this activity even during the Civil War.

In the 1840s several Wesleyan Methodist ministers in North Carolina—Jesse McBride, Adam Crooks, and J. C. Bacon were often mentioned—were notorious agitators, according to local authorities. They were harassed and at times arrested. McBride, after conviction, managed to flee to the North.[15]

Others from this area are relatively well known; some, in opposing slavery, nevertheless evinced racist views, but others were moved by feelings of compassion and a sense of common humanity, as well as a belief that slavery was an albatross hindering the state's progress. While Hinton Rowan Helper exiled himself and Benjamin Hedrick, after being fired from the University of North Carolina, also went north, and still others like Eli W. Caruthers, confined their anti-slavery views to private writings or to family conversation, there were instances of forthright defiance of authorities at grave peril. Daniel R. Goodloe did choose to go north; there he affiliated himself with the Abolitionist movement and became assistant editor of the *National Era* in Washington.

Daniel Worth, on the other hand, remained in his North Carolina home and continued his anti-slavery agitation. Finally, in December 1859, in the midst of the terror unleashed after John Brown's assault, Worth was arrested. He was charged with sedition—"making slaves and free negroes dissatisfied with their condition"—and also with distributing Helper's *Impending Crisis*, which was aimed at persuading Southern whites that not the slaves but the slaveowners were the source of their difficulties.

Worth was required to post bond coming to $10,000, a very considerable sum in those days. He refused and therefore spent the winter of 1859–60 in prison. At this same period several other white men, perhaps as many as ten, were arrested on charges similar to those filed against Worth. The *Raleigh Standard* was writing by early 1860 that as many as two hundred copies of Greeley's subversive *New York Tribune* were circulating in North Carolina.

Worth was convicted of sedition and sentenced to a year in jail; because of his age he was not lashed. After he had spent a difficult time in a freezing cell, the Supreme Court, on appeal, had him released on $3,000 bail. Worth went to New York, collected money to reimburse the bondsman, lost an appeal, and remained in the North. He spent his final years attacking slavery and injustice; he died in 1867.[16]

Eli Caruthers has already been noted. Caruthers (1793–1865), a Presbyterian minister, was active in community affairs in Greensboro, and occasionally published books. His views were anti-slavery, but these he did not publish. He did produce a long manuscript between 1840 and 1850 called "American Slavery and the Immediate Duty of Southern Slaveholders"; he revised this in his final year, but it remained unpublished.

The manuscript began with the assertion that in the United States "slavery originated in avarice, falsehood and cruelty." It affirmed the equal value of all people in the eyes of God and stated that this included the African American. Caruthers wanted an end to slavery but was vague as to how this might be accomplished. It appears that his views were well known to his wide circle of friends. He viewed the Civil War as God's judgment upon the slaveholding South and felt that the Confederate cause was "both unjust and without hope of success."[17]

More outspoken against slavery, though hostile to Northern abolitionism, was Samuel M. Janney of Virginia. Janney, a Quaker, privately wanted immediate abolition, but his public advocacy was more moderate. Still, since he insisted that masters had no just claim to slave property, he was indicted in 1850, but when he turned his case into a defense of the Bill of Rights, the proceedings were quashed, though he was warned to curb his pen. By the late 1850s he seems to have concluded that seeking emancipation through converting those who ruled Virginia was hopeless. Still, according to his biographer, his anti-slavery views and his insistence that Black people could function well if freed met wide acceptance, thus showing that "Virginians in the 1840's were more opposed to slavery and more receptive to anti-slavery agitation than has been generally believed."[18]

Levi Coffin, the North Carolinian who left the realm of slavery to become one of the most effective battlers against slavery, stated in his reminiscences that almost as distasteful to him as slavery was racism and the discrimination against Black people. In this invaluable source, Coffin told of a white man whom he called "Jones" from Louisville, Kentucky, who made a practice of helping slaves to flee. He was arrested, convicted, and sentenced to two years in jail. He appealed and was let out on bail; he forfeited bail and moved to Ohio. Coffin knew him in Cincinnati as a physician and therefore used a pseudonym in his case.

Two other white fighters against slavery were described by Coffin. One was John Fairfield of Virginia, who spent most of his life assisting slaves to flee. Coffin, in referring to Fairfield's activity, wrote, "There are several other such cases on record."

Among the exploits of Fairfield was one in which he helped twenty-eight slaves to flee from Virginia to Ohio. Fairfield devoted himself to this activity for at least twelve years. He went to the South, heavily armed, in slave-freeing expeditions. Coffin, a pacifist, would not directly assist Fairfield in this kind of work. Coffin stated that Fairfield, when in Cincinnati, "made his home among the colored people."

According to Coffin, Fairfield was arrested more than once and was jailed (in Kentucky) at least once, but managed to escape. He let those who joined him know that resistance would be offered if would-be captors came within range (as did Harriet Tubman). In one encounter he was wounded. Coffin wrote: "He often had to endure privation and hardship, but he was ready to undergo any suffering for the sake of effecting his object."

For a time, Fairfield lived in Randolph County, Indiana, "in the midst of a large settlement of colored people where he was well known." Coffin believed that Fairfield was one of the several white men reported as involved in numerous slave conspiracies and uprisings in the late 1850s. He closed: "With all his faults and misguided impulses, and wicked ways, he was a brave man, he never betrayed a trust that was reposed in him and he was a true friend to the oppressed and suffering slave."

Coffin is the main source for details about another white martyr in the effort to further African American liberation. This was Richard Dillingham, an Ohio Quaker. He is known to have taught Black students in southern Ohio; it was from them that he learned what slavery was. In December 1848 several Black people asked Dillingham to go to Nashville and help liberate relatives. Dillingham went; three slaves fled with him in a hired wagon. The driver betrayed them, and Dillingham was jailed. His cell, twelve by fifteen feet, was shared by six other prisoners. He was tried in April 1849 and convicted; prior to sentence he informed the court that he had acted on his own and that he "was prompted to it by feelings of humanity." He was sentenced to three years at hard labor, spent some months breaking rocks, contracted cholera, and died in the summer of 1850. One of Dillingham's prison letters to his wife told of some Black fellow prisoners, "of as noble mind as ever the Anglo-Saxon race were possessed of." Coffin wrote: "His name is remembered among the unsung heroes who, without glory or renown, have yielded up their lives in the furtherance of Right and Liberty."

Of himself, Coffin wrote:

Besides aiding fugitives, I often assisted the poor and destitute among the free colored people of our city [Cincinnati], visiting the sick and afflicted among them who seemed to be neglected by the white people and was often accused by those who were prejudiced against colored people, of thinking more of the colored race than of the white. To such accusations I generally replied that I was no respecter of color or race, that the negroes had souls equally as precious as ours, that Christ had died for them as well as for us and that we were all alike in the divine sight.

Coffin added: "I often gave them employment in preference to whites, not that I felt any greater attachment to them on account of their color, but because I knew that they were often unjustly refused and neglected."

Coffin is the main source concerning another of the not-inconsiderable number of white people who participated in the monumental struggle against slavery and did so despite peril and sacrifice. This was James Connelly, who was on the staff of the *Cincinnati Commercial* in the 1840s. For several days he secreted and cared for two fugitive slaves—a man and a woman—in a hideaway behind his office. In his absence the hideaway was discovered. The fugitives were ordered to surrender; they refused and the man was killed, the woman captured.

Connelly defied a writ for his arrest; he went to New York and found employment with the *New York Sun*. In a few months he was tracked down and returned to Cincinnati. He was convicted in that city but fined rather lightly and sentenced to but twenty days in prison. There he was visited by friendly people; indeed, delegations from both a Methodist and a Unitarian conference paid respects—Horace Mann among them. Upon his release he was hailed by many and serenaded by a band. Clearly, the days of slavery were numbered.[19] Lives such as those sketched by Coffin—as well as his own—are a throbbing part of the tradition of egalitarianism, which, despite everything, has been one of the splendid, if neglected, features of the history of the United States.

16

From Liberty Party to Republican Party

In the politics of the ten or fifteen years prior to the Civil War, racism and anti-racism played a significant role. Those who held power in the slave-holding states intensified repression and propaganda. In the remaining states efforts looking toward compromise and, in effect, acquiescence with the status quo tended to dominate the scene and to control most forms by which opinion was created and dispensed.

Nevertheless, in the South, significant challenges to traditional parties and attitudes did surface, and in the North, despite all efforts at restraint, discontent with the political, economic, and ideological mainstream grew. In fact, by the mid-1850s, turmoil, not placidity, was characteristic.

Left-wing forces in Northern politics were minor in the 1840s, but their influence grew as the years passed; they were characterized by opposition to slavery and the questioning of racism. While some recent literature, exemplified by the work of James B. Stewart, James M. McPherson, and Eric Foner in particular, has brought forward this development, the contrary attitude, particularly emphasizing the apparent omnipotence of racism, remains dominant. I believe that the challenging viewpoint is valid.

While moral suasionists, political activists, and advocates of militant resistance were present in the anti-slavery movement from its earliest appearance, the latter two groups tended to grow in relative importance as the slave system and those who opposed it matured. One of the earliest manifestations of political emphasis saw the founding of the Liberty party late in 1839. This political component, undergoing appropriate alterations, persisted and developed until it triumphed with the Republican party. While the level of slavery's rejection varied in the course of this development, the opposition to slavery's expansion, if not its existence, always was present. Comprehending the nature of the slave system, its supporters were correct

in insisting that confining it meant in effect eliminating it, albeit less per-
emptorily.

Anti-slavery and, to a lesser degree, opposition to slavery's expansion
carried with them some hostility to racism. This hostility might be partial
even in anti-slavery; it certainly was partial in opposition to slavery's expansion, where, in fact, racism might be present. At the same time, opposition to racism also could be and was present in the opposition to slavery's
expansion.

In the Liberty party the anti-racism was explicit. Thus the convention of
the party in Buffalo in 1843 adopted the following resolutions in preparation
for the next year's elections:

1. *Resolved*, That human brotherhood is a cardinal doctrine of true Democracy,
as well as of pure Christianity, which spurns all inconsistent limitations; and neither
the political party which repudiates it, nor the political system which is not based
upon it, nor controlled in its practical workings by it, can be truly Democratic or
permanent.

2. *Resolved*, That the Liberty party, placing itself upon this broad principle, will
demand the absolute and unconditional divorce of the General Government from
Slavery, and also the restoration of equality of rights, among men, in every State
where the party exists, or may exist.

The fourth resolution made the anti-racist commitment especially clear:
"That the Liberty party has not been organized merely for the overthrow
of Slavery. Its first decided effort must indeed be directed against slaveholding, as the grossest form and the most revolting manifestation of Despotism; but it will also carry out the principles of Equal Rights, into all
their practical consequences and applications, and support every just measure conducive to individual and social freedom."[1] Further, it was at this
Liberty party convention of 1843 that for the first time in the history of the
United States, on such an occasion, there were African American delegates,
speakers, and officials.

In various elections in 1843 the Liberty party received almost 65,000
votes, contrasted with a little over 7,000 three years earlier. Its 1844 platform reaffirmed a belief in human equality and promised to seek the elimination of racist laws and practices in the North. In the 1840s some anti-
racist victories were won, notably the removal in 1843 of the law banning
interracial marriage in Massachusetts. Other efforts, such as those seeking
an end to Jim Crow militia or the elimination of discriminatory voting
provisions, failed. A notable success in 1849, following a powerful showing
of Free Soil strength in the preceding year, made possible the repeal of
Ohio's Black Laws, among the most obnoxious to exist anywhere in the
North. This removed legal barriers to African American migration, attendance in public schools, and testimony against whites in courts.[2]

Very explicit and principled in its anti-racism was the argument of Charles

Sumner in December 1849 before the Massachusetts Supreme Court urging that Boston desegregate its Smith School—a part, but a segregated part, of the city's public school system. Sumner was soon to be a U.S. senator. Serving with Sumner was the African American lawyer, Robert Morris, of whom more later. The case is known as *Sarah C. Roberts v. The City of Boston*. It was brought on behalf of the five-year-old Sarah by her father, Benjamin Roberts, after years of vigorous Black-white agitation. The court, through Chief Justice Lemuel Shaw, ruled against Roberts, but by legislative act in 1855 Massachusetts illegalized segregation in any of its public schools.

Though the Sumner appeal was noted by the Warren Court in its 1954 *Brown v. Topeka* decision, the latter did not go so far as did Sumner, especially when he emphasized the harmful effects of segregation upon the white children. Sumner insisted that relegating an "*entire race*" to separation on the assumption that its members "possess certain moral or intellectual qualities" that rendered this separation "proper" was erroneous "and therefore illegal." Those who justified the separation, Sumner continued, did so as not violating "any principle of Equality" since the excluded students "have equal advantages of instruction" with the others. Factually, this was false; five schools for white children intervened between Sarah's home and her school, and an official investigating committee reported that its rooms were "too small" and its equipment was "shattered and neglected." Further, said Sumner, equivalency was impossible, for separation was insulting. Whatever the equipment, whatever the instruction, the fact of enforced separation was wrong. "It is a mockery to call it an equivalent."

In any case, Sumner argued, the Black children had a right to equality, and that must mean that they "have an equal right with white children to the public schools." He continued that schools provided for Jews in cities like Rome and Frankfurt might be as good as others, "but this compulsory segregation from the mass of citizens is of itself an *inequality* which we condemn with our whole souls." Sumner suggested, moreover, that the logic of separation by color (and in Europe by religion) might well justify segregation here by religion or by nationality, too, and perhaps by class. The point was that not exclusion but equality was needed.

Finally, Sumner took up the argument that racial discrimination was good for both colored people and whites, just as some said that slavery was "for the mutual benefit of master and slave, and of the country where it exists." On the contrary, "Nothing unjust, nothing ungenerous can be for the benefit of any person, or any thing." Further, of course segregation "injures the blacks," but "the whites themselves are injured by separation." Here followed Sumner's most powerful paragraph, still not appreciated in the practice of the law in the United States:

With the law as their monitor, the [white children] are taught to regard a portion of the human family, children of God, created in his image, co-equals in his love, as a separate and degraded class.... Their hearts, while yet tender with childhood, are necessarily hardened by this conduct, and their subsequent lives, perhaps, bear enduring testimony to this legalized uncharitableness.... Their characters are debased, and they become less fit for the magnanimous duties of a good citizen.

The eloquence of Sumner's closing remarks to the court remains moving more than fourteen decades after they were uttered:

> I have occupied much of your time, but I have not yet exhausted the topics. Still, which way soever we turn, we are brought back to one single proposition—*the equality of men before the law*. This stands as the mighty guardian of the colored children in this case. It is the constant, ever-present, tutelary genius of this Commonwealth, frowning upon every privilege of birth, upon every distinction of race, upon every institution of caste. You cannot slight it or avoid it. You cannot restrain it. It remains that you should welcome it. Do this, and your words will be a "charter freehold of rejoicing" to a race which has earned by much suffering a title to much regard. Your judgment will become a sacred landmark, not in jurisprudence only, but in the history of Freedom, giving precious encouragement to all the weary and heavy-laden wayfarers in this great cause. Massachusetts will then, through you, have a fresh title to regard and be once more, as in times past, an example to the whole land.[3]

In a recent study of the Liberty party in the Northwest, Vernon Wolpe emphasized its sectarian character, with members searching for "purity" and the salvation of their own souls as a primary concern, though it cost them political effectiveness. With this theme, the book is entitled *Forlorn Hope of Freedom*, and the party certainly was minuscule in size. Still, Wolpe did suggest that its existence was consequential as an example, as a kind of living conscience.

Its members were not only vehemently anti-slavery; they also were profoundly egalitarian. They sought the elimination of racist laws and practices and conducted themselves in accordance with these principles. This was true in the cases of Theodore Weld, John Rankin, Gamaliel Bailey, and others now less well known, such as Augustus Wattles, the Reverend Samuel Crothers, and the Reverend Dyer Burgess—most of them originally Southerners.

The Liberty party did have pockets of considerable strength in sections of Illinois, Michigan, Ohio, and Wisconsin. As a body it insisted that "the interests and rights of the free colored population of these United States should never be considered by us as less important or sacred than our own." Its organ in Wisconsin held that the Bible "distinctly informs us that mankind have a common origin." The Anti-Slavery Society of Michigan sought not only the abolition of slavery but also the elevation of "their colored brethren" to their "proper rank as MEN." When the Female Anti-Slavery Society of Dundee, Illinois, presented a freedom banner as an award for meritorious conduct to the Reverend W. B. Dodge of Mill Creek in 1847, he, in accepting it, explained that those who supported the Liberty party not only sought slavery's termination but also wanted "to bring the colored man on the platform of the white man."[4]

The whole question of the development of anti-slavery politics and its relationship to racism or anti-racism is a matter of dispute. The view that remains dominant was summarized this way by C. Vann Woodward: "The successful anti-slavery movement embraced anti-Negro recruits and their prejudices, and triumphed over slavery in the name of white supremacy."[5] George M. Fredrickson did not quite agree with this position and noted that there were some Republicans "who came close to accepting the radical abolitionist premise of racial equality." But the central point of his position was this: "That in the debate over slavery's extension spokesmen for all positions made racial appeals would seem to suggest that differences in racial philosophy had little to do with the ideological origins of the Civil War."[6] The evidence, I believe, not only clearly refutes the Woodward position as quoted; it also places in serious doubt the somewhat amended outlook of Fredrickson.

The still-dominant outlook is based heavily on the work of James Rawley and Eugene Berwanger noted earlier, but both exaggerated the significance of racism, omitted its opposition, and even inadvertently brought forward statistics shown to be faulty.[7] Eric Foner earlier had rejected such one-sided versions. Certainly, racism existed within Republican party ranks, but Foner correctly emphasized that there did exist "fundamental differences between the two parties' racial attitudes." The Republicans "did develop a policy which recognized the essential humanity of the Negro and demanded protection for certain basic rights which the Democrats denied him." Foner pointed to the fact that leading Republicans had supported the rights of the free Black population and had defended fugitive slaves, thus further differentiating themselves from their opponents.[8]

That Black people like Frederick Douglass, John M. Langston, and John S. Rock supported the Republicans, as did many other Abolitionists, also emphasizes the reality of this distinction. The Republican attitude often was patronizing and sometimes worse, and people like Frederick Douglass did not fail to condemn this, often publicly and sometimes privately, as Douglass did, for example, in a letter to Charles Sumner. Douglass knew that "aversion to blacks" might be a reason at times for opposing slavery's extension, but he campaigned for the Republican party because, as he said in 1860, "It cannot be denied that the anti-slavery element in the Northern States is a vital element of the Republican party."[9]

On the commitment to equal rights by leading Republicans in the pre–Civil War period, one has the examples of Henry Wilson, Charles Sumner, George W. Julian, Joshua R. Giddings, and John P. Hale. This will be examined in subsequent pages.

Lincoln himself, of course, had great limitations in his attitude toward the African Americans, not only in terms of present-day standards but also— as this work has emphasized—by comparison to many of his contemporaries and predecessors. But with all this in mind, it is to be observed that in his debates with Stephen Douglas he attacked him precisely because Senator Douglas denied the "humanity of the negro"; it was, said Lincoln, Douglas's "utter indifference" to that point that separated him from "a great mass of mankind" who "consider slavery a great moral wrong."[10]

Paul Angle, in his definitive study of the Lincoln-Douglas debates, emphasized that in them Lincoln "attacked the morality of the slave system" and that "unlike Douglas, Lincoln looked forward to a time when slavery would no longer stain American democracy and when the Negro would at least have an equal chance to advance to the limits of his capabilities."[11] Perhaps one gets closest to Lincoln's views in this passage from his speech, August 21, 1858, replying to Douglas:

I agree with Judge Douglas that he [the African American] is not my equal in many respects—certainly not in color, perhaps not in moral or intellectual endowment. But in the right to eat the bread, without leave of anybody else, which his own hand earns, *he is my equal and the equal of Judge Douglas, and the equal of every living man.*[12]

The italics are in the original, and the contemporary recorder added that this was followed by "Great Applause."

A year earlier, Lincoln, in speaking of the Declaration of Independence, referred to it as representing a goal toward which humanity should strive, "and even though never perfectly attained, constantly approximated, and thereby constantly spreading and deepening its influence and augmenting the happiness and value of life to people *of all colors* everywhere." Here, too, Lincoln added: "The Republicans inculcate, with whatever of ability they can, that the negro is a man; that his bondage is cruelly wrong, and that the field of his oppression ought not to be enlarged."[13]

Sharper than Lincoln's statements and relevant to the question of racism, public opinion, and Republicanism are the words of an editorial in the *Cleveland Leader*, November 26, 1857:

Sen. Douglas insulted the colored race in one of his low, demagogical speeches in Chicago. It drew the colored people of that city upon him. In reply to the Senator's fling in regard to the intellectual capacities of the Negro race, they have challenged the learned Little Giant to meet Fred Douglass in a debate on that question. The white Douglas will not dare accept the challenge so fairly given. He knows that as far as manners are concerned he is not equal to nine tenths of the black race, for the reason that they will never unnecessarily insult or injure an unfortunate human being. We can give names of scores of colored men who are superior in intellect to this vaunted champion of the amalgamated Democracy.[14]

The remarks in this Cleveland newspaper bring to mind the statement in Congress by Thaddeus Stevens early in the post–Civil War period. In the House Stevens listened to a Representative Brooks, a New York Democrat, discoursing on the theme of Black people as being creatures quite separate from white people. Stevens remarked that he thought that Black people had souls even as had the New York congressman, and in terms of intellect, Stevens suggested that Brooks might want to debate with Frederick Douglass on some mutually agreed-upon subject (and Brooks might himself select the judges of this contest); Stevens opined that Brooks would not do well in this contest.[15]

Relevant to the question of the pre–Civil War Republican party are studies of its attitude during the war and early in the Reconstruction era. The later period is beyond the scope of the present volume, but here attention should be called to a recent work that, as Michael Lee Benedict pointed out, did "implicitly challenge the view promoted by C. Vann Woodward, Eugene Berwanger, Larry Gara, and others that Republicans were racists not fully committed to equal rights."[16] In his important study of this question, John M. Rozett concluded:

> If indeed the Republican party did represent to a predominant degree those who at the very least had a distaste for the ill-treatment of the black man instead of Negrophobes who desired to contain slavery because they feared the dispersion of blacks, then the South did have something to fear from the election of Lincoln. Southerners had built their defense of the peculiar institution on the denial of the black man's rights, and even the beginnings of a moral conscience in the nation threatened their position. From this viewpoint, the South's reaction to free soil agitation and the Republican ascendancy can be seen not as an irrational act in response to a non-existent threat from a handful of unpopular abolitionists, but as a response to the long-feared crack in the southern defense of slavery. Even though most Republicans did not espouse full equality for the black man, they did adopt a position of limited equality and of moral judgment which the South could neither accept nor tolerate.[17]

This observation needs some amendment, I believe, but its essence is correct. It was not "the South" that became agitated; it was the predominant component of the slaveholding class. One of the class's main concerns was the diverse rather than monolithic reality of that "South." Further, the Abolitionists were far from a "handful" by the 1850s; on the contrary, they numbered in the hundreds of thousands, and their views were being received with greater and greater seriousness as those years passed. Very much a basic part of that process, as Rozett's observation indicates, was a growing alteration in the national attitude toward the African American population.

Years ago, Emil Olbrich showed that when the question of Black enfranchisement arose at Northern state conventions in the pre–Civil War generation, while a negative vote eventuated, the minority in favor of such enfranchisement was significant. Further, he observed that in the debates rejection of disfranchisement often was advocated and that at times this was accompanied by renunciation of the idea of African American inferiority. This was true, he showed, in the New York State convention even in 1821 and again in its 1846 convention. The same was true in the 1837 Pennsylvania convention and those in Michigan, Indiana, Ohio, and Wisconsin in the 1850s.[18]

Let us observe some of the relevant remarks in several of these debates. In the New York State convention of 1846 on the revision of the constitution, at least eight of the delegates—two each from Delaware and Madison counties and one each from Onondaga, Orleans, Seneca, and Wyoming counties—spoke in favor of no color distinction in voting rights. One, Benjamin F. Bruce of Madison, did so "energetically" according to the summary by the reporters at one point, and on another day Bruce "made an impassioned appeal in behalf of equal rights."[19]

The reports of the debates and proceedings of the Ohio State conventions in 1850–51 are very rich in material reflecting hostility to discrimination on the basis of race, and often on the basis of gender also. There also is evidence of contrary feeling, especially in the remarks of individual delegates. But in the reporting of petitions from citizens, those rejecting racism very much outnumber others.

Of the petitions opposing racism, notice may be taken of one from 54 citizens of Clinton County on May 13, 1850. When debate ensued as to whether or not the petition should be accepted by the convention, the presenter stated that it offered "the views of a considerable portion of his constituency" and that they were "of respectable character," but that they were "comparatively however, a small portion of the people of his district." Several of the delegates who voted to receive the petition carefully added that they were opposed to its purpose, but one, a Mr. Humphreyville, made clear that he agreed with its contents. One of the delegates who stated that he opposed the content of the petition did add, however, that "there was a very respectable portion of the community" who favored it, and he was sure that they were "honest" people. There followed an anti-racist petition from 51 citizens of Fairview. Another petition from Jonas Wilson and 20 other Black people from Warren County also was received. A few days later came petitions from 50 people in Stark and Portage counties asking that suffrage be granted to all regardless of color or sex. Another, offered on May 21, again from Portage County, was signed by 102 people asking that "the new constitution may accord to all the members of our commonwealth equal rights, political and social, without regard to sex or color." Others of a similar character were then offered from "some sixty or seventy persons" who were the neighbors of the presenting delegate and were described by him as "very respectable persons." Similarly, a petition came from a group whose numbers were not given, but who were described as coming from the Yearly Meeting of the Green Plains Friends. Like action continued for several additional days, mostly from white petitioners (male and female), but with some petitions coming from "colored" people.

One of the delegates, a Mr. Hunter, made a fairly prolonged speech accompanying the presentation of a petition of similar character from 27 "legal voters" in Ashtabula County. He had been asked whether petitions of this character were framed in respectable language. Yes, he said, they were, and he added that it would be well for delegates to remember that they were to use "respectable" language when referring to these petitioners—citizens of the state they were representing. Hunter continued that for some twenty years he had known the people of Ashtabula County, and "I can confidently say that those who sympathize with the sentiment of this petition (and they constitute a very large majority of the people of the county) are not an impulsive and excitable people," as some had charged. On the contrary, "They are as sober, industrious, well-behaved, intelligent, moral and religious a class of persons as can be found in the State of Ohio or any other State." He made it clear that these sentiments were his own, for he felt them "to be founded upon the principles of right and justice."[20]

In the Indiana convention of 1850 to consider revising the state's constitution, the opinion of most of the delegates clearly was hostile to the Black population. Still, there were some who differed, like Edward R. May from DeKalb and Steuben districts, Daniel Crumbacker of Lake and Porter, William S. Holman of Dearborn, Joseph Robinson of Decatur, Othniel L. Clark of Tippecanoe, Milton Gregg of Jefferson, and the well-known Robert Dale Owen of Posey.

May, for example, insisted that the African people were people, not brutes; he thought, therefore, that this meant that their rights could not be denied without serious compromise of the nation's principles. Crumbacker was more forceful, insisting that Africans had shown aptitude for accomplishment despite severe obstacles and that retaining, not to speak of intensifying, such obstacles ill fitted a nation that boasted of itself as "an asylum for the oppressed of all nations." He insisted, "Of one flesh and one blood were created all the inhabitants of the earth." Perhaps, he did add, separation of races was ideal—he was not sure. But while they all lived in the same state, a policy of oppression was wrong and self-defeating. Robinson, too, while no egalitarian, did plead for restraint of repression, for "when it is remembered that we are the pirates, that we have torn them from their families and chained them here in servitude, I do think that it comes with an ill grace for any member of this Convention, to talk about a distinction which God himself does not recognize." Clark said that he believed in the Declaration of Independence, and therefore "I am pledged, sir, to recognize by law, the negro, as a man, and not to deny him the great and essential rights of humanity." Would gentlemen, Clark asked, so permit their prejudices to mislead their judgment "that they will trample upon the

institutions of our forefathers, and rend in twain the very citadel of liberty?"
Gregg informed the convention that in Madison, where he lived, he knew
"a great many" Black people "whose sober and industrious habits are worthy of all praise, whose moral characters stand above reproach, whose regard
for truth and veracity may well serve as models for others in higher life."
They had built churches and schools, they labored diligently; "Shall we
paralyze the efforts of these men to do good?"[21]

Vigorous attacks marked 1857 events in the Wisconsin legislature. There
consideration was given to a Senate bill aiming at extending the right of
suffrage. Despite its announced purpose, the first section of that bill excluded
Black men and all women from the suffrage. The majority of the Judiciary
Committee of the Assembly submitted its report on that bill on February
27, 1857. This majority (of three members) urged that section one of the
bill, which limited the suffrage, be altered so that it would read: "Every
person of the age of 21 years, or upwards, who shall have resided in the
State of Wisconsin for one year next preceding any election, shall be deemed
a qualified elector at such election."

Arguing for this, so far as the African American was concerned, the
majority denounced "the barbarous and unmanly dogma that human rights
are qualities of color." Quite apart from the difficulty of determining who
was "white," the report continued (with great optimism, one must add)
that in any case the nature of modern civilization's development "prove[s]
that the period of clannish prejudice, of national animosities, of religious
bigotry, of cutaneous aristocracy, is passing away." Those who persisted
in holding such prejudices, said this 1857 document, were "fossil men."
"Eagle-eyed science," it added, "does not recognize the distinction of color."

The report continued that political equality "has nothing to do with any
man's social choices." A person "may refuse to associate with one man
because he is a native American, with another because he is a Dutchman,
or on account of any other whim." This was the logic of the Know-Nothing
person. "Are our individual or national hatreds to be the charter of human
rights in this great Republic?"

This majority went on to declare that it realized its amendment would
enfranchise women. So be it. It denied the validity of any argument denying
women the vote. In any case, it suggested that this total enfranchisement
would "awaken discussion" and thus "stimulate the intellectual and moral
powers of the individuals and the masses." Let all who were not infants
and not mentally deficient vote—"let the majority rule. Vox populi, vox
Dei."

The author of this report was Joseph T. Mills, born in 1812 in Kentucky;
as a lawyer he moved to Illinois in 1831 and to Wisconsin in 1843. He was
elected to the Wisconsin Assembly in 1856, 1857, and 1862 and again in
1879; from 1865 to 1877 he served as a circuit judge. The views he held

and vigorously espoused were not only those of the majority of an Assembly committee; they were views known to the people among whom he lived, and those views certainly were repeatedly favored by the (male white) voters of Grant County, Wisconsin.[22]

Fortunately, a detailed historical overview of this Wisconsin development has been made by Michael J. McManus.[23] McManus observed that the question of extending the suffrage to Black men was rejected in 1846 by a popular vote of 14,615 to 7,664. The question remained alive and became acute in the 1850s. At a state convention of the infant Republican party in September 1855, the delegates unanimously adopted this resolution: "That the fundamental principles of the Republican party are based upon the equal rights of all men; that these principles are utterly hostile to the proscription of any on account of birthplace, religion or color."

The concern reflected by this resolution was in part induced and stimulated by significant collective action by the African American population in Wisconsin. A petition "numerously signed," as a contemporary source noted, was presented by Black residents of the state to the legislature in September 1857, asking that their disfranchisement—"this heel of oppression"—be terminated. They declared their belief in the enfranchisement of "men of foreign birth, immigrating to this asylum of the oppressed," and they insisted "that the same rights and blessings should be extended to us." Was it right, was it just, was it "common sense," they asked, "that we should be subject to taxation without representation?"[24]

In 1856 the Wisconsin Senate urged this enfranchisement, but the Assembly rejected it. The Senate again passed a bill enfranchising Black men; this was referred to the Assembly, the result being the committee report summarized earlier. The Senate balked at accepting this report, basically because of its call for the enfranchisement of women. Democrats opposed the measure giving Black men the suffrage. The question was then submitted to the judgment of the electorate. It was rejected in 1857 by a vote of 45,157 to 31,964, which should be compared with the vote of 1846. In the campaign, Republican candidates tended to avoid this question, but its press did not. Although Berwanger declared that "Republican editors remained strangely silent about Negro suffrage," McManus showed that he was wrong. On the contrary, that press reported Black meetings in support of enfranchisement and itself supported the effort. This was true despite vicious attacks upon the measure and upon the Republicans for supporting it from the Democratic party press.

Further, McManus reported that about 74 percent of the negative vote came from Democrats and that over 61 percent of all Republicans participating in the election voted in favor of Black political equality. McManus found: "Timeworn racial assumptions obviously were being disclaimed or called into question by many Wisconsin residents.... It seems beyond question that a significant number of Republicans would countenance measures favorable to Negroes if provided the opportunity to do so." His final words were as follows: "It is certain that those who view the Republicans as basically racist have ignored significant evidence to the contrary."

17

The Crisis Decade

On the federal level, in Congress, similar developments in attitudes toward the African American people may be illustrated in the persons of several Republican leaders. Joshua R. Giddings (1795–1864) of Ohio was elected as a Whig from the Western Reserve in 1838; his experiences in Washington and the growing concern over slavery moved him steadily toward a position just short of the political Abolitionists. The tremendous excitement engendered by the slave uprising in 1839 aboard the *Amistad* and the litigation therefrom, which resulted in the slaves being declared free in 1841—and the central role in that case of John Quincy Adams, then Giddings's colleague in the House—furthered this move. The climax came that same year 1841 with the uprising of the slaves aboard the domestic slave-trading vessel, the *Creole*. The rebels in this case made it to the Bahamas, British territory in which slavery had been abolished recently. Despite desperate—even war-threatening—demands upon England from Secretary of State John C. Calhoun, the rebels retained their freedom.

Giddings, on the floor of the House, defended the rebels and compared them with the Republic's revolutionary fathers. For this, he was censured by the House, resigned, and was overwhelmingly returned to his seat in a special election. By December 1848 Giddings, now a Free Soiler, having been appalled by the sight of a slave coffle driven through the streets of the capital, introduced a bill that called for a plebiscite, to be participated in by "all the male inhabitants" of the District of Columbia, where the question would be for or against slavery therein. This provoked Representative Patrick W. Tomkins to inquire with some asperity whether the honorable gentleman from Ohio meant that slaves and the "free colored" also should vote. Giddings replied with elaborate courtesy—not failing to face the Louisiana congressman—that as he "looked abroad upon the family of men," he could discover "no distinctions among people which justified giving one man the control over another's liberty."

Of course, the House disdained treating Giddings's proposal seriously, but the latter's evolution reflected the motion in significant sections of the population. Giddings excoriated the Mexican War, and in the 1851 campaign to enfranchise the Black men of Ohio, he was a fervent partisan. He fought—without success—in Congress to eliminate racist provisions within the proposed Homestead Act, and in 1854 he denounced the exclusionary provisions of New Mexico's constitution.

By this time Giddings was a Republican. In 1856 he told his congressional colleagues that the Declaration of Independence applied to "*all men*, embracing high and low, rich and poor . . . of light complexion, of dark complexion, of mixed complexion." In December of that year he asserted that the Republican party held exactly that belief and therefore proposed legislation to repeal the Fugitive Slave Law, to abolish slavery in the District of Columbia—where states' rights did not apply—and to prohibit slavery in the federal territories and slave trading on the coastal waters.

Giddings was especially incensed by Chief Justice Taney's assumption in the Dred Scott case (1857) of the innate inferiority of African-derived peoples. Indeed, by 1857 he had come to the conclusion that only through "successful slave insurrections could the problems of bondage in America be solved." Hence from an 1841 defense of slave rebels he had moved—shortly before John Brown's effort—to believing not only in the justice of slave rebellion but in its necessity if slavery was to be terminated.

Giddings's careful biographer—a basic source for the material summarized in the preceding paragraphs—found that although there never was from him any expression of "open racism," publicly or privately, and although he repeatedly insisted upon what the removal of chains might accomplish, citing Frederick Douglass and Charles L. Remond, he still retained a patronizing view.[1] One must accept the conclusion of such an expert; still, one must add that the Congress of the United States would profit very much at the end of the twentieth century, in its confrontation with racism, if it contained more members like Joshua R. Giddings, who died in 1864.

The career of George W. Julian (1817–1899) of Indiana also is reflective of this mounting attack in leading political circles, not only upon slavery but also upon racism. Elected to the state legislature in 1845 as a Whig, he soon moved left and became prominent in the infant Free Soil party. A coalition of "conscience" Democrats and Free Soilers succeeded in sending Julian to Congress (1849–51). The next year he was the Free Soil party's vice-presidential candidate with John P. Hale, the presidential candidate, of whom more will be said later.

Julian was a founding member of the Republican party and was again in Congress, 1861–71, playing a significant role in the Civil War and Reconstruction. Julian's public expressions of his anti-racist beliefs were at least as forthright as those of Giddings, his father-in-law. The two of them were part of a general radical approach. Prior to the creation of the Republican party, for example, in a speech at a Free Soil convention in Indianapolis, May 25, 1853, Julian said:

It is especially true of anti-slavery men, that whilst they wage war against chattel slavery in the South, they wage war against wages slavery in the North. They are advocates of land reform, of the rights of labor in opposition to the exactions of capital, and are exerting themselves to the utmost in the cause of the downtrodden humanity, whether white or black or whatever the form of degradation under which it groans.

In this same speech he ridiculed arguments in favor of the colonization of African Americans as put forth by "Southern men and their minions." In these arguments, he said, they insisted on the great "improvability" of the African-derived peoples and told of the glories of Ethiopia and Egypt— "colored peoples"—all of which "cannot fail to strike the common sense of the most unreflective as virtually surrendering the main prop of their system."

Two years later, speaking again in Indianapolis, he reiterated the theme that the forces of opposition to slavery had as a "central life-giving principle . . . the equal brotherhood of all men before their common Father." Their mission, he said, "is the practical vindication of this truth." Indeed, in Congress on May 14, 1850, Julian had excoriated concepts of white supremacy and had remarked: "I will not undertake to combat these absurdities of its [slavery's] champions; for it has been said truly, that to argue with men who have renounced the use and authority of reason, and whose philosophy consists of holding humanity in contempt, is like administering medicine to the dead, or endeavoring to convert an atheist by Scripture."[2]

The egalitarian position of such a significant politician and future Republican party leader as Senator Benjamin Wade of Ohio was repeatedly stressed. On February 6, 1854, a Kentucky senator asked him if he was in fact "a believer in the Declaration of Independence and in the doctrines of God which declare all men are equal." Did he mean, the Kentuckian continued, "that the slave is equal in regard to those free laborers that he speaks of in the North?" Wade replied:

Certainly, certainly. The slave in my judgment, is equal to anybody else, but is degraded by the nefarious acts and selfishness of the master, who compels him, by open force and without right, to serve him alone. That, sir, is my doctrine. When you speak of equality before the law, or equality before the Almighty God, I do not suppose you stand one whit higher than the meanest slave you have. That is my judgment.

On March 3, 1854, Wade denounced the "unwarrantable prejudice" against Black people that kept them from enjoying, as he insisted they should, all political and civil rights.[3]

John P. Hale (1806–1873), in the Senate as an Independent from New Hampshire (1847–53) and as a Republican (1855–64), had, his biographer stated, "a genuine concern for the Negro's welfare."[4] In his own state, Hale remarked in the Senate on March 5, 1858, Black people were "industrious, patient, exhibiting very many amiable and excellent traits of character"— this in response to racist baiting from a Mississippi senator. In the same speech he emphasized that his opposition to allowing Oregon to enter the Union was based upon racist provisions in its constitution. He continued:

Providence has placed them here; they are a part of our people; and they are here on God Almighty's earth, which He made for His children to dwell upon, of every race and every nation; and I do not believe that it is morally or politically right for us to say to these people, whom Providence of God, or our own avarice, or the avarice of our own ancestors, has brought here, that they shall be subjected to perpetual disabilities.

In this same speech Hale sounded an oft-repeated note: "I ask if a republic, or a republican form of government, is one that makes fundamental distinctions between races?" Later, during the war, on March 18, 1862, urging an immediate end to slavery in the District of Columbia, he especially denounced not only slavery but racist discrimination. The latter placed fearful obstacles before people and then denounced them because they had not achieved that which other people not so handicapped might have done. Slavery, he said, was an "awful sin"; racism, he added, was an "awful injustice."[5]

Henry Wilson of Massachusetts—noted in earlier pages—in the Senate in the 1850s, when pressed by Southern colleagues, would deny a belief in the intellectual and moral equality of Blacks as compared with white people. Nevertheless, even then he denounced the prejudice of "this proud and domineering white race of ours." He insisted in this pre–Civil War period that the African Americans should have full equality before the law and the opportunity to "improve all the faculties that God has given them." On February 23, 1855, Wilson told a Southern senator: "To me, sir, the proudest master and the lowliest bondsman are alike brethren and fellow-countrymen." He insisted that "slavery is a violation of the holy commands to love our neighbor, and to do unto others as we would that others should do unto us." By 1860 Wilson was expressing the opinion in correspondence that the intelligence and industriousness of Black people were not inferior to those of the general population in the country; he especially wanted all the Northern states to cleanse their statutes of any evidence of racism.[6]

For a final example of significant Republican officeholders who denounced not only slavery but racism and racist-based inhuman treatment, consider the Reverend Owen Lovejoy, brother of the martyred Elijah. Owen Lovejoy (1811–1864) for many years was pastor of the Congregational Church in Princeton, Illinois. From 1857 to his death he also served in the House.

On February 21, 1859, Congressman Lovejoy decried the betrayal of the Declaration of Independence by the Democratic party with its insistence that the African American had "no rights which another is bound to regard." He asked: "Was ever so much diabolism compressed into one sentence?" The Democrats not only rejected Jefferson, he declared, they quarreled with God. "If there is any one dissatisfied with the fact that there is a whole race of human beings with the rights of human beings, created with a skin not colored like our own, let him go mouth to the heavens, and mutter his blasphemies in the ear of the god who made us all."

Lovejoy went on that he had been charged with the crime of assisting fugitive slaves. As to that, he announced in Congress his guilt. Yes, let it be known that Lovejoy lived "at Princeton, Illinois, three quarters of a mile east of the village," and, he went on, Owen Lovejoy "aids every fugitive that came to his door and asks it." As for those who would keep him from such Christian service and perhaps would want to jail him for criminal behavior, "I bid you defiance in the name of God!"[7] In 1860 Lovejoy vehemently attacked slavery in the House despite being verbally assaulted and insulted by a surrounding crowd of some twenty screaming representatives of slaveholding states.[8] It was this defiant one that Illinois folk sent to Congress until he died in 1864.

While the decade preceding the Civil War saw these kinds of speeches being made in Congress, these same years witnessed sharper and sharper attacks upon racism outside those halls. A biographer of Wendell Phillips observed that in these years, "in Lewis Hayden's dignified awareness of his own worth, in the resourcefulness of Harriet Tubman, and the triumphs of men like Anthony Burns, Frederick Douglass, and William Wells Brown, Phillips discovered at first hand the qualities of courage, purpose, and persistence that he ascribed [in one of his better-known public addresses] to the legendary Toussaint." It was at this time that Lydia Maria Child wrote to Phillips (July 2, 1860): "Please see to it that I am buried in some ground belonging to the *colored people* ... as the *last* testimony it is in my power to bear against the wicked, cruel, and absurd prejudice, which so grievously oppressed them in a country that boasts loudly of its free institutions."[9]

It was also in the 1850s in the United States that organized Marxism appeared. One of its features was utter rejection of racism—though this is not to say that there were no lapses from individuals within Socialist and Communist organizations. Just before the Civil War, in fact, the first Communist club appeared in the Western Hemisphere. There had earlier been a grouping of largely German émigrés after the defeated 1848 revolution who formed in the United States a European Communist League. In October

1857 some members of this league created a Communist Club in New York City. The constitution of this club pledged adherence to "the complete equality" of all, without distinction as to color or gender. In a public meeting sponsored by the club in New York City in the summer of 1858, the following resolution was adopted: "We recognize no distinction as to nationality or race, caste or status, color or sex."

The influence of this club remains obscure, although of course Marx and Engels had significant influence. Both contributed regular columns quite often to the powerful *New York Tribune* just before, during, and for some years after the Civil War. There were Southern politicians in the 1850s who denounced the agitation and statements of Communist groups in the United States; association of abolitionism with communism recurred fairly often in slaveholding propaganda.[10]

It was in the 1850s that the unequivocally egalitarian Gilbert Haven first expressed his views.[11] The author of a work devoted to this Methodist church figure correctly called him "an authentic racial equalitarian." It was passage of the Fugitive Slave Law that radicalized him. Soon thereafter, Haven delivered a sermon, "The Higher Law," in Amenia, New York, in November 1850. He observed here that some claimed that the African American people, being "beneath the grade of man," had no love of liberty. This, he thought, was absurd; witness, he urged, the extraordinary efforts to obtain freedom connoted by the exploits of Henry "Box" Brown and Ellen and William Craft. These "have made illustrious the annals of the world." Despite the just-enacted law, they must aid the fugitive. "It is a duty we owe to him as our brother, of our own flesh and blood, made in the same image as ourselves, by the same God, endowed with the same nature and rights, responsible to the same justice, and heir to the same immortality."

The passage of the Kansas-Nebraska bill led to a sermon in Wilbraham, Massachusetts, in May 1854, devoted largely to denouncing "a pride of caste" where a mere difference in complexion had become twisted into a "sinful aversion." Soon after Sumner was struck down on the Senate floor, Haven told a congregation in Westfield, Massachusetts, June 11, 1856, that the outrageous assault had its "primal root in our fixed repugnance" to those in chains. For the salvation of all of them, they must be "the upholders of the great sentiment of perfect human equality and brotherhood."

His sermon, "Caste the Corner-Stone," delivered repeatedly in the 1850s, contained some of the strongest anti-racist language ever to be uttered. For example, this "prejudice against color ... is a sin at our own door, in our own hearts. It makes us naked before our enemies ... it is the most general, deep-rooted, unnatural and destructive of all the sins of the nation." Haven here declared that the people slandered by racism were a talented folk whose characteristics were "of the highest rank." Whence stemmed the prejudice against them? It arose from "their social condition," from their enslavement;

it was necessary to abolish that atrocity and thus make possible a nation flourishing in equality.

It was necessary for those in the North, he went on, to combat this sinful prejudice, else they could not effectively fight to end slavery. What should they do? They must rid their churches and "our workshops, our stores, our juries, our halls of legislation, our family relations" of the "iniquity." He made clear that he practiced this in his daily life, in his personal relationships; thus he welcomed Black people into his home and told how splendid it was to have that home visited by Sojourner Truth, "an admirable guest, full of genius and grace."

Haven balked at nothing. Some raised the "alarm" of intermarriage. Where was the cause of alarm? he demanded. When two people married, that was the act of those two people. Interference with this was insolence; it was insufferable. Haven compared the rejection of the Black to the demeaning of women. He suggested that the African American was a John the Apostle, perhaps "milder than the rest, yet superior to all of them in many of the highest traits of the soul."

In the *Methodist Quarterly Review* of 1859 Haven maintained that notions of human inequality were the foundation for "all monarchies and aristocracies" and served as "that chief of the doctrines of the devils" emanating from slaveholding states and churches rationalizing slavery— "that a man can be born the property of another man." Haven demanded absolute and complete political, economic, and social equality. He denounced colonizationism as reeking with racism and similarly castigated anti-miscegenation laws. In the *Liberator* (November 6, 1857), he demanded that those opposed to slavery show in their lives their belief in "the unity of man." "Blacks," he continued, "must serve in our workshops, our schools, our pulpits, and as our physicians."

As a Methodist minister, Haven publicly rebuked a notice printed in the church's regional weekly, *Zion's Herald*, which warned members against welcoming to their pulpits the Black woman, Sojourner Truth, because she had associated with radicals "of the socialist, Garrisonian stamp." Not only did Haven, speaking in Westfield, Massachusetts, denounce the weekly, but he went on to hail the radicals for "being the first to fraternize with her on terms of perfect equality (in which great duty they have been teachers of Christ to this too prejudiced Church)." It is not too much to claim that an indicator of the great change produced by the next few tumultuous years was Gilbert Haven being appointed editor of *Zion's Herald* in 1867. Immediately after the martyrdom of John Brown, he stated that the bells then tolling mournfully would soon be "changed to merry peals of gladness over the glorious consummation of Universal Emancipation, for which he laid down his heroic life, and received his eternal crown."

There are glimpses of this outlook and even something of its fervor emanating from time to time from Southern church and political circles in this decade, despite the fact that the 1850s witnessed intensive repression. For example, late in 1856 one finds an unnamed Baptist clergyman in Georgia stating that he had himself preached to mixed congregations and that "we, Baptists of the South, have no hesitation in avowing our belief that God 'hath made of one blood all nations.' " This minister from Georgia continued: "The negro is a man . . . when converted the negro is as gladly welcomed into our churches as a brother, as if he were of pure Anglo-Saxon blood."[12]

W. G. Bean, back in 1935, had called attention to an occasional public rejection by Southern politicians of the repudiation of Jeffersonianism that had become the vogue in dominant Southern circles.[13] He instanced the speech in 1857 of Congressman L. D. Evans of Texas. Evans suggested that a doctrine of human inequality might do for a medieval society, "but," he said (meaning Thomas Dew of Virginia and James Henry Hammond of South Carolina), "emanating from the lips of a Virginia professor, or a statesman of Carolina, it startles the ear, and shocks the moral sense of a republican patriot!" Evans went on to suggest some effort to transform the slave society into a kind of feudal one; he thought that this, as a temporary arrangement, might preserve the Black people's "natural equality" and that it might, hopefully, somehow move on to a state of "perfect equality."

Charles Sellers in 1960 noted the serious questioning of slavery late in the institution's lifetime by some leading slaveowners. He added that at times "the racist argument was attacked with surprising vehemence." Perhaps the data in this work will indicate that the vehemence was not all that surprising. Sellers cited the views expressed by the dissident North Carolinian, Daniel R. Goodloe, in his 1858 book, *The Southern Platform*. "The African," Goodloe wrote—after having left the South to become an editor of the emancipationist paper, the *National Era*, in Washington—"is endowed with faculties as lofty, with perceptions as quick, with sensibilities as acute, and with natures as susceptible of improvement, as we are, who boast of a fairer skin." Indeed, Goodloe thought that if the Black people had the advantages white people had, "they would, as a mass, reach as high an elevation in the scale of moral refinement, and attain as great distinction on the broad theatre of intellectual achievement as ourselves."[14]

Eric Foner wrote that "the Republicans did develop a policy which recognized the essential humanity of the Negro"; but, he remarked, "the Republican stand on race relations went against the prevailing opinion of the 1850's and proved a distinct political liability in a racist society." Still, the changes brought about as that decade proceeded were reflected in this editorial paragraph appearing in the party's chief organ, the *New York Tribune*, May 9, 1857 (and quoted by Foner): "They have in fact ceased to be Africans. Just as our native-born white population have ceased to be Englishmen, Irishmen, or Germans, they are becoming black Americans just as we have become white Americans."

Foner emphasized that many of the leaders of the Republican party had "long histories of support of Negro rights"; further, that "many of the areas of the North which gave the Republicans their largest majorities had distinguished themselves in the past by their endorsement of Negro suffrage and opposition to Negro exclusion laws"—as was shown in earlier pages of this work. In a sharp paragraph whose direction contradicted an earlier remark about "distinct political liability," Foner declared that "fundamentally it [what he had called 'the mainstream of Republican opinion'] asserted that Negroes are human beings and citizens of the United States, entitled to the natural rights of life, liberty and property." This, Foner remarked, was a "considerable step forward," bearing in mind "the racism that pervaded the society."[15]

There was indeed this pervasive racism; but the fact is that the "mainstream" of a party that nearly won a national election in 1856 and did win such an election in 1860 had moved to the point summarized in this language. That posture and its acceptance by that "mainstream" were achieved by very great effort, Black and white, Northern and Southern—indeed, international.

Relevant is the fact that Charles Sumner's devastating assault upon "The Barbarism of Slavery," delivered in the Senate on June 14, 1860, troubled some of the Republican leaders and editors of some Republican newspapers, but, as David Donald pointed out, it was printed in full in many newspapers. Donald noted that "rural areas of the North and West welcomed it" and that "so great was the reaction in Sumner's favor that the same party managers who treated him cooly in June warmly solicited his aid in August."

Sumner's speech was extremely popular in Republican ranks. That speech not only excoriated the enslavement of the African American people; it also expressed doubts as to their alleged inferiority and insisted, in any case, that even if such inferiority did exist, that would add to the duty of a decent civilization to assist them "by a generous charity"; it certainly did not justify using against them "the bludgeon and chain."[16]

The high point of the rejection of slavery and of at least the questioning of racism was symbolized by John Brown. Perhaps I will be forgiven if I quote my own language at this point: "John Brown truly believed that all people were created in God's image and that Black men and women were the brothers and sisters of those who were white. Brown actively sought out Black people, lived among them, listened to them, learned from them." This is why, I think, Shields Green, the young recent fugitive from slavery, listening to John Brown detail his plan to Frederick Douglass in an effort to get Douglass to join him, decided—unlike Douglass—to "go with the old man." This is why he and other Black men chose to go with him into the lion's den and to share his martyrdom.

Lydia Maria Child had written in the *Liberator*, May 20, 1842, that "great political changes may be forced by the pressure of external forces." She had in mind the ending of slavery, but she warned, prophetically, that if such change came "without a corresponding change in the moral sentiment of a nation," the cancer would not be excised. Twenty years of effort and developing external forces did produce monumental change, even in moral sentiment, so that a political party with an anti-slavery essence and a rejection of at least the most putrid aspects of racism did become the leading party in a great civil war testing the survivability of the Republic.

This same Mrs. Child, having lived to see the betrayal of Reconstruction, suggested in 1878 that this could be explained, in considerable part, because "emancipation was not the result of a popular *moral sentiment*, but of a miserable 'military necessity.' "[17] Still, emancipation had become a military necessity, and in time of war there is no greater urgency. Opposition to slavery and its twin, racism, reached a high point during that war and for some years thereafter. That slavery was undone was the result, in part, of an incessant hammering away at it—and against racism.

18

The Civil War and Emancipation

"I am one of those," said Frederick Douglass at the Thirtieth Annual Meeting of the American Anti-Slavery Society in December 1863, "who believe that the work of the American Anti-Slavery Society will not have been completed until the black men of the South, and the black men of the North, shall have been admitted fully and completely, into the body politic of America." He was confident that the demise of slavery was soon to occur: "But a mightier work than the abolition of slavery now looms for the Abolitionist."

Douglass recalled that in founding the society, it was agreed that its purpose included the ending of slavery, certainly, but a crusade against racism was also a commitment. He went on: "When we have taken the chains off the slave, as I believe we shall do, we shall find a harder resistance to the second purpose of this great association than we have found even upon slavery itself."[1]

Even while Douglass was speaking, the New York *Journal of Commerce*, a fierce foe of abolitionism, remarked that with the issuance of the Emancipation Proclamation, "the opposition is no longer to the Slave; it is to the Negro." Theodore Tilton, an Abolitionist and editor of the important weekly, the *Independent*, in citing this, went on to agree that the argument about slavery was over; "The needful plea now," he added, "is for the Negro."[2]

With the commencement of the Civil War, those who had fought against slavery were persuaded that the war's basic source lay in that institution and that a positive outcome of the war required the ending of slavery. But while this seemed clear to such partisans, the first months of the conflict showed no movement toward slavery's termination and no battle victory for the Union. Indeed, as casualties (in the beginning only among white people) mounted and despair appeared, an intensification of anti-Negro feeling was apparent. Not atypical was the attitude expressed by William Parham, born free in 1839 and by the end of the 1850s a teacher at a school for African American children in Cincinnati. By the early 1860s he had given up hope of the land ever abandoning its colorphobia. As late as September 1862, he wrote a friend, "You do not know how much I yearn to be a *man*." He had concluded that to realize that feeling, perhaps he had to leave the country. But in less than a year he gave up the idea of migrating "at least for the present," as he wrote the same friend in August 1863. "The present aspect of things in this country," he then wrote, "the outrage and injustice to which we are still subject, notwithstanding, gives evidence of coming to a better day." Aware of his own considerable education, he concluded: "When this war is over the next war will be against prejudice which is conquered by intellect, and we shall need all the talent that we have among us or can possibly command."[3]

In the 1860 presidential campaign, the centrality of the slavery question, especially of slavery's expansionism, was clear, and the fact that the Republican party, alone of the four parties in contention, represented opinion hostile not only to slavery's expansion but also to slavery itself was palpable. This determined the fact that the majority of Abolitionists hoped for Lincoln's election; this united, for example, Garrison and Douglass.

At this period of crisis, the sensitivity of the slaveholding class to anything suggesting the humanity of the African American was extreme. Illustrative was the comment in a letter from Charles Sumner to the Duchess of Argyle, dated Boston, September 3, 1860: "That chance word from Ld. Brougham at the Statistical Congress has produced considerable commotion here. . . . It has shot far and wide the truth of the common humanity of the negro."[4]

This "word" referred to two paragraphs in the *London Times*, July 21, 1860, following a lengthy account of the International Statistical Congress then meeting in London. The reader was reminded that at the congress's opening, Lord Brougham had "called the attention of Mr. Dallas to the fact that one of the delegates was a man of colour, in a manner which seemed offensive to Mr. Dallas." Lord Brougham, said the *Times*, "made the following explanation: 'I exceedingly regret that the observations I made on the first day have been interpreted into something disrespectful to the United States. No one who has known me will accuse me of such an intention. I respect our brethren of the United States, even when I differ from them.' " Lord Brougham continued with comments that probably did not assuage Mr. Dallas:

When I called attention in the presence of our friend, Mr. Dallas, to the, in my opinion, important statistical fact that a most respectable coloured gentleman from Canada, was a member of the Congress, I only called attention to it just as I would the attention of our excellent friend the representative of the Brazils, who is here today; and, God knows, I do not entertain the slightest disrespect for the Brazils. I ought also to have called the attention of the Count de Ripaldi (the Spanish representative) to the same subject; they have colonies, and they have persons of various colours in their possessions. I call his attention to it hereby.[5]

During the early 1860s former slaves like William Wells Brown and William Craft, as well as English Abolitionists like George Thompson and American Abolitionists like Moncure Conway—of a very distinguished Virginia family—were not only attacking slavery but also polemizing against racism. Illustrative is the influential work of Conway, whose views were published in London in 1864. In *Testimonies Concerning Slavery* this self-exiled Virginian devoted a chapter to attacking concepts of African American inferiority. He found African Americans, he declared, highly imaginative and very artistic people, who were the creators of "the only original melodies we have." Their morality, he thought, was at least the equal of that of other people. He prophesied that "a vast deal of high art [was] yet to come out of that people in America." He also made clear his rejection of the idea that interracial marriage would be harmful; on the contrary, "I for one, am firmly persuaded that the mixture of the blacks and whites is good."[6]

In 1860 Louisa May Alcott wrote a novella whose theme was precisely Conway's point on intermarriage. Alcott offered the story for publication in the year she wrote it, and it was then refused because, she said, "it is antislavery and the dear South must not be offended." But it was published serially in the *Boston Commonwealth* between January 24 and February 21, 1863. In its final line the heroine rejects the belated apologies of her friends who had snubbed her because of her choice of a Black man as her husband: "Put off the old delusions that blind you to the light," she tells them, "and come up here to me."[7]

In the 1860 presidential campaign—not unlike several since—the "Negro question" was prominent. Indeed, some propaganda stated that Lincoln and particularly Hannibal Hamlin, his vice presidential running mate, were Black. A result was that some figures of stature and integrity faced up to this matter of racism. Notable was the long essay by James Russell Lowell on "The Election in November," which appeared in the October issue of the *Atlantic Monthly*, which Lowell edited, and to which attention was called earlier.

Lowell, in explaining his preference for the Republican party, placed great emphasis upon its hostility to the enslavement of human beings, however limited its proposals against it, in contrast to the other parties. A main section of Lowell's argument was devoted to an insistence upon the reality of the humanity of the African American. A lengthy extract is warranted because of the distinction of its author, the consequence of the journal publishing it, and the light it throws upon a viewpoint that by then had become quite widespread:

A great deal is said, to be sure, about the rights of the South; but has any such right been infringed? When a man invests money in any species of property, he assumes the risks to which it is liable. If he buy a house, it may be burned; if a ship, it may be wrecked; if a horse or an ox, it may die. Now the disadvantage of the Southern kind of property is—how shall we say it so as not to violate our Constitutional obligations?—that it is exceptional. When it leaves Virginia, it is a thing; when it arrives in Boston, it becomes a man, speaks human language, appeals to the justice of the same God whom we all acknowledge, weeps at the memory of wife and children left behind—in short, hath the same organs and dimensions that a Christian hath—and is not distinguishable from ordinary Christians, except, perhaps, by a simpler and more earnest faith.

There are people at the North who believe that, beside *meum* and *tuum*, there is also such a thing as *suum*—who are old-fashioned enough, or weak enough, to have their feelings touched by these things, to think that human nature is older and more sacred than any claim of property whatever, and that it has rights at least as much to be respected as any hypothetical one of our Southern brethren.

This, no doubt, makes it harder to recover a fugitive chattel; but the existence of human nature in a man here and there is surely one of those accidents to be counted on at least as often as fire, shipwreck, or the cattle disease; and the man who chooses to put his money into these images of his Maker cut in ebony should be content to take the incident risks along with the advantages. We should be very sorry to deem this risk capable of diminution; for we think that the claims of a common manhood upon us should be at least as strong as those of Freemasonry, and that those whom the law of man turns away should find in the larger charity of the law of God and Nature a readier welcome and surer sanctuary.

We shall continue to think the Negro a man, and on Southern evidence, too, so long as he is counted in the population represented on the floor of Congress—for three fifths of perfect manhood would be a high average even among white men; so long as he is hanged or worse, as an example and terror to others—for we do not punish one animal for the moral improvement of the rest; so long as he is considered capable of religious instruction—for we fancy the gorillas would make short work with a missionary; so long as there are fears of insurrection—for we have never heard of a combined effort at revolt in a menagerie.

During the war the activities of the already-noticed American Missionary Association were of consequence. As it had supported voluntary educational work in the antebellum South, often at great risk, so it continued this effort during the war. Illustrative is the work of Charles P. Day, a teacher in upstate New York, who opened a school near Hampton, Virginia, early in 1862. As he wrote to Simeon S. Jocelyn, one of the founders of the association, on April 4, 1862, he undertook this because he believed that the nation owed "a work of love to their colored brothers at the South, for the part we have taken (for I believe the North as well as the South are to blame in this) in helping to tread down him who is our brother."[8]

At its 1865 meeting the association approved suffrage and full citizenship rights for the African American man. Lewis Tappan notably was committed to absolute equality and attacked, for example, those who balked at intermarriage. In fact, the association employed interracial couples in its work in the United States and later in Africa.

A study of the association's work in Hampton found that the volunteers were convinced that the Black people were "human beings like themselves" and that they "could and should be free." The first worker at Hampton, coming there late in 1861, was Lewis Lockwood; he lived with Black people, and they greeted each other as "brother" and "sister." The practice of praying, eating, and, usually, living together was customary during the war period. A result was deep conviction of the equality of Blacks and whites.

When Lockwood fell ill in 1862, he was replaced by S. S. Jocelyn. Characteristic of the latter's reports was this: "I have found their love of freedom strong. Their desire for learning and the aptitude of the children and adults to learn are remarkable. . . . The religious knowledge, experience, character, unusual intelligence and gifts of numbers among them, have surprised the missionary teachers and visitors."[9]

The Civil War crusade for education was a Black-white effort; the teachers were of both colors, and together they faced serious peril and occasionally martyrdom. When white teachers were refused housing in white-controlled facilities, as often happened, Black families shared their very modest accommodations, despite the danger this entailed.

This egalitarian effort continued into the 1890s and beyond. Du Bois paid beautiful tribute to these extraordinary men and women, some of whom he knew personally. Here is one of his paragraphs:

Behind the mists of ruin and rapine waved the calico dresses of women who dared, and after the hoarse mouthings of the field guns rang the rhythm of the alphabet. Rich and poor they were, serious and curious. Bereaved now of father, now of brother, now of more than these, they came seeking a life work in planting New England schoolhouses among the white and black of the South. They did their work well.[10]

The books by Richardson and Engs cited earlier record the nearly universal testimony repudiating racism coming from these teachers. Other studies, including some hostile to the efforts, concur. This educational crusade, while cut short by the slanders and violence of the dominant classes, constituted a notable instance of anti-racist commitment.[11]

Especially thorough is a 1981 work by Robert C. Morris.[12] Typically, one teacher, William Allen, after seven months' experience, entered in his diary (June 11, 1864): "I do not think that there is any inferiority to white children." Colonel John Eaton (1829–1906), in his 1864 report as superintendent in the Freedmen's Department of the Army, included the results of a questionnaire submitted to teachers of Black people, asking especially their views as to the capacity to learn. Without exception, the replies affirmed this capacity as being at least the equal of that of others; not a few expressed surprise at this discovery. The Board of Education of the Army's Department of the Gulf, in its 1864 report, commented upon the schools for freed people in this way: "A marked influence of these schools is seen upon the white people in the lessening prejudice, and in the reluctant admission of the African's ability to learn, and his consequent fitness for places in the world, from which we have hitherto excluded him."

The general superintendent of freedman's education, John W. Alvord, in his official semiannual report in July 1867, concluded that the experience, covering broad areas and thousands of subjects in the face of serious obstacles, had proved the existence of "equal endowments" among the African American people and of "equality common to all mankind." Publicly, Alvord added that doubts about "the ability of colored children to learn, with capacity for higher attainment were rapidly passing away." No wonder that such efforts and the social reorganization that made them possible had to be terminated by any means necessary if a society approximating that of 1860 were to be restored.

There were instances—how numerous is uncertain—of individual initiatives toward educating Black people in the South during the war. An example is the effort of Esther Hill Hawks, M.D., originally from New Hampshire and of anti-slavery persuasion. In the 1850s she married a physician, John Milton Hawks, and settled with him in Florida, where she "clandestinely taught a school for black children." During the Union occupation of Jacksonville in 1864, she taught Black and white youngsters. This effort lasted four months until objection by some white parents forced the school's closing. Dr. Hawks stated that she was delighted with the "ability and eagerness to learn" of the Black children. She added, *"I love them,"* but, alas, the effort was short-lived.[13] White women taught Black people in Louisville, Kentucky, during the war. Stores, restaurants, and boarding houses were closed to them, but Black people welcomed them.[14]

By now a considerable literature exists on the African American people and the Civil War in the United States. After initial resistance, their participation was permitted. The result was the enlistment of about 200,000 Black men as soldiers, several thousand as sailors, and about 250,000 more as workers for the Army and the Navy—as cooks, draymen, fortification builders, nurses, guides, and what were then called "pioneers," now known as combat engineers.[15] Their activity was vital to the success of Lincoln's government. During the war years significant advances in the position of the Black people were achieved: an end to the slave trade, the abolition of slavery in the District of Columbia, the repeal of the Fugitive Slave Law, and the elimination of various racist laws and practices in some cities and states, including laws involving transportation, judicial procedure, suffrage, education, and marriage. These were partial, often poorly enforced, and spotty—in this or that city or state. But they did occur. The movement challenging racism finally led to the Civil War amendments, the Civil Rights

Acts of the 1860s, and the beginnings of actual citizenship. All of these advances resulted from the needs of combat, the realities of diplomatic relationships, and the necessity of national survival. All also represented some challenge to the mythology as well as the practice of racism.

The participation of the African American population in the Civil War effort, especially as soldiers, had a particularly dramatic impact upon racist stereotypes. Those who had led in the Abolitionist movement—even those of a pacifist outlook, like Garrison—knew that forcing the participation of Black people would have this effect. Hence they fought for it individually— outstanding was Frederick Douglass—and collectively in meetings, conventions, and petitions.

The role of Black men as fighters generally evoked expressions of an anti-racist character, mixed quite often with surprise. Of special consequence in demonstrating the anti-racist impact of joint Black-white combat has been the quite recent work of Joseph T. Glatthaar.[16] In the first of his books, Glatthaar wrote of a "wide range of racial attitudes" among the white soldiers. Some were vicious, even murderous, in their colorphobia. His work and other evidences have demonstrated this; there were cases, especially ones involving unspeakable maltreatment of Black women by some Union soldiers, that rival the worst atrocities committed later in the Philippines, Haiti, and Vietnam. Yet Glatthaar did find that "a fairly sizable proportion of the troops" came to advocate "social and political equality." This resulted because many of the white soldiers saw the Blacks' passion for freedom, their eagerness for learning, and their exemplary conduct in combat. Further, many white soldiers, including escaped prisoners, were helped by Black people who fed them and guided them; in one case a Black man gave his own shoes to a barefoot soldier.

Glatthaar wrote: "No doubt, everyone except the most close-minded soldiers who participated in the Savannah and Carolina campaigns returned home with an advanced opinion of Southern blacks." There were cases of white soldiers who prevented segregationist acts, as in the instance of an effort to Jim Crow Black soldiers on a naval transport. By way of a kind of summary, Glatthaar quoted one white officer: "What they [the Black troops] have done for the army entitles them to their freedom, or whatever else they may desire." Glatthaar's final words in dealing with the subject in his *March to the Sea* were the following:

By the end of the Carolina campaign, even though a majority of the troops in Sherman's army still bore some sort of racial prejudice, most soldiers would agree with an officer who wrote [March 27, 1865]: "the more we become acquainted with the negro character, both as men and Christians, the more we are impelled to respect them."[17]

In his more recent and more expansive volume, Glatthaar offered significant information on the impact joint combat experience had upon racist concepts. Glatthaar believed that most of the white officers with Black troops were infected with racism, but probably less so than many of their contemporaries. Of course, most of them wanted to preserve the Republic and to help end slavery; some were actively anti-racist.

One, Carlos P. Lyman, wrote his sister early in 1865 that he was engaged in "the best cause that man ever fought for in the preservation of the Union . . . and the equal freedom of all men in this country, *regardless of color!*" Another, serving as a surgeon with the United States Colored Troops, wrote in September 1864 that he was "tired of war," but he added, "I don't want an inglorious peace. The peace I want is one based upon equality, freedom, to all white black or copper color."[18]

Prejudice certainly existed, but "after just a few days nearly all the officers were excited over the progress and promise of the troops." One quite innocently wrote his mother late in the war that his Black troops were "much more intelligent than I had supposed."[19]

Captain Charles Augustus Hill wrote his wife in November 1863, after a period of service with Black troops: "A great many have the idea that the entire negro race are vastly their inferiors—a few weeks of calm unprejudiced life here would disabuse them I think—I have a more elevated opinion of their abilities than I ever had before." He concluded: "I *know* that many of them are vastly *superiors* of those (many of those) who would condemn them all to a life of degradation." This same Captain Hill wrote his wife one month later, as the first anniversary of the Emancipation Proclamation neared: "Do you remember how it was with the Emancipation Proclamation? How many tho't 'twould be the ruin of the nation and all that?" None now could be so blind as not to see the enormous benefit it had brought the nation; indeed, it converted "a bleak future into a bright one." In fact, he believed, in freeing slaves and making inevitable the reality of Black soldiers, the proclamation "under the Providence of God" had "*saved*" the nation.[20]

More and more, summarized Glatthaar, as the struggle continued, "Unionists and their troops were hesitantly casting aside much of their racial blinders." In the case of some of the white officers, like Penrose Hallowell, Horace Bumstead, and Dr. Burt G. Wilder, the war experience produced a strong rejection of racism and a lifelong commitment to active involvement in the anti-racist movement. This persisted into the twentieth century and is matter for a subsequent study.[21]

One of the officers who served with Black troops, Thomas Wentworth Higginson (1827–1911), left in his classical *Army Life in a Black Regiment* a magnificent account. Higginson concluded: "Till the blacks were armed, there was no guarantee of their freedom. It was their demeanor under arms that shamed the nation into recognizing them as men—intensely human."

Major-General David Hunter, who had authorized Higginson to raise his regiment, reported in the spring of 1863 that its men "proved brave, active, enduring and energetic." They "never disgraced their uniform by pillage or cruelty"; indeed, "even our enemies, though more anxious to find fault with these than any other portion of our troops, have not been able to allege against them a single violation of the rules of civilized warfare."[22]

Two other quite recently published volumes provided additional evidence of the positive impact upon white officers of their participation in combat with Black soldiers. Both of the men chronicled in these books stayed on in the South for some time after the war and continued their anti-racist commitment in strong support of radical Reconstruction despite serious threats to their lives. One, John Emory Bryant, wrote: "I had a chance to see how black soldiers will fight and I can assure you that no men can do better." Similarly, Marshall Harvey Twitchell, originally from Vermont, served as a captain with the Black soldiers leading the final assault that brought Lee's surrender. He thought that these soldiers were "splendid"; they excelled "even the best white troops I had ever seen."[23]

Additional evidence of anti-racist developments in the war years appeared in cities and states of the South and of the North. Many among the German population in St. Louis before the war had troubled slaveowners who suspected them of anti-slavery views. A leader of the community, Friedrich Münch, described as a "farmer, politician and publicist," was editor of the newspaper, *Anzeiger des Westens*. An editorial in its issue of March 31, 1862, contained these lines: "Were we allowed to tell the owners of human beings what we thought of black servitude? Were we allowed to tell the slaves, or even to indicate to them through silent conduct, that we regarded them as *human* beings and that they had human rights, too?" The editorial continued that "not very long ago," when "a respected German . . . let slip a simple comment that blacks were *people*, too," he was visited by a group of slaveowners, "intensively grilled," and made to understand that such views were unwelcome. Indeed, in 1861 "a so-called vigilance committee was formed" to oversee "our deeds and speech," and the Germans were labelled "thieves of Negroes." The Germans had witnessed terrible cruelty toward the slaves—"the screams of those being whipped assailed our ears." Slavery was damnable. "If we reconcile ourselves to the notion of free labor alongside slave labor and continuing so into the future, then we will be guilty of holding our own state back from the progress of the free states and we shall never win full freedom for ourselves or our descendants."[24]

Often whites who participated in efforts to produce a less inhuman South themselves reflected some degree of white supremacist thinking. Yet here, too, characteristic was a rejection of the oppression resting upon such supremacist attitudes. The rejection carried with it an insistence upon the humanity of the African American.

A good representative of this type is Hugh Lennox Bond of Maryland, a leading attorney and a judge of Baltimore's Criminal Court from 1860 to 1867. Bond was an outstanding figure in Maryland's Union party, which led in creating the constitution of 1864 that emancipated over 80,000 slaves. During these years Bond was also a significant force in creating the Baltimore Association for the Moral and Educational Improvement of the Colored People; by 1867 it conducted eighty schools in the city and environs and enrolled about six thousand students.

Bond's approach was that of a devout Christian; while he never did achieve a belief in actual equality of Blacks and whites, he did vehemently reject any suggestion that Black people were less human than whites or that their political and educational rights ought to be circumscribed. As the historian who most fully analyzed Bond's views put it, at their center was Bond's conviction that Blacks and whites were members of God's "single family of man"; that in the United States they shared a "common country" and had "mutual interests." Black people, Bond said at a public meeting in Maryland soon after the war, were "citizens of the Republic," and if anything less than their full citizenship rights came out of the slaughter, then all efforts were a "mere mockery." Bond's efforts failed in his lifetime, but with all the limitations of his outlook, he did labor to eradicate not only slavery but the meanest features of its legacy. As such, Bond is part of the anti-racist tradition of the United States.[25]

The activity of General John M. Palmer, commander of Union forces in Kentucky in the last year of the war, reflected a person who not only detested slavery but who intended to root out racist discrimination. Becoming convinced that city officials in Louisville had unjustly imprisoned Black people, he appointed a Black man, the Reverend Thomas James, to inspect the city's jails and report back to him. James found many Black men held unjustly and treated barbarously—"some had iron bars on their legs, reaching from the hip to the ankles and fastened on with iron straps." They were released, and when threats appeared against James, General Palmer let it be known that "if James is killed, I will hold responsible for the act every man who fills an office under your city government. I will hang them higher than Haman was hung, and I have 15,000 troops behind me to carry out the order."

Palmer provided passes freely to any Black person wanting to go north; by April 1865 about two hundred a week were being issued. By the end of the spring of 1865 slavery was finished in Kentucky because of this exodus, though officially slavery did not end there until the ratification of the Thirteenth Amendment in December 1865. On July 4, 1865, General Palmer told about twenty thousand Black people celebrating the day with new vigor that "you are free"; they were "my countrymen," and the army under his command would "defend your right to freedom." No wonder a contemporary noted that "pandemonium broke out."[26]

Knowing the particular history of New Orleans, one might expect that the war years would witness significant challenges not only to slavery but also to racism. They did. The militancy of the Black population, slave and free, was intense, and in the closing years of the war, collaboration between whites who hated slavery and rejected racism was marked. Among the white people leading in this activity—on literary, agitational, and political fronts—were C. Le Maistre, J. C. Houzeau, and Thomas J. Durant in particular.

All vigorously and explicitly rejected racism and favored not only political and civil equality for Black people but also the distribution of land to them. The advocacy of the enfranchisement of women also appeared among these advanced figures. Full justice to the developments in this city from 1862 to 1866 has not yet been done, but a dissertation and an article bring forward the main facts: the advocacy of Black-white unity, full African American equality, and collaboration in life and in work between Blacks and whites.[27]

In the North the war greatly stimulated the advocacy of equality and the passage of laws directed against discrimination. Ohio in 1864–65 provided for the establishment of a considerable number of schools for Black youngsters, repealed an 1859 act that had restricted Black suffrage, and abrogated a later law that had barred Black immigrants. Cincinnati eliminated segregated street cars.[28]

In Pennsylvania anti–Jim Crow legislation finally was enacted in 1867. This resulted from insistent agitation and organized protests, led especially by the Pennsylvania State Equal Rights League. Among white people a decisive role was played by Morrow B. Lowry, a state senator representing Erie and Crawford counties. He introduced a bill to bar discrimination on public means of travel in 1861 and stayed with the effort for six years.

Illustrative of his views was a speech delivered in the Pennsylvania Senate on January 19, 1865. He then affirmed: "I stand for the absolute equality of all men before the law. This is God's eternal law—this is divine ethics, 'God hath made of one blood all nations of men.' " Slavery, he said, was the progenitor of "a diabolical prejudice against the black men," and the war to end slavery must also be a war to exterminate that product of slavery.[29]

Earlier, the use of Jim Crow street cars in San Francisco was declared illegal in a ruling in October 1864 made by Judge C. C. Pratt of the Twelfth District Court of California. Judge Pratt said that such discriminatory practice was "the invocation of prejudices which have no holier origin than in brutal propensities, and a willingness to assist in perpetuating a relic of barbarism."[30]

A striking example of how the anti-slavery essence of the Civil War carried over into anti-racism is afforded by developments in various religious denominations in the North. John R. McKivigan's work is especially illuminating on this. He observed that "many northern churchmen [supported] calls to repeal state and local legislation that barred blacks from the polls in most states and forced their children into racially separated public schools." The *Freewill Baptist Quarterly* in January 1865 insisted that churches were "duty bound to testify against prejudices which deprive [Black people] of their rights and equality before human law. When they are eman-cipated the struggle is not over. It is yet a long march to the millennium."

The Church Anti-Slavery Society, formed in this period, sought to cleanse its own denominations of racist practices. It feared, said an 1863 pro-nouncement, that "every other door in the nation would be opened to the negro before the pew door." Many individual congregations and wider groupings moved toward integration. McKivingan summarized:

The New England and Erie conferences of the Methodist Episcopal Church, for example, removed all discriminatory rules against black members. In 1863 white Episcopalians in Philadelphia admitted black delegates to the conventions for the first time. Numerous New England Congregational churches voted to abolish the custom of negro pews.

McKivingan emphasized that, nevertheless, "many northern churches con-tinued to discriminate against blacks," but added that the positive actions taken by others were important reflections and stimuli of widespread anti-racist developments.[31]

Theodore Tilton (1835–1907), noted earlier, was editor of the important Congregationalist weekly the *Independent*. In its issue of June 25, 1863, he characterized the war as one "for social equality, for rights, for justice, for freedom." A month earlier, speaking at the Cooper Institute in New York City, he had insisted that no proof existed to support the notion of the inferiority of Black people. God, he said, was no respecter of persons, why should men be? All regulations, all laws reflecting concepts of inequality should be undone.

With emancipation recently announced, he said, Black people came "into the light and liberty of sons of God! My countrymen," he urged, "give them a greeting of good cheer!" Make them welcome, he pleaded: "For they come guided of Him whose reward is with Him—who has said, 'Inasmuch as ye do it unto the least of these, my little ones, ye do it unto me.' "[32]

Eloquent and unequivocal in its attack upon racism was a sermon deliv-ered by Henry Ward Beecher at his Brooklyn, New York, church early in 1865 and published in full in the *Independent* on February 23. Otto Olsen characterized Beecher as "essentially a moderate reformer who remained closely attuned to respectable opinion in the North." Olsen observed that Beecher did not favor emancipation until well into 1862 and that in the postwar period he assumed a posture favorable to Johnsonian Reconstruc-tion. I believe that all this makes even more significant his powerful attack upon racism in this 1865 address.

He began by remarking that the African Americans were "remarkably endowed with moral susceptibilities." This suggested to him "that if ever again we are to have prophets and seers and rapt mystics, we shall find them of their blood"—a quite remarkable prophecy of Du Bois and Martin Luther King, Jr.

Men must at once proceed to "removing wrongs and disabilities" from them, for "we are to recognize this people as a part of that human family for which Christ died. From the face of that truth will fly away all those guilty and hideous lies which have denied their humanity and ranked them with beasts." Beecher insisted: "Once admit that he is a *man*, and then whatever you would think of the white man, think of him."

Beecher here urged their full citizenship, equal education, and even that they be given land for their sustenance. He refused to deny or to affirm racial equality: "I am willing to take my chance with him. Are you willing to do the same? Or, are you afraid that he will outrun you in a fair race?"

With some daring, Beecher denounced laws prohibiting intermarriage. He had no opinion, he said, as to whether this would deteriorate one or the other race; he did not think that physiologists could speak on this with confidence. He closed with characteristic eloquence:

> I accept him as my brother, because Christ is his Redeemer and mine, and God is his Father and mine; he is my blood kindred. And I assert for him, in the name of Christianity, in the name of liberty, and in the name of civilization, the rights that God gave him, that men have taken away from him, and that it is your privilege to restore to him.[33]

If Beecher tended to bend with the wind, a man of the cloth who certainly did not was Gilbert Haven, noted earlier. Haven, destined in 1872 to be Methodist bishop of Georgia, was unanimously elected editor of the Boston-based *Zion's Herald*, probably the leading religious publication in New England, in 1867. His motto for that publication was "No Caste in the Church of God."

Appearing in Boston in May 1863 at the Annual Meeting of the Church Anti-Slavery Society (George Cheever, Frederick Douglass, and Henry Wilson were on the platform), Haven argued that"the end of slavery was only the necessary first step toward overcoming all forms of racial injustice." Haven feared, as he said in 1864, that overcoming racism "may take a longer time and greater struggles to destroy" than slavery, but, if the nation was faithful to God's teaching, he was sure that it would "triumph over both."

No one since Anthony Benezet a century earlier had so fiercely denounced racism as did Gilbert Haven. In a sermon at Charlestown, Massachusetts, April 2, 1863, he confidently announced that "the tide sweeps with increasing force and volume against these deep and ancient prejudices. They will be overwhelmed." He recalled the 1862 resolution unanimously adopted by the Methodist Episcopal Church: "We deprecate the unchristian spirit of caste so prevalent throughout the North, and even among many professed anti-slavery men with respect to people of color, and we can never regard our reformatory work accomplished till they enjoy equal rights and privileges with other classes."

The church must lead, he said, in eliminating all distinctions among people. At a mass meeting in Boston in June 1863, he pleaded: "Uproot and expel the iniquitous prejudice from your souls." Cast out this foul thing, "out of our stores, our shops, our families, our pews, and our pulpits, yea, and first of all, out of our own hearts."[34]

Union victories in the summer of 1864 led him to hope that "we shall welcome them [Black people] as brothers and sisters, and the long nightmare of our fears and hates will break up." A little later that year (September 11), he warned that if the "nightmare" was not terminated, "as sure as there is a god in heaven, there will be another war in America; a war more fierce, more bloody, more fatal than this—a war of races and extermination."

Welcoming the new year in 1865, he said, "To the removal of this prejudice every lover of Christ and his country should devote himself." A Jim Crow army of a Republic fighting against slavery was an absurdity and a sin. Indeed, in every aspect of life, public and private, "We must grant them [Black people] civil equality and fraternity." He thought, or at least hoped, that military victory would lead swiftly to racism's end, that the land's highest positions would be graced by Black people, and that, perhaps within a decade after peace, intermarriage "will be frequent."

He hailed what he saw as a new dedication to real equality. "Let our land be really free, really equal, really cleansed of racism" was the theme of his magnificent Boston sermon, July 9, 1865, on "Peace: Her Gifts and Demands." He was confident that if the cleansing really went forward, "The negro will rise to posts of honor and authority in all the land; will sit in Congress ... and men will smile at the idea of distinction of color as they now do at the divinity of slavery."[35]

In Boston on December 31, 1862, a mass meeting that had gathered in anticipation of the announcement of the Final Proclamation of Emancipation to be issued on January 1, 1863, heard a poem, "Boston Hymn," written for that occasion by Ralph Waldo Emerson. In it were these lines:

> Pay ransom to the owner,
> And fill the bag to the brim.
> Who is the owner? The slave is the owner,
> And ever was, Pay him!

Garrison observed that these lines "won loudest applause" from the large crowd.[36]

By the emancipation year Harper's Weekly was editorializing: "How utterly undeserving this mad hatred of the colored race is every sober man in this country knows."[37] To combat "this mad hatred" was a central purpose in the minds of those who created the Nation magazine. A group of anti-slavery men in New England, who in 1863 had constituted themselves a Committee for Recruiting Negro Troops, pledged $16,000 for that magazine, stipulating that it was to be "devoted to the equal rights of all men." Those backing the creation of the magazine understood that its purpose—to quote its 1865 prospectus—would be "the removal of all artificial distinctions between [the Negro] and the rest of the population." This did not eventuate, and by 1866 former Abolitionists had withdrawn their support; that, however, is another matter. The point here was this belief, backed by considerable funding, that the magazine's main purpose was to combat racist discrimination in much the same way that the *Liberator* had combatted slavery.[38]

The Civil War revitalized an organized labor movement in the North. Components of this effort were fearful of the possibility of competition from newly freed African American people. On the other hand, there had been a tradition, going back to abolitionism, of some sense of the need for unity of all those who labored, regardless of color (and, in some cases, of gender). Shortly before the war this concept was represented especially by William H. Sylvis of the International Molders Union and Andrew C. Cameron, editor of the Chicago-based *Workingmen's Advocate*.[39]

During and immediately after the war this policy of unity of Black and white was advocated forcefully by the Boston *Daily Evening Voice* (1864–67), a publication of the organized printers of the city. It had a considerable circulation; George E. McNeil in his book *The Labor Movement* (1888) called it "the most important" of the labor papers of its time. This paper strongly advocated the rights of women and the enhancement of public education. But its outstanding feature was its passionate call for Black-white unity among working people, its support for Black political and economic equality, and its denunciation of the Reconstruction policies of President Andrew Johnson. Typical of its position was this editorial paragraph from its issue of January 13, 1866:

> If the workingmen have learned anything, it is that there can be no hope of their success but in union—the union of all that labor. How mad and suicidal, then, to hold up one hand for the degradation of the Negro while the other is raised for the elevation of the white laborer! Capital knows no difference between white and black laborers and the labor movement cannot make any, without undermining its own platform and tearing down the walls of its own defence.[40]

The material presented here helps explain the sense of optimism among some who had spent much of their lives fighting not only against slavery but also against its main rationalization. Garrison, for example, wrote in the *Liberator* June 12, 1863 "Of the multitudinous disparaging allegations that have been brought against the slave population by the enemies of impartial freedom, not one has been verified by the war"; that is, the Black people had shown themselves eager for freedom and yearning for education and as soldiers had demonstrated "a courage for attack, and a disregard of danger and death, unsurpassed in the annals of warfare."

Whittier wrote to Garrison that with emancipation, the Black people must have "a fair field for development and improvement...the last vestige of that hateful prejudice which has been the strongest external support" of slavery must be undone. Whites must, Whittier went on, lift themselves "at once" to the "heartfelt recognition of the brotherhood of man." "At once" was quite swift. Garrison did not suggest this; still, his view in the closing period of the war indicated great optimism on this score. He wrote a British friend in 1864 that "with the abolition of slavery in the South, prejudice or 'color phobia,' the natural product of the system, will gradually disappear."[41] This may well help explain Garrison's decision—in the face of appeals from Douglass and Phillips—to disband the American Anti-Slavery Society with the close of 1865 and the adoption of the Thirteenth Amendment, though both Douglass and Phillips reminded him that the society had pledged itself at its creation not only to fight for the emancipation of the slaves but also for the extirpation of racism.

At the federal level, meanwhile, the climax of the Thirteenth Amendment came as act after act was passed aimed both at slavery and at some of its vestiges. Crowning the defeat of the Confederacy, with its explicit commitment both to slavery and to racism, was the fact that some half a million African American men and women had fought in the Army and the Navy of the United States, had labored in a score of capacities for these forces, had supplied vital information to them, and had demonstrated that the salvation of the nation required an end to slavery and that to both of these connected purposes their own contribution had been indispensable.

Indicating the intent of the dominant force in the U.S. Congress were the preliminary report and the final report of the Freedmen's Inquiry Commission created by War Department order on March 16, 1863. The formal origin under the aegis of Secretary of War Edwin Stanton did not belie a decisive influence in the commission's makeup and creation of Senator Charles Sumner. Sumner's opposition to slavery and to racism was as intense as has ever marked a white person in the United States.

The commission members were Dr. Samuel Gridley Howe, Colonel James McKaye, and Robert Dale Owen. Howe (1801–1876) had been a leading Abolitionist, a dedicated revolutionary (having participated in the Greek War for Independence), and a supporter of John Brown and was the husband of Julia Ward Howe. Owen (1801–1877), the other decisive member of the commission, was the son of the Utopian Socialist Robert Owen, an associate of the very radical Frances Wright, and a strong emancipationist.

The commission in its preliminary report (June 1863) stated: "Every aggression, every act of injustice committed by a Northern man against unoffending fugitives from despotism, every insult offered by the base prejudice of our race to a colored man because of his African descent, is not only a breach of humanity, an offense against civilization, but is also an act which gives aid and comfort to the enemy." In its final report the commission urged an end "to the depressing influence of disgraceful prejudice" and support for the policy of plantation confiscation to be followed by the distribution of land to the South's impoverished—Blacks and whites. In short, the commission sought, as its historian has written, to "root out the social evil of race prejudice."[42] To paralyze this "disgraceful prejudice" and to lay the groundwork for a Republic worthy of the promise of the Declaration of Independence was the intent of the majority of that Congress that finally enacted the amendment abolishing slavery, effective in December 1865, passed the Civil Rights Act of 1866, and enacted the Fourteenth Amendment to the Constitution.

Evocative of this stance were the words of George W. Julian of Indiana. He had said in 1855: "Let the brotherhood of all men, without regard to race, color, religion, or birthplace, be the platform on which all may gather." Ten years later (February 7, 1865), in the House, chronicling the acts that had been passed "wiping out our code of national slave laws," Julian said that Congress had thereby "opened the way for further and inevitable measures of justice, looking for his [the Black man's] complete emancipation from the dominion of Anglo-Saxon prejudice, the repeal of all special legislation intended for his injury, and his absolute restoration to equal rights with the white man as a citizen as well as a soldier." On January 16, 1866, in arguing for enfranchising the Black men in the District of Columbia, Julian demanded that "one rule be adopted for white and black"; he went on, "And let us, if possible, dispossess our minds, utterly, of the vile spirit of caste which has brought upon our country all its woes."[43]

Increasingly, then, racism was explicitly protested and attacked, as we have seen, in churches and in legislative halls. Recurring, too, were attacks upon long-standing customs of exclusion like, for example, that practiced by the Young Men's Association of Albany, New York, which had barred Black people from attendance. Lecturers now would refuse to appear unless such practices were abandoned.[44]

In 1863 John S. Rock (1825–1866), a Boston attorney and physician and a leader in the anti-slavery and anti-racist effort, visited at the home of his friend, Charles Sumner. He brought up the matter of Sumner's support for the effort to qualify Rock to practice before the U.S. Supreme Court. Late in 1864 Senator Sumner wrote to Chief Justice Salmon P. Chase recommending Rock for such admission, noting that he was supported in this request by Governor John A. Andrew of Massachusetts. Sumner here described Rock as "an estimable colored lawyer." Sumner added: "Of course, the admission of a colored lawyer to the bar of the Supreme Court would make it difficult for any restriction on account of color to be maintained anywhere."

Sumner had the pleasure of presenting Rock to the Court on February

1, 1865, when he was admitted to plead before its bar. At this time he was leading the effort to enfranchise the Black man and to break up the great Southern plantations and distribute the land to those whose unpaid labor had made it fruitful. On March 29, 1865, he wrote to Garrison: "Our last battle approaches," having in mind these purposes. "Its countersign will be Equality before the law—without distinction of color. The good cause must triumph."[45]

Under Johnsonian Reconstruction, when black laws were passed in several former Confederate states, their repeal was sought at once in Congress. Senator Henry Wilson, in introducing legislation for that purpose, said that Congress must assure that the emancipated slave "is a freeman indeed; that he can go where he pleases, work when and for whom he pleases; that he can sue and be sued; that he can lease and buy and sell and own property, real and personal; that he can go into the schools and educate himself and his children; that the rights and guarantees of the good old common law are his, and that he walks the earth, proud and erect in the conscious dignity of a freeman." It was necessary, said the Massachusetts senator—and for this the blood of 600,000 men had been shed—"that these enfranchised men shall be free indeed, not serfs, not peons, and that no black laws nor unfriendly legislation shall linger on the statute book of any Commonwealth in America."[46]

In continuing the struggle against racism, Senator Wilson made clear his belief that such an effort was part of the battle against elitism in general. In debate with the intensely racist Senator Edgar Cowan of Pennsylvania—who had caricatured the whole matter of equality and had mockingly asked if this meant equally tall or equally heavy or equally wealthy—Wilson replied that the Pennsylvanian knew that what was meant was equality of rights, of the law, of citizenship. Further, Senator Cowan knew that Wilson advocated the rights of the Black man "because the black man was the most oppressed type of the toiling masses of this country." Wilson continued: "I tell you, sir, that the man who is the enemy of the black laboring man is the enemy of the white laboring man the world over. The same influences that go to keep down and crush down the rights of the poor black man bear down and oppress the poor white laboring man." The "negro drivers," said Senator Wilson, "had just as much contempt for the toiling white millions of the country as they had for their own black slaves." Senator Cowan had sneered at the physical features and mental capacities of Black people. Wilson thought that there "are many negroes who have hearts quite as good as the heart of that Senator; and I know some of them with brains quite as capacious and quite as well trained as his own."[47]

Quite the opposite of Cowan of Pennsylvania was Thaddeus Stevens of Pennsylvania. He, like Wilson, had suggested to a racist colleague in the House that he knew Black people who would stand up very well in debate with him. Speaking in the House on December 18, 1865, this very powerful figure and key force in creating the Civil War amendments denounced those who pandered "to the lowest prejudices of the ignorant [and] repeat the cuckoo cry, 'This is a white man's government.' Demagogues of all parties, even some in high authority, gravely shout, 'This is the white man's government.' " They contradicted the Declaration of Independence. Those who carried through the Revolution "were prevented by slavery" from perfecting the government; they waited "but never relinquished the idea of its final completion." Now "it is our duty to complete their work." Most certainly, Stevens insisted, "This is not a 'white man's government.' " That idea, he said, "is political blasphemy." On the contrary, "Equal rights to all the privileges of the government is innate in every immortal being, no matter what the shape or color of the tabernacle which it inhabits."

Thaddeus Stevens lived with a Black woman, Lydia Hamilton Smith—always addressed as Mrs. Smith—from 1848 to his death twenty years later. When death was approaching, he made certain that his remains would not be interred in a segregated cemetery. He directed that upon his tombstone be carved these words:

> I repose in this quiet and secluded spot,
> Not from any natural preference for solitude
> But, finding other Cemeteries limited as to Race by Charter Rules,
> I have chosen this that I might illustrate in my death
> The Principles which I advocated
>   Through a long life.
> EQUALITY OF MAN BEFORE HIS CREATOR[48]

With slavery ended, the drive to extirpate racism reached a more desperate and a higher level. A subsequent volume is projected that will examine that effort from the time the Illinois lawyer was assassinated to the time when a young Du Bois, undertaking his historic work at the *Crisis* in 1910 and participating in the First All-Races Congress in London in 1911, later witnessed Wilson's crusade for democracy descending into a resurgent racism in the United States.

The youngster who, a generation ago, could not believe that John Brown, a white man, had died to make Black people free may now see that John Brown was not unique in his commitment to human equality, and not even in his martyrdom. He may now see the past in a new light. Let that illumination help fashion a more humane future for the United States of America.

Notes

Introduction

1. I published a suggestion, "Anti-Racism in U.S. History: An Introduction," in *Black Scholar* (1975), 6:15–22. Another essay, with the same title but more material, edited by Benjamin Bowser, is in *Sage Race Relations Abstract* (1987), 12:3–22. The decision to concentrate on anti-racism among white people owes much to a conversation some years ago with John Hope Franklin.

2. A doctoral dissertation being prepared by Toby Terrar in the history department of the University of California in Los Angeles treats this strand in Catholicism up to the seventeenth century. I appreciate his sharing his findings with me.

3. See Haim Cohn, *Human Rights in Jewish Law* (New York, 1984). On this question I was helped by Rabbi Brad Artson of Mission Viejo, California.

4. Harriet Martineau, *Society in America*, 4th ed., 2 vols. (New York and London, 1837), 1:371.

5. Roger-Henri Gaurrand, "Private Spaces," in Phillipe Arnès and Georges Duby, eds., *A History of Private Life*, 4 vols. (Cambridge, Mass., 1987–1990), 4:359.

6. An outstanding example is the influential work of Nicholas Caussin, *The Holy Court; or, The Christian Institution of Men of Quality* (first published in 1626; an English edition, translated by Basil Brooke, appeared in London in 1977).

7. On ancient society and racism, see H. C. Baldry, *The Unity of Mankind in Greek Thought* (New York, 1965); and two books by Frank M. Snowden, Jr., *Blacks in Antiquity: Ethiopians in the Greco-Roman Experience* (Cambridge, Mass., 1970) and *Before Color Prejudice: The Ancient View of Blacks* (Cambridge, Mass., 1983). On ideas of the innate inferiority of the poor, see Edgar S. Furniss, *The Position of the Laborer in a System of Nationalism* (reprinted, New York, 1965); and Eli F. Heckscher, *Mercantilism* (first published in Sweden in 1931), rev. edition, 2 vols. (London, 1955), especially vol. 2. Also see Oliver C. Cox, *Caste, Class, and Race* (New York, 1948); Cox, *The Foundations of Capitalism* (New York, 1959); and I. M. Rubinow, "Poverty," in *Encyclopedia of the Social Sciences* (New York, 1934), vol. 13. In general, see Alain Locke and Bernhard J. Stern, eds., *When Peoples Meet* (New York, 1942). On concepts of women, see Julia O'Faolain and Lauro

Martines, *Not in God's Image: Women in History from the Greeks to the Victorians* (New York, 1973). For the relatively recent development of racial thought in South Africa, see W. M. Freund, "Race in the Social Structure of South Africa to 1836," *Race and Class* (London) (Summer 1976), 18:53–67.

Chapter 1

1. See Raymond Starr and Robert Detweiler, eds., *Race, Prejudice, and the Origins of Slavery in America* (Cambridge, Mass., 1975). This book reprints essays by nine scholars; it also contains a helpful "additional readings section." No mention, however, is made of Louis Ruchames, "The Sources of Racial Thought in America," *JNH* (1967), 52:251–72, nor of Joseph Boskin, "Race Relations in 17-Century America," *Sociology and Social Research* (1965), 49:446–55. Also see Alden T. Vaughan, "The Origins Debate: Slavery and Racism in 17th Century Virginia," *VMHB* (1989), 97:311–54.

2. The classical assault upon the racism dominating the history profession in the United States until World War II was W. E. B. Du Bois's *Black Reconstruction* (New York, 1935). Carter G. Woodson devoted his life to countering racist historiography. James Hugo Johnston's book—originally a dissertation at the University of Chicago in 1937—was finally published in 1970 at Amherst, Massachusetts, as *Race Relations in Virginia and Miscegenation in the South, 1776–1860.*

3. James M. McPherson, *The Struggle for Equality: Abolitionists and the Negro in the Civil War and Reconstruction* (Princeton, N.J., 1964); Ralph G. Morrow, "The Pro-Slavery Argument Revisited," *MVHR* (1961), 48:79–94. A critical analysis of the Phillipsian "white supremacy" theme in Southern history forms a chapter in my *Toward Negro Freedom* (New York, 1956), pp. 182–91.

4. Winthrop D. Jordan, *White over Black: American Attitudes toward the Negro, 1550–1812* (Chapel Hill, N.C., 1968), p. xi.

5. Eric Foner, *Politics and Ideology in the Age of the Civil War* (New York, 1980), p. 77.

6. H. Shelton Smith, *In His Image, But . . . Racism in Southern Religion, 1780–1910* (Durham, N.C., 1972), p. vii.

7. See James B. Stewart, "Evangelicalism and the Radical Strain in Southern Anti-Slavery Thought during the 1820's," *JSH* (1973), 39:379–96.

8. Ira Berlin, *Slaves without Masters: The Free Negro in the Antebellum South* (New York, 1974), pp. 261–68; quotation, p. 269.

9. Warren M. Billings, "The Cases of Fernando and Elizabeth Key: A Note on the Status of Blacks in 17th Century Virginia," *WMQ* (1973), 30:67–74.

10. See my "Resistance and Afro-American History," in G. Y. Okihiro, ed., *In Resistance: Studies in African, Caribbean, and Afro-American History* (Amherst, Mass., 1986), p. 17.

11. Roger Fischer, "Racial Segregation in Ante-Bellum New Orleans," *AHR* (1969), 74:926–37.

12. V. Jacque Voegeli, *Free But Not Equal* (Chicago, 1962); Eugene H. Berwanger, *The Frontier against Slavery* (Urbana, Ill., 1967); James A. Rawley, *Race and Politics* (Philadelphia, 1969); Phyllis Field, *The Politics of Race in New York* (Ithaca, N.Y., 1982), p. 22.

13. *New York Times Book Review*, December 10, 1989, p. 3.

14. John S. Haller, Jr., *Outcasts from Evolution: Scientific Attitudes of Racial Inferiority, 1859–1900* (Urbana, Ill., 1971), p. 210.

15. Robert M. Miller, "Southern White Protestantism and the Negro, 1865–1965," in Charles E. Wynes, ed., *The Negro in the South since 1865: Selected Essays* (University, Ala., 1965), pp. 232–33.

16. Thomas Graham, "Harriet Beecher Stowe and the Question of Race," *NEQ* (1973), 46:614–22.

17. Ralph E. Luker, "Bushnell in Black and White," *NEQ* (1972), 45:408–16.

18. L. B. Scherer, "A New Look at *Personal Slavery Established*," *WMQ* (1973), 30:645–52.

19. John Hope Franklin, *Racial Equality in America* (Chicago, 1976); see especially pp. 17, 39, 51–52, 54–55.

Chapter 2

1. Jeffrey Brooke Allen, "Were Southern White Critics of Slavery Racists?" *JSH* (1978), 44:169–90; "The Racial Thoughts of White North Carolina Opponents of Slavery," *NCHR* (1982), 59:49–66; the quotations are from pp. 169–70 and p. 66, respectively.

2. Gary B. Mills, "Miscegenation and the Free Negro in Ante-Bellum 'Anglo' Alabama: A Re-Examination of Southern Race Relations," *JAH* (1981), 68:16–34; quotation, p. 20.

3. Michael C. Coleman, "Not Race But Grace: Presbyterian Missionaries and American Indians, 1837–1893," *JAH* (1980), 67:41–60.

4. David Edwin Harrell, Jr., *White Sects and Black Men in the Recent South* (Nashville, 1970).

5. James McBride Dabbs, *The Southern Heritage* (New York, 1958), pp. 112–13.

6. James Hugo Johnston, *Race Relations in Virginia and Miscegenation in the South, 1776–1860* (Amherst, Mass., 1970); the quotations in the following paragraphs are from pp. 7, 11, 97, 97–98, 107–8, 188.

7. Writing of "lower-class" white people in the United States, Herbert Gutman commented: "Their racial beliefs still await careful study." *The Black Family in Slavery and Freedom, 1750–1925* (New York, 1976), p. 541.

8. For details on the 1816 conspiracy and the involvement of Boxley—whose views anticipated those of John Brown—see my *American Negro Slave Revolts* (New York, 1943), pp. 255–57.

9. This kind of evidence brought forward by Johnston in *Race Relations in Virginia* makes quite inappropriate Winthrop Jordan's prefatory remarks that Johnston's work suffers from downplaying "*racial* distinctions" (italics in original) and not observing that "virtually all whites then (and most now) were unwilling to have blacks in America and at the same time be free." His views as to the past are shown to be dubious by the work he introduces; his parenthetic remarks about the feelings of "most" whites in the present are at best extraordinary.

10. Mechal Sobel, *The World They Made Together: Black and White Values in Eighteenth-Century Virginia* (Princeton, N.J., 1987).

11. Stephen Innes, *Reviews in American History* (1989), 17:22–28. Innes did,

however, state that the book was "imaginative" and contained "fresh insights." A very positive review by Rhys Isaac is in *AHR* (1989), 94:1175–76.

12. In a letter dated Haifa, Israel, November 30, 1989; italics in original.

13. Sobel, *World They Made Together*, pp. 5, 45.

14. T. H. Breen, "A Changing Labor Force and Race Relations in Virginia,1660–1710," *Journal of Social History* (1973), 7:3–25; quotation, p. 18.

Chapter 3

1. Basil Hall, *Travels in North America, in the Years 1827 and 1828*, 3d ed., 3 vols. (London, 1830), 3:190–91.

2. James S. Buckingham, *The Slave States of America*, 2 vols.(London, 1842), 2:112.

3. Carl Bridenbaugh, *Myths and Realities: Societies of the Colonial South* (Baton Rouge, 1952), p. 169. Observe that the bride of Du Bois was Nina Gomer, daughter of a German mother and a Black father, living on a farm in Iowa. The marriage took place in Cedar Rapids in 1896; Du Bois nowhere comments on the arrangements for this ceremony nor any other circumstance of this event.

4. See Silvio A. Bedini, *The Life of Benjamin Banneker* (New York, 1972).

5. On the Banneker-Jefferson exchange of 1792, see Herbert Aptheker, *A Documentary History of the Negro People in the United States* (New York, 1951; reissued in four volumes, Secaucus, N.J., 1989–90), 1:22–25. See also William Cohen, "Jefferson and the Problem of Slavery," *JAH* (1969), 56:503–26. Jefferson's letter to Chastellux is in Julian Boyd, ed., *The Papers of Thomas Jefferson* (Princeton, N.J., 1953), 8:186. Also see Fawn Brodie, *Thomas Jefferson: An Intimate History* (New York, 1974), p. 159.

6. Kenneth M. Stampp, *The Peculiar Institution* (New York, 1956); quotations are from pp. 212, 337, 235–36.

7. James M. McPherson, *The Struggle for Equality: Abolitionists and the Negro in the Civil War and Reconstruction* (Princeton, N.J., 1964); quotations are from pp. 135, 136, 153.

8. John L. Thomas, ed., *Slavery Attacked: The Abolitionist Crusade* (Englewood Cliffs, N.J., 1965).

9. Winthrop D. Jordan, *White over Black: American Attitudes toward the Negro, 1550–1812* (Chapel Hill, N.C., 1968), p. 11.

10. Richard Baxter, *A Christian Directory; or A Summ of Practical Theologie, and Cases of Conscience* (London, 1673), p. 557.

11. The material in the preceding two paragraphs is in Jordan, *White over Black*, pp. 12–13 (italics in original), 188–89. The Pennsylvania statement in the following paragraph is in Jordan, p. 361. Similar statements from these kinds of societies will be offered in subsequent pages.

12. H. Shelton Smith, *In His Image, But . . . Racism in Southern Religion, 1780–1910* (Durham, N.C., 1972), pp. 5, 6, 9, 11, 13, 18–19, 36, 51.

13. Ira Berlin, *Slaves without Masters: The Free Negro in the Antebellum South* (New York, 1974); quotations are from pp. 48, 43–44, 68–69, 74, 306, 129, 144, 260–64. On Lemuel Haynes, see Richard Newman, ed., *Black Preacher to White America: The Collected Writings of Lemuel Haynes*, introduction by Helen McLam (Brooklyn, N.Y., 1990); and Richard Newman, *Lemuel Haynes, A Bio-Bibliography*

(Brooklyn, N.Y., 1990). On Margaret Douglas, see my *Abolitionism* (Boston, 1989), p. 117.

14. Mechal Sobel, *The World They Made Together: Black and White Values in Eighteenth-Century Virginia* (Princeton, N.J., 1987), pp. 3, 5, 11, 45.

15. Carl Degler, *The Other South: Southern Dissenters in the Nineteenth Century* (New York, 1974); quotations are from pp. 4, 7.

Chapter 4

1. In 1947 this author's commission as a major in the Army of the United States was taken from him by order of the president; one of the proofs of his subversiveness was his alleged closeness with Negro people. At the 40th annual conference of the National Association for the Advancement of Colored People (1949), William H. Hastie—then Governor of the Virgin Islands—"protested against the attempt to label as 'subversive' persons who maintain social friendships across color lines." *The Crisis*, August-September, 1949, 56:248.

2. Gary B. Mills, "Miscegenation and the Free Negro in Ante-Bellum 'Anglo' Alabama: A Re-Examination of Southern Race Relations," *JAH* (1981), 68:16–34.

3. Orville V. Burton, "Ungrateful Servants? Edgefield's Black Reconstruction: Part I of the Total History of Edgefield County, South Carolina" (Ph.D. diss., Princeton University, 1976); quotations are from pp. iii, iv, 51, 56, 58. Burton saw the fear among "the elite" of integration as important in producing the violence they instigated against Radical Reconstruction. I used this work in its dissertation form; it has been published as *In My Father's House Are Many Mansions: Family and Community in Edgefield, South Carolina* (Chapel Hill, N.C. 1985).

4. James Hugo Johnston, *Race Relations in Virginia and Miscegenation in the South, 1776–1860* (Amherst, Mass., 1970), originally a dissertation at the University of Chicago in 1937. Perhaps it is worth noting that his dissertation was influential with this writer, then a graduate student at Columbia University. My use in the paragraphs that follow refers very nearly to the entire volume.

5. Carter G. Woodson, "The Beginnings of Miscegenation," *JNH* (1918), 3:335–53.

6. Alan Watson, *Slave Law in the Americas* (Athens, Ga., 1989) pp. 76–82; quotation, p. 81. Watson noted similar records in Louisiana.

7. Edmund S. Morgan, *American Slavery, American Freedom: The Ordeal of Colonial Virginia* (New York, 1975), p. 336.

8. Allan Kulikoff, *Tobacco and Slaves: The Development of Southern Cultures in the Chesapeake, 1680–1800* (Chapel Hill, N.C., 1986), pp. 386–87.

9. Herbert G. Gutman, *The Black Family in Slavery and Freedom, 1750–1925* (New York, 1976), p. 389.

10. Kenneth M. Stampp, *The Peculiar Institution* (New York, 1956), pp. 350–51, 355. Note that Richard M. Johnson (1780–1850), a member of Congress and vice president under Van Buren, lived openly with a Black woman and had two daughters with her. One wonders if anything like that would be possible in today's Washington.

11. James M. McPherson, *The Struggle For Equality: Abolitionists and the Negro in the Civil War and Reconstruction* (Princeton, N.J., 1964), pp. 148–49.

12. On Miner, see Josephine F. Pacheco in P. S. Foner and Josephine F. Pacheco,

Three Who Dared (Westport, Conn., 1984), p. 187. About forty years ago, this writer asked Carter G. Woodson what might be the solution to the "problem." Woodson replied that continued intermarriage would, in the long run, terminate its existence.

13. Winthrop D. Jordan, *White over Black: American Attitudes toward the Negro, 1550–1812* (Chapel Hill, N.C., 1968), pp. 137, 163, 139–40, 146.

14. Ira Berlin, *Slaves without Masters: The Free Negro in the Antebellum South* (New York, 1974), pp. 261, 265, 267.

15. Louise B. Hill, "George F. Clarke," *FHQ* (1943), 21:192–253; quotation, p. 199.

16. Joel Williamson, *New People: Miscegenation and Mulattoes in the United States* (New York, 1980); quotations, pp. 7, 16–17. Stronger on this reality of sexual relations between Blacks and whites in the antebellum South is Williamson's essay, "Black Self-Assertion before and after Emancipation," in Nathan Huggins, Martin Kilson, and Daniel Fox, eds., *Key Issues in the Afro-American Experience*, 2 vols. (New York, 1977), 1:213–39, especially 210, 217, 223.

17. Burton, "Ungrateful Servants?"

18. James H. Croushore and David M. Potter, eds., *John William De Forest: A Union Officer in the Reconstruction* (New Haven, Conn., 1948), p. 138; noted in Williamson, *New People*, p. 89.

19. Peter Wood, *Black Majority: Negroes in Colonial South Carolina from 1670 through the Stono Rebellion* (New York, 1974); quotations, pp. 98–99, 234.

20. Robert C. Twombley and Richard H. Moore, "The Negro in Seventeenth Century Massachusetts," *WMQ* (1967), 24:224–42; quotations, pp. 235, 237. Twombley and Moore called attention to cases of Black slaves and white servants fleeing together; they often worked together at similar employment.

21. Mechal Sobel, *The World They Made Together: Black and White Values in Eighteenth-Century Virginia* (Princeton, N.J., 1987), p. 45.

22. For other notices of miscegenation prior to the Civil War, see Carl Bridenbaugh, *Myths and Realities: Societies of the Colonial South* (Baton Rouge, 1952), p. 388; Edward R. Turner, *The Negro in Pennsylvania* (Washington, D.C., 1910), pp. 194–96; Marcus W. Jernegan, *Laboring and Dependent Classes in Colonial America* (1931; reprinted, New York, 1960), who called attention to "the question of intermarriage between servant and slave" (p. 55); John Hope Franklin, *The Free Negro in North Carolina, 1790–1860* (Chapel Hill, N.C., 1943), pp. 35–38; Letitia Woods Brown, *Free Negroes in the District of Columbia, 1790–1846* (New York, 1972), pp. 29, 30, 67–74; Edgar J. McManus, *Black Bondage in the North* (Syracuse, N.Y., 1973), pp. 63–64; David Fowler, *Northern Attitudes toward Interracial Marriage, 1780–1930* (New York, 1987), pp. 38–39; Marina Wikramanayake, *A World in Shadow: The Free Black in Antebellum South Carolina* (Columbia, S.C., 1973), pp. 69–70, 75–78; Guion G. Johnson, *Ante-Bellum North Carolina* (Chapel Hill, N.C., 1937), pp. 588–93; John W. Blassingame, *Black New Orleans, 1860–1880* (Chicago, 1971), p. 17; H. E. Sterkx, *The Free Negro in Ante-Bellum Louisiana* (Rutherford, N.J., 1972), pp. 133, 252, 255; Robert C. Reinders, *End of an Era: New Orleans, 1850–1860* (New Orleans, 1964), pp. 30–31; Roger A. Fischer, "Racial Segregation in Ante-Bellum New Orleans," *AHR* (1969), 74:926–37, especially pp. 934–35.

Chapter 5

1. On the 1663 conspiracy, see Herbert Aptheker, *American Negro Slave Revolts* (New York, 1943), pp. 164–65. Recall also Crispus Attucks, and Moses Sash in Shays's Rebellion.

2. Peter Wood, *Black Majority: Negroes in Colonial South Carolina from 1670 through the Stono Rebellion* (New York, 1974), pp. 243–45.

3. Gerald W. Mullin, *Flight and Rebellion: Slave Resistance in Eighteenth-Century Virginia* (New York, 1972), especially pp. 83–123.

4. Lathan A. Windley, comp., *Runaway Slave Advertisements: A Documentary History from the 1730s to 1790*, 4 vols. (Westport, Conn., 1983). There is an analysis of this collection in my *Racism, Imperialism, and Peace* (Minneapolis, 1987), pp. 25–49.

5. Letitia Woods Brown, *Free Negroes in the District of Columbia, 1790–1846* (New York, 1972), p. 37.

6. Carter G. Woodson, "The Beginnings of Miscegenation," *JNH* (1918), 3:347.

7. See Aptheker, *American Negro Slave Revolts*, pp. 103, 104n, 111.

8. This corrects my account, ibid., p. 216; see Derek N. Kerr, "Petty Felony, Slave Defiance, and Frontier Villainy" (Ph.D. diss., Tulane University, 1988), pp. 152–92, 317–63.

9. See Aptheker, *American Negro Slave Revolts*, pp. 218–26, on Gabriel's conspiracy. Douglas R. Egerton, "Gabriel's Conspiracy and the Election of 1800," *JSH* (1990), 56:191–214, named Alexander Beddenhurst and Charles Quersey as the whites probably involved. He believed that there was "plenty of proof" of white involvement (p. 213).

10. The material on slave unrest and white sympathy is documented in Aptheker, *American Negro Slave Revolts*; on the implication of whites in the Vesey plot, see my *To Be Free* (New York, 1948), p. 45.

11. Lawrence D. Reddick, "The Negro in the New Orleans Press" (Ph.D. diss., University of Chicago, 1939), pp. 59–68. For the ensuing material, up to the discussion of David Walker, see Aptheker, *American Negro Slave Revolts*, and *To Be Free*, pp. 25–30.

12. The material on David Walker's *Appeal to the Colored Citizens of the World* is now fairly abundant; see my *Abolitionism* (Boston, 1989), p. 99.

13. Much of my *Abolitionism* details and documents the preceding paragraphs.

14. Edward L. Briddner, "The Fugitive Slave of Maryland," *Md. Hist. Mag.* (1971), 66:33–59; quotation, pp. 48–49.

15. On Bailey and Fee, see Eliza Wigham, *The Anti-Slavery Cause in America* (London, 1863), pp. 46–57; *Annual Report of the American Anti-Slavery Society by the Executive Committee for the Year Ending May 1, 1860* (New York, 1861), pp. 167–68, 174–77. See also Lowell H. Harrison, *The Anti-Slavery Movement in Kentucky* (Lexington, Ky., 1978), pp. 64–71.

16. On the Bowers case, see Barbara Jeanne Fields, *Slavery and Freedom on the Middle Ground: Maryland during the Nineteenth Century* (New Haven, Conn., 1985), pp. 63–65.

17. Helen T. Catterall, ed., *Judicial Cases Concerning American Slavery and the Negro*, 5 vols. (Washington, D.C., 1926–37); cases on 1:186; 1:210–11; 1:216; 1:216–18; 1:219–21; 1:247; 4:187.

Chapter 6

1. *Richmond Enquirer*, February 9, 1832.

2. Harriet Martineau, *Society in America*, 4th ed., 2 vols. (New York and London, 1837), 1:371.

3. Lorenzo J. Greene, "The New England Negro as Seen in Advertisements for Runaway Slaves," *JNH* (1944), 29:125–47.

4. Michael P. Johnson, "Runaway Slaves and the Slave Communities in South Carolina, 1799–1830," *WMQ* (1981), 38:418–41.

5. Lathan A. Windley, *Runaway Slave Advertisements: A Documentary History from the 1730s to 1790*, 4 vols. (Westport, Conn., 1983), 1:11, 350, 336–67, 373, 404; 2:411; 3:271, 279; 4:26.

6. Gerald W. Mullin, *Flight and Rebellion: Slave Resistance in Eighteenth-Century Virginia* (New York, 1972), chap. 3; Peter Wood, *Black Majority: Negroes in Colonial South Carolina from 1670 through the Stono Rebellion* (New York, 1974), pp. 105, 110, 113, 198, 44n, and app. A.

7. Marcus W. Jernegan, *Laboring and Dependent Classes in Colonial America* (1931; reprinted, New York, 1960); L. P. Stavisky, "Negro Craftsmanship in Early America," *AHR* (1949), 54:315–25. A good recent study of skilled slaves is by Bayly E. Marks, "Skilled Blacks in Antebellum St. Mary's County, Maryland," *JSH* (1987), 53:537–64.

8. On Grégoire, see Ruth F. Necheles, *The Abbé Grégoire* (Westport, Conn., 1971); Henri Grégoire, *An Enquiry Concerning the Intellectual and Moral Faculties and Literature of Negroes: Followed with an Account of the Life and Works of Fifteen Negroes and Mulattoes Distinguished in Science, Literature, and the Arts* (Brooklyn, N.Y., 1810; reprinted, College Park, Md., 1967).

9. Joyce Blackburn, *George Wythe of Williamsburg* (New York, 1975), p. 134. It is likely that the slave involved was Wythe's son. He mastered Greek, Latin, and elements of science. The sordid story of the slave's murder formed the final pages of Blackburn's biography. On Jefferson, see Fawn Brodie, *Thomas Jefferson: An Intimate History* (New York, 1974), especially p. 159. Also see Robert McColley, *Slavery and Jeffersonian Virginia* (Urbana, Ill., 1964), pp. 35–36; and William Cohen, "Jefferson and the Problem of Slavery," *JAH* (1969), 56:503–26.

10. This is dated August 22, 1787, as spoken at the Constitutional Convention, Robert A. Rutland, ed., *The Papers of George Mason 1725–1792*, 3 vols. (Chapel Hill, N.C., 1970), 3:965–66.

Chapter 7

1. There is an excellent treatment of Phyllis Wheatley in Sidney Kaplan and Emma Nogrady Kaplan, *The Black Presence in the Era of the American Revolution*, rev. ed. (Amherst, Mass., 1989), pp. 170–91. For a somewhat different treatment, see Saunders Redding in Rayford W. Logan and Michael R. Winston, eds., *Dictionary of American Negro Biography* (New York, 1982), pp. 640–42; hereafter Logan and Winston, *DANB*.

2. This is from Benjamin Rush, *Observations upon Negro Slavery* (Philadelphia, 1794). On Crawford, see Lewis Leary, "Charles Crawford," *PMHB* (1959), 83:302.

3. On Derham (or Durham), see L. H. Butterfield, ed., *Letters of Benjamin Rush*

2 vols. (Princeton, N.J., 1951), 1:497–98. Also see the sketch by Betty L. Plummer in Logan and Winston, *DANB*, pp. 205–6. On Fuller, see Kaplan and Kaplan, *Black Presence*, pp. 148–49. Also see Rayford Logan in Logan and Winston, *DANB*, pp. 247–48, and Gary B. Nash, *Forging Freedom: The Formation of Philadelphia's Black Community, 1720–1840* (Cambridge, Mass., 1988), p. 107.

4. See Silvio A. Bedini, *The Life of Benjamin Banneker* (New York, 1972), p. 151, and Nash, *Forging Freedom*, p. 307 n. 26.

5. The Pemberton letter is in the Historical Society of Pennsylvania; Ellen Slack, its archivist, kindly sent me a copy. On Banneker, see also Kaplan and Kaplan, *Black Presence*, pp. 132–51.

6. Parker Pillsbury, *Acts of the Anti-Slavery Apostles* (Concord, N.H., 1883; reprinted, New York, 1969), especially pp. 481, 484, 487.

7. See Richard Newman, *Lemuel Haynes: A Bio-Bibliography* (New York, 1984); and Richard Newman, ed., *Black Preacher to White America: The Collected Writings of Lemuel Haynes* (Brooklyn, N.Y., 1990). A good account is in Kaplan and Kaplan, *Black Presence*, pp. 119–30.

8. On Twilight, see "The Iron-willed Black Schoolmaster and His Granite Academy," *Middlebury College News Letter*, Spring 1974; unsigned, but written by its editor, Gregor Hileman. Deborah Van Hodge of Middlebury College kindly sent me a copy; she also supplied the information on Twilight Hall. See the account of Twilight by Clarence G. Contee, Jr., in Logan and Winston, *DANB*, p. 613.

9. Pennington's *The Fugitive Blacksmith* was first published in London in 1849; it has been reprinted often. See the essay on him by Rayford W. Logan in Logan and Winston, *DANB*, pp. 488–90. The Heidelberg material is in Horatio T. Strother, *The Underground Railroad in Connecticut* (Middletown, Conn., 1962), p. 146. Also see Herbert Aptheker, *A Documentary History of the Negro People in the United States* (New York, 1951; reissued in four volumes, Secaucus, N.J., 1989–90), 1:329, 341. For an excellent study of Pennington (and other influential Black ministers of the nineteenth century), see David E. Swift, *Black Prophets of Justice: Activist Clergy before the Civil War* (Baton Rouge, 1989).

10. Margaret Burr Des Champs, "John Chavis as a Preacher to Whites," *NCHR* (1955), 32:165–72; quotation, p. 172. See also Edgar W. Knight, "Notes on John Chavis," *NCHR* (1930), 7:326–45.

11. Carter G. Woodson, *The History of the Negro Church* (Washington, D.C., 1921), remains very useful. See also W. H. Brooks, "The Evolution of the Negro Baptist Church," *JNH* (1922), 7:11–22.

12. See Ira Berlin, *Slaves without Masters: The Free Negro in the Antebellum South* (New York, 1974), pp. 60–69.

13. W. Harrison Daniel, "Virginia Baptists and the Negro in the Early Republic," *VMHB* (1972), 80:60–69.

14. See Albert J. Raboteau, "The Slave Church in the Era of the American Revolution," in Ira Berlin and Ronald Hoffman, eds., *Slavery and Freedom in the Age of the American Revolution* (Urbana, Ill., 1986), pp. 197–213.

15. See Randy Jay Sparks, *A Mingled Yarn: Race and Religion in Mississippi, 1800–1876* (Ph.D. diss., Rice University, 1988), pp. v, 36, 38–39.

16. Kenneth K. Bailey, "Protestantism and Afro-Americans in the Old South: Another Look," *JSH* (1975), 41:451–72; quotations, pp. 452, 471.

17. Letitia Woods Brown, *Free Negroes in the District of Columbia, 1790–1846* (New York, 1972), pp. 44–45.

18. John Hebron Moore, "Simon Gray, Riverman: A Slave Almost Free," *MVHR* (1962), 49:472–84. See also Horace S. Fulkerson, *Random Recollections of Early Days in Mississippi*, ed. Percy L. Rainwater (Baton Rouge, 1937), pp. 130–31.

19. Charles B. Dew, "David Ross and the Oxford Iron Works: A Study of Industrial Slavery in the Early Nineteenth Century," *WMQ* (1974), 31:189–224; quotation, p. 202.

20. See Edmund Berkley, Jr., "Prophet without Honor: Christopher McPherson, Free Man of Color," *VMHB* (1969), 77:180–90. Also see Berlin, *Slaves without Masters*, pp. 76–78.

21. Nash, *Forging Freedom*, p. 149. See Rayford Logan on Forten in Logan and Winston, *DANB*, pp. 234–35. There are numerous references to Forten in Aptheker, *Documentary History*, vol. 1.

22. William Willis, *A History of the Law, the Courts, and the Lawyers of Maine* (Bangor, 1863), pp. 552–53.

23. Charles S. Brown, Jr., "The Genesis of the Negro Lawyers in New England," *NHB* (April 1959), 22:147–52.

24. William Cheek and Aimee Lee Cheek, *John Mercer Langston and the Fight for Black Freedom, 1829–1865* (Urbana, Ill., 1989), p. 227. In Langston's acceptance, racism was present; one of the examiners remarked on his rather light complexion.

25. See Charles S. Brown, "Genesis of the Negro Lawyers," and Clarence Contee's account in Logan and Winston, *DANB*, pp. 454–55.

26. See James Monroe Trotter, *Music and Some Highly Musical People* (Boston, 1881; reprinted, New York, 1968), pp. 100–106 for the Lucas family; pp. 66–87 for Elizabeth Taylor Greenfield; pp. 130–35 for Thomas Bowers. See also Raymond Lemieux on the Lucas family in Logan and Winston, *DANB*, pp. 405–6; and A. W. Akins on Bowers, *DANB*, p. 54. Cleveland Lucas went to Liberia in 1860; he composed its national anthem and died there in 1872.

Chapter 8

1. See John Hope Franklin, *The Free Negro in North Carolina, 1790–1860* (Chapel Hill, N.C., 1943), pp. 31–32.

2. Loren Schweninger, ed., *From Tennessee Slave to St. Louis Entrepreneur: The Autobiography of James Thomas* (Columbia, Mo., 1984). The foreword by John Hope Franklin summarizes much of the literature characteristic of this volume.

3. Marina Wikramanayake, *A World in Shadow: The Free Black in South Carolina* (Columbia, S.C., 1973), pp. 69–70, 75–78, 110; quotation, p. 78.

4. H. E. Sterkx, *The Free Negro in Ante-Bellum Louisiana* (Rutherford, N.J., 1972), pp. 232, 237, 242.

5. Juliet E. K. Walker, *Free Frank: A Black Pioneer on the Ante-Bellum Frontier* (Lexington, Ky., 1983). Some of the free Black people became so "successful" as to follow questionable habits not unlike those of white class brothers; see William R. Hogan and Edwin A. Davis, eds., *William Johnson's Natchez*, 2 vols. (Baton Rouge, 1951).

6. See Donnie D. Bellamy, "Free Blacks in Antebellum Missiouri, 1820–1860," *Missouri Historical Review* (1972), 67:198–226.

7. Ira Berlin, *Slaves without Masters: The Free Negro in the Antebellum South* (New York, 1974), p. 362, quoting from the *Richmond Dispatch*, February 15 and March 9, 1853.

8. George Stephen, *The Niger Trade Considered in Conexion with the African Blockade* (London, 1849), quoted in Philip D. Curtin, *The Image of Africa: British Ideas and Action, 1780–1850* (Madison, Wis., 1964), p. 382.

9. Loren Schweningen, "Prosperous Blacks in the South, 1790–1880," *AHR* (1990), 95:31–56; quotation, p. 40.

10. Robert S. Starobin, *Industrial Slavery in the Old South* (New York, 1970), pp. 137–45; quotations, pp. 137, 143.

11. See my *To Be Free: Studies in Afro-American History* (New York, 1948), pp. 113–35; quotations, pp. 113, 116, 117.

12. W. Jeffrey Bolster, " 'To Feel Like a Man': Black Seamen in the Northern States, 1800–1860," *JAH* (1990), 76:1173–99; quotations, pp. 1179, 1180–81, 1183.

13. Lorenzo J. Greene, "The Negro in the War of 1812 and the Civil War," *NHB* (1951), 14:133–38. Leon Litwack called attention to this, citing Greene, but he mistakenly attributed the enlightened views to Perry instead of to Chauncey; *North of Slavery* (Chicago, 1961), p. 52.

14. Kenneth W. Porter, "Negro Labor in the Western Cattle Industry, 1866–1900," in Milton Cantor, ed., *Black Labor in America* (Westport, Conn., 1969), pp. 24–52; quotation, p. 51.

Chapter 9

1. The first extended presentation of this view by Du Bois was in his *The Negro* (New York, 1915). African Americans leading the anti-slavery and anti-racist movements before the Civil War, like William Wells Brown and Frederick Douglass, insisted that "the ancient Egyptians were not white people"; see P. S. Foner, ed., *The Life and Writings of Frederick Douglass* (New York, 1952), 2:296. Recently the work of Cheikh Anta Diop on the Negroid features of ancient Egyptian civilization has been especially influential. See his *The African Origin of Civilization: Myth or Reality?*, trans. Mercer Cook (New York, 1974; first published in Paris in 1955). Surprisingly, Du Bois is not in the bibliography of this book. See also Ivan Van Sertima, ed., *Egypt Revisited* (New Brunswick, N.J., 1989), and the reportage of Joye Mercer in *Black Issues in Higher Education*, February 28, 1991. Related in the work of Paul H. D. Kaplan, *The Rise of the Black Magus in Western Art* (Ann Arbor, Mich., 1985); see also his bibliographical comments in the introduction. Important in confirming this approach is Martin Bernal, *Black Athena: The Afroasiatic Roots of Classical Civilization*, vol. 1, *The Fabrication of Ancient Greece* (New Brunswick, N.J., 1989).

2. The writings are voluminous. See especially A. J. R. Russell-Wood, "Iberian Expansion and the Issue of Black Slavery: Changing Portuguese Attitudes, 1440–1770," *AHR* (1978), 83:16–42; Lewis Hanke, *The Spanish Struggle for Justice in the Conquest of America* (Philadelphia, 1949); and Lewis Hanke, "Pope Paul IV and the American Indians," *Harvard Theological Review* (1937), 30:65–102. Also

see Silvio Zavala, *The Defense of Human Rights in Latin America: Sixteenth to Eighteenth Centuries* (Paris, 1964).

3. In translation, this was published in Edinburgh in 1798 in the third volume of *The Works of Don Francisco de Quevedo*, pp. 106–8. I am obliged to Professor Sidney Kaplan of the University of Massachusetts, Amherst, for calling this to my attention.

Basil Davidson has shown convincingly that in the fifteenth century, Portuguese made no distinction as to the humanity of the Africans and themselves, and that business partnerships and intermarriage were common. See his "Slaves or Captives? Some Notes on Fantasy and Fact," in Nathan Huggins, Martin Kilson, and Daniel Fox, eds., *Key Issues in the Afro-American Experience*, 2 vols. (New York, 1971), 1:54–73, especially 65–66.

4. J. H. Plumb, *New York Review of Books*, March 13, 1969. Margharita Laski, writing from England, and taking issue with Plumb, offered evidence that Sir Thomas Roe, London's ambassador to the great mogul, in rejecting gifts, made clear that he thought it was wrong "to make the Image of God fellow to a Beast" and that among God's images some were in Black. Sir Thomas was writing in 1616 and 1617; *New York Review of Books*, July 10, 1969.

5. Winthrop D. Jordan, *White over Black: American Attitudes toward the Negro, 1550–1812* (Chapel Hill, N.C., 1968), pp. 15–16, 20.

6. This is in Browne's 1646 work commonly called *Vulgar Errors*, in Geoffrey Keynes, ed., *The Works of Sir Thomas Browne*, 4 vols. (Chicago, 1964), 2:460–85; quotations, pp. 472–74.

7. William D. Stump, "The English View Negro Slavery to 1780" (Ph.D. diss., University of Missouri, 1962); quotations pp. 132, 134, 148, 158–59, 209–10, 259. This work is not cited by Jordan, *White over Black*, or Davis.

8. Quoted by Frank Klingberg, *An Appraisal of the Negro in Colonial South Carolina* (Washington, D.C., 1941), p. 36.

9. See H. A. Wyndham, *The Atlantic and Slavery* (London, 1935), p. 236.

10. Emory G. Evans, ed., "A Question of Complexion," *VMBH* (1963), 71:411–15.

11. On Wallace and Philmore, see David B. Davis, "New Sidelights on Early Antislavery Radicalism," *WMQ* (1971), 28:585–94.

12. See Claudine Hunting, "The *Philosophes* and Black Slavery," *JHI* (1978), 39:405–18. John Chester Miller stated, "Where human rights were concerned, the Enlightenment studiously ignored skin coloration," *The Wolf By the Ears* (New York, 1977), p. 4; see the chapter in that book, "The Question of Racial Inferiority," pp. 46–59. Also see David Geggus, "Racial Equality, Slavery, and Colonial Secession during the Constituent Assembly," *AHR* (1989), 94:1290–1308.

13. For the preceding three paragraphs, see Thomas E. Drake, *Quakers and Slavery in America* (New Haven, Conn., 1950), chap. 1; J. Herbert Fritz, "The Germantown Anti-Slavery Petition of 1688," *Mennonite Quarterly Review* (1959), 33:42–59; and my article "The Quakers and Negro Slavery" (1940), reprinted in *Toward Negro Freedom* (New York, 1956), pp. 10–35.

14. Richard Baxter, *Chapters from a Christian Directory; or, a Sermon of Practical Theology and Cases of Conscience*, ed. Jeannette Tawney (London, 1925), pp. 15, 27–38. David B. Davis, *The Problem of Slavery in Western Culture* (Ithaca, N.Y., 1966), pp. 203, 333–39, commented on Baxter's denunciation of slavery and

the slave trade and emphasized that Baxter urged obedience upon the slaves. Davis did not notice, however, Baxter's insistence upon the African's equality with his owner. See also Mary S. Locke, *Anti-Slavery in America . . . 1619–1808* (Boston, 1901), pp. 15–16.

15. Milton Cantor, "The Image of the Negro in Colonial Literature," *NEQ* (1963), 36:452–77; quotation, p. 471.

16. A convenient source for this protest is Roger Bruns, ed., *Am I Not a Man and a Brother? The Anti-Slavery Crusade of Revolutionary America* (New York, 1977), pp. 3–5. This valuable book reprints, in full or in generous excerpts, several of the works discussed in the pages that follow.

17. Drake, *Quakers and Slavery in America*, pp. 16–17, 120–21. Drake found that Friends as a whole did not reject racism. There were, however, some cases of African Americans being admitted to membership and a few instances of intermarriage. Even Quaker burial practices generally were discriminatory.

18. Keith's pamphlet was reprinted in *PMHB* (1889), 13:265–70. The quotation is from p. 266; italics in original. Keith later was disowned and joined a group called "Christian Quakers." It is possible, but not certain, that his strong anti-slavery position may have been the cause. Keith's pamphlet is also printed in full in the valuable collection edited by Louis Ruchames, *Racial Thought in America: From the Puritans to Abraham Lincoln* (Amherst, Mass., 1969), pp. 41–45.

19. This is in *JNH* (1937), 22:488–93. See also *Friends Intelligencer* (Philadelphia, 1874), 31:91–92.

20. There are sketches of the lives of Southby and Farmer in the *Friend* (Philadelphia, 1855), 28:293, 301, 309, 316. Farmer was disowned for broadcasting his views without permission. Southby seems to have died in 1718 after being told to stop his efforts.

21. Sewall's broadside was published in Massachusetts Historical Society, *Collections*, ser. 5, vol. 7 (Boston, 1897), pp. 19–20. The small volume of Sewall's work edited by Sidney Kaplan, with introduction, notes, and bibliography, surely is definitive; it was published by the University of Massachusetts Press, Amherst, 1969.

22. There is a likeness of Lay, at an advanced age, in Bruns, *Am I Not a Man?* p. 47.

23. See Robert Vaux, *Memoirs of the Lives of Benjamin Lay and Ralph Sandiford* (Philadelphia, 1815). Vaux devoted a larger work to Lay; this *Life* was published in Philadelphia in 1817. Some of the preceding three paragraphs are based, in part, upon my 1940 "Quakers and Negro Slavery," reprinted in *Toward Negro Freedom*.

24. Betty Wood, *Slavery in Colonial Georgia, 1730–1775* (Athens, Ga., 1984), p. 30. In the late 1730s slave unrest threatened the existence of South Carolina.

25. See George W. Pilcher, "Samuel Davies and the Instruction of Negroes in Virginia," *VMHB* (1966) 74:293–300; quotation, p. 295.

26. Woolman's *Some Considerations* was first published in 1753 by James Chatten; it was reprinted in an edition of fifty-two pages by Benjamin Franklin in Philadelphia in 1762 and in a thirty-five-page edition by Thomas Maund in Baltimore in 1821. Woolman's works were edited by John Greenleaf Whittier and published in Boston in 1871. Other editions were published in 1922 and 1954. Probably the best edition—used here—was edited by Phillips P. Moulton, *The Journal and Major Essays of John Woolman* (New York, 1971).

27. Locke, *Anti-Slavery in America*, p. 28. Locke's book was a product of Albert

Bushnell Hart's seminar; it was Radcliffe College Monographs no. 11. Du Bois's *Suppression of the African Slave-Trade* (New York, 1896) also was a product of Hart's seminar. Hart merits a biography.

28. Benezet's statement was quoted by George S. Brookes in *Friend Anthony Benezet* (Philadelphia, 1937), pp. 46–47. Yet, a page earlier, Brookes wrote that Benezet's "profoundly spiritual nature daily contemplated their [the slaves'] natural dullness"—a reflection of the author's limitations to be explained, perhaps, by the date at which he was writing. Moses Brown, a Rhode Island Quaker who taught Black people in Providence about this time, also declared that ideas of their inferiority were false; see M. Kraus, "Slavery Reform in the Eighteenth Century: An Aspect of Transatlantic Intellectual Cooperation," *PMHB* (1936), 60:62.

29. Anthony Benezet, *A Caution and Warning to Great-Britain and Her Colonies* (Philadelphia, 1767), pp. 11–12. See Roger Bruns, "Anthony Benezet's Assertion of Negro Equality," *JNH* (1971), 56:23–39; and Nancy Slocum Hornick, "Anthony Benezet and the Africans' School: Toward a Theory of Equality," *PMHB* (1975), 99:399–421. There is a generous selection from Benezet's writings and correspondence in Bruns, *Am I Not a Man?* pp. 79–99, 111–27, 137–41, 145–84, 193–99, 262–69, 302–16.

30. [Anthony Benezet,] *The Potent Enemies of America Laid Open* (Philadelphia, 1774), quoted by Locke, *Anti-Slavery in America*, p. 48.

31. This is from the pamphlet version of Dickinson's *Letters* often reprinted in the United States and England; see *Anti-Slavery in America*, p. 61.

32. Sydney V. James, *A People among Peoples: Quaker Benevolence in Eighteenth-Century America* (Cambridge, Mass., 1963), pp. 222, 235–36. The Philadelphia school also taught the children of poor white parents.

33. Quoted by David Grimsted, "Anglo-American Racism and Phyllis Wheatley," in Ronald Hoffman and Peter J. Albert, eds., *Women in the Age of American Revolution* (Charlottesville, Va., 1989), pp. 392–93n.

34. David B. Davis, *The Problem of Slavery in the Age of Revolution, 1770–1823* (Ithaca, N.Y., 1975), p. 272.

35. James Beattie's *Elements of Moral Philosophy* was written in 1778, but first published in 1792. I used the third edition (Edinburgh, 1817). Pages 22–74 of volume 2 are devoted to slavery and the character of the African; quotations are from pp. 24, 30–31, 42, 46, 56–57, 65.

Chapter 10

1. See Albert C. Outler, ed., *John Wesley: A Representative Collection of His Writings* (New York, 1964), pp. 85–86. Wesley's *Thoughts upon Slavery* was also printed in Dublin in 1775 and in New York City in 1834.

2. Rush's pamphlet was originally published in 1773 by J. Dunlap; later that year it was printed by Hodge and Shober in New York City, and in 1775 by J. P. Spooner in Norwich, Connecticut. Arno Press in New York City reprinted the pamphlet in 1967 together with a second pamphlet from Rush inspired by Richard Nisbet's attack upon him, to be discussed hereafter.

3. The *Answer* was published by Dunlap in Philadelphia. It made a pamphlet of fifty-four pages—twenty more than in the one Nisbet had attacked. Some twenty

years later, Rush came to very strange conclusions as to the source of the skin color in Africans; this will be commented upon in later pages.

4. Duncan J. McLeod, *Slavery, Race, and the American Revolution* (London, 1974), p. 12. See, to the contrary, extracts from a sermon offered in 1774 by James Allen four pages further along in MacLeod's book.

5. This is in the documents section of the *JNH* (1929), 14:493–95. It was edited by Lorenzo J. Greene, who stated that the essay appeared in the *Connecticut Journal and New Haven Post-Boy*, July 6, 1770. Trumbull's essay was published without this attribution in Roger Bruns, ed., *Am I Not a Man and a Brother? The Antislavery Crusade of Revolutionary America, 1688–1788* (New York, 1977), pp. 143–45. The Trumbull satire strikingly resembles that penned by Benjamin Franklin almost twenty years later, to be noticed hereafter.

6. Howard's charge is in Don Higginbotham and W. S. Price, Jr., "Was It Murder for a White Man to Kill a Slave?" *WMQ* (1979), 36:593–601.

7. *Some Historical Account of Guinea* was a book of nearly two hundred pages; it was published in Philadelphia in 1771 by J. Crukshank. It was an enlarged version of some of Benezet's publications of the 1760s, to which attention has been called. An extract is in Bruns, *Am I Not a Man?* pp. 145–84.

8. In 1773, according to Bruns (*Am I Not a Man?* p. 200), Swan revised his pamphlet "at the request of several blacks in Boston." In this form it was dedicated to the governor and legislature of Massachusetts; accompanying it was "the blacks' own petition against slavery." The 1773 version of Swan's work was printed in Boston by J. Greenleaf. The 1773 petitions from slaves in Massachusetts are in Herbert Aptheker, *A Documentary History of the Negro People in the United States* (New York, 1951; reissued in four volumes, Secaucus, N.J., 1989–90), 1:6–8.

9. David Cooper, *A Mite Cast into the Treasury; or, Observations on Slave-Keeping.* No publisher is given for this twenty-one-page pamphlet issued in Philadelphia in 1772. This appears on its title page: "To Be Had at Most of the Booksellers in Town." Extracts are in Bruns, *Am I Not a Man?* pp. 184–91. In 1773 Cooper published, anonymously, another attack upon slavery, *A Serious Address to the Rulers of America*; this also attacked racism.

10. Winthrop D. Jordan, *White over Black: American Attitudes toward the Negro, 1550–1812* (Chapel Hill, N.C., 1968), p. 255.

11. [Theodore Parsons and Eliphalet Pearson], *A Forensic Dispute on the Legality of Enslaving the Africans, Held at the Public Commencement in Cambridge, New-England, July 21, 1773, by Two Candidates for the Bachelor's Degree* (Boston: 1773). A portion of this forty-eight-page pamphlet is in Bruns, *Am I Not a Man?* pp. 278–90. See Bernard Rosenthal, "Puritan Conscience and New England Slavery," *NEQ* (1973), 46:62–68. This is insightful on the debate and on the thought of the Mathers, Samuel Sewall, and Nathaniel Appleton.

12. Albert H. Smyth, ed., *The Writings of Benjamin Franklin* 10 vols. (New York, 1907), 6:222.

13. Quoted in Bernard Bailyn, *The Ideological Origins of the American Revolution* (Cambridge, Mass., 1967), p. 243; italics in original.

14. P. S. Foner, ed., *The Complete Writings of Thomas Paine*, 2 vols. (New York, 1951), 2:16–19. Also see Moncure D. Conway, ed., *The Writings of Thomas Paine*, 4 vols. (New York, 1894), 1:4–9.

15. Betty Wood, *Slavery in Colonial Georgia, 1730–1775* (Athens, Ga., 1984),

p. 201. Wood noted that this document followed shortly after the appearance of slave unrest in Georgia. McIntosh did not free his own slaves; in the 1780s he ardently defended slavery. For evidence of the slave unrest in Georgia at this time, see Herbert Aptheker, *American Negro Slave Revolts* (New York, 1943), pp. 199–200.

16. Hopkins's *Dialogue* was published by J. P. Spooner in Norwich. It was reprinted in New York City in 1785 by Robert Hodge with an appendix containing the constitution of the newly created New York Society for the Manumission of Slaves, of which John Jay and Alexander Hamilton were officers.

17. This quotation is from an essay "On the African Slave Trade" in the *Providence Gazette and Country Journal*, quoted by Davis S. Lovejoy, "Samuel Hopkins: Religion, Slavery, and the Revolution," *NEQ* (1967), 40:235. In 1793 Hopkins again published anti-slavery and anti-racist opinions. His work was reprinted into the 1850s.

18. R. Scarborough, *The Opposition to Slavery in Georgia prior to 1860* (1933; reprinted, New York, 1968), pp. 62–63.

19. Nathan Bangs, *The Life of the Rev. Freeborn Garretson, Compiled from His Printed and Manuscript Journal* (1829); 4th ed., New York, 1839); quotation, p. 40.

20. Richard Morris, *Alexander Hamilton and the Founding of the Nation* (New York, 1957), p. 454.

21. Quoted by his son, William Jay, in *Miscellaneous Writings on Slavery* (Boston, 1853), p. 147.

22. See Sidney Kaplan and Emma Nogrady Kaplan, *The Black Presence in the Era of the American Revolution*, rev. ed. (Amherst, Mass., 1989), pp. 244–48.

23. See *Proceedings of the Massachusetts Historical Society* (Boston, 1874), 43:294.

24. The petitioners were from Frederick County; the original is in the Virginia State Archives and is printed in Bruns, *Am I Not a Man?* pp. 506–7.

25. See Thomas R. Moseley, "A History of the New-York Manumission Society, 1785–1849" (Ph.D. diss., New York University, 1963); italics in original. Educational exhibitions by this society produced significant anti-racist views; these will be noticed in subsequent pages.

26. James Dana, *The African Slave Trade: A Discourse* (New Haven, Conn., 1791); Z. Swift, *An Oration on Domestic Slavery* (Hartford, Conn., 1791). See Mary S. Locke, *Anti-Slavery* (Boston, 1901), pp. 167, 180–81; and David B. Davis, *The Problem of Slavery in the Age of Revolution, 1770–1823* (Ithaca, N.Y., 1975), pp. 327, 552.

27. Marguerite F. Melcher, *The Shaker Adventure* (Princeton, N.J., 1941), pp. 175–76.

28. J. P. Brissot de Warville, *New Travels in the United States of America*, trans. Mara S. Vamos and Durand Echeverria, ed. Durand Echeverria (Cambridge, Mass., 1964). The book was first published in France in 1791; it was translated by Joel Barlow and published in London in 1792. By 1797 there were editions in England, Holland, and Sweden. Echeverria in his introduction stated that Brissot "repeatedly insisted . . . that Negroes had just as great moral and intellectual capacities as their white masters." See pp. xxii, 232–37, 241.

29. *American Museum* (Philadelphia, April 1789), 5:377–81; (July 1789), 6:77–80. George Fishman kindly assisted me in getting copies of these essays.

Chapter 11

1. On O'Kelly, see Jeffrey B. Allen, "The Racist Thought of White North Carolina Opponents of Slavery," *NCHR* (1982), 59:52–53.

2. On Nisbet's later thoughts, see David Grimsted, "Anglo-American Racism and Phyllis Wheatley," in Ronald Hoffman and Peter J. Albert, eds., *Women in the Age of the American Revolution* (Charlottesville, Va., 1989), p. 409.

3. *Speech of William Pinkney, Esq., in the House of Delegates of Maryland, at Their Session in November, 1798* (Philadelphia: 1790); the speech also appeared in the *American Museum* (1789), 1:80–89. See Ira Berlin, *Slaves without Masters: The Free Negro in the Antebellum South* (New York, 1974), p. 88; and Grimsted, "Anglo-American Racism and Phyllis Wheatley," pp. 408, 430.

4. The constitution was published in Baltimore in 1789 by Goddard and Angell; see Letitia Woods Brown, *Free Negroes in the District of Columbia, 1790–1846* (New York, 1972), p. 54.

5. From 1794 to 1803 the *Minutes of the Proceedings* were published in Philadelphia by Z. Poulson, Jr. Thereafter, until the final convention, held in Philadelphia in 1837, the minutes had varied publishers. The proceedings for 1826 and 1827 were published by Benjamin Lundy in Baltimore. For the 1796 quotation, see Brown, *Free Negroes in the District of Columbia*, pp. 58–59.

6. Winthrop D. Jordan, *White over Black: American Attitudes toward the Negro, 1550–1812* (Chapel Hill, N.C., 1968), pp. 446–47.

7. Betty Fladeland, *Abolitionists and Working-Class Problems in the Age of Industrialization* (Baton Rouge, 1984), pp. 21, 26.

8. Quoted by Stephen B. Weeks, *Southern Quakers and Slavery* (Baltimore, 1896), p. 22. See also Allen, "Racist Thought," p. 52.

9. Quoted by John Richard Alden, *The South in the Revolution, 1763–1789* (Baton Rouge, 1957), p. 344n.

10. See William C. Bruce, *John Randolph of Roanoke* (New York, 1922), pp. 104–5. Also see Willie Lee Rose, *Slavery and Freedom*, ed. W. W. Freehling (New York, 1982), pp. 9–10.

11. John Hope Franklin, *The Free Negro in North Carolina, 1790–1860* (Chapel Hill, N.C., 1943), p. 11.

12. "Constantia's" essay may be consulted conveniently in Paul Lauter, ed., *The Heath Anthology of American Literature*, 2 vols. (Lexington, Mass., 1990), 1:1032–39. Abigail Adams's quotation is from Charles F. Adams, ed., *Letters of Mrs. Adams, the Wife of John Adams*, 3d ed. (Boston, 1841), 1:24.

13. See my "Militant Abolitionism," first published in *JNH* in 1941, reprinted in *To Be Free* (New York, 1948), pp. 43–44, 199–200.

14. Quoted by Allen, "Racist Thought," pp. 52–53.

15. See W. E. Juhnke, "Franklin's View of the Negro and Slavery," *Pennsylvania History* (1974), 41:375–90.

16. The satire is in Lauter, *Heath Anthology*, 1:819–21. See also Juhnke, "Franklin's View of the Negro," and Matthew T. Mellon, *Early American Views on Negro Slavery* (Boston, 1934), especially pp. 28–36.

17. Jedidiah Morse, *The American Geography; or, A View of the Present Situation of the United States of America* (Elizabeth Town, N.J., 1789), p. 67. It is

quoted by Dwight L. Dumond, *Anti-Slavery: The Crusade for Freedom in America* (Ann Arbor, Mich., 1961), p. 386n.

18. Mary S. Locke, *Anti-Slavery in America...1619–1808* (Boston, 1901), p. 167, called attention to this essay but did not quote it. She stated that it was the work of Henri Grégoire and was translated by Phyllis Wheatley. The quotations are from the *American Museum*, January 1791, p. 53, and December 1791, p. 303.

19. The *Defence of Warner Mifflin* was dated Kent, Delaware, November 1796; it was printed by Samuel Sansom that year in Philadelphia. In 1798 Mifflin published *A Serious Expostulation with the Members of the House of Representatives*, which was reprinted widely. The *Defense* was published, in part, in the *Friends' Miscellany* (Philadelphia), April 1834. It is given in full in Hilda Justice's *Life and Ancestry of Warner Mifflin* (Philadelphia, 1905), pp. 77–100. On the reception of Mifflin's petition, see David B. Davis, *The Problem of Slavery in the Age of Revolution, 1770–1823* (Ithaca, N.Y., 1975), p. 101.

20. Rice's pamphlet was issued in facsimile by the University of Kentucky Associates (Lexington, 1956). See also H. Shelton Smith, *In His Image, But...Racism in Southern Religion, 1780–1910* (Durham, N.C., 1972), pp. 56–58. In addition to the frequent reprinting of Rice's work, it was cited and quoted repeatedly by anti-slavery people and organizations until the Civil War.

21. See Henry Adams, *The Life of Albert Gallatin*, 2 vols. (Philadelphia, 1879), 1:109; 2:585, 662. In 1792 first appeared Gilbert Imlay's *A Topographical Description of the Western Territory of North America*; this was a very widely read book, which reached its third printing, revised, in London in 1797. Ten of its pages (221–31) were devoted to excoriating Jefferson for permitting himself to doubt the equality of Black people, a view called "puerile" and "inconsistent" with Jefferson's general outlook. "How long," Imlay demanded, "is the world to be tantalized with such paltry sophistry and nonsense!" Quotations are from pp. 227 and 231 of the edition published in New York City in 1969. See Robert Rusk, "Adventures of Gilbert Imlay," *Indiana University Studies* (1923), no. 57, 10:1–26.

22. See Robert D. Sayre, "The Evolution of Early Abolitionism: The American Convention for Promoting the Abolition of Slavery" (Ph.D. diss., Ohio State University, 1987), pp. 59, 69, 74.

23. L. H. Butterfield, ed., *Letters of Benjamin Rush*, 2 vols. (Princeton, N.J., 1951), 2:756–58.

24. H. Aptheker, ed., "An Unpublished Benjamin Rush Manuscript," *PMHB* (1947), 71:68–69. See Donald J. D'Elia, "Dr. Benjamin Rush and the Negro," *JHI* (1969), 30:413–22. Also see J. A. Woods, ed., "Correspondence of Benjamin Rush and Granville Sharp," *Journal of American Studies* (England) (1967), 1:1–38. In 1797 Rush came to the conclusion that the African's color might be the result of some disease. If this were true, he thought it likely that a "cure" could be found. Butterfield, the editor of his letters, correctly referred to this as "astonishing"; it did not, however, change Rush's ideas as to the vicious falsity of ideas of inferiority. Ronald Takaki, *Iron Cages: Race and Culture in Nineteenth-Century America* (New York, 1979), while noting Rush's rejection of racism, omitted any reference to Rush's actual activity in opposition to slavery and racism and concentrated on this "disease" that Rush the physician thought that he had discovered. At one point, Takaki wrote of Rush as being similar to Thomas Jefferson: "Critics of slavery, yet slaveholders themselves, both men were white nationalists" (p. 15). Calling Rush a slaveowner

(he owned one slave, whom he manumitted) like Jefferrson is similar to calling the corner grocer and Donald Trump property owners. The differences between Rush and Jefferson in attitudes toward the African American and in activity to terminate slavery and discrimination were profound. Calling Jefferson a "white nationalist" is probably sound; applying this to Rush is highly dubious. Rush's paper on skin color was "Observations Intended to Favour a Supposition That the Black Color (As It Is Called) of the Negroes Is Derived from Leprosy." It was published in *Transactions of the American Philosophical Society* (1799), 4:287–97.

25. Thomas E. Drake, *JNH* (1947), 32:110–12.

26. Barrow's *Circular Letter* was printed for the author in Norfolk, Virginia, by Willett and O'Connor in 1798. It was reprinted in *WMQ* (1963), 20:440–51, with a helpful introduction by Carlos R. Allen, Jr. Italics in original. Strangely, it is missing from Dwight L. Dumond's indispensable *Bibliography of Anti-Slavery in America* (Ann Arbor, Mich., 1961).

27. White is quoted in William Stanton, *The Leopard's Spots: Scientific Attitudes toward Race in America, 1815–59* (Chicago, 1960), pp. 17–18. Stanton's book does not do justice to the rejection of racism that characterized several of the scientists in the period covered; future pages will show this.

28. Ruth F. Necheles, "Grégoire and the Egalitarian Movement," in Harold E. Pagliaro, ed., *Racism in the Eighteenth Century* (Cleveland, 1973), p. 356. See also Necheles, *The Abbé Grégoire* (Westport, Conn., 1971), especially pp. 82, 85, 178, 200, 227, 261–63, 285–87.

Chapter 12

1. See Herbert Aptheker, *American Negro Slave Revolts* (New York, 1943). On maroons, see my "Maroons within the Present Limits of the U.S.," *JNH* (1939), 24:167–84. In *American Negro Slave Revolts* I expressed doubts about allegations of white involvement in the Gabriel conspiracy for reasons there elucidated. That there almost certainly was such involvement has been shown by Douglas R. Egerton, "Gabriel's Conspiracy and the Election of 1800," *JSH* (1990), 56:191–214.

2. See Aptheker, *American Negro Slave Revolts*, pp. 219–224, for content, sources, and context of this correspondence.

3. St. George Tucker, *Letter to a Member of the General Assembly of Virginia, on the Late Conspiracy of the Slaves* (Baltimore, 1801). Du Bois's 1906 Niagara Address is in Herbert Aptheker, *A Documentary History of the Negro People in the United States* (New York, 1951; reissued in four volumes, Secaucus, N.J., 1989–90), 2:907–10. It should be noted that John Drayton of South Carolina, while defending slavery, denied Jefferson's suggestion of African inferiority in his *A View of South Carolina*. See David Grimsted, "Anglo-American Racism and Phyllis Wheatley," in Ronald Hoffman and Peter J. Albert, eds., *Women in the Age of the American Revolution* (Charlottesville, Va., 1989), p. 434.

4. See Christine Bolt, *Victorian Attitudes to Race* (London, 1971), especially pp. 227–29; also William Baker, "Wilberforce on the Idea of Negro Inferiority," *JHI* (1970), 31:433–40. On Brougham, see Peter D. Garside, "Scotland and the 'Philosophical' Historians," *JHI* (1975), 36:497–512; quotation, p. 507.

5. Henri Grégoire, *An Enquiry Concerning the Intellectual and Moral Faculties and Literature of Negroes: Followed with an Account of the Life and Works of*

Fifteen Negroes and Mulattoes Distinguished in Science, Literature, and the Arts,
(Brooklyn, N.Y., 1810; reprinted, College Park, Md., 1967): pp. 47, 42, 249.

6. Philip D. Curtin, *The Image of Africa: British Ideas and Action, 1780–1850,*
(Madison, Wis., 1964), pp. 47, 55, 382.

7. I used the edition translated by John Black, 2 vols. (London, 1814). The
quotation is from 1:235.

8. Beverly Wilson Palmer, ed., *The Selected Letters of Charles Sumner,* 2 vols.
(Boston, 1990), 1:301, 303.

9. See Philip S. Foner, *Alexander von Humboldt on Slavery in the United States,*
trans. by Ingo Schwarz (Berlin, DDR, n.d.).

10. See A. Nikoljukin, ed., *A Russian Discovery of America* (Moscow, 1986);
and D. Tumarkin, ed., *Travels to New Guinea* (Moscow, 1982).

11. James Malvin, "The Impact of Slavery in British Radical Politics, 1787–
1838," in V. Rubin and A. Tuden, eds., *Comparative Perspectives on Slavery,* Annals
of the New York Academy of Sciences, vol. 292 (New York, 1977), pp. 343–67; I.
McCalman, "Anti-Slavery and Ultra-Radicalism," *Slavery and Abolition* (London)
(1986), 7:118–28.

12. The printer of Barrow's pamphlet was D. and C. Bradford. It is rare; a copy
was kindly supplied me by the library of Cornell University. Its preface is dated
Montgomery County, Ky., August 27, 1807. The quotations are from pp. 19, 20,
45; italics in original. On Barrow, see H. Shelton Smith, *In His Image, But . . .
Racism in Southern Religion, 1780–1910* (Durham, N.C., 1972), pp. 49–53; David
B. Davis, *The Problem of Slavery in the Age of Revolution, 1770–1823* (Ithaca,
N.Y., 1975), pp. 201–3; Lowell H. Harrison, *The Antislavery Movement in Ken-
tucky* (Lexington, Ky., 1978), pp. 28–29.

13. Elias Hicks, *Observation of the Slavery of the Africans and their Descendants.
Recommended to the Serious Perusal and Important Consideration of the Citizens
of the United States of America* (New York: Samuel Wood, 1811; another printing
was made in 1814). See Henry Wilbur, *The Life and Labors of Elias Hicks* (Philadelphia, 1910), and Bliss Forbush, *Elias Hicks* (New York, 1956). Davis, *Problems
of Slavery in the Age of Revolution,* in its index, confuses Elias Hicks with Isaac
Hicks, a New York banker.

14. Monte A. Calvert, "The Abolition Society of Delaware," *Delaware History*
(1963), 10:301–20; quotation, p. 303. This article is hostile toward later Abolitionist
societies, which were "hasty, violent and radical" (p. 320). A similar attitude char-
acterizes Patrick Sowle, "The North Carolina Manumission Society, 1814–1834,"
NCHR (1965), 42:47–69. The same view is in Gordon E. Finnie, "The Antislavery
Movement in the Upper South before 1840," *JSH* (1969), 35:343–60. See my *Abolitionism* (Boston, 1989), pp. 1–4.

15. Duncan J. McLeod, *Slavery, Race, and the American Revolution* (London,
1974), pp. 144–45.

16. Merton L. Dillon, *Benjamin Lundy and the Struggle for Negro Freedom*
(Urbana, Ill., 1966). Subsequent quotations are from pp. 18–19, 30–31, 61, 177;
italics in original.

17. Jesse Torrey, *A Portraiture of Domestic Slavery in the United States* (written
in 1816, published by the author in Philadelphia in 1817); John Kenrick, *Horrors
of Slavery* (Cambridge, Mass.: Hilliard and Metcalf, 1817); John Rankin, *Letters
on American Slavery* (Boston: Garrison and Knapp, 1983). Kenrick and Rankin

continued as influential Abolitionists through the 1830s. See Alice D. Adams, *The Neglected Period of Anti-Slavery in America (1808–1831)* (Boston, 1908). p. 78; and Davis, *Problem of Slavery in the Age of Revolution*, pp. 332–33.

18. "The African Chief" is in Paul Lauter, ed., *The Heath Anthology of American Literature*, 2 vols. (Lexington, Mass., 1990), 1:670–72.

19. Thomas R. Moseley, "A History of the New-York Manumission Society, 1785–1849" (Ph.D. diss., New York University, 1963), pp. 200–204.

20. Randolph A. Roth, "The First Radical Abolitionists: The Reverend James Milligan and the Reformed Presbyterian Church of Vermont," *NEQ* (1982), 55:540–63; see especially pp. 540, 558.

21. Jeffrey Brooke Allen, "The Racial Thoughts of White North Carolina Opponents of Slavery, 1789–1876," *NCHR* (1982) 65:49–66; quotations, pp. 54, 55.

22. The *Address* is printed in Carl Degler, *The Other South: Southern Dissenters in the Nineteenth Century* (New York, 1974), p. 33; italics in original.

23. The preceding three paragraphs are based on Walter B. Possey, "The Slavery Question in the Presbyterian Church in the Old Southwest," *JSH* (1949), 15:310–24.

24. James B. Stewart, "Evangelicalism and the Radical Strain in Southern Anti-Slavery Thought during the 1820's," *JSH* (1973), 39:379–96; quotations, pp. 382, 392.

25. Josephus Wheaton, *The Equality of Mankind and the Evils of Slavery Illustrated: A Sermon Delivered on the Day of the Annual Fast, April 6, 1820* (Boston: Crocker and Brewster, 1820). This is rare; a copy was kindly supplied by the Library of Congress. Extracts from it are in D. L. Dumond, *Anti-slavery: The Crusade for Freedom in America* (Ann Arbor, Mich., 1961), pp. 142–49. In the index of Dumond's book, the name is rendered incorrectly. Other than the information in the text, I have not been able to learn more about Wheaton. Quotations are from pp. 11, 15, 17, 18 of his sermon; italics in original.

26. Degler, *Other South*, p. 20.

27. Jeffrey Brooke Allen, "Were Southern White Critics of Slavery Racists?" *JSH* (1978), 44:172–73.

28. Rankin's *Letters on American Slavery*, while written in 1820, were first published in 1833 in Boston by Garrison and Knapp. The edition here used is the third, published in Newburyport, Mass., by Charles Whipple. A fifth edition was published in 1838 in Boston by Isaac Knapp. The 1836 edition was reprinted by Greenwood Press (Westport, Conn.) in 1970. Quotations are from pp. 11, 18, 19, 27, 28–29. Early in the nineteenth century, John Gloucester created in Philadelphia the first Black Presbyterian congregation in the United States. He died in 1822; by 1819 he had succeeded in purchasing the freedom of his wife and six children (at a total cost of $1,500). See Gary B. Nash, *Forging Freedom: The Formation of Philadelphia's Black Community 1720–1840*, (Cambridge, Mass. 1988), pp. 199–201.

29. James Duncan, *A Treatise on Slavery. In Which Is Set Forth the Evil of Slaveholding Both from the Light of Nature and Divine Revelation* (Vevay: Indiana Register Office, 1824, 88 pp.). This was reissued in 1840 by both the Cincinnati Anti-Slavery Society and the American Anti-Slavery Society in New York. A four-page extract, called "The Slave-Holder's Prayer," was widely circulated by the latter society.

30. Adams, *The Neglected Period* p. 71.

31. A sermon by a Presbyterian minister, the Reverend Edwin Griffin of New Brunswick, New Jersey, was thus summarized in the *African Repository* (Washington) in March 1825, 1:7–12. I am indebted to George Fishman for calling this to my attention.

32. See George M. Fredrickson, "A Man But Not A Brother: Lincoln and Racial Equality," *JSH* (1975), 41:42. In February 1849, as Fredrickson wrote, Clay declared that even if the African people were intellectually inferior to white people (Clay was not sure), this did not justify slavery, else those more intelligent than others might enslave the latter, regardless of color.

Chapter 13

1. Quoted by Carl Degler, *The Other South: Southern Dissenters in the Nineteenth Century* (New York, 1974), p. 20.

2. *Niles' Weekly Register* (Baltimore), January 16, 1830, p. 357; italics in original. For documentation of the preceding paragraphs, see Herbert Aptheker, *American Negro Slave Revolts* (New York, 1943), pp. 264–92; and Aptheker, *Abolitionism*, (Boston, 1989), especially pp. 58–76.

3. My *Abolitionism* was part of a series; hence its size was strictly limited.

4. See Lawrence T. Lesick, *The Lane Rebels: Evangelicalism and Antislavery in America* (Metuchen, N.J., 1980), pp. 88–89.

5. Charles Beecher, ed., *Autobiography of Lyman Beecher*, 2 vols. (New York, 1864), 2:32–35.

6. Milton Rugoff, *The Beechers: An American Family in the Nineteenth Century* (New York, 1981), pp. 65–66.

7. From an obituary notice in 1844 of the death of Mrs. Weed, quoted by Dwight L. Dumond, *Antislavery: The Crusade for Freedom in America* (Ann Arbor, Mich., 1961), p. 280.

8. G. H. Barnes and D. L. Dumond, eds., *The Letters of Theodore Dwight Weld, Angelina Grimké Weld and Sarah Grimké, 1822–1844*, 2 vols. (New York, 1934) 1:211.

9. Ibid., 1:273; italics in original. The Reverend Asa Mahan was a Lane Seminary trustee; he supported the Lane Rebels and became president of Oberlin College.

10. There is a splendid chapter on Oberlin and racism in William Cheek and Aimee Lee Cheek, *John Mercer Langston and the Fight for Black Freedom, 1829–65* (Urbana, Ill., 1989), pp. 84–118; the quotation is on p. 100.

11. Quoted from the Finney Papers by Charles P. Cole, Jr., *The Social Ideas of the Northern Evangelists, 1826–1860* (New York, 1954), pp. 207–8. In context, it is clear that Cole felt that Finney was right.

12. For this Tappan objection, see Bertram Wyatt-Brown, *Lewis Tappan* (Cleveland, 1969), p. 177.

13. Robert Samuel Fletcher, *A History of Oberlin College from Its Foundation through the Civil War*, 2 vols. (Oberlin, 1943). Fletcher observed that "in a surprising number of instances masters sent their own children to Oberlin." Harriet Beecher Stowe assisted the school. It appears that Black students did not exceed 5 percent of the enrollment; in student activities they "seem always to have been welcome." See 1:170–78; 2:523–26; quotations, 2:523, 526, 528, 767. Italics in original.

14. See Philip Detweiler, "Congressional Debate on Slavery and the Declaration

of Independence, 1819–1821," *AHR* (1958), 63:598–616. Despite its title, this essay contains important material going back to the eighteenth century.

15. An illustration is John Hersey, *An Appeal to Christians on the Subject of Slavery* (Baltimore: 1833). Of its 124 pages, 36 consist of quotations from this debate. It is now rare; a copy was kindly sent to me by the Drew Theological Seminary.

16. In the Virginia State Library there is a bound volume entitled "Virginia Slavery Debate of 1831." This contains the entire record; it is this that I used. This legislature passed laws further restricting slaves and free Black people. There was serious consideration of colonization, and a small appropriation for this purpose was made. There was profound questioning of slavery; even the ideas of both quick and more gradual emancipation were discussed, but no action looking toward slavery's termination was taken. There also was a serious debate on slavery in the Virginia press; it lasted several weeks and then disappeared, never again to reappear in that press. Several of the speeches were published in an appendix to Joseph C. Robert, *The Road from Monticello: A Study of the Virginia Slavery Debate of 1832* (Durham, N.C., 1941). A section of my "Nat Turner's Slave Rebellion" (Master's thesis, Columbia University, 1937) contains a detailed examination of these debates. See also Aptheker, *American Negro Slave Revolts*, pp. 314–15. A penetrating study by Alison Goodyear Freehling is the fullest account now available: *Drift toward Dissolution: The Virginia Slavery Debate of 1831–1832* (Baton Rouge, 1982). This work paid attention to what it called "Negrophobia," but did not observe the presence of significant questioning of racism itself.

17. Robert M. Cover, *Justice Accused: Antislavery and the Judicial Process* (New Haven, Conn., 1975), especially pp. 246–47.

Chapter 14

1. See my "The struggle within the Ranks," *Masses and Mainstream*, February, 1950, 3:47–57.

2. See my "Militant Abolitionism," *JNH* (1941), 26:438–84.

3. Austin Wiley, *The History of the Antislavery Cause in State and Nation* (1860; reprinted by Negro Universities Press, New York, 1969), pp. 45–46. This development in Maine was especially noted by John C. Calhoun; see my *Abolitionism* (Boston, 1989), p. 24.

4. Louis Ruchames, "Race, Marriage, and Abolition in Massachusetts," *JNH* (1955), 40:250–73; quotation, p. 250.

5. Ronald G. Walters, *The Anti-Slavery Appeal: American Abolitionism after 1830* (Baltimore, 1975), pp. xiii, 57, 65,

6. On Parker's racism, see, for example, Douglas Stange, *Patterns of Antislavery among American Unitarians, 1851–1860* (Rutherford, N.J., 1977), p. 163.

7. John L. Thomas, ed., *Slavery Attacked: The Abolitionist Crusade* (Englewood Cliffs, N.J., 1965), p. 1.

8. Barnes and Dumond, eds., *The Letters of Theodore Dwight Weld, Angelina Grimké Weld and Sarah Grimké, 1822–1844*, 2 vols. (New York, 1934) 1:124–25.

9. Carleton Mabee, *Black Freedom: The Nonviolent Abolitionists from 1830 through the Civil War* (New York, 1970), pp. 91–184.

10. *Liberator*, November 19, 1836.

11. Beverly Wilson Palmer, ed., *The Selected Letters of Charles Sumner*, 2 vols. (Boston, 1990), 1:91, 125, 129–30; italics in original. On Emerson protesting segregation, see Len Gougeon, *Virtue's Hero: Emerson, Antislavery, and Reform* (Athens, Ga., 1990), pp. 16–17.

12. Richard A. Abbott, *Cobbler in Congress: The Life of Henry Wilson* (Lexington, Ky., 1972), pp. 21–23.

13. *Sentinel of Freedom* (Newark, N.J.), July 15, 1834. See George Fishman, "The African-American Struggle for Freedom and Equality in New Jersey, 1624–1850" (Ph.D. diss., Temple University, 1990), pp. 438–39. Also see G. Fishman, "New Jersey's Abolition Voice," *NHB* (January 1968), 31–18–19. Other information was kindly sent me by Dr. Fishman in a letter dated January 2, 1991.

14. *American Anti-Slavery Almanac* (1840), p. 21; italics in original.

15. *Liberator*, May 7, 1831. The letter to Webb is quoted by Leon Litwack, *North of Slavery* (Chicago, 1961), p. 106.

16. Quoted by Dorothy B. Porter, "The Educational Activities of Negro Literary Societies, 1828–1846," *JNH* (1936), 5:555–76. In this important essay, Porter noted that the *Liberator* often published poems and essays from members of such societies.

17. Du Bois in his eulogy of Florence Kelley, edited by the present writer, in *Social Work* (1966), 11:99–100. Du Bois spoke on March 11, 1932.

18. See Louis Ruchames, ed., *The Letters of William Lloyd Garrison* (Cambridge, Mass., 1971), 2:294, 334. See also p. 227, and Garrison to Gerrit Smith, March 7, 1835, in W. M. Merrill, ed. *The Letters of William Lloyd Garrison*, 1:459–63. On American Indians and the Irish, see Ruchames, *Letters of Garrison*, 2:105–6, 268, 285. See also William Lloyd Garrison, *Thoughts on African Colonization* (1832; reprinted, New York, 1968).

19. See Anthony J. Barker, *Captain Charles Stuart, Anglo-American Abolitionist* (Baton Rouge, 1986).

20. The 1833 edition was published in Boston by Allen and Ticknor; the book was reissued in New York City in 1836 by John S. Taylor.

21. The 1968 reprint was published by Arno Press in New York.

22. The quotations from Child are from the source cited in note 20, pp. 135, 169, 170, 203, 206, 214. Her sixth chapter was on "Intellect of the Negroes." Child wrote of John Kenrick that he "aroused many minds to think and act upon the subject." She added that he published occasionally on the question in local newspapers and circulated relevant pamphlets at his own expense. Dwight L. Dumond, *Bibliography of Antislavery in America* (Ann Arbor, Mich., 1961), p. 71, listed a pamphlet by him *Horrors of Slavery*, published in 1817 in Cambridge. Dumond also spoke of Kenrick's financial contributions and stated that he was associated with the New England Anti-Slavery Society created in 1832. There are two brief notices of him in David B. Davis, *The Problem of Slavery in the Age of Revolution, 1770–1823* (Ithaca, N.Y., 1979), pp. 332–33. Davis wrote me that he had no further information.

23. Julius Lewin, *The Struggle for Racial Equality* (London, 1967), p. 29.

24. Laura S. Haviland, *A Woman's Life Work: Including Thirty Years' Service on the Underground Railroad and in the War* (Grand Rapids, Mich., 1881). On Fairbank, see my *Abolitionism* (Boston, 1989), pp. 108–9, 114, 115, 177 n. 28.

25. Samuel J. May, *Some Recollections of our Anti-Slavery Conflict* (Boston, 1869; reprinted, New York, 1968); quotations from pp. 18, 270–72, 399.

26. No compiler is named in the book, but it is catalogued under Ames's name and is so attributed in Dwight L. Dumond, *Bibliography of Antislavery in America.* The material cited here is on pages 22 and 158–60 of *"Liberty": The Image and Superscription on Every Coin Issued by the United States* (New York, 1837). Another illustration of Abolitionist concern to refute racism is S. B. Treadwell, *American Liberties and American Slavery Morally and Politically Illustrated* (1838; reprinted, New York, 1969), especially pp. 189, 223, 238.

27. Charles Olcott, *Two Lectures on the Subject of Slavery and Abolition* (Massillon, Ohio, 1838; published by the author); quotations from pp. 36, 55, 56, 75; italics in original. This idea of compensating the slaves for their unrequited labor, after emancipation, recurs in the literature. It reappears in the demands of the Civil Rights movement after the Second World War. The concept deserves extended historical treatment.

28. *Herald of Freedom*, November 10, 1838, in L. Ruchames, ed., *The Abolitionists: A Collection of Their Writing* (New York, 1963), p. 157; italics in original.

29. William Jay, *Inquiry into the Character and Tendency of the American Colonization and American Anti-Slavery Societies*, first published in New York City in 1835. By 1840 it was in its tenth edition and was published by the American Anti-Slavery Society. Most of Jay's essays appear in his *Miscellaneous Writings on Slavery* (Boston, 1853). I have used that edition; quotation, p. 30.

30. Donald G. Mathews, "The Methodist Mission to the Slaves, 1829–1844," *JAH* (1965), 51:615–31; quotations, pp. 627, 631.

31. Gerda Lerner, *The Grimké Sisters from South Carolina: Rebels against Slavery* (Boston, 1967), especially pp. 132–33, 156–57, 161, 251–56. See Aptheker, *Abolitionism*, pp. 58–93.

32. Grimké's *Appeal* was published in New York City in 1836; it was reprinted in New York City in 1969; quotation, p. 30; italics in original.

33. *The Anti-Slavery Catechism* was published in Newburyport, Mass.; excerpts are in Thomas, *Slavery Attacked*; quotations, pp. 66, 68.

34. These remarks are from the essay, "Slavery," dated Boston, December 20, 1836, in *The Works of William E. Channing* (Boston, 1895), pp. 688–743; quotations, pp. 691, 693, 695. Channing's later work reiterated rejection of racism, as did his final address, August 1842, ibid., p. 915.

35. Edward Price, "The Black Voting Rights Issue in Pennsylvania, 1780–1900," *PMHB* (1976), 100:356–73; quotation, pp. 360–61. Also see Edward Price, "Let the Law Be Just: The Quest for Racial Equality in Pennsylvania, 1780–1915" (Ph.D. diss., State University of Pennsylvania, 1973), pp. 104–23. Earle was quoted on p. 110. For protests against disfranchisement at this time from Black people in Pennsylvania, see Herbert Aptheker, *A Documentary History of the Negro People in the United States* (New York, 1951; reissued in four volumes, Secaucus, N.J., 1989–90), 1:176–83, 208–9.

36. J. Herman Schauinger, *William Gaston: Carolinian* (Milwaukee, 1949), pp. 184, 1–2.

37. Letter dated April 14, 1841, in Bertram Wyatt-Brown, *Lewis Tappan* (Cleveland, 1969), p. 217.

38. The italics are in the original account. The story is told by John S. Patterson,

"A Garrisonian Discussion of Prejudice: 'Not One Dared to Rise,' " *NEQ* (1975), 48:564–70. Patterson presents it as supporting the recent literature, which showed "a heightened awareness of its [abolitionism's] blemishes." I think, rather, that the incident and the *Liberator*'s full report show the seriousness with which the movement confronted racism, as well as the difficulties this posed. On Edmund Quincy, see, for example, J. B. Stewart, *Wendell Phillips* (Baton Rouge, 1986), pp. 103, 296.

39. *The Legion of Liberty! And Force of Truth, Containing the Thought, Words, and Deeds of Some Prominent Apostles, Champions, and Martyrs*, 2d ed. (New York: American Anti-Slavery Society, 1843; reprinted, New York, 1969); quotation, pp. 17–18. Park's *Travels in the Interior of Africa* was published in London in 1799.

40. Armistead's *A Tribute for the Negro* was republished in 1900 in London and in 1969 in Westport, Connecticut. Earlier the society had produced brief pamphlets, called "Tracts," like no. 9, "Prejudice against Color," printed in 1839. Belatedly the American Tract Society in Cincinnati began to issue anti-slavery pamphlets; one issued in 1860 was by B. P. Aydelot, *Prejudice against Color*.

41. This 1846 pamphlet was reprinted in Jay, *Miscellaneous Writings on Slavery*, pp. 409–52; quotations, pp. 440–41; italics in original. Frederick Douglass offered a glowing eulogy of William Jay in 1854; see P. S. Foner, ed., *Douglass*, vol. 5 (1975), pp. 430–49.

42. See Reginald Horsman, "Scientific Racism and the American Indian in the Mid-Nineteenth Century," *AQ* (1975), 27:152–68.

43. Leslie D. Stephens, "Forget Their Color: J. Peter Lesley on Slavery and the South," *NEQ* (1980), 53:212–21; quotation, p. 215. In 1863 Lesley thought that the Black people were "a great race" quite "on a par" with "the other great races." He suggested that land be given them, else freed people would not be really free. During his last years he altered these views.

44. Burt G. Wilder, "Jeffries Wyman," in David Starr Jordan, ed., *Leading American Men of Science* (New York, 1910), pp. 171–208; quotation, p. 192. Wilder, a physician and a Civil War veteran, was a leading anti-racist in the early twentieth century and a participant in founding the National Association for the Advancement of Colored People (NAACP). It should be noted that into the 1830s it was seriously argued that the orangutan and the chimpanzee were of the human species; see Philip D. Curtin, *The Image of Africa: British Ideas and Action, 1780–1850* (Madison, Wis., 1964), p. 368, and L. Gougeon, "Abolition, the Emersons, and 1837," *NEQ* (1981), 54:355–56 n. Gougeon wrote of the rejection of the African orangutan identification.

45. See Curtin, *Image of Africa*, pp. 232, 386.

46. David A. Gerber, *Black Ohio and the Color Line, 1860–1915* (Urbana, Ill., 1976), pp. 12–13. In 1856 John Mercer Langston was elected town clerk in Brownhelm, Ohio, as an Independent Democrat. Charles Fairfield, a white man, nominated him. See William Cheek and Aimee Lee Cheek, *John Mercer Langston and the Fight for Black Freedom, 1829–65* (Urbana, Ill., 1989), pp. 259–62. The source for the *Cleveland Herald* quotation is *Annals of Cleveland, 1818–1935: A Digest and Index of the Newspaper Record of Events and Opinions*, by workers of the Ohio W.P.A. (Cleveland, 1938), vol. 28, pt. 1, p. 186.

47. See Joe M. Richardson, *Christian Reconstruction: The American Missionary Association and Southern Blacks, 1861–1890* (Athens, Ga., 1986).

48. John G. Fee, *An Antislavery Manual* (Maysville, Ky., 1848; reprinted, New York, 1969); quotations, p. 171; see pp. 206–11.

49. The information on Jones is based on the record made in 1945 by Abner C. Wright, Chemung County historian, and published as "Underground Railroad Activities in Elmira," *Chemung Historical Journal*, August 1985, pp. 1755–59.

50. See Priscilla Thompson, "Harriet Tubman, Thomas Garrett, and the Underground Railroad," *Delaware History* (1986), 22:1–22. On Garrett, see also William Still, *The Underground Railroad: A Record* (Philadelphia, 1872), pp. 623–43. This contains several letters from Garrett to Still. Still's book of over eight hundred pages, with splendid illustrations, is a monument to human capacity, endurance, and fellowship.

51. See the essay on Miner by Josephine Pacheco in P. S. Foner and J. F. Pacheco, *Three Who Dared* (Westport, Conn., 1984), pp. 101–204; quotations from pp. 117, 140, 187. Myrtilla Miner died in 1864. For a time the Miner School was connected with Howard University. In 1929 it became Miner Teachers College; in 1955 (after the *Brown* decision) it merged with Wilson Teachers College to become the District of Columbia Teachers College. There now is a Miner Elementary School in Washington, D.C.

Chapter 15

1. For example, Louise K. Barnett, *The Ignoble Savage: American Literary Racism, 1790–1890* (Westport, Conn., 1975); Jean Fagan Yellin, *The Intricate Knot: Black Figures in American Literature, 1776–1863* (New York, 1972).

2. Herman Melville, in a review of Parkman in the *Literary World*, March 31, 1849, quoted in Barnett, *Ignoble Savage*, p. 171.

3. Yellin, *Intricate Knot*, pp. 215–41; quotation, p. 224. See the powerful presentation by Sidney Kaplan in *American Studies in Black and White: Selected Essays, 1949–1989*, edited by Allan D. Austin (Amherst, 1991), pp. 144–97.

4. Severn Duvall, " 'Uncle Tom's Cabin': The Sinister Side of the Patriarchy," *New England Review* (1963), 36:5. Compare Huck's refusal to turn in Jim. On Stowe's novel it is to be observed that some contemporaries regretted that its emphasis upon Christian resignation might have a quieting effect upon the nation's conscience. This was the reaction, for example, of William G. Allen, an Afro-American living in England as a refugee. See Yellin, *Intricate Knot*, p. 139.

5. The announcement was published in Middletown, Connecticut, *Sentinel and Witness*, October 20, 1850, quoted in Horatio T. Strother, *The Underground Railroad in Connecticut* (Middletown, Conn., 1962), p. 102.

6. Bradford Terry, ed., *The Writings of Henry David Thoreau*, 19 vols. (1906; reprinted, New York, 1968), 17:437–38. On Emerson, see Len Gougeon, *Virtue's Hero: Emerson Antislavery, and Reform* (Athens, Ga., 1990).

7. See the two volumes of *The Anti-Slavery Papers of James Russell Lowell* (no editor given; Boston, 1902); quotations are from 1:16; see also 2:194–201.

8. For Lowell on Prichard, see his *Anti-Slavery Papers*, 2:25–32. On Mary Putnam, see my *Abolitionism* (Boston, 1989), pp. 84–85. On Crukshank and Prichard, see Philip D. Curtin, *The Image of Africa: British Ideas and Action, 1780–1850* (Madison, Wis., 1964), pp. 252, 387, 400–401.

9. Beverly Wilson Palmer, ed., *The Selected Letters of Charles Sumner*, 2 vols.

(Boston, 1990), 1:415, 499; David Livingstone, *Missionary Travels and Researches in South Africa* (New York, 1858), especially chap. 19; the quotation is from p. 399.

10. Yellin, *Intricate Knot*, pp. 87–120.

11. *Ford v. Ford* (1846), in Helen T. Catterall, ed., *Judicial Cases Concerning American Slavery and the Negro*, 5 vols. (Washington, D.C., 1926–37), 2:530; see also 2:479, 514, 534, 585. On the question of slaves as humans and as property that plagued Southern courts, see Robert M. Cover, *Justice Accused: Anti-Slavery and the Judicial Process* (New Haven, Conn., 1975). While there was breast-beating, legal formalism prevailed.

12. L. Minor Blackford, *Mine Eyes Have Seen the Glory: The Story of a Virginia Lady, Mary Berkeley Minor Blackford, Who Taught Her Sons to Hate Slavery and to Love the Union* (Cambridge, Mass., 1954), pp. 16–47; quotation, p. 47. Compare this paragraph with the mention of Mary Blackford, "who did oppose slavery in principle," in Elizabeth Fox-Genovese, *Within the Plantation Household: Black and White Women of the Old South* (Chapel Hill, N.C., 1988), p. 366.

13. Charles B. Rousseve, *The Negro in Louisiana: Aspects of His History and His Literature* (New Orleans, 1937), p. 41. Roger Shugg referred to displays of "the darkest Abolitionist proclivities," citing the *New Orleans Picayune*, December 16, 1860; another Louisiana paper (*Franklin Banner*, September 1, 1860) reported the arrest of several white people in the state who "hurrahed for Lincoln"; *Origins of Class Struggle in Louisiana* (Baton Rouge, 1939), p. 146.

14. Peyton McCrary, *Abraham Lincoln and Reconstruction in Louisiana* (Princeton, N.J., 1978), p. 21. The Abbé Adrian Emmanuel Rouquette preached against slavery from the pulpit of St. Louis Cathedral. See Geraldine Mary McTigue, "Forms of Racial Interaction in Louisiana 1860–1880" (Ph.D. diss., Yale University, 1975), p. 31.

15. See Gail Williams O'Brien, *The Legal Fraternity and the Making of a New South Community, 1848–1882* (Athens, Ga., 1986), pp. 38–45; Martin Cranford, "Political Society in a Southern Mountain Community, Ashe County, N.C., 1850–1861," *JSH* (1989), 55:373–90. Cranford stated that Bacon was accused of complicity in a slave outbreak in 1851 that resulted in the death of the county's sheriff. See also Aptheker, *Abolitionism*, p. 117.

16. John Spencer Bassett, *Anti-Slavery Leaders of North Carolina* (Baltimore, 1898), remains indispensable. On Worth, see pp. 25–26. Also see N. J. Tolbert, "Daniel Worth: Tar Heel Abolitionist," *NCHR* (1962), 39:284–304. Compare Carl Degler, *The Other South: Southern Dissenters in the Nineteenth Century* (New York, 1974) p. 89.

17. George Troxler, "Eli Caruthers: A Silent Dissenter in the Old South," *Journal of Presbyterian History* (1967), 45:95–111; quotations, pp. 108, 109.

18. Patricia Hicken, "Gentle Agitator: Samuel M. Janney and the Anti-Slavery Movement in Virginia, 1842–1851," *JSH* (1971), 37:159–90; quotation, p. 189. In general, see James Oakes, *The Ruling Race: A History of American Slaveholders* (New York, 1982), pp. 109–10, 117, 184–85.

19. Levi Coffin, *Reminiscences of Levi Coffin, the Reputed President of the Undeground Railroad* (Cincinnati, [1876]; 3d ed., 1898), pp. 428–46 (on Fairfield), 713–18 (on Dillingham), 582–88 (on Connelly).

Chapter 16

1. The Liberty party resolutions are in *Emancipation Extra, Tract no. 1* (September 1843), quoted in John L. Thomas, ed., *Slavery Attacked: The Abolitionist Crusade* (Englewood Cliffs, N.J., 1965), pp. 94–95.

2. See Charles H. Wesley, "The Participation of Negroes in Anti-Slavery Political Parties," *JHN* (1944), 29:32–74, especially pp. 44–46.

3. Sumner's remarks to the court are in his *Works*, 2:327–76; italics in original. Warmly appreciative of Sumner's efforts is Leonard W. Levy and Harlan B. Phillips, "The Roberts Case," *AHR* (1956), 59:510–18. Judge Samuel Shaw's decision is briefly evaluated in Robert M. Cover, *Justice Accused: Antislavery and the Judicial Process* (New Haven, Conn., 1975), p. 267. The case is *Roberts v. City of Boston* (1849), 59 Mass. (5 Cush.) 198. Shaw's decision may be found in Helen T. Catterall, ed., *Judicial Cases Concerning American Slavery and the Negro*, 5 vols. (Washington, D.C., 1926–37), 4:512–14. David Donald's treatment of the case is brief and rather cold; *Charles Sumner and the Coming of the Civil War* (New York, 1960), pp. 180–81. Donald noted that Sumner served without fee in this case. See also the acute remarks on *Roberts* in Richard Kluger, *Simple Justice* (New York, 1976), pp. 75–77.

4. Vernon L. Wolpe, *Forlorn Hope of Freedom: The Liberty Party in the Old Northwest, 1836–1848* (Kent, Ohio, 1990); quotations, pp. 58, 105, 13, 56. In 1855 George B. Vashon was the Liberty party's candidate for attorney-general of New York, the first Black candidate for public office on a statewide ticket. Earlier, Vashon had been on the faculty of the integrated, coeducational Central College in McGrawsville, New York; the college existed from 1849 to 1858. See William Cheek and Aimee Lee Cheek, *John Mercer Langston and the Fight for Black Freedom, 1829–65* (Urbana, Ill., 1989), p. 122. On George B. Vashon (1824–1878), see Joan R. Sherman in Rayford W. Logan and Michael R. Winston, eds., *Dictionary of American Negro Biography* (New York, 1982), p. 617.

5. C. Vann Woodward, *American Counterpoint: Slavery and Racism in the North-South Dialogue* (Boston, 1971), p. 148.

6. George M. Fredrickson, *The Arrogance of Race* (Middletown, Conn., 1988), p. 60.

7. See especially John M. Rozett, "Racism and Republican Emergence in Illinois, 1848–1860: A Re-Evaluation of Republican Negrophobia," *Civil War History* (1976), 27:101–15.

8. Eric Foner, *Free Soil, Free Labor, Free Men: The Ideology of the Republican Party before the Civil War* (New York, 1970).

9. Douglass in a letter to Sumner, April 24, 1855, complained that Sumner did not recognize "the entire manhood and social equality of the colored people"; Donald, *Charles Sumner*, p. 235n. But the two men respected each other, and their relationship became very close as the years passed and the struggle continued. See P. S. Foner, ed., *Douglass*, 2:490–93, quoting *Douglass' Monthly*, August 1860, where Douglass especially commended Sumner.

10. Lincoln's speech at Peoria, October 16, 1854, in Roy Basler, ed., *The Works of Abraham Lincoln* (New Brunswick, N.J., 1953), 2:256, 261, 231.

11. Paul M. Angle, ed., *Created Equal? The Complete Lincoln-Douglas Debates of 1858* (Chicago, 1958), p. xxix.

12. Basler, *Works of Abraham Lincoln*, 2:16. Important material on Lincoln's evolving position on Black people is in Peyton McCrary, *Abraham Lincoln and Reconstruction: The Louisiana Experiment* (Princeton, N.J., 1978). See also Fredrickson, *Arrogance of Race*, pp. 54–72. Fredrickson compared Lincoln's position with that of Henry Clay. On Clay, see Douglass's estimate in Foner, *Life and Writings of Frederick Douglass*, 5:234–36.

13. Speech in Springfield, June 26, 1857, in Basler, *Works of Abraham Lincoln*, 2:398–410; quotations, 406, 409; italics added.

14. In *Annals of Cleveland, 1818–1835: A Digest and Index of the Newspaper Record of Events and Opinions*, by workers of the Ohio W.P.A. (Cleveland, 1938), 40:133.

15. Stevens's statement appears in Thomas F. Woodley, *Thaddeus Stevens* (Harrisburg, Pa., 1934), pp. 557–58. Indicative of the date of this book, Stevens's biographer here identifies "Fred Douglass" as being Stevens's barber in Lancaster. The encounter between Stevens and Brooks occurred December 18, 1867; see *Congressional Globe*, 40th Cong., 2d sess., p. 267.

16. Michael Lee Benedict, "Equality and Expediency in the Reconstruction Era," *Civil War History* (1977), 23:322–35; quotation, p. 325. Benedict was referring particularly to James C. Mohr, ed., *Radical Republicans in the North: State Politics during Reconstruction* (Baltimore, 1976).

17. Rozett, "Racism and Republican Emergence in Illinois," p. 115.

18. Emil Olbrich, "The Development of Sentiment on Negro Suffrage to 1860," *Bulletin of the University of Wisconsin* (1912), History Series no. 477, pp. 33, 60, 75, 94, 101, 103, 117. Also see E. R. Turner, *The Negro in Pennsylvania, 1689–1861* (Washington, D.C., 1911), p. 177; and Rowland Berthoff, "Conventional Morality, Free Blacks, Women, and Business Corporations as Unequal Persons, 1820–1870," *JAH* (1989), 76:753–84, especially pp. 765–69.

19. S. Crosswell and R. Sutton, reporters, *Debates and Proceedings of the New-York State Convention, for the Revision of the Constitution* (Albany, 1846); quotations from pp. 776, 785. I am indebted to the kindness of Sidney Kaplan of the University of Massachusetts, Amherst, for making available copies of the New York, Ohio, and Indiana convention reports.

20. J. V. Smith, official reporter, *Report of the Debates and Proceedings of the Convention for the Revision of the Constitution of the State of Ohio, 1850–1851* (Columbus, 1851). Material is summarized and quoted from pp. 57, 58, 59, 75, 107, 108, 191, 236, 313, 337–38, 726.

21. *Report of the Debates and Proceedings of the Convention for the Revision of the Constitution of the State of Indiana, 1850* (Indianapolis, 1850); quotations from pp. 245, 563, 568, 571, 593.

22. *Report of Majority of Judiciary Committee, Made to the Assembly, March 2, 1857*; quotations from pp. 3, 4, 5, 12. The information on Mills is in the "Biographical Sketches" of the *Wisconsin Blue Book* (Madison, 1879), p. 473. I am indebted to Clarence Kailin of Madison, Wisconsin, for copies of this material.

23. Michael J. McManus, "Wisconsin Republicans and Negro Suffrage Attitudes and Behavior, 1857," *Civil War History* (1979), 25:36–54; quotations, pp. 38, 39, 53, 49, 53–54.

24. *Liberator*, October 23, 1857, in Herbert Aptheker, *A Documentary History of the Negro People in the United States* (New York, 1951; reissued in four volumes, Secaucus, N.J., 1989–90), 1:395–96; italics in original.

Chapter 17

1. James Brewer Stewart, *Joshua R. Giddings and the Tactics of Radical Politics* (Cleveland, 1970).

2. Lydia Maria Child, ed., *Speeches on Political Questions by George W. Julian* (New York, 1872), pp. 95–96, 103, 105.

3. Benjamin Wade in *Congressional Globe*, 33d Cong., 1st sess. p. 339, and March 3, 1854, appendix, p. 311.

4. Richard H. Sewell, *John P. Hale and the Politics of Abolition* (Cambridge, Mass., 1965), pp. 209–11.

5. Hale is quoted from the *Congressional Globe*, March 5, 1858, p. 1970; March 18, 1862, p. 1268.

6. Henry Wilson, *Congressional Globe*, 33d Cong., 2d sess., Appendix, p. 238. See Richard A. Abbott, *Cobbler in Congress: The Life of Henry Wilson* (Lexington, Ky., 1972), pp. 158–59.

7. Owen Lovejoy, *Congressional Globe*, 35th Cong., 2d sess., Appendix, p. 199. The last sentence in this quotation was printed in uppercase type in the *Globe*.

8. The 1860 speech, "The Barbarism of Slavery," gained national attention and in pamphlet form was printed in German as well as English. See Edward Magdol, *Owen Lovejoy: Abolitionist in Congress* (New Brunswick, N.J., 1967), pp. 233–43. See also the *Annual Report of the American Anti-Slavery Society for Year Ending May 1, 1860* (reprinted, New York, 1969), p. 252. In a eulogy of Lovejoy, his very close friend, Ichabod Codding, said: "He saw from the beginning that the Negro possessed our common human nature, and that in his rights were involved the rights of man, the principle of popular government." Magdol, *Owen Lovejoy*, p. 409.

9. Irving H. Bartlett, *Wendell and Ann Phillips: The Community of Reform, 1840–1880* (New York, 1979), pp. 66, 68; italics in original. See also pp. 62, 64–65. Mrs. Child was buried near the graves of two former slaves in Wayland, Massachusetts, in 1880.

10. Karl Marx and Frederick Engels, *The Civil War in the United States*, ed. Richard Enmale [Herbert Morais] (New York, 1938), contains most of their war columns, several of which emphasized the significance of the African American. See also Karl Marx and Frederick Engels, *Collected Works* (Moscow, 1985), vol. 20 (1864–1868), especially pp. 5–13, 19–21, 99–100. Karl Obermann's biography, *Joseph Weydemeyer* (New York, 1947), is helpful. See also P. S. Foner, "Peter H. Clark, Pioneer Black Socialist," in his *Essays in Afro-American History* (Philadelphia, 1978), pp. 156–57; and my two essays, originally published in 1939 and 1954, "Class Conflicts in the South, 1850–1860" and "The Labor Movement in the South during Slavery," reprinted in Bettina Aptheker, ed., *The Unfolding Drama: Studies in U.S. History* (New York, 1978), pp. 29–66. Edward Channing called attention to the creation of Social Democratic Societies of Working Men in Richmond, Baltimore, and New York City in the 1850s. These not only called for an end to slavery but also for universal suffrage, the eight-hour day for workers, taxing church property, government ownership of railroads, and some other reforms not yet achieved

as the twentieth century nears its end. *A History of the United States*, vol. 6 (New York, 1926), pp. 126–28.

11. The two main sources for Gilbert Haven are Gilbert Haven, *Sermons, Speeches, and Letters on Slavery and Its War* (Boston, 1869; reprinted, New York, 1969), and William Gravely, *Gilbert Haven, Methodist Abolitionist: A Study in Race, Religion, and Reform, 1850–1880* (Nashville, 1973).

12. Quoted by Ruth Scarborough, *The Opposition to Slavery in Georgia prior to 1860* (1933; reprinted, New York, 1968), pp. 231–32.

13. W. G. Bean, "Anti-Jeffersonianism in the Ante-Bellum South," *NCHR* (1935), 12:111.

14. Charles G. Sellers, Jr., "The Travail of Slavery," in Charles G. Sellers, ed., *The Southerner as American* (Chapel Hill, N.C., 1960), p. 65. Sellers mistakenly referred to Goodloe as a Virginian. Goodloe's work is *The Southern Platform: or, Manual of the Southern Sentiment on Slavery* (Boston, 1858); the quotation is on p. 93. Carl Degler, *The Other South: Southern Dissenters in the Nineteenth Century* (New York, 1974), frequently mentioned Goodloe and called attention to his significance as an anti-slavery figure who retained advanced policies after the war, but he did not notice Goodloe's sharp attack on racism. Soon after the war began, a professor of chemistry, identified only as Boynton, was dismissed from the University of Mississippi for Lincoln sympathies; see Georgia Lee Tatum, *Disloyalty in the Confederacy* (Chapel Hill, N.C., 1934), p. 89.

15. Eric Foner, *Free Soil, Free Labor, Free Men: The Ideology of the Republican Party before the Civil War* (New York, 1970), pp. 261–300; quotations, pp. 261, 262.

16. David Donald, *Charles Sumner and the Coming of the Civil War* (New York, 1960), pp. 356–63; quotations, pp. 356, 358, 362.

17. On John Brown, see my *Abolitionism* (Boston, 1989), pp. 123ff.; on Lydia Maria Child in 1878, see James M. McPherson, *The Struggle for Equality: Abolitionists and the Negro in the Civil War and Reconstruction* (Princeton, N.J., 1964), p. 431.

Chapter 18

1. P. S. Foner, ed., *Douglass*, 3:379.

2. The *Journal of Commerce* was paraphrased by Theodore Tilton in his *The Negro* (New York, 1863), this being the text of a speech at Cooper Institute, New York City, May 12, 1863; see Gilbert Osofsky, ed., *The Burden of Race: A Documentary History of Negro-White Relations in America* (New York, 1967), p. 101.

3. William Parham to Jacob White in David A. Gerber, *Black Ohio and the Color Line, 1860–1915* (Urbana, Ill., 1976), pp. 41–43. The addressee, Jacob C. White, Jr. (1837–1902), was then principal of the Roberts Vaux School in Philadelphia. Parham's remarks are strikingly similar to those of the young Du Bois.

4. Beverly Wilson Palmer, ed., *The Selected Letters of Charles Sumner*, 2 vols. (Boston, 1990), 2:34. The editor noted that Sumner was referring to a story in the *London Times*, but gave no date. Sidney Kaplan very kindly searched the *Times* for me and sent me a copy of the issue quoted here.

5. *London Times*, July 21, 1860, p. 9. Henry Peter Brougham (1778–1868) had been prominent in the anti-slave-trade efforts in Parliament. He was lord chancellor

(1830–34) and active in scientific efforts. He chaired the Statistical Congress. George M. Dallas was then U.S. minister to Great Britain; in 1845–49 he had been vice president of the United States. An attempt to learn the name of the "coloured gentleman from Canada" has not been successful.

6. Moncure D. Conway, *Testimonies Concerning Slavery* (London, 1864; reprinted, New York: Arno Press, 1969). See especially pp. 56–79; the quotations are from pp. 71, 76. On William Wells Brown, see W. Edward Farrison, *William Wells Brown: Author and Reformer* (Chicago, 1969), pp. 363, 367–68.

7. Alcott's novella was reprinted, with editorial note by Lorenzo D. Turner, in *JNH* (1929), 14:495–522.

8. See Joe M. Richardson, *Christian Reconstruction: The American Missionary Association and Southern Blacks, 1861–1890* (Athens, Ga., 1986), p. 10.

9. Robert F. Engs, *Freedom's First Generation: Black Hampton, Virginia, 1861–1890* (Philadelphia, 1978), pp. 46, 50.

10. W. E. B. Du Bois, "The Freedmen's Bureau," *Atlantic Monthly* (March 1901), 88:358. Two such women are immortalized in his novel, *The Quest of the Silver Fleece* (1911); see my note in the Kraus edition of that book (New York, 1974), p. 12 n. 8.

11. In addition to Richardson, *Christian Reconstruction*, and Engs, *Freedom's First Generation*, see Henry L. Swint, *The Northern Teacher in the South, 1862–1870* (Nashville, 1941). Swint was unfriendly to the effort, but he reported: "Practically all the teachers seem to have agreed that the Negro was very intelligent and that he learned very quickly" (p. 66). Also see Willie Lee Rose, *Rehearsal for Reconstruction: The Port Royal Experiment* (Indianapolis, 1964), especially p. 88.

12. Robert C. Morris, *Reading, 'Riting, and Reconstruction: The Education of Freedmen in the South, 1861–1870* (Chicago, 1981); quotations from pp. 17–18, 31, 51. John Eaton had been superintendent of schools in Toledo. His later career included the positions of U.S. commissioner of education, president of Marietta College, and superintendent of the public-school system in Puerto Rico. Important additional evidence on repudiation of racism is in Wayne E. Reilly, ed., *Sarah Jane Foster, Teacher of the Freedmen: A Diary and Letters* (Charlottesville, Va., 1990).

13. Gerald Schwartz, "An Integrated Free School in Civil War Florida," *FHQ* (1982), 61:155–61; italics in original.

14. George C. Wright, *Life behind a Veil: Blacks in Louisville, Kentucky, 1865–1930* (Baton Rouge, 1985), pp. 29–30.

15. Contributing to the literature on Black participation in the Civil War were George W. Williams, Joseph T. Wilson, W. E.B. Du Bois, the present writer, Benjamin Quarles, Charles H. Wesley, John Hope Franklin, Dudley T. Cornish, and James M. McPherson. See Herbert Aptheker, *A Documentary History of the Negro People in the United States* (New York, 1951; reissued in four volumes, Secaucus, N.J., 1989–90), especially 1:450–532.

16. Joseph T. Glatthaar, *The March to the Sea and Beyond: Sherman's Troops in the Savannah and Carolinas Campaign* (New York, 1985); and *Forged in Battle: The Civil War Alliance of Black Soldiers and White Officers* (New York, 1990).

17. Glatthaar, *March to the Sea*, pp. 52–65; quotations, pp. 53, 63, 65.

18. Glatthaar, *Forged in Battle*, p. 81; italics in original. The surgeon was James O. Moore.

19. Ibid., pp. 85, 87; the surprised one was Warren Goodale.

20. Ibid., pp. 96–97; italics in original.

21. Ibid., pp. 206, 258–59.

22. I used the Michigan State University Press edition (Lansing, 1960) of Higginson's 1870 volume. It contains a fine introduction by Howard Mumford Jones. The quotations are from pp. xi and 190. See especially pp. 189–203.

23. Ruth Currie-McDaniel, *Carpetbagger of Conscience: A Biography of John Emery Bryant* (Athens, Ga., 1987), `p. 35; Ted Tunnell, ed., *Carpetbagger from Vermont: The Autobiography of Marshall Harvey Twitchell* (Baton Rouge, 1989), p. 82.

24. Steven Rowan, trans., James N. Primm, commentator, *Germans for a Free Missouri: Translations from the St. Louis Radical Press, 1857–1862* (Columbia, Mo., 1983), pp. 316–17; italics in original.

25. Richard Paul Fuke, "Hugh Lennox Bond and Radical Republican Ideology," *JSH* (1979), 44:569–86. See also Fuke, "The Baltimore Association," *Md. Hist. Mag.* (1971), 66:369–404.

26. Wright, *Life behind a Veil*, pp. 18–19.

27. Geraldine Mary McTigue, "Forms of Racial Interaction in Louisiana, 1860–1880" (Ph.D. diss., Yale University, 1975); William P. Connor, "Reconstruction Rebels: The New Orleans *Tribune* in Post-War Louisiana," *Louisiana History* (1980), 21:159–81. Especially informative is Jean-Charles Houzeau, *My Passage at the New Orleans "Tribune,"* first published in French in 1870. See the edition edited by David C. Rankin, trans. G. F. Denault (Louisiana State University Press, Baton Rouge, 1984).

28. See William Cheek and Aimee Lee Cheek, *John Mercer Langston and the Fight for Black Freedom, 1829–65* (Urbana, Ill., 1989), p. 440.

29. Lowry's speech, in full, is in the *Liberator*, February 3, 1865. On this effort in Pennsylvania, see P. S. Foner, *Essays in Afro-American History* (Philadelphia, 1978), pp. 57–65. See also Aptheker, *Documentary History*, 1:502–6.

30. *San Francisco Bulletin*, October 3, 1864, quoted by P. S. Foner, "The Battle to End Discrimination against Negroes in Philadelphia Street Cars," *Pa. Hist.* (1973), 40:283. See J. M. McPherson, "Abolitionists and the Civil Rights Act of 1875," *JAH* (1965), 51:493–510, especially 495 for anti-racist acts in various cities and states during the war.

31. John R. McKivingan, *The War Against Proslavery Religion: Abolitionism and the Northern Churches* (Ithaca, N.Y., 1984), pp. 197–98. The *Liberator*, June 7, 1864, reported on anti-racist developments in Northern churches.

32. Tilton's speech was reprinted in a pamphlet issued in 1863, abstracted in Osofsky, *Burden of Race*, pp. 100–104.

33. Otto Olsen, ed., *The Negro Question: From Slavery to Caste, 1863–1910* (New York, 1971), pp. 55–57, 69, 70.

34. William Gravely, *Gilbert Haven, Methodist Abolitionist: A Study in Race, Religion, and Reform, 1850–1880* (Nashville, 1973), pp. 110, 119.

35. Gilbert Haven, *Sermon, Speeches, and Letters on Slavery and Its War* (Boston, 1869; reprinted, New York, 1969), pp. 351, 369, 372, 473, 509, 581, 601.

36. *Life of Garrison*, by his sons, 4:69.

37. Quoted in Carl Sandburg, *Abraham Lincoln: The War Years*, 4 vols. (N.Y., 1939), 2:418. The anti-draft riots in New York City had numerous causes and results, but their most ghastly feature was the mass killings of African Americans.

The outbreak explains the phrase "mad hatred." See Iver Bernstein, *The New York City Draft Riots* (New York, 1990).

38. See William M. Armstrong, "The Freedmen's Movement and the Founding of *The Nation,*" *JAH* (1967), 53:708–36, especially pp. 708, 721. Also see Rollo Ogden, ed., *Life and Letters of Edwin L. Godkin*, 2 vols. (New York, 1907), 1:248, 250.

39. See my *Abolitionism* (Boston, 1989), pp. 35–45, 168 n. 29.

40. See P. S. Foner, "A Labor Voice for Black Equality," *Science and Society* (1974), 38:308–25; quotation, p. 320. Also see Foner, *History of the Labor Movement in the United States* (New York, 1947), 1:349.

41. Whittier's letter is in Garrison, *Letters,* 4:89; it was dated November 24, 1863. Garrison's letter is in *Letters,* 4:118.

42. The commission's preliminary report is printed in *War of the Rebellion: Official Records,* ser. 3, vol. 3, pp. 430–54; the final report is in ser. 4, vol. 4, pp. 289–382. See John G. Sprout, "Blueprint for Radical Reconstruction," *JSH* (1957), 23:25–44; quotations, pp. 37, 39, 41, 43.

43. Lydia Maria Child, ed., *Speeches on Political Questions by George W. Julian* (New York, 1872), pp. 125, 236, 300.

44. See George W. Curtis to Charles Sumner, March 21, 1864, and Sumner's letter to the secretary of the association, April 16, 1864, in Beverly Wilson Palmer, ed., *The Selected Letters of Charles Sumner,* 2 vols. (Boston, 1990), 2:233–34.

45. Ibid., 2:259–60, 281.

46. *Congressional Globe,* December 21, 1865, pp. 111, 112.

47. *Congressional Globe,* January 22, 1866, pp. 343, 344. On Senator Cowan, see LaWanda Cox and John H. Cox, *Politics, Principle, and Prejudice, 1865–1866* (New York, 1963), especially pp. 216–17.

48. Fawn Brodie, *Thaddeus Stevens, Scourge of the South* (New York, 1959). See especially chapter 7 ("Lydia"), pp. 86–93; on the tombstone, see p. 306. Stevens's speech of December 18, 1865, is in the *Congressional Globe,* 39th Cong., 1st sess., pp. 72–75.

There is a powerful editorial by E. L. Godkin in the *Nation* (1865), 1:520–21, "The One Humanity," which attacked "the white man's country" demagogy as being "the lowest conception of government" and continued, very much like Stevens, to deny concepts of racism. Alas, Godkin and the *Nation* did not stand firm on this position as the postbellum years unfolded.

Bibliographic Comment

A basic source for this book was the vast literature produced by the anti-slavery movement, especially its pamphlet deluge. Here the indispensable guide was Dwight Lowell Dumond, *A Bibliography of Antislavery in America* (Ann Arbor, Mich., 1961). Very rare, indeed, was the discovery of a relevant source that Dumond had missed.

Newspapers were of importance; Garrison's *Liberator* was a gold mine. The four-volume life of Garrison compiled by his sons, Wendell Phillips Garrison and Francis Jackson Garrison (New York, 1885–89), remains an important supplement. Magazines like the *American Museum, Niles' Weekly Register,* and the *Independent* were important. The *Congressional Globe* was essential.

Collections of correspondence were basic sources; especially important were those of Benjamin Rush by Lyman H. Butterfield; of the Grimké sisters and Theodore D. Weld by Dwight Lowell Dumond and Gilbert H. Barnes; of Garrison by Louis Ruchames and Walter Merrill; of Lydia Maria Child by Milton Meltzer, Patricia Holland, and Francine Karson; of Frederick Douglass by Philip S. Foner; and of Charles Sumner by Beverly Wilson Palmer. The speeches and writings of George W. Julian, Gilbert Haven, Wendell Phillips, and James Russell Lowell were important sources; so were certain memoirs, like those of Levi Coffin. The documents published by William Still on the Underground Railroad were vital.

Certain dissertations were especially useful. These included those by Lawrence D. Reddick, Thomas R. Moseley, Geraldine Mary McTigue, and William D. Stump; full details on the works by these authors are in the reference notes.

Historians whose work was of importance have been referred to in the reference notes. I want to call special attention, however, to the publications of the late Louis Ruchames and to those coming from Philip S. Foner, Sidney Kaplan, Merton L. Dillon, James B. Stewart, and James M. McPherson.

The four-volume compilation by the late Lathan A. Windley of *Runaway Slave Advertisements* is a tribute to those who sought freedom and to Windley's indefatigability. The 1937 dissertation by James Hugo Johnston (finally published in 1970) was a pathbreaking book.

Index